Envisioning reform

CW01651038

Envisioning reform: Enhancing UN accountability in the twenty-first century

Edited by Sumihiro Kuyama and Michael Ross Fowler

United Nations University Press

TOKYO • NEW YORK • PARIS

© United Nations University, 2009

The views expressed in this publication are those of the authors and do not necessarily reflect the views of the United Nations University.

United Nations University Press
United Nations University, 53-70, Jingumae 5-chome,
Shibuya-ku, Tokyo 150-8925, Japan
Tel: +81-3-5467-1212 Fax: +81-3-3406-7345
E-mail: sales@unu.edu general enquiries: press@unu.edu
http://www.unu.edu

United Nations University Office at the United Nations, New York
2 United Nations Plaza, Room DC2-2062, New York, NY 10017, USA
Tel: +1-212-963-6387 Fax: +1-212-371-9454
E-mail: unuona@ony.unu.edu

United Nations University Press is the publishing division of the United Nations University.

Cover design by Andrew Corbett

Cover photograph from UN Photo by John Isaac

Printed in Hong Kong

ISBN 978-92-808-1170-4

Library of Congress Cataloging-in-Publication Data

Envisioning reform : enhancing UN accountability in the twenty-first century / edited by Sumihiro Kuyama and Michael Ross Fowler.
p. cm.
Includes bibliographical references and index.
ISBN 978-9280811704 (pbk.)
1. United Nations—Reform. 2. United Nations—Management. I. Kuyama, Sumihiro. II. Fowler, Michael Ross.
JZ4995.E68 2009
352.3′572113—dc22 2009022010

Contents

Tables and figures viii

Contributors x

Foreword xvi
Konrad Osterwalder

Abbreviations xviii

Introduction 1
Sumihiro Kuyama and Michael Ross Fowler

1 Making the United Nations accountable: Managerial and political perspectives 19
Edward C. Luck

Part I: General analysis of accountability in the UN context 35

2 Bringing the different United Nations to account 37
Michael Ross Fowler

3 Conceptual analysis of accountability: The structure of accountability in the process of responsibility 73
Hirohide Takikawa

4 Legitimacy and accountability of the United Nations 97
Jochen Prantl

5 Accountability of the United Nations from the perspective of international law 116
Kyoji Kawasaki

Part II: Managerial accountability 133

6 Managerial accountability and the UN system 135
Tadanori Inomata

7 UN management reform as a basis for enhancing accountability 162
Hideaki Shiroyama

8 A ladder of accountability: Analysis of subconcepts of managerial accountability in the United Nations 174
Ikuyo Hasuo

Part III: Political accountability 191

9 Enhancing the political accountability of the United Nations via multi-stakeholder synergy 193
Tatsuro Kunugi

10 Democratic accountability in UN field operations 215
Kazuo Takahashi

Part IV: Case studies of accountability 227

11 Accountability and NPM reforms in the European Union: Implications for UN reform 229
Koji Fukuda

12 Improving accountability and legitimacy in the European Union 253
Michael Reiterer

13 The World Bank Inspection Panel: Participation and accountability 271
Edith Brown Weiss, Peter L. Lallas and Anna S. Herken

14 Improving accountability at the Asian Development Bank 303
Suresh Nanwani

Part V: Conclusion 325

Conclusion 327
Michael Ross Fowler and Sumihiro Kuyama

Appendix I: Commentaries made at the United Nations University Tokyo Symposium on Accountability 343
Tetsuo Sato, Mariko Shoji and Mikoto Usui

Appendix II: Areas for further study 359

Index 361

Tables and figures

Tables

5.1 Basic aspects behind UN accountability from the perspective of international law 117
6.1 Total budget of the UN system 140
6.2 Policies, principles and guidelines developed by the Inter-Agency Standing Committee 143
6.3 Multilateral resources available for environment activities, 2006 156
6.4 Expenditures on normative and operational environmental activities within the UN system 157
11.1 Chronological overview of accountability reforms in the European Union 236
11.2 Modern understanding of accountability 237
11.3 Agencies of the European Union 244
11.4 Evolution of accountability mechanisms in the European Union: Measures and institutions 245
13.1 Eligibility and investigation 281

Figures

3.1 The structure of accountability 77
3.2 The process of responsibility 87
3.3 The process of responsibility (revised version) 89
4.1 Formal meetings and informal consultations, 1972–1982 ... 106
4.2 Formal meetings and informal consultations, 1988–2002 ... 107

4.3	Legitimacy and accountability gap of the Security Council: Causes	109
6.1	Current institutional scheme of disaster reduction and response	145
6.2	Sphere of competence of entities related to international humanitarian assistance at disaster management stages	146
6.3	Share of expenditures on operational activities of the UN system by sector, 2003	149
6.4	Fragmented landscape of environmental governance within the UN system	151
8.1	The fundamental concept of accountability	177
8.2	The fundamental concept of managerial accountability in government	178
8.3	Stewart's model	180
8.4	Conclusion: UN model of a ladder of accountability	186
13.1	Geographical distribution of requests, as of 30 June 2008	287
13.2	Policies most often raised in requests, as of 30 June 2008	288

Contributors

Edith Brown Weiss is Francis Cabell Brown Professor of International Law at Georgetown University Law Center, former Chair of the World Bank Inspection Panel (2003–2007), a vice-presidential-level appointment, and former President of the American Society of International Law. She is the author/co-author of many books and articles, including *In Fairness to Future Generations* (in English, Japanese, French, Spanish and Chinese), *Engaging Countries: Strengthening Compliance with International Environmental Accords* and *Fresh Water and International Economic Law*. She has received national and international awards for her work from the American Bar Association, American Society of International Law, IUCN and Free University of Brussels, Center for International Environmental Law and International Studies Association.

Michael Ross Fowler is Professor of Political Science at the University of Louisville, where he specializes in international law, organization and negotiation. A graduate of Dartmouth College, the University of Virginia and Harvard Law School, he is the author of five books, including *Law, Power, and the Sovereign State: The Evolution and Application of the Concept of Sovereignty* and the forthcoming *Bribes, Bullets, and Intimidation: Narcotics Trafficking in Central America*. Michael Fowler has published in various journals, including *International Studies Perspectives*, *Review of International Studies* and *Harvard Negotiation Law Review*. Twice a Fulbright Scholar to Japan, and a lecturer in Australia, China, Costa Rica, Ecuador, Mexico, Panama and Venezuela, Michael Fowler was also one of the first American academics selected to teach officials in Laos and Viet Nam.

Koji Fukuda is Professor of International Public Administration at the Graduate School of Political Science, School of Political Science and Economics, and Director of the Waseda Institute for EU Studies at Waseda University, Tokyo, Japan. Koji Fukuda is also a member of the executive committee of the Japan Association of EU Studies. He was a research fellow at the College of Europe in Bruges (1992–1993). He has written a number of journal articles and books, including *The Administrative Structure and Policy Processes in the European Communities* (Seibundo, 1992), and *European Governance after Nice* (Routledge/Curzon, 2003).

Ikuyo Hasuo is Associate Professor of Political Science at Osaka University, School of International Public Policy, where she specializes in international public administration, theory of international organization and UN studies. She obtained an MA in law and diplomacy from the Fletcher School of Law and Diplomacy, Tufts University, USA, and a doctor of laws (LLD) from Hitotsubashi University, Japan. She was also a 2006 Fulbright Scholar at Columbia University. She has published in various academic journals and books, including *Kokusai Seiji* (*International Relations*) and *Kokusai Anzenhosho* (*International Security Studies*). Ikuyo Hasuo has occupied a variety of posts, including appointments as an international civil servant (1993–2002) and a senior consultant (2005) at UNESCO, Paris, as well as Director of a Japanese chapter of Transparency International (2005–present).

Anna S. Herken is the principal adviser to the Secretary-General of the European Bank for Reconstruction and Development and a former Assistant Executive Secretary of the Inspection Panel of the World Bank. Prior to this she served, *inter alia*, for the German High Level G-8 Task Force and as deputy head of the International Sustainability Division and deputy head of the International Trade Division in the German government. Other previous experience includes the World Trade Organization and the World Bank. Anna Herken is a lawyer and received her education in the United States, Germany and France.

Tadanori Inomata is an Inspector of the Joint Inspection Unit, the only independent and system-wide oversight body within the UN system, where he issued inspection reports on UN humanitarian emergency assistance and disaster reduction as well as environmental governance within the UN system. Prior to this he served as Japanese spokesman on the Montreal Protocol and Japanese Ambassador to Costa Rica. From 1999 to 2002 he taught as full Professor of International Public Administration and Transnational Relations in the Graduate School of International Cooperation Studies, Kobe University, Japan, and wrote various academic treatises on environment, peacekeeping and interdisciplinary aspects of the governance and management of UN system organizations. He was a professional staff member at the Organisation for Economic Co-operation and Development and the UN Conference on Trade and Development, respectively, in the 1970s and 1980s.

Kyoji Kawasaki is Professor of Public International Law at the Graduate School of Law, Hitotsubashi University, where he specializes in state responsibility and peaceful settlement of international disputes. Kyoji Kawasaki has published various articles in English on state responsibility and *jus cogens* in such journals as the *Hitotsubashi Journal of Law and Politics* (Tokyo, Japan) and *In.Law* (Perugia, Italy). He graduated from Hitotsubashi University, and has conducted research at the University of Pisa, Italy, and the University of Paris II, France.

Tatsuro Kunugi is Visiting Professor at the United Nations University/ Institute of Advanced Studies and representative of the International Cooperation Research Association. Formerly he was a Professor at the International Christian University (1990–2004); UN Assistant Secretary-General (1984–1990) (Special Representative of the Secretary-General for humanitarian assistance to Cambodia; Deputy Executive Director, UN Population Fund); Minister, Permanent Mission of Japan in Geneva (1976–1983); and senior legal adviser, UN Peacekeeping Missions in the Middle East (1971–1976). He has a PhD from Columbia University and a diploma from The Hague Academy of International Law. His publications in English include *Towards a More Effective UN*; *Codes of Conduct for Partnership in Governance*; "Globalization and Synergistic Responses"; and "Redressing Security Deficits in Our Divided World".

Sumihiro Kuyama is Visiting Professor at the United Nations University. Prior to this he was a member, including its Chair, of the Joint Inspection Unit of the UN system for 10 years, after serving as a member of the Advisory Committee on Administrative and Budgetary Questions (ACABQ) and the Chair of the Fifth Committee of the UN General Assembly in his capacity as a diplomat at the Permanent Mission of Japan to the UN; he was also UN Assistant Secretary-General for nine years. He is the author and coauthor of many articles and reports relating to enhancing UN effectiveness and efficiency, focusing in particular on management reforms including results-based management, information management, knowledge management, governance and oversight, as well as the managerial review of the WHO, ILO, UNESCO, UNHCR, UNU, etc.

Peter L. Lallas is Executive Secretary of the Inspection Panel of the World Bank, an independent accountability mechanism that investigates complaints ("requests for inspection") from people affected by World Bank projects. Previously he was Director of the International Environmental Law office of the US Environmental Protection Agency, visiting expert in international law at the UN Food and Agricultural Organization and counsellor in international and European law in a

Brussels-based law office. A graduate of Harvard Law School, he has taught as Adjunct Professor on international and environmental law and policy themes, and authored and co-authored many publications in these fields.

Edward C. Luck is Senior Vice President and Director of Studies at the International Peace Institute and Special Adviser to UN Secretary-General Ban Ki-moon. He is currently on public service leave as Professor of Practice in International and Public Affairs at Columbia University.

Suresh Nanwani is presently Principal Human Resource Specialist in the Asian Development Bank (ADB). He was the associate Secretary of the ADB Compliance Review Panel from 2003 to June 2008, and previously senior counsel and deputy head of the ADB law and policy reform group, and counsel in the European Bank for Reconstruction and Development. He co-authored the ADB Accountability Mechanism policy paper. He advises institutions on establishing and operating accountability mechanisms. His publications in various journals and lectures and presentations in many countries cover law and policy reform; law and practice of international financial institutions; accountability mechanisms of multilateral development banks; and institutional governance and responsibility.

Jochen Prantl is Acting Director of the Centre for International Studies, senior research fellow in international relations and fellow of Nuffield College, University of Oxford. In 2007 he was awarded the Zvi Meitar/Vice-Chancellor Oxford University Research Prize in the Social Sciences. His recent books include *The UN Security Council and Informal Groups of States: Complementing or Competing for Governance?* (Oxford University Press, 2006), and *ECOSOC Ad Hoc Advisory Groups on African Countries Emerging from Conflict: The Silent Avant-garde* (United Nations, 2006). Jochen Prantl holds degrees in political science, Spanish and history of art from the University of Bonn (MA) and in international relations from the University of Oxford (DPhil).

Michael Reiterer, appointed in 2005 as Adjunct Professor of International Politics at the University of Innsbruck, Austria, specializes in EU-Asia relations in general and EU-Japan in particular, the Asia-Europe Meeting (ASEM), interregionalism and EU foreign and foreign trade policy. The author of two books (*The Diplomatic Protection of Refugees by Their State of Asylum* and *Asia – Europe: Do They Meet?*), he has also published about 90 articles in international journals. In addition to a *doctor juris* of the University of Innsbruck, Michael Reiterer holds diplomas in international relations from the Johns Hopkins University, Bologna Center and the Graduate Institute for International Studies, Geneva, Switzerland. He has lectured at various universities and participated in academic conferences in Europe, the United States, China, Singapore, South Korea, the Philippines and Japan.

He is also an official of the European Commission, serving presently as Ambassador to Switzerland and the Principality of Lichtenstein.

Tetsuo Sato is Professor of International Law and Organization at the Graduate School of Law, Hitotsubashi University, Tokyo, Japan. He holds an LLB, LLM and PhD (Hitotsubashi University), and an MA in law and diplomacy (Fletcher School of Law and Diplomacy, Tufts University, USA; Fulbright Scholarship grantee). His publications include *Creative Evolution of International Organizations* (in Japanese) (Keiso Shobo, 1993), which received the twenty-fourth Mineichiro Adachi Award, *Evolving Constitutions of International Organizations* (Kluwer Law International, 1996) and *The Law of International Organizations* (in Japanese) (Yuhikaku, 2005). He has authored many articles, including "The Legitimacy of Security Council Activities under Chapter VII of the UN Charter since the End of the Cold War", in Jean-Marc Coicaud and Veijo Heiskanen, eds, *The Legitimacy of International Organizations* (United Nations University Press, 2001).

Hideaki Shiroyama is Professor of Public Administration at the Graduate School of Law and Politics, University of Tokyo, where he specializes in international administration, policy process and science/technology and public policy. His recent publications include "Japan's Policy and Interface Arrangement with International Organizations: Financial and Other Resource Flows", in Glenn D. Hook and Harukiyo Hasegawa, eds, *Japanese Responses to Globalization: Politics, Security, Economics and Business* (Palgrave Macmillan, 2006), and "The Harmonization of Automobile Environmental Standards between Japan, the United States and Europe: The 'Depoliticizing Strategy' by Industry and the Dynamics between Firms and Governments in a Transnational Context", *Pacific Review* 20(3), 2007.

Mariko Shoji is a Professor in the Faculty of International Studies at Keiai University, where she specializes in international organization, law and politics. Her recent publications include *Global Public Policy* (Koyo Shobo, 2007); "The Challenge for Democracy: A New Approach on Security Problems", *Daxiyangguo – Revista Portuguesa de Estudios Asiáticos*, Universidade Técnica de Lisboa 8, 2005; "Preventive Diplomacy and the Reform of the UN", in Hideo Sato, ed., *Containing Conflict: Cases in Preventive Diplomacy* (Japan Center for International Exchange); and "The UN and East Asian Regional Security: A Japanese Perspective", in Soo-Gil Park and Sung-Hack Kang, eds, *UN, PKO and East Asian Security: Currents, Trends and Prospects* (Korean Academic Council on the United Nations System, 2002). She has been an executive board member since 2004 of the Japan Association for United Nations Studies, and since 2006 of the Peace Studies Association of Japan.

Kazuo Takahashi is Visiting Professor at the United Nations University and the National Graduate Institute for Policy Studies (Tokyo). Prior to this he was Professor at the

International Christian University (Tokyo) after occupying various senior positions at the OECD, the Foundation for Advanced Studies on International Development (Tokyo), etc. He is the author/editor of many publications, including *Agenda for International Development* and *Capacity Development for Peacebuilding*. He has a PhD from Columbia University and serves as President of the Society of Researchers of International Development, as well as a governing board member of the Society for International Development and the International Development Center of Japan. Within the overall framework of global public goods, his current research topics include peacebuilding, water resource management and social trust.

Hirohide Takikawa is Associate Professor of Philosophy of Law at the Graduate School of Law, Osaka City University. He is the author of a book in Japanese, *Sekinin no Imi to Seido* (*The Significance of Responsibility*) (Keiso shobo, 2003), and numerous articles, including "Can We Justify the Welfare State in an Age of Globalization? Toward Complex Borders", *Archiv für Rechts und Sozialphilosophie* 92(1), 2006. A graduate of the University of Tokyo and a former visiting scholar at Harvard University, Hirohide Takikawa's research interests include responsibility, equality, globalization and political obligation.

Mikoto Usui is Professor Emeritus at Tsukuba University. He is currently Professor of International Relations at Seisa University Faculty of Noosphere Sciences *cum* Visiting Professor at the United Nations University/Institute of Advanced Studies. His latest publications in English include "Business-society Interaction towards Sustainable Development", in J. F. Green and W. B. Chambers, eds, *The Politics of Participation in Sustainable Development Governance* (United Nations University Press, 2006); "The Private Business Sector in Global Environmental Diplomacy", in N. Kanie and P. M. Haas, eds, *Emerging Forces in Environmental Governance* (United Nations University Press, 2004); "Sustainable Development Diplomacy in the Private Sector: An Integrative Perspective on Game Change Strategies at Multiple Levels", *International Negotiation* 8(2), 2002; and co-editor with R. U. Ayres, *Eco-Restructuring* (United Nations University Press, 1999). A graduate of the Massachusetts Institute of Technology Graduate School of Economics (USA), after working for 20 years in the United Nations, New York, UNIDO, Vienna, and then the Organisation for Economic Co-operation and Development, Paris, he repatriated to teach at Tsukuba, Keio and Shukutoku Universities in Japan, specializing in economics, inter-cultural communication/negotiation and global governance.

In addition to the above contributors, the volume editors also wish to acknowledge the contribution made, at the 2006 UNU Tokyo Symposium on Accountability, by Prof. **Yozo Yokota**, who is currently Special Adviser to the Rector of UNU and Professor of Chuo University Law School, Tokyo. Prof. Yokota has a PhD from the University of Tokyo.

Foreword

Konrad Osterwalder

For the UN system the cardinal importance of accountability urgently calls for more attention by scholars and practitioners and more thorough and creative analytical studies than are currently found within either the international organization literature or the ongoing councils of policymakers. This study, a wide-ranging appraisal of the problems of, and possible future policy directions for, UN accountability by a highly qualified group of persons, forms a notable initial contribution that is expected to lead to further significant developments in this field.

Attention to the manner in which the United Nations manages its affairs is by no means a brand new endeavour. Large and small Member States, independently and collectively, have periodically attempted to bring the Organization to account in various ways, with certain useful consequences. To take one important example, under a mandate from the UN General Assembly as well as from the legislative organs in the other UN organizations, results-based management, as a symbol of improved public administration, has increasingly been introduced into the UN system.

And yet these initial forays have been neither comprehensive nor wholly satisfying. The extent of UN programmes and institutions has expanded dramatically, far outpacing the resources devoted to accountability. Further, as more attention has been paid in the post–Cold War era to improving global governance, the notion of a "democratic deficit" – which gained much intellectual attention in the 1990s – has been supplemented by the twin idea of an "accountability gap". In the context of international organizations, however, accountability has proven to be a remarkably slippery and elusive concept. The small circle of analysts who have written on UN accountability have tended to define the term differently, to focus on different problems and to suggest rather different approaches and possible reforms.

Within that context, in October 2006 the United Nations University (UNU) took the initiative of hosting the Tokyo Symposium on Accountability. This workshop brought together scholars with expertise in philosophy, political science, public administration, international law, international organization and international relations as well as practitioners from the European Union, the World Bank, the Asian Development Bank and the Joint Inspection Unit of the UN system. Alongside opening addresses by then UNU Rector Hans van Ginkel and Masato Kitera, Ambassador in Charge of UN Affairs in the Ministry of Foreign Affairs of Japan, the keynote contribution was provided by Edward Luck, then Director of the Center on International Organization of the School of International and Public Affairs at Columbia University. The seminar was organized into four sessions focused on general analysis, managerial accountability, political (democratic) accountability and case studies; each was overseen by a chair and a discussant, all of them notable figures in the related field.

This book has emerged basically from the seminar contributions and the discussions of the participants. Its purpose is to clarify, through its chapters, key concepts and issues, identify pertinent questions, draw on the experiences of comparable organizations and suggest a framework for better understanding of accountability in the UN context, as well as to point the way towards areas for further examination.

It is our hope that this volume will stimulate further study and considerations on this important subject. We hope that future analyses involving more disciplines and expertise can stand on the shoulders of these initial contributors, bringing additional elements and ideas into play that will reach beyond the necessarily tentative discussions and conclusions drawn in this book. We at the United Nations University see this process as a very valuable contribution to the vital process of enhancing UN accountability.

Prof. Dr. Konrad Osterwalder
Rector, United Nations University;
United Nations Under-Secretary-General

Abbreviations

ABM	activity-based management [EU]
ACABQ	Advisory Committee on Administrative and Budgetary Questions [UN]
ACC	Administrative Committee on Coordination (now CEB) [UN]
ADB	Asian Development Bank
ADPC	Asian Disaster Preparedness Center
AfDB	African Development Bank
AIDCO	EuropeAid Co-operation Office
ASEAN	Association of Southeast Asian Nations
CAP	Consolidated Appeals Process
CCA	Common Country Assessment
CEB	Chief Executives Board for Coordination [UN]
CEO	chief executive officer
CSD	Commission on Sustainable Development [UN]
DAC	OECD Development Assistance Committee
DG	Director-General [UN]
DG	directorate-general [EU]
DPKO	Department of Peacekeeping Operations [UN]
EBRD	European Bank for Reconstruction and Development
EC	European Commission
ECE	Economic Commission for Europe
ECJ	European Court of Justice
ECOSOC	Economic and Social Council [UN]
EEC	European Economic Community
EFSA	European Food Safety Authority
ESCAP	Economic and Social Commission for Asia and the Pacific

ESCWA	Economic and Social Commission for Western Asia
EU	European Union
EUROJUST	European Judicial Cooperation Office
EUROPOL	European Police Office
FAO	Food and Agricultural Organization
GA	General Assembly [UN]
GAO	Government Accountability Office [US]
GC	Global Compact [UN]
GEF	Global Environment Facility
GEMS	Global Environment Monitoring System
G-77	Group of 77
IACSD	Inter-Agency Committee on Sustainable Development [UN]
IASC	Inter-Agency Standing Committee [UN]
IATF	Inter-Agency Task Force for Disaster Reduction [UN]
IBRD	International Bank for Reconstruction and Development
ICJ	International Court of Justice
ICRC	International Committee of the Red Cross
ICT	international criminal tribunal
ICTY	International Criminal Tribunal for the Former Yugoslavia
IDA	International Development Association
IDB	Inter-American Development Bank
IDP	internally displaced person
IFC	International Finance Corporation
IFRC	International Federation of Red Cross and Red Crescent Societies
IGO	intergovernmental organization
ILA	International Law Association
ILC	International Law Commission [UN]
ILO	International Labour Organization
IMF	International Monetary Fund
IMO	International Maritime Organization
IOC	International Oceanographic Commission
IOM	International Organization for Migration
IRIN	Integrated Regional Information Networks [UN]
IT	information technology
ITU	International Telecommunication Union
JBIC	Japan Bank for International Cooperation
JICA	Japan International Cooperation Agency
JIU	Joint Inspection Unit [UN]
MDB	multilateral development bank
MDG	Millennium Development Goal
MEAs	multilateral environmental agreements
MEP	member of the European Parliament
MIGA	Multilateral Investment Guarantee Agency
NATO	North Atlantic Treaty Organization
NGO	non-governmental organization
NPM	new public management

OAS	Organization of American States
OCHA	Office for the Coordination of Humanitarian Affairs [UN]
ODA	official development assistance
OECD	Organisation for Economic Co-operation and Development
OHCHR	Office of the UN High Commissioner for Human Rights
OLAF	European Anti-Fraud Office
PAHO	Pan American Health Organization
PKO	peacekeeping operation
PPBS	planning-programming-budgeting system [UN]
R2P	responsibility to protect
RBB	results-based budgeting [UN]
RBBM	results-based budgeting and management [UN]
RBM	results-based management [UN]
ROAR	Result-Oriented Annual Report [UNDP]
SC	Security Council [UN]
SG	Secretary-General [UN]
SMART	specific, measurable, achievable, relevant and time-bound (objectives) [UN]
TNC	transnational corporation
UNAIDS	Joint UN Programme on HIV/AIDS
UNAMI	UN Assistance Mission for Iraq
UNAMIR	UN Assistance Mission for Rwanda
UNAT	UN Administrative Tribunal
UNCCD	UN Convention to Combat Desertification
UNCED	UN Conference on Environment and Development
UNCLOS	UN Convention on the Law of the Sea
UNCTAD	UN Conference on Trade and Development
UNDAC	UN Disaster Assessment and Coordination
UNDAF	UN Development Assistance Framework
UNDMT	UN Disaster Management Team
UNDP	UN Development Programme
UNESCO	UN Educational, Scientific and Cultural Organization
UNEP	UN Environment Programme
UNFCCC	UN Framework Convention on Climate Change
UNFIP	UN Fund for International Partnerships
UNFPA	UN Population Fund
UN-HABITAT	UN Human Settlements Programme
UNHCR	Office of the UN High Commissioner for Refugees
UNICEF	UN Children's Fund
UNITAR	UN Institute for Training and Research
UNJLC	UN Joint Logistic Centre
UNMIBH	UN Mission in Bosnia and Herzegovina
UNO	UN Organization
UNOPS	UN Office for Project Services
UNRWA	UN Relief and Works Agency for Palestine Refugees in the Near East
UNTAC	UN Transitional Authority in Cambodia

UNU	United Nations University
UNU-IAS	UNU Institute of Advanced Studies
UNWTO	World Tourism Organization
US AID	US Agency for International Development
VFM	value for money
WFP	World Food Programme
WHO	World Health Organization
WIPO	World Intellectual Property Organization
WMO	World Meteorological Organization
WSSD	World Summit on Sustainable Development
WTO	World Trade Organization

Introduction

Sumihiro Kuyama and Michael Ross Fowler

In the face of the numerous global challenges existing in the world today, promoting more effective global governance has come to the forefront of the international agenda, and the UN organizations are expected to play a key role in the way international affairs are managed. As a vital precondition, however, UN organizations must themselves improve their efficiency and effectiveness. In this context, and in the context of UN reform in general, a growing demand has been placed in recent years on enhancing, among other items, the accountability of the UN organizations.

The UN General Assembly, for instance, has adopted a number of relevant resolutions, including resolution 60/260 in which it emphasized the importance of strengthened accountability in the Organization and of ensuring greater accountability of the Secretary-General to the Member States, *inter alia*, for the effective and efficient implementation of legislative mandates and the best use of human and financial resources. In addition to these resolutions, the former Secretary-General Kofi Annan, at the conclusion of his annual report presented to his last General Assembly session (September 2006–August 2007), reiterated the importance of accountability by stating that the Organization can become stronger and more effective only if it is better managed and more clearly accountable. Likewise, Secretary-General Ban Ki-moon clearly emphasized UN accountability upon taking the oath of office,[1] and he has been committed to strengthening accountability since then.[2]

It is noted that this attention from within the Organization reflects dissatisfaction and criticism from without. Close observers have long argued

Envisioning reform: Enhancing UN accountability in the twenty-first century, Kuyama and Fowler (eds), United Nations University Press, 2009, ISBN 978-92-808-1170-4

that the Organization is unaccountable, or at least insufficiently accountable. Thus illuminating the contours of the subject of UN accountability in a comprehensive manner, describing in particular its problems and future policy direction, is a vital step to productive analysis of a common body of issues leading, eventually, to useful recommendations for reform.

Since, to date, the concept of UN accountability has often been rather loosely employed and only infrequently defined, development of more robust analysis of this important subject would certainly be of great value to both practitioners and academics concerned with UN accountability.[3] To contribute to this, the United Nations University (UNU) initiated a project to study, evaluate and eventually make tangible and practical recommendations concerning UN accountability. As a first step, in October 2006 the UNU convened the Tokyo Symposium on Accountability, followed by another public forum in November 2007 in New York to keep up the momentum originated in Tokyo. These brought together an array of relevant academics and practitioners to explore what different approaches to UN accountability might be found within diverse disciplines and practices, and to see whether a common approach to accountability, including its definition, is feasible in the UN context as the basis for the ultimate objective of enhancing its accountability. Experts from the World Bank and two other international institutions (the European Union and Asian Development Bank) were also invited to share the experiences that their organizations have had with their respective efforts to enhance accountability.

This volume is the upshot of the Tokyo symposium, but stimulated by the symposium discussions, with each author reflecting further and refining their thoughts in order to turn their contributions into the chapters herein. The book thus aims, in the main, to fill out the current understanding of the conceptual matters relating to accountability as it may apply to the United Nations, together with relevant practices and experiences for enhancing UN accountability. The chapter authors, drawn from an assortment of academic disciplines and with an array of practical and scholarly experiences in relevant fields, were asked to reflect on the problems and possible policy directions or approaches for UN accountability, to analyse particular aspects of accountability or to examine the concept in the related contexts of other international organizations that have wrestled with accountability concerns. While the authors hail from a number of different countries, this volume also aims to add to the English-language literature the perspectives of noted Japanese scholars and practitioners, and various of the chapters reference Japanese contributions to or perspectives on UN reform in general and accountability issues in particular.

It is to be noted here that, in light of the divergent views, approaches and perspectives on an array of issues related to accountability, no attempt was made to adopt an a priori common approach for all the chapters with regard to basic issues such as the definition of the term. Instead, the matter was left to each author to present on the basis of his or her own perspective to see, as referred to already, if a common ground[4] could be found to help to facilitate meaningful debates and policy formulations for strengthening the accountability of the UN system organizations to improve their relevance, efficiency and effectiveness. In the conclusion we then trace the basic convergence on the definition of accountability that eventually may have emerged.

With that background in mind, and before introducing the outline of this book, we here briefly discuss some matters, primarily conceptual, that are further elaborated in the chapters that follow: the definition of accountability, the question of who bears accountability for what and to whom, and the distinction, in the main, between managerial accountability and political accountability in the UN context.

The concept of accountability

Despite frequent use of the term, *accountability* is an "elusive concept whose meaning and characteristics differ depending upon the context".[5] This is certainly true in the UN context, and, as Edward Luck observes in chapter 1, "there is no generally accepted understanding of what accountability entails or how it could best be measured, assessed or instilled in the Organization". It could be noted in this context that divergent views and opinions on the concept of accountability would depend, to a large extent, upon differences among the academic disciplines and perspectives of public administration, political science, international relations, international law and others.

Nevertheless, it is commonly enunciated that, at least from the perspective of democratic theory, a few factors, especially *authorization* (besides, for instance, *support* and *impact*),[6] constitute a foundation for accountability. Namely, an individual, group or organization entrusted with some financial, human or other resources ought subsequently to give an account of the use (or non-use) of the resources. Here, existence of a superior authority is presupposed, even if implicitly, in the form of the one that provides the resources (in addition to guidance and direction). Of fundamental importance for grasping properly the concept of accountability in the UN context is to recall that government representatives, in adopting the UN Charter, are assumed to have acknowledged, even if tacitly, the authority of "a global demos", that is, "the peoples of the United Nations".[7] As alluded to already, Secretary-General Ban Ki-moon, in his address on taking the oath of office, declared "Ultimately, we are all – Secretariat and Member States alike – accountable to 'we the peoples'."[8]

Having noted these fundamental points, however, inevitably discussions on the question of accountability in the UN context quickly become more complicated. For instance, not only is the UN system fragmented and immense in the size and scope of its activities, but it contains a number of distinct power centres, including the Member States, the legislative organs (Security Council, General Assembly, etc.) and the specialized agencies (see chapter 2).

Furthermore, the norms to be used in bringing the distinct parts of the UN system to account are not well defined, particularly with respect to the more politicized dimension of the Organization. How exactly might the Security Council be made more accountable to the General Assembly or to the rest of the Member States? Who is accountable for the security of UN peacekeepers and civilian personnel posted to dangerous parts of the world? Who ought to be brought to account when the United Nations fails to act, and what are the standards to be used in situations of nonfeasance as well as misfeasance? These and many other specific questions remain contentious and not yet clearly answered.

Moreover, within the UN system use of the term accountability has too often been accompanied by negative connotations. Within this highly political organization, accountability has itself often become politicized and caught up in larger disagreements between North and South, and the discord sometimes evident among the Security Council, the General Assembly and the Secretariat. If approached positively and constructively, accountability could help to create a climate conducive to needed changes in organizational culture. It could alter the way that people act and interact, the ways in which things get done.[9]

At present, however, observers find very little positive to say about accountability at the United Nations. It is generally agreed that the Organization should be brought to account, in Edward Luck's phrase, "for its failure to act in some cases, as well as for its wrong choices, ill-conceived strategies, or failed implementation in other instances" (see chapter 1). More specific examples abound. For instance, the Independent Panel on the Safety and Security of UN Personnel in Iraq noted "a major deficiency identified ... is the lack of accountability for the decisions and positions taken by UN managers with regard to the security of UN staff".[10] Similarly, the Independent Inquiry Committee concluded, "The Oil-for-Food Program overtaxed the UN's fragile oversight and accountability mechanisms, revealing significant flaws that urgently need to be addressed if confidence in the United Nations is to be restored."[11]

The common thread that links together such comments is the perception that there exists, at the United Nations, an accountability "deficit" or "gap", defined as a gap between a valid claim for accountability by, for example, a certain deserving group and the actual practice by an entity that ought to be accountable.[12] The former party could be termed the *accountability holder*, who is holding someone else accountable, and the latter could be the *accountability holdee*.[13] In such a complex system as that found in the United Nations, a leading issue is that accountability holdees have often failed to assess carefully what has occurred, and even less frequently have they communicated a comprehensible report to accountability holders. Under the circumstances, closing or narrowing such an accountability "gap", or enhancing accountability, is a key element of effective UN reform.

Managerial accountability and political accountability

To facilitate consideration of accountability in the context of the UN organizations, we believe it is advisable to divide the subject into two broad clusters of notions: managerial accountability and political accountability.

The term *managerial accountability* – a management norm sometimes also referred to as *internal accountability* – may be familiar to students of business or public administration, and could be defined, in the most general and simple terms, as accountability relating to managerial functions within public or private entities or organizations.[14] More specifically, managerial accountability in the context of the UN system is focused upon accountability of those provided with delegated authority (i.e. Secretariat officials, including executive heads such as the Secretary-General), and holding them accountable *for* the actions (or the lack of actions) taken in accordance with given mandates or responsibilities with respect to programmes and financial, human and/or other resources, as well as *for* the performance and the manner in which the related resources were managed.

Management ought to occur in an ethical, transparent, efficient and non-corrupt manner. A key component of effective managerial accountability, however, involves delegation of authority in the Secretariat. Given a proper delegation of authority, managerial accountability is applicable at all levels, from the executive heads down to lower levels of managers/staff members, and it is imperative that the accountabilities of all officials in the Secretariat be established in an unambiguous manner with due regard to the line-management structure.[15] While the Oil-for-Food Programme has been cited as a most notorious example of problematic managerial accountability in the United Nations in recent years, persistent questions have been raised as well with respect to managerial problems in various peacekeeping missions and within an array of other UN programmes, agencies and offices. Furthermore, it may be worth noting that the so-called oil-for-food scandal contained an element of a lack of adequate legislative oversight in addition to managerial weaknesses, a point raised later.

Meanwhile, *political accountability* focuses upon the need for an organization to account for its behaviour, such as decisions made and actions or inactions taken, *to* the constituencies and stakeholders that are impacted. How wise and effective have the organization's policies and mandated programme actions been to achieve the intended objectives and results? *Political accountability* could be described, in general, as organizational accountability; that is, it encompasses the accountability of legislative organs (member states) and secretariats to relevant constituencies and stakeholders. These would include, ultimately, the "peoples of the United Nations", but more specifically they would be comprised of any groups or individuals significantly affected by decisions made and actions or inactions taken by the United Nations – as Edward Luck put it, "by what it chooses to do or not to do, as well as by how well it does it" (see chapter 1).

An important feature inherent in making the United Nations more politically accountable is a participatory factor. Namely, the political accountability of the Organization could be enhanced if *relevant* stakeholders that are affected in major ways by a particular decision, programme or action were involved, directly or indirectly, to the extent practically possible, in decision-making processes, i.e. in devising or revising the policies and mandates of the organizations in the UN system.

To date, apart from the multilateral development banks (such as the World Bank and the Asian Development Bank), just a few organizations in the UN system have adopted the practice of involving non-state stakeholders (i.e. stakeholders other than government representatives) in decision-making processes, even indirectly. These include the International Labour Organization (ILO), which has traditionally maintained a tripartite system – that is, a system of its governing body being composed of governments, employers and workers – and UNAIDS, the Joint UN Programme on HIV/AIDs, which operates its governing body (Programme Coordinating Board) with the participation of an array of stakeholders, namely representatives of five NGOs (including associations of people living with HIV) in addition to 22 governments and 10 UNAIDS co-sponsors. Furthermore, the UN Commission on Sustainable Development (CSD), a functional commission of the UN Economic and Social Council (ECOSOC) consisting of 53 Member States, provides space for the participation in its meetings of non-state actors, with the overall purpose of informing the Commission's decision-making processes.[16]

Political accountability and managerial accountability are functionally distinct. However, both of the key actors in the UN context, the secretariats and the legislative organs (Member States), are involved, or should be involved, in both varieties of accountability, sometimes in the intricate manner indicated below.

With respect to the functions under political accountability, the legislative organs are primarily accountable for the mandates established (as well as the results achieved). However, the reality is more complex than such a simple statement suggests. In many instances, a mandate is established on the basis of, or by selecting, a certain policy from a basket of policy options, which *de facto* the secretariats more often than not prepare, with or without delegated authority. Thus, although the policies of the UN organizations are supposed to be formulated, in principle, by the legislative organs, in practice, as one expert has noted, "civil servants do make policy. Typically, they disclaim that they are doing any such thing. They insist that they are merely filling in the administrative details of overall policies established by their political superiors."[17]

With respect to the functions under managerial accountability, the secretariats themselves are mainly accountable for various management functions, including management concerning the implementation of authorized or mandated programmes. Nevertheless, legislative organs are also expected to perform legislative or governance oversight, meaning that the Member States oversee the secretariats in their management or implementation of the mandated programmes, assisted often by oversight mechanisms.[18]

What one could conclude from this is that legislative organs (Member Sates) and secretariats (as well as oversight mechanisms) have a "shared responsibility"[19] in strengthening the accountability of the UN organizations. This further underscores that, while distinguishing between managerial and political accountability may be analytically useful, there exists a legitimate need to treat both varieties of accountability in a comprehensive and holistic manner to enhance UN accountability.

A final introductory point concerning political accountability is that one finds the term used, in general, more or less interchangeably with democratic accountability, as referred to, for instance, in a paper by the US Agency for International Development (US AID).[20] However, a number of the authors in this volume take issue with that usage, and suggest that the concepts ought to be distinguished from one another. For instance, Tatsuro Kunugi asserts that political accountability is broader than democratic accountability, as elaborated in chapter 9. Michael

Reiterer suggests in his chapter that the term democratic accountability is used instead of political accountability when the *democratic* element is emphasized over the political process. Kazuo Takahashi is also in favour of using the term democratic accountability for the purpose of the analysis of the issues that are of concern in the context of UN reform, as indicated in his chapter. On the other hand, among other authors in this volume, Edward Luck argues forcefully in his keynote chapter that the term *political accountability* ought to be preferred to *democratic accountability* on the grounds that the former is "value-neutral". Pending further consideration of the matter, the term *political accountability*, defined broadly as accountability applicable to any kind of political form including, of course, democratic accountability, is used in this book unless the term democratic accountability (instead of political accountability) is used explicitly by the authors in a specific context.

Outline of the volume

The initial keynote contribution by Edward Luck provides a substantive overview of the question of accountability in the UN context, observing first of all that the credibility of the United Nations depends on a concerted effort to repair the deficits in political and managerial accountability. While Luck sees some modest progress in improving managerial accountability in the wake of the oil-for-food scandal, he declares that "the challenge of boosting political accountability remains little understood and largely problematic".

Part I: General analysis of accountability in the UN context

The first part of the book lays out certain cardinal issues related to accountability in the UN context: *inter alia*, problems, definitions and conceptual linkages or distinctions between accountability, on the one hand, and terms such as responsibility, legitimacy, etc., on the other. First, political scientist Michael Fowler sketches out the problems that the Organization has confronted in the past and will probably continue to confront in the future in enhancing its accountability. He asks "who in the Organization might be accountable to whom?", identifies the multidimensional nature of the United Nations and its implications for accountability and suggests that different accountability challenges confront "the United Nations of the Member States" or "the legislative United Nations", including what he calls "the executive United Nations" (that is, the Security Council as a "core decision-making group"), "the United Nations of the Secretariat" and "the umbrella United Nations". Then, in analysing the widespread perception of an accountability gap at the United Nations, he points to the minimal constitutional guidance in the Charter, the lack of a political tradition of accountability, the shortcomings of UN reports and the absence of a well-defined line-management structure. He is also sceptical that further "democratization" of the Organization holds the key to enhanced accountability.

With Luck and Fowler having identified certain of the key problems associated with UN accountability, in chapter 3 Hirohide Takikawa, writing from the perspective of philosophy of law, explores approaches to the central issue of the definition of accountability. After noting the elusive quality of accountability, Takikawa suggests a core definition and then clarifies the concept by focusing on how accountability might be structured and how a process of responsibility might be envisioned. Takikawa finds the essence of accountability in the "obligation to explain and justify one's actions". To the three basic questions of "who should be accountable, for what and to whom?", Takikawa urges that we consider as well "why (on what rule) is someone accountable, and how does he or she explain and justify?" Based on this, he further analyses a number of related conceptual issues, including the relationship between accountability and such concepts as liability, responsibility, transparency, legitimacy and democracy.

Of particular importance in the UN context, Takikawa notes that, in addition to positive laws, custom, practices and political culture may shape accountability rules. To those who would enhance UN political accountability via the increased involvement of those outside the Organization affected by its decisions, Takikawa cautions that, while the term *stakeholder* may be readily defined, it can be difficult to determine who is sufficiently affected by a decision to qualify for inclusion in that category. In applying his ideas to the UN context, Takikawa also notes that accountability processes consume time, money and effort. Becoming overly accountable could cause inefficiencies, just as the lack of accountability could. Thus, while the United Nations may affect the global demos, it cannot realistically be accountable to everyone.

In chapter 4 Jochen Prantl examines, from the perspective of international relations, the question of linkages between UN legitimacy and accountability, taking the Security Council as a specific case and focusing upon a few aspects "that have been understudied". By legitimacy, Prantl refers "primarily to the justification of legal and political authority exercised by an international institution through its procedures (or input) and output". He emphasizes the effectiveness of UN institutions in terms of solving global challenges as a precondition for an authority delegated to the United Nations. He also focuses upon the need to allow "a flexible participation of stakeholders" in order to enhance the legitimacy and accountability of the United Nations. In this context, and on practical grounds, informal or *ad hoc* mechanisms, in particular informal groupings of states (such as contact groups, core groups, groups of friends), are hinted as possible options. Prantl concludes that "adopting less rigid rules and more flexible procedures is the avenue . . . [to] pursue to make the United Nations . . . more legitimate and accountable".

In the final chapter in part I, Kyoji Kawasaki, writing from the perspective of international law, discusses one specific facet of the "multifaceted phenomenon" of UN accountability, namely legal accountability. By referring principally to the work of the International Law Commission in the context of UN accountability, he discusses the concept of responsibility, based on the proposition that "for the purpose of international law, responsibility of an entity arises from the violation of an obligation owed by the entity" and concludes that "in order to get the whole picture . . . we should look at . . . the accountability and responsibility of the Member States to the UN organizations as well as to the peoples of the United Nations".

Part II: Managerial accountability

The second part of this volume focuses on questions of managerial accountability, including the impact of new public management (NPM) on the United Nations. Based on an extensive review of the cases of humanitarian assistance and environmental governance as examples, Tadanori Inomata, in chapter 6, identifies "lacunae" of accountability at the level of the UN system due to a lack of a system-wide management and governance framework. In this context, he also refers to a "lack of intergovernmental ownership in inter-agency coordination", as well as a "lack of coherence in governance", and declares that results-based management (RBM), adopted by the UN General Assembly as a basic benchmarking framework, "would not ensure system-wide strategic planning and resource management [which is supposed to facilitate system-wide managerial accountability] unless the governing bodies or the Member States adopt common objectives applicable throughout the UN system".

In the next chapter, from the perspective of public administration, Hideaki Shiroyama analyses the management methods of the UN organizations, using NPM as a frame of reference. Shiroyama points out that important aspects of the management reforms introduced under former Secretary-General Kofi Annan included the trial "introduction" of results-based budgeting (RBB) (and eventually results-based management, as referred to in chapter 6) and the efforts to manage development via the Millennium Development Goals (MDGs). In this context, and on the basis of extensive empirical research, Shiroyama identifies important challenges, in particular in evaluation. He notes: "If an international organization is to be managed as a system, conscious and continuous efforts must be made to determine indicators for evaluation. However, indicators are frequently established hastily and without an essential understanding of the activities of the Organization, making evaluation ineffective." In addition to presenting a number of related recommendations aimed at ensuring enhanced managerial accountability in the United Nations, Shiroyama observes that managerial effectiveness of the UN organizations, including the state of their accountability, actually depends to a substantial extent on the manner in which the Member States behave. Here one can see how the contributions of Inomata and Shiroyama nicely converge.

Also grounding her work in the field of public administration, Ikuyo Hasuo briefly provides a historical review of the evolution of programme budgeting at the United Nations, and then describes the background underlying the need to enhance UN accountability. In this context, she focuses her analysis on the conceptual aspects of managerial accountability. Specifically, Hasuo examines the historical evolution of the subconcepts of managerial accountability by making reference to J. D. Stewart's "ladder of accountability" model as a yardstick. She concludes that, at present, the United Nations is at the stage of "performance-based accountability". Furthermore, based on her analysis using an Organisation for Economic Co-operation and Development (OECD) study as a point of reference, she also concludes that "NPM serves as a basis for the concept of managerial accountability in the United Nations". However, she indicates that, with the increased introduction and application of NPM in the context of results-based management, the promotion of delegation of authority in human resources management and similar advances, other issues, such as reforms of the administration of justice, will inevitably become essential.

Part III: Political accountability

While issues of political accountability are one focus of earlier contributions, including the Luck chapter and some of those in part I, the third part of the volume focuses on two additional dimensions of, or perspectives on, political accountability at the United Nations. (Political accountability is defined here as accountability applicable to any kind of political form, including one with a "democratic" feature, implying that political accountability is thus "value-neutral" and a "broader" concept than "democratic accountability".) The chapters in part III are supplemented by the case studies in part IV; the studies therein are basically focused on the aspect of political accountability, as defined above, rather than managerial accountability. In chapter 9 Tatsuro Kunugi, having defined political accountability as "an emerging principle of global governance transcending the existing omni-governmental multilateralism of the United Nations", examines a number of cases, including the Declaration of Accountability for Global Governance made at San Francisco (on the occasion of the fiftieth anniversary of signing the UN Charter)[21] and other codes of conduct that facilitate the enhancement of accountability and effectiveness of global governance with participation of non-state actors. Kunugi further analyses "transformative but non-structural changes proposed in the Cardoso report" for strengthening the United Nations, such as "multi-stakeholder partnerships" and "multi-constituency processes", since such measures would have the effect of enhancing the accountability and legitimacy of the United Nations.

One area in which the political accountability of the United Nations has often been criticized involves its field operations. In chapter 10 Kazuo Takahashi identifies "a tension between field operations and democratization" at the level of programme countries that has been brought about through "the consecutive emphasis on highly interventionist approaches of development cooperation" (namely "structural adjustment" in the 1980s, and "governance" in the 1990s and beyond). Based on this, Takahashi proceeds to argue that it is essential to address the question of UN accountability with the increasing emergence of field operations in mind. Thus his analysis focuses specifically on the question of democratic accountability,[22] by a grouping of the major field operations (i.e. "development cooperation, humanitarian intervention and PKO with UN interim administrations") against three components of democracy, namely "[popular] participation [in decision-making], transparency [in governance] and rule of law", and concludes that democratic accountability of field operations raises specific types of issues which will require special attention in the context of UN reform.

Part IV: Case studies of accountability

The fourth part of the book involves case studies of accountability, in an aim to draw on the experiences of the European Union, the World Bank and the Asian Development Bank to shed light on how the United Nations might enhance its accountability.

In chapter 11 Koji Fukuda begins with a comprehensive consideration of conceptual aspects of accountability, together with discussions of how NPM reforms (which are specified by Fukuda as "NPM-guided public sector governance reforms") have been introduced into the European Union (EU) and have succeeded in enhancing its accountability. Among the various points identified, one may wish to note in particular that NPM in the European Union has had a positive impact on managerial reforms in general as well as in countering the EU's perceived lack of accountability (the democratic deficit in its mechanisms and policy processes); the critical importance of accountability to the citizenry; and the need to institutionalize both managerial and political accountability. Fukuda concludes that lessons learned from the EU experiences, taking NPM as a frame of reference for enhancing accountability, will be applicable to the United Nations, and submits a number of suggestions including, in particular, the reform of the decision-making process supported by a system of stakeholders' participation.

The chapter by Michael Reiterer complements nicely that of Fukuda. Having noted that accountability is regarded as an instrument to overcome the "disenchantment of many of the EU's citizens", Reiterer presents a detailed account of the state of affairs of the European Union, separately, on democratic and political accountability, as well as on legal accountability. In this context, he observes that the European Union "was pushed to deal in its reform process with both aspects of accountability, managerial and political", since it was "clear that management reform [was] only part of the story". Reiterer further notes that European citizens "advocated more democratic control over the political goals of the process, the process itself and over the use of the financial means used in pursuit of the goals". Following this, he observes that there exist "some parallels" between the United Nations and the European Union concerning a number of aspects, including "a loss of confidence by key stakeholders, and of morale by staff". He cautions, however, against an overstatement of "the parallels" because of the differences in respect of the very nature as well as the administrative culture of the two institutions.

Having acknowledged that part of the "increasing concern about accountability of institutions . . . focuses on international financial institutions, and in particular the World Bank and other multilateral development banks", Edith Brown Weiss, Peter Lallas and Anna Herken point out that "There is broad consensus that institutions need to be legitimate, both in the eyes of those who established them and in the eyes of those whom they serve or affect, and that accountability is a necessary condition for institutions to be legitimate." They observe that the "growing attention to the need for accountability in international institutions" and "to the effectiveness of . . . complaint and response mechanisms . . . may be characterized as an emerging part of . . . 'global administrative law', or the structural and normative frameworks which govern the operation of institutions at the international level".

In this context, in light of many concerns raised by civil society, the Inspection Panel, which "is intended to enhance the legitimacy of the World Bank", was created in 1993 as a body independent of Bank management to promote "participation and accountability" by providing "a forum within the World Bank Group for people who believe that they have been, or are likely to be, harmed by World Bank-funded projects or programmes to bring their concerns directly to the Bank's board of executive directors". The authors contend that "it has provided a forum for communities around the world to give voice to their concerns about the adverse social and environmental impacts of projects funded by the World Bank, to establish the facts in relation to these concerns and to report findings to the decision-making chamber of the Bank for consideration and action". They note that "Since the Inspection Panel was established more than 14 years ago, all multilateral development banks and several national export and investment agencies have now established similar instruments, in good part modelled after the Inspection Panel." And having described in detail the panel's history, purpose, structure, process and impact, together with case presentations, they conclude that "the panel provides an entryway for people and civil society into the decision-making process of a major international institution", and that "The panel's experience has considerable relevance for future efforts within the UN system to establish or strengthen institutions for ensuring accountability."

In the final chapter among the case studies, Suresh Nanwani focuses on the measures that have been put in place to improve accountability at the Asian Development Bank (ADB). Nanwani offers a detailed description of the evolution of the ADB mechanisms relevant to accountability. In this context, the "ripple effects" of the World Bank Inspection Panel on other multilateral development banks (MDBs) are acknowledged. These have contributed, in the case of the ADB, to "providing a system that is more responsive to the needs of people affected by ADB-assisted projects". He points out, however, that the ADB accountability mechanism is the first, among MDBs, which has introduced "two related but separate phases" in which private individuals can file claims for problem-solving/consultation, followed by requests for investigation/compliance review. He also concludes by presenting basically the same message as provided by other contributors, especially in part IV: "That the window of access has been opened to individuals by the creation of any MDB accountability mechanism is groundbreaking, as for the first time citizens are given a voice and an opportunity to participate in the decision-making processes of an international organization which consists of member states and to which individuals are not parties even though they are project beneficiaries."

Concluding remarks

As Rosemary Righter has noted, "organizations that are unaccountable finish up by being irresponsible if not corrupt, unresponsive to opportunities, and unintelligible to the public".[23] More than six decades after the founding of the United Nations, important work remains to be done with respect to the organization's accountability. As former Secretary-General Kofi Annan noted, and as has been eventually endorsed by Secretary-General Ban Ki-moon, "A key ingredient of any successful organization is an ethical and accountable culture pervading its staff from top to bottom."[24] Perceptions of UN efficiency, effectiveness and credibility are closely related to accountability. And such perceptions will influence global governance and, in particular, the question of whether the United Nations will receive the necessary resources and be assigned tasks that will place it at the centre of international relations in the twenty-first century.

In this regard the Tokyo Symposium on Accountability, capped by the further efforts of the participants to turn their contributions into the chapters of this book, might be envisioned as a triggering input for setting up a *horizontal information network*[25] aimed at focusing attention on one central problem of global governance: deficiencies in UN accountability. This initial undertaking, reaching out not only to scholars from different relevant disciplines but also to officials and practitioners from the United Nations and other international organizations, has started to establish relationships among participants and encourage information exchange about ongoing problems, research and policies, including identifying different institutional and procedural approaches that might help to close the UN accountability gap. Our hope is that by focusing attention on issues and problems, common themes and best practices, as well as areas of at least preliminary shared perceptions identified first in the Tokyo symposium, then gaining wider circulation through this volume, we will start the process of creating an inclusive, ever-widening network of individuals, groups and institutions interested in the problems of UN accountability and what might be done about them.

The important subject of accountability at, and of, the organizations in the UN system certainly warrants more serious attention than it has yet been accorded. It is hoped that this volume will serve not only to identify key issues and raise pertinent questions that practitioners and academics can draw on in future endeavours, but also that it may eventually contribute to enhancing the accountability of the UN organizations.

Notes

1. United Nations (2006) Press Release SG/2119, GA/10558, 14 December.
2. For instance, in a recent report to the General Assembly prepared in response to General Assembly resolution 61/245 (entitled "Comprehensive Review of Governance and Oversight within the United Nations and Its Funds, Programmes and Specialized Agencies"), the Secretary-General proposed an "accountability architecture" focusing on achievement of results and management of risks by holding "managers and staff at all levels accountable". See United Nations (2008) "Accountability Framework, Enterprise Risk Management and Internal Control Framework, and Results-based Management", Doc. A/62/701, 19 February, summary.
3. The latest Advisory Committee on Administrative and Budgetary Questions (ACABQ) report comments on the Secretary-General's report (note 2 above) that it does not address "the measures implemented with the aim of strengthening accountability in the secretariat. The Advisory Committee would have expected that information would be provided on concrete cases where accountability measures had been applied and remedial action taken" (para. 7); "lack of clarity in the definition of accountability is one of the fundamental weaknesses in the Secretary-General's accountability architecture" (para. 9); and "the issues of accountability, internal control and management practices... should be further discussed with the other organizations of the UN system" (para. 37). United Nations (2008) Advisory Committee on Administrative and Budgetary Questions, Report A/63/457, 29 September.
4. In this connection a good analogy is given by Mary Kaldor, who notes that there does not exist any commonly agreed definition of civil society, but that establishing a common perspective on the concept based on studies and debates on the various definitions and related matters will eventually provide a common ground on which further advances could be expected in various respects, including better policy formulation. Kaldor, Mary (2003) *Global Civil Society: An Answer to War*, Cambridge: Polity Press.
5. US General Accounting Office (1995) "Block Grants: Issues in Designing Accountability Provisions", GAO/AIMD-95-226, September, p. 4. (Effective from 7 July 2004 the GAO's legal name became the Government Accountability Office.)
6. "Normatively, from the perspective of democratic theory, three different sets of justifications are commonly enunciated for demands by one entity that another [entity] be held accountable:
   - authorization, by which one entity authorizes another to act [on behalf of the former];
   - support – those who provide financial or political support to [another entity] have a claim to hold [it] accountable; and,
   - impact – those who are 'choice-determining' [decision-making] for some people should be accountable for their actions." Keohane, Robert O. (2002) "Global Governance and Democratic Accountability", in David Held and Mathias Koenig-Archibugi, eds, *Global Governance and Public Accountability*, Malden, MA: Blackwell, pp. 130–159, available at www.lse.ac.uk. http://www.lse.ac.uk.
7. On this issue, however, Prantl, for example, in his chapter argues that "UN politics remains essentially unaccounted by 'we the peoples of the United Nations'. Although the first seven words of the UN Charter, inspired by the preamble of the US Constitution,

seem to underline the democratic foundations of the Organization, reflecting the collective will of mankind, a brief look into the proceedings of the San Francisco Conference tells us otherwise."

8. United Nations, note 1 above.
9. United Nations (2004) "Delegation of Authority and Accountability", Report of the UN Joint Inspection Unit, JIU/REP/2004/7, p. 13.
10. United Nations (2003) "Report of the Independent Panel on the Safety and Security of UN Personnel in Iraq", 20 October, available at www.un.org/News/dh/iraq/safety-security-un-personnel-iraq.pdf, p. 3.
11. Independent Inquiry Committee (2005) "Second Interim Report", 29 March, available at www.iic-offp.org.
12. In this context, Kunugi asserts in his chapter that "the exercise of power by one set of actors is subject to responsiveness [accountability] to those over whom their power is exercised. Two functional dimensions are transparency in reporting on the exercise and enforceability of responsiveness that can be imposed on power holders. Most of the time neither of these two dimensions seems to be available in the case of the Security Council's political sphere."
13. Behn, Robert D. (2001) *Rethinking Democratic Accountability*, Washington, DC: Brookings Institution, p. 220.
14. Hasuo in her chapter, citing Day and Klein (1987), notes that "unlike political accountability, the most distinctive feature of managerial accountability is that, as a neutral, technical exercise, it can be found within any kind of political framework". Day, Patricia and Rudolf Klein (1987) *Accountability: Five Public Services*, London and New York: Tavistock Publications.
15. United Nations, note 9 above.
16. Since the creation of the CSD in December 1992 by the UN General Assembly to ensure effective follow-up to the UN Conference on Environment and Development (UNCED, also known as the Earth Summit), nine major groups of civil society recognized by "Agenda 21" (women, children and youth, indigenous people, NGOs, local authorities, workers and trade unions, business and industry, scientific and technological communities and farmers) have been given important roles to play as partners in sustainable development. There are currently two categories of major group organizations that can participate in the meetings of the CSD: organizations in consultative status with the ECOSOC, and those accredited to the CSD roster. See UN Department of Economic and Social Affairs, Division for Sustainable Development (2008) "Commission on Sustainable Development", available at www.un.org/esa/sustdev/csd/poly.htm.
17. Behn, note 13 above, p. 64.
18. Kuyama, Sumihiro (2001) "Enhancing Governance Oversight Role", UN Doc. JIU/REP/2001/4.
19. In this connection, Mark Bovens refers to "a paradox of shared responsibility" in "complex organizations", stating that "as the responsibility for any given instance of conduct is scattered across more people, the discrete responsibility of every individual diminishes proportionately". Bovens, Mark (1998) *The Quest for Responsibility*, Cambridge: Cambridge University Press, p. 46. Edward Luck also refers to the matter in his chapter, citing the Oil-for-Food Programme in which "the Secretariat was responsible for implementing the mandate agreed by the Security Council, but it was the latter that was to exercise [legislative] oversight. In the end, neither fully upheld its end of the bargain, leading to endless finger-pointing when the scandal broke. Shared responsibility invited a lack of accountability on both sides."
20. See Brinkerhoff, Derick W. (2001) "Taking Account of Accountability: A Conceptual Overview and Strategic Options", US Agency for International Development, March.

21. According to Kunugi, "the opinion was widely shared by the drafters of the declaration of accountability that acceptance of popular sovereignty, in place of state sovereignty, as the basis of the United Nations would constitute a conceptual breakthrough for the adaptation of the United Nations as a universal political organization for the twenty-first century, which should play a pivotal role for global governance".
22. For the rationale for his use of the term "democratic accountability", see his chapter.
23. Righter, Rosemary (1995) *Utopia Lost: The United Nations and World Order*, New York: Twentieth Century Fund, p. 281.
24. Annan, Kofi (2006) *Investing in the United Nations: For a Stronger Organization Worldwide*, UN Doc. A/60/692, 7 March, p. 13, Box 1.
25. For more on this phrase see Slaughter, Anne-Marie (2004) *A New World Order*, Princeton, NJ: Princeton University Press, p. 3.

1

Making the United Nations accountable: Managerial and political perspectives

Edward C. Luck

> A key ingredient of any successful Organization is an ethical and accountable culture pervading its staff from top to bottom. (Secretary-General Kofi Annan[1])

> Ultimately, we are all – Secretariat and Members States alike – accountable to "we the peoples". (Secretary-General-Designate Ban Ki-moon[2])

In these two brief statements, the outgoing and incoming Secretaries-General capture the essence of two distinct, but complementary, notions of accountability. On the one hand, the staff of any organization must be held accountable for the efficiency, competence and integrity with which they carry out the tasks they have been assigned. On the other hand, the Organization as a whole, including its top managers and the members of its governing board or boards, should be accountable to a much wider array of constituencies and stakeholders. In a market, for example, a firm may be highly efficient at producing a particular product, but if there is fading demand for it then those decision-makers who failed to recognize and adjust to changing market conditions and consumer preferences should be held responsible for their mismanagement. Likewise, in a responsive or democratic society a government will not be returned to power if, at election time, the people decide that it has pursued the wrong priorities, even if it has done so diligently and honestly.

In recent years the accountability of the United Nations has been brought into question on both levels. For the purposes of this chapter, the first level will be labelled "managerial accountability" and the second

Envisioning reform: Enhancing UN accountability in the twenty-first century, Kuyama and Fowler (eds), United Nations University Press, 2009, ISBN 978-92-808-1170-4

"political accountability". This chapter posits that the credibility of the world body depends on a concerted effort to repair both dimensions of its accountability deficit; that, spurred by the revelations of the oil-for-food scandal, there has been some, as yet quite modest, progress on the managerial front; but that the challenge of boosting political accountability remains little understood and largely problematic. The purpose of the chapter is to provide a brief introduction to some of the policy dilemmas endemic to this quest, particularly on the political side. To this end, it will present far more questions than answers.

Introduction: The accountability test

This story, like so many involving the United Nations, begins with a paradox. Whatever the prevailing doubts about the UN's accountability, the Member States have not been shy about assigning it ever broader and weightier tasks. A case in point was the Outcome Document agreed at the September 2005 global summit meeting, the largest gathering of heads of state and government in history. Its 178 paragraphs read like a comprehensive laundry list of the world's problems and aspirations.[3] Yet, in underlining "the urgent need to substantially improve the United Nations oversight and management processes",[4] the Member States sounded rather uncertain of its capacity to get the job done. Pledging "to enhance the relevance, effectiveness, efficiency, accountability and credibility of the United Nations system",[5] the heads of state and government emphasized that "we need an efficient, effective and accountable Secretariat".[6] Less clear was what they were prepared to do to enhance the Organization's political accountability, and whether adding one more tranche of ambitious goals would simply widen the gap between words and deeds, expectations and performance.

The paradox, of course, is that at this point, for all of the summitry, public confidence in the UN's effectiveness appears to be at an all-time low. A February 2006 Gallup survey found 64 per cent of Americans declaring UN performance to be poor, compared to only 30 per cent labelling it good – the worst finding in the more than half a century that Gallup has been posing the question.[7] Three-quarters of the respondents to a September 2006 US poll by Luntz Maslansky Strategic Research believed that the United Nations is no longer "effective" and "needs to be held more accountable".[8] While Americans are particularly vocal in their doubts about the United Nations, they are hardly alone. In a 2004 survey, Pew found less favourable views of the United Nations in Turkey, Pakistan, Jordan and Morocco – the only developing countries included in the poll – than in the United States.[9] When asked by the Standard Eurobarometer on behalf of the European Commission in September 2005 whether they tend to trust the United Nations, 37 per cent in France, 39 per cent in Italy, 40 per cent in Germany, 43 per cent in Spain, 48 per cent in Croatia, 50 per cent in Turkey and 62 per cent in Greece said they did not.[10] The Independent Inquiry Committee into the UN Oil-for-Food Programme, led by Paul Volcker, reached similar conclusions. According to its September 2005 report, at the world body there "appears to be a pervasive culture resistant to accountability and prone to escaping responsibility".[11]

Nevertheless, while the United Nations may be failing the accountability test, both US polls discovered large majorities favouring a major role for the United Nations in world affairs, a finding also endorsed by the Volcker inquiry. As Volcker subsequently wrote, the United States and others "simply cannot have it both ways: calling upon the UN to respond to large challenges while failing to insist upon the management capacity and integrity to meet those responsibilities".[12] If "we the peoples" were so discouraged that they had given up on the United Nations, then trying to identify ways of bolstering its accountability would be a truly academic exercise. But today, as in earlier bouts of despair about the current state of the world body, the hope for a stronger, more effective and more credible United Nations has not been extinguished.

Nevertheless, the marked dissonance between the public's preference for multilateral action through the United Nations and its doubts about the latter's accountability and effectiveness may help to explain the hollowness of public and governmental support for the world body. As long as the United Nations is perceived to be unaccountable, it will be hard to convince national leaders and legislators to invest heavily in its programmes and activities. Hence material resources to tackle its ambitious agenda will remain far short of what is required, contributing to a further deterioration of performance. Likewise, it is difficult to improve the performance and effectiveness of an institution – or firm or individual for that matter – that cannot be held accountable for its mistakes and failings. That principle, of course, is a prerequisite for effective democratic governance. It is altogether fitting, therefore, that accountability has emerged as a key theme, or at least buzzword, in recent commentary about the United Nations, its reform and its future.

How to make the United Nations more accountable, however, remains elusive. Few would dispute that the United Nations, like any other public institution, should be fully accountable for its failure to act in some cases, as well as for its wrong choices, ill-conceived strategies or failed implementation in other instances. But there is no generally accepted understanding of what accountability entails or how it could best be measured, assessed or instilled in the Organization. Who should be accountable to whom for what? Apportioning responsibility is no easy task in an intergovernmental body whose board consists of 192 disparate and sovereign Member States, which has a chief administrative officer instead of a CEO, whose work is carried out by a dizzying array of programmes, funds and agencies, often in partnership with civil society, and whose resources are frequently unpredictable and habitually inadequate for the mandates it has been assigned. None of this would matter a great deal if the UN's work was of marginal consequence and fading relevance. But at a point when the United Nations is coming to play an increasingly ubiquitous and even indispensable role in addressing critical public policy challenges, its persistent accountability deficits threaten to undermine the prospects for sustained and effective international cooperation when it is most needed. That is why the initiative by the United Nations University to clarify these issues, to identify and learn from best practices in other international bodies and around the UN system and to identify options for enhanced accountability mechanisms both inside and outside the world body is most timely and welcome.

Managerial and political accountability

As noted earlier, it is analytically useful to think of two kinds of accountability, one managerial and one political.[13] The former applies to managers, from the Secretary-General to lower-level administrators in the Secretariat to the heads of agencies, funds and programmes. The latter applies both to these managers and to the intergovernmental bodies and the Member States themselves. Political accountability concerns results achieved and the wisdom of mandates, as well as how efficiently and faithfully they are implemented.

Managerial accountability is familiar to even the most casual student of administration, management and governance, whether in the private or the public sector. Managers need to report fully and regularly to some higher authority, whether to a board, executive committee or higher-level manager. Various internal and external oversight or auditing bodies may be employed to supplement these hierarchical channels in ensuring transparency, integrity and efficiency. As chief administrative officer, the Secretary-General is responsible to the General Assembly for the work of the Organization and to the other principal intergovernmental organs for those functions they entrust to him (article 98 of the Charter). Agency heads often report to their own intergovernmental boards. This side of accountability is reasonably straightforward, although, as discussed below, more complicated in the United Nations than in most other institutions.

Political accountability, or what some would call democratic accountability, refers to the need for the intergovernmental bodies, as well as the Secretariat, to be answerable to the multiple and diverse constituencies and stakeholders affected by UN action or inaction, by what it chooses to do or not to do as well as by how well it does it. These groups certainly include the Member States, though some will be more affected than others by UN performance in different policy spheres. For example, the states bordering on a conflict will have a higher stake in its resolution than those distant ones that have few direct interests in the region. The same could be said about various economic and social issues. Political accountability, however, having both transnational and intra-state dimensions, reaches far beyond the 192 governments represented in the Assembly. In many cases, Member States and the Secretariat alike share the burden and responsibility for carrying out decisions of the intergovernmental organs. For instance, in the Oil-for-Food Programme the Secretariat was responsible for implementing the mandate agreed by the Security Council, but it was the latter that was to exercise oversight. In the end, neither fully upheld its end of the bargain, leading to endless finger-pointing when the scandal broke. Shared responsibility invited a lack of accountability on both sides.

As a global and virtually universal organization with an unceasingly broad agenda, the United Nations – quite literally – is accountable to the world. Some authors, especially those who see the United Nations as a stepping-stone towards world government, prefer to use "democratic" accountability instead of "political" accountability. Because people the world over are affected by what the United Nations does or, too often, fails to do, everyone is a stakeholder of the world body. Therefore, the closer and more directly the interests and concerns of individuals can be represented and voiced in UN forums, the more accountable to its ultimate constituents the Organization will become.[14] When he was Secretary-General, for instance, Kofi Annan championed the notion of human security, on the principle that the world body needs to take account of the security concerns of individuals as well as those of states. But is the United Nations democratic, or can it even aspire to be a truly democratic organization? This author has his doubts, as the United Nations was structured to be the pre-eminent intergovernmental body, with no mention of democracy or representation in the Charter.[15] Even the term "sovereign equality" was agreed at the founding conference in San Francisco to refer to equal status before international law, not to voting rights in the General Assembly.[16]

Yes, as the quote from Secretary-General Ban at the outset affirms, the Secretariat and the Member States alike are ultimately accountable to "we the peoples". But, given the UN's structure and purpose, the only way to attain this, in this author's view, is through responsive and democratic Member States. Domestic mechanisms should exist through which Member States can be held accountable by their citizens for their policies towards and within the United Nations. To suggest that there are ways the United Nations could be restructured, for example by adding a people's, parliamentary or non-governmental organization body to parallel the General Assembly to make it more "democratic", could be dangerous as well as impractical. The risk would be both to existing democratic processes within states and to the coherence and authority of the UN's intergovernmental organs. Therefore, the value-neutral term of "political" accountability is preferred for this analysis.[17]

Accountability for all seasons

Few concepts have been invoked with greater frequency or less precision around the United Nations in recent times than accountability. The term has proven especially handy and malleable in the course of the sweeping reform drive launched by Kofi Annan in September 2003. But in the process it has become a lightning rod for controversy, especially in the frequently divisive intergovernmental debates over management reform and the proposed expansion of the Security Council. For developed countries, the prime concern has been to ensure that the Secretariat (and the General Assembly's Fifth Committee) is accountable for the productive and honest use of the Organization's material and human resources. As the primary financial contributors to the Organization, and themselves accountable to their taxpayers and parliaments, they often act as if – at least on financial matters – accountability should be to them, first and foremost. They tend to place a higher priority on managerial than political accountability. The developing country majority, caucusing as the 131-member G-77 plus China group, naturally see things in a starkly different light. They are prone to stressing the political accountability of select membership bodies, like the Security Council, to the membership as a whole. On this, their views tend to coincide with those of the many developed countries that do not happen to have the good fortune to have been self-nominated as a permanent member of the Security Council in 1945. In the hotly contested battle over how to reform the Security Council, most Member States, Secretary-General Kofi Annan and his High-level Panel on Threats, Challenges and Change argued vigorously that the present members of the Council, particularly the permanent ones, are currently unaccountable to the larger membership and their deliberations remain insufficiently transparent. What greater accountability would look like in terms of the Council's composition, procedures and working methods, however, remains a matter of conjecture and heated debate.[18]

The growing deployment of UN military and civilian personnel in peace operations and humanitarian missions around the world has raised a series of complex accountability challenges.[19] As the number of UN personnel in the field has come to exceed by far those at headquarters in an age of acute terrorist threats, questions about accountability for their security have been posed sharply and painfully. The bombing of UN headquarters in Baghdad in August 2003, which killed the head of the UN Assistance Mission for IRAQ (UNAMI), Sergio Vieira de Mello, and 21 of his colleagues, is still described by Kofi Annan as the low point of his decade-long tenure.[20] It prompted a lot of soul-searching in New York and a sweeping and highly critical review of UN security procedures.[21] In an immediate and managerial sense, accountability should rest with the Secretary-General, of course. But what of the Member States, particularly those on the Security Council, which negotiate the mandates for UN missions and then fail to provide them with sufficient funding, personnel and security measures? Nowhere can the overlap between managerial and political accountability be seen more starkly than in the UN's peace operations in the field, whether in Rwanda, Srebrenica or Baghdad.

Peacekeeping poses risks not only for UN civilian personnel but also for the soldiers contributed by Member States and the local population they seek to protect.[22] As the United Nations seeks to recruit a record number of blue helmets, police and civilian personnel to fulfil the ambitious and high-risk peace operations authorized by the Security Council in recent months, potential troop-contributing countries are asking pointed questions about who will be accountable for any lapses in oversight, communications, mission planning or adjustments to changing circumstances on the ground. The stakes for those governments that respond to the UN's call, for the UN's credibility and reputation and, most importantly, for the victims of the conflicts themselves are very high. In recent years there has been a dismaying surge in reports of sexual abuse by peacekeepers, civilian as well as military, of the very women and children they were supposed to protect.[23]

The September 2005 Outcome Document from the global summit took a potentially historic step towards achieving a consensus on the doctrine of a responsibility to protect. The gathered heads of state and government agreed that "each individual State has the responsibility to protect its populations from genocide, war crimes, ethnic cleansing and crimes against humanity".[24] But, in the next paragraph, they asserted that "the international community, through the United Nations, also has the responsibility" to take appropriate measures "to help protect populations" from these acts. The latter paragraph, however, is heavily caveated and its invocation would depend on the results of multilateral decision-making processes: no automaticity here. What remains unclear, then, is who is responsible when the United Nations and the so-called international community fail collectively to uphold their side of the equation even in well-publicized situations of genocide, as in Darfur. The question of whether or how international leaders and national decision-makers should be held accountable for such failures of will has hardly entered the mainstream debate, much less produced any convergence of views. The International Criminal Court, for example, is understandably focused on the commission of illegal and repugnant acts, not on those who look the other way.

Aside from these more existential matters of political accountability, which have always plagued the notion of collective decision-making in a world of sovereign nation-states, the United Nations has also suffered from more prosaic but highly damaging deficits in managerial accountability. Ongoing investigations of UN procurement practices, much like the Volcker-led inquiry into the Oil-for-Food Programme, have aimed at centres of alleged impunity in which managers have not been held properly accountable despite the relatively large and growing sums involved. In 2005–2006 Secretary-General Kofi Annan announced a series of steps, such as an Ethics Office, whistleblower protection, financial disclosure statements and enhanced auditing.[25] His successor, Ban Ki-moon, has promised further steps. How stubborn the longstanding culture of unaccountability will prove to be remains to be seen.

Traditionally, the incoming Secretary-General has enjoyed a honeymoon period in which to restructure top posts to fit his priorities and management style.[26] Secretary-General Ban has indicated that he plans to introduce a major restructuring of the UN's political departments, as well as pursuing the management reform process initiated by Kofi Annan. There is substantial unfinished business on the latter front, as in mid-2006 the General Assembly and its Fifth Committee rebuffed much of Kofi Annan's broad-ranging package of management, budgetary and human resources reforms.[27] Again, starkly different interpretations of accountability standards and processes fed the deep mistrust between developed and developing countries, and between the latter and the Secretariat, that downed the reform proposals. Not only were the Secretary-General's far-reaching proposals set aside, but, in the process, the Assembly ended a two-decades-old practice of deciding budgetary matters by consensus. Thus the most important and durable product of the mid-1980s' reform effort has been lost: a high price for the current lack of trust, transparency and accountability in the world body. This setback served to underline the depth of North–South differences over the meaning of accountability, as well as their policy consequences.

As these disparate examples suggest, accountability – or more often the lack of it – has become a pervasive and central challenge to UN reformers, managers and Member States. The more popular the concept has become, however, the harder it has been to refine and articulate its content and definition. At this point, as the examples above illustrate, accountability means quite different things to different people.

Accountability in the UN context

The United Nations is not the first institution to try to refine the notion of accountability in the policy realm. A number of NGOs are dedicated to improving the accountability of public institutions. For example, the Humanitarian Accountability Partnership suggests that "accountability is the countervailing force which confronts power and ensures that it is exercised responsibly".[28] Though evocative, this formulation fails to provide a rigorous or measurable standard. A 2003 report by the Global Accountability Project, *Power Without Accountability*, comes closer to providing a usable definition. It begins with a variation of the dictionary definition: "At its simplest, accountability refers to a process by which individuals or organizations are answerable for their actions and the consequences that follow from them."[29] It then differentiates between "traditional" and "stakeholder" approaches that roughly correspond to the managerial and political models noted above, though the report favours a democratic standard based on the voice and access of individuals to the decision-making processes of intergovernmental bodies, as if the latter were components of a world government.

During the recent reform drive, the United Nations itself tried to come up with a usable definition of accountability. The Independent Steering Committee on the Comprehensive Review of Governance and Oversight within the United Nations and Its Funds, Programmes and Specialized Agencies was established by Secretary-General Annan upon a request contained in the Outcome Document of the September 2005 World Summit. In the glossary of its report,[30] the Committee defines accountability as "the responsibility to justify money spent, decisions made, and activities performed by an individual or an organization". The report outlines a proposed UN Code of Governance based on best practices. The latter, it notes, "are therefore a means to help ensure that the UN Code of Governance is implemented and that those responsible are held accountable".

These findings of the Independent Steering Committee certainly help clarify the notion of accountability in a management context. However, there are several reasons to treat this definition as the starting point, not the end, of the quest for greater clarity.

- One, the United Nations is criticized as often for what it has failed to do or to respond to as for "money spent, decisions made, and activities performed". The UN's management and governance lapses, in both the Secretariat and the Security Council, on the implementation of the Oil-for-Food Programme come to mind. As noted above, the Security Council's lack of will in dealing with the humanitarian calamities in Rwanda, Srebrenica and Darfur surely raises accountability issues that far transcend, in the public's eye, those stemming from garden-variety management shortcomings.
- Two, the Independent Steering Committee's definition seems more apt for management accountability than for political accountability, and for the Secretariat than for intergovernmental bodies. In an organization as intrinsically political as the United Nations, it makes little sense to employ standard management criteria for assessing whether it has succeeded in carrying out those mandates that are highly political or have a more aspirational or symbolic quality. In other words, one-size-fits-all standards are unlikely to work across the board in a UN context.
- Three, under this definition it is not entirely clear for what the United Nations is being held accountable. Since the proposed code is to be based on best practices, it sounds as if these would form the standard or basis for judgement. As long as the UN entity could reasonably claim to have followed the best practices then known, it could not be held responsible or accountable for any inadequacies in the results achieved. That may be an acceptable standard for accounting purposes, but hardly sufficient for political expectations and demands. The latter, like the policy challenges facing the United Nations, are highly dynamic. Current practices and standards are often insufficient to get the job done in such an unpredictable policy environment, particularly when the UN's assigned task and policy preferences involve prevention.
- Four, while the report's definition encompasses the standard dictionary meaning of having to give account or be answerable, it tells us nothing about what happens next. Are there rewards for good performance and punishments for bad? Are there increments along the way? Who determines these and who is capable of carrying them out? Some authors emphasize that accountability entails imposing significant costs or disincentives for failure, while Robert Behn goes so far as to assert that "accountability means punishment".[31] Neither punishment nor reward, of course, comes easily or surely for the United Nations.

As noted earlier, it is no secret that the often murky managerial and governance relationships between the Member States and the Secretariat contribute to both the perception and the reality of a lack of accountability in the world body. According to the report, "transparency and disclosure concern the framework and context for the accountability of the governing body, its members and the executive management in the entity".[32] It goes on to underline that "the General Assembly is the Governing Body of the Secretariat". But how does one hold a body of 192 states accountable? Given the universal character and one-state, one-vote rules not only of the Assembly but also of its Fifth Committee that handles management and budgetary matters, is not this proposition equivalent to declaring the world to be responsible and accountable? As early as 1945, when the United Nations had only 51 members, the UN's Preparatory Commission recognized that "a large body like the General Assembly, or the Administrative and Budgetary Committee of the Assembly, would find it difficult to deal adequately with the budget and related administrative matters".[33] One can imagine what the Commission would have said about the oversight capacities of an Assembly with 192 members! Yet, as demonstrated once again in the breakdown of the consensus process in 2006, many Member States, particularly the developing countries, insist that these questions be addressed only by committees of the whole, where each of them has a voice and vote equal to those of the largest contributors.

To get a fuller perspective on why accountability has been so problematic for the United Nations, it would be helpful to consider the steps that would need to be taken to ensure effective and sustainable accountability in an institution devoted to public policy. For such a body, delivery matters more than good intentions. The following seven steps therefore suggest themselves.

- One, the mandate or policy task to be undertaken must be defined, articulated and communicated with sufficient clarity, precision and timeliness that all of the relevant players and stakeholders have a clear and common understanding of what is being undertaken. Ambiguity about the nature, scope or means for carrying out the mandate should be kept to a minimum. But the intergovernmental bodies that produce the UN's core mandates thrive on creative ambiguity, even vagueness, in the pursuit of convergence and consensus among the Member States.
- Two, the results or performance must be measurable in some generally accepted way, as well as in a timely manner. The second dictionary definition of accountable is "explainable" or "capable of being accounted for". Even when not hampered by purposeful ambiguity, UN resolutions are often general, aspirational or indicative of a policy direction more than of specific, actionable, policy measures or steps. For example, the most precise mandates in the Millennium Declaration were those for the Millennium Development Goals, but it required considerable work and no little controversy to have them translated into more

specific and measurable targets that could spur policy action. Seven years later, controversy persists on whether and how much progress is being made towards these goals and deadlines. The 178 paragraphs of the 2005 Outcome Document are every bit as general and hortatory. Outcomes in the peace and security realm tend to be even less measurable, partly because one can never know what would have happened if the United Nations had acted in a different way or be fully confident that the remnants of past conflicts will not spark renewed trouble at some future point. The United Nations tends to address dynamic, not static, situations.

- Three, there must be some agreed or generally acceptable means of conducting the measurement and assessment of results achieved, and of communicating these findings to the relevant parties and stakeholders. This needs to be done, of course, in a credible, accessible, timely and authoritative manner. Results-based or performance-based budgeting has provided a partial answer to this challenge, but it has worked far better in some policy sectors than others. On the whole, it appears to have added more to managerial than to political accountability; on core development and security issues of wide visibility and high public concern, these techniques have been less productive. In part, this reflects the UN's modest role as one of many actors in these fields, in which it often exercises relatively little control over events and developments. On its own, it generally is in no position to deliver on its promises.
- Four, beyond these questions about who should be responsible for what lies the matter of to whom they should be accountable. By its very nature, the United Nations tends to deal with controversial issues whose resolution favours some parties more than others, whether the question relates to development, social matters or security. More and more, the United Nations is seeking to address the problems affecting individuals and groups, not just states. In human rights and humanitarian affairs, the state may be the problem and UN actions may be applauded on one level and condemned on another. There may be multiple constituencies, with a range of views and values, to whom the United Nations is accountable.
- Five, whichever constituency is deemed to have a legitimate stake in the outcome should also have a reliable means of aggregating and communicating its collective judgement about the success of the UN programme or action. Again, UN leaders have increasingly identified its core mission as coming to the aid of the poor, vulnerable, abused and disenfranchised. Fair enough, but by definition these groups may be the least able to assemble and develop a collective viewpoint or have the means of communicating it to international officials or other Member

States in a timely, accurate and assured manner. Who speaks for the poor, the displaced and the suppressed? Many diplomats in the General Assembly claim to, as do any number of Northern-based NGOs. But such contentions are highly political, sometimes self-interested and hard to verify. Articulate and energetic NGOs are being established at an impressive rate in much of the developing world, and South-South NGO networks are growing as well.[34] Their credentials and independence from government influence are not always unambiguous, and they tend to be in short supply where most needed in underdeveloped and oppressive societies where the United Nations seeks to make the most difference.

- Six, there needs to be some generally accepted means of determining, calibrating and applying appropriate incentives or sanctions in each case. This has proven to be a particularly high and stubborn hurdle for the UN system. The United Nations relies on others to carry out many of its field and operational activities, whether in peacekeeping, humanitarian assistance, human rights or development. As the repugnant abuses by UN blue helmets noted above have illustrated, it is difficult for the United Nations to hold individual soldiers or officers accountable when their chain of command goes to their capitals, not to Turtle Bay. The United Nations has no legal authority to prosecute its own employees, while its management culture often favours ignoring all but the most serious transgressions and passing on poor performers to other departments or programmes. Much of the Secretariat, moreover, seems convinced that the existing avenues for redress for employees facing disciplinary action are unfair, antiquated and biased towards managers.[35] On the intergovernmental level, Member States, not surprisingly, show little appetite for sanctions or even naming-and-shaming tactics to keep other Member States accountable.
- Seven, in theory Member States have some powerful tools for ensuring that the Secretary-General, his top managers and those of the programmes, funds and agencies are held accountable. But the practice of permitting a Secretary-General to serve two terms is deeply ingrained among the Member States, especially since the United States unilaterally denied Boutros Boutros-Ghali a second term. The Charter has no provision for impeachment, or even for the terms and conditions of the office. The power of the purse is hard to exercise in a 192-member body, especially when the large majority have little financial stake in the Organization. Some major contributors would prefer to move more rapidly towards voluntary funding, precisely to ensure fuller accountability. However, there is much resistance to that trend in the General Assembly, where most states already complain incessantly about the financial pressures exerted by the wealthier countries. The heavy

reliance on voluntary funding raises a managerial dilemma as well, for it reduces the Secretary-General's, as well as the General Assembly's, leverage and control over those vast portions of the UN system – as much as 80 per cent of its posts and spending – funded through voluntary or extra-budgetary channels.[36] Hence, in the name of political accountability, the prospects for managerial accountability have been compromised and its scope has been narrowed.

None of this suggests that accountability is impossible in the UN system or that these barriers are immutable. The United Nations is a dynamic and adaptable place.[37] These seven points do help explain, however, why notions of accountability from other contexts, such as the private sector or national governments, may fit the United Nations awkwardly and imperfectly at best. They also underline why managerial accountability is easier to achieve, even to define, than political accountability. In such an obsessively political environment, of course, the distinction between what is managerial and what is political is rarely clean cut. The United Nations needs to do far better at both. It cannot move with assurance down either path, moreover, without substantial progress on the other. This will require a degree of joint effort and mutual confidence between the Member States and the Secretariat that has too often been lacking in recent years. To function properly and to be sustainable, accountability in the UN system demands a degree of the very trust that it is – ironically – designed to produce. With new leadership at the United Nations and changing political dynamics in key capitals, it just may be time for what has been a downward cycle to reverse itself, as steps towards greater transparency, trust and accountability become mutually reinforcing. If so, then the long-awaited renovation of the world body could begin to move from the realm of theory to the plane of practice.

Acknowledgements

This is a revised and expanded version of the keynote address to the United Nations University (UNU) Tokyo Symposium on Accountability on 16 October 2006.

Notes

1. Annan, Kofi (2006) *Investing in the United Nations for a Stronger Organization Worldwide*, A/60/692, 7 March, p. 13, Box 1.
2. Ban Ki-moon (2006) "Address on Taking the Oath of Office", SG/2119, GA/10558, 14 December.

3. United Nations (2005) Outcome Document, 2005 World Summit Meeting, A/RES/60/1, 16 September.
4. Ibid., para. 164.
5. Ibid., para. 15.
6. Ibid., para. 161.
7. Gallup (2006) *Gallup Organization Poll*, Princeton University, 6–9 February.
8. *PR Newswire* (2006) "Americans Grade the U.N.: 'Get It Together or Get Out'; Americans Vote 'No Confidence' on UN", *PR Newswire*, 11 September.
9. Pew Research Center for the People and the Press (2004) "A Year After Iraq War: A Nine Country Survey", 16 March, available at http://people-press.org/reports/display.php3?ReportID=206.
10. European Commission (2005) "Standard Eurobarometer 63: Public Opinion in the European Union", Luxembourg: Office for Official Publications of the European Communities, September, available at http://ec.europe.ec/public_opinion/archives/eb/eb63/eb63_en.htm.
11. United Nations (2005) *Report of the Independent Inquiry Committee: The Management of the United Nations Oil-for-Food Programme*, vol. I, 7 September, p. 61, available at www.iic-offp.org/Mgmt_Report.htm.
12. Volcker, Paul A. (2006) "Introduction", in Jeffrey A. Meyer and Mark G. Califano, eds, *Good Intentions Corrupted: The Oil-for-Food Scandal and the Threat to the United Nations*, New York: Public Affairs, p. ix.
13. The Committee on the Accountability of International Organizations of the International Law Association (ILA) differentiates between four kinds of accountability: legal, political, administrative and financial. The notion of managerial accountability presented in this chapter encompasses both the administrative and financial categories used by the ILA Committee. In this chapter, legal accountability will be addressed only to the extent that it has political implications. The ILA Committee notes the underdevelopment of "legal theory concerning the international legal responsibility of international organizations". International Law Association (2004) "Accountability of International Organizations", *International Law Organizations Law Review* 1, p. 255.
14. In his contribution to this volume, Hirohide Takikawa counsels that accountability should not be equated with democracy. He introduces the intriguing term of "indirect democratic accountability".
15. Many authors, among them Jochen Prantl in this volume, have pointed out the proclivity of international organizations, including the United Nations, to be undemocratic in their own governance.
16. Russell, Ruth B. (1958) *A History of the United Nations Charter: The Role of the United States 1940–1945*, Washington, DC: Brookings Institution, p. 672.
17. Also writing in this volume, Tatsuro Kunugi rejects the term "democratic" accountability for quite different reasons. He finds it to be too narrow because it does not take into account the broader civil society actors, such as non-state actors, academia, media, NGOs, etc. The chapters by Michael Fowler and Jochen Prantl also reject the notion of "democratic" accountability.
18. For a recent discussion of the ongoing intergovernmental debate over Security Council reform, see Luck, Edward C. (2006) *UN Security Council: Practice and Promise*, London: Routledge, pp. 111–126.
19. For trends in numbers of deployed peacekeepers and in the top 10 contributors of troops and police personnel see ibid., pp. 38–39 and 175–176.
20. For a pointed account of this episode see Traub, James (2006) *The Best of Intentions: Kofi Annan and the UN in the Era of American World Power*, New York: Farrar, Straus and Giroux, pp. 189–199.

21. See United Nations (2003) *Report of the Independent Panel on the Safety and Security of UN Personnel in Iraq*, 20 October, New York: United Nations; United Nations (2004) *Report of the Security in Iraq Accountability Panel* (SIAP), 3 March, New York: United Nations.
22. For a provocative discussion of the doctrine of operational necessity in this regard, see the chapter by Kyoji Kawasaki in this volume.
23. Luck, note 18 above, pp. 88–89.
24. United Nations, note 3 above, p. 31, para. 138.
25. For a summary of some of these measures see United Nations, note 1 above, pp. 13–14, Box 1.
26. The historical record, Secretary-General by Secretary-General, is usefully documented in Myint-U, Thant, and Amy Scott (2006) *A Brief History of the UN Secretariat*, 27 November, New York: International Peace Academy.
27. A/RES/60/283, 7 July 2006. For the proposals of Secretary-General Kofi Annan being considered by the Assembly see United Nations, note 1 above. For press accounts of the initial action in the Assembly's Fifth Committee see Lynch, Colum (2006) "Developing Nations Thwart Annan's Plan for Reform at U.N.", *Washington Post*, 29 April; Hoge, Warren (2006) "Third World Bloc Thwarts U.N. Reform Plan", *New York Times*, 29 April.
28. See homepage of the Humanitarian Accountability Partnership International, Geneva, Switzerland, available at www.hapinternational.org/en/page.php?IDpage=64&IDcat=10.
29. Kovach, Hetty, Caroline Neligan and Simon Burall (2003) *Power Without Accountability?*, London: One World Trust, p. 3.
30. See United Nations (2006) "Report of the Independent Steering Committee", UN Doc. A/60/883/Add.1, 28 August.
31. Behn, Robert D. (2001) *Rethinking Democratic Accountability*, Washington, DC: Brookings Institution Press, p. 3.
32. United Nations, note 30 above, p. 39.
33. United Nations (1946) *Report of the Preparatory Commission of the United Nations*, London: United Nations, p. 106.
34. While this chapter is largely focused on accountability at headquarters, Kazuo Takahashi's chapter in this volume raises the essential dimension of the need to boost civil society participation and greater transparency in UN operations in the field.
35. For ambitious plans for restructuring and reorienting the UN's internal justice system see United Nations (2006) "Report of the Redesign Panel on the United Nations System of Administration of Justice", UN Doc. A/61/205, 28 July.
36. On the breakdown of the founding concept of "the expenses of the organization" see the useful chapter by Tadanori Inomata in this volume.
37. As this author has documented elsewhere, the history of change in the UN system suggests that the world body is as adaptable to changing circumstances, opportunities and demands as it is resistant to formal structural reform steps. See Luck, Edward C. (2007) "Principal Organs", in Thomas Weiss and Sam Daws, eds, *The Oxford Handbook on the United Nations*, Oxford: Oxford University Press; Luck, Edward C. (2003) "Reforming the United Nations: Lessons from a History in Progress", Occasional Paper Series, New Haven, CT: Academic Council on the United Nations System.

Part I

General analysis of accountability in the UN context

2

Bringing the different United Nations to account

Michael Ross Fowler

Introduction

The post–Cold War era has been marked by a series of diverse issues that have arisen somewhere within the UN system and have raised grave questions regarding the Organization's accountability. In the early 1990s charges of corruption and mismanagement dogged peacekeeping missions in Cambodia, Somalia and the Balkans.[1] In 1994 the wholly inadequate UN responses to events in Rwanda proved to be a key factor in the killing of approximately 800,000 people, and yet no UN actor, and certainly not the Security Council or its permanent members, squarely accepted blame for the failure to act effectively.[2] The following year the Serb army massacred civilians at the supposed UN "safe area" of Srebrenica in Bosnia and Herzegovina. Here, despite the fact that neither a peace agreement nor a ceasefire existed, peacekeepers had been deployed in inadequate numbers. While the United Nations published a report that detailed the organization's failures in Srebrenica,[3] no officials were cited as having been responsible and disciplined or punished.[4] Indeed, later ventures, such as the military operation in Sierra Leone, also progressed with a clearly insufficient peacekeeping force, raising serious questions as to whether the lessons of Srebrenica had been duly absorbed.[5]

In 2004 and 2005 revelations of fraud, corruption, mismanagement and faulty oversight badly tarnished the Oil-for-Food Programme in Iraq[6] and eventually led to the conviction of a UN procurement officer on

Envisioning reform: Enhancing UN accountability in the twenty-first century, Kuyama and Fowler (eds), United Nations University Press, 2009, ISBN 978-92-808-1170-4

charges of receiving nearly $1 million in kickbacks from the companies with which he was contracting.[7] After former US federal prosecutor Robert Appleton led an investigation into bribery, bid rigging, overcharges and misappropriated funds in peacekeeping operations, a 2007 report concluded: "The task force identified multiple instances of fraud and corruption with aggregate value in excess of $610 million."[8] In 2008 internal audits at the UN Office for Internal Oversight Services turned up millions of dollars that had allegedly been wasted during the UN peacekeeping operation in Sudan.[9]

During the early twenty-first century charges of sexual exploitation by UN personnel in Africa and the Balkans[10] drew considerable public attention as well. A 2005 UN report concluded that "Sexual exploitation and abuse by military, civilian policy and civilian peacekeeping personnel is not a new phenomenon" and often brings with it "a continued downward spiral of further prostitution, with its attendant violence, desperation, disease, and further dependency". This causes local and international public disillusionment with an organization "mandated to enter into a broken society to help it, not to break the trust placed in it by the local population".[11] A 2008 report authored by the non-governmental organization Save the Children concluded that sexual abuse of children takes place in every emergency zone, with abuse by UN peacekeepers a particular problem.[12] After observing that "Few UN agencies and NGOs collect detailed information on the abuse of children by their own personnel, and even fewer make this information publicly available",[13] Save the Children noted that the impact of past efforts to curb the problem had yet to be seen at the grassroots level.[14]

The crescendo of scandals, followed by mounting evidence that public confidence in the United Nations is receding,[15] has stimulated scholars to focus upon how the Organization might become more accountable. In attempting to shed light on the difficulties involved in bringing such a vast global international organization to account,[16] this chapter addresses the following questions.

- How should accountability be conceived of within the United Nations?
- Who in the Organization might be accountable to whom?
- What is the "accountability gap"?
- What are the principal obstacles to improved future accountability?
- Would further democratizing the United Nations be likely to enhance accountability?

Accountability within the United Nations

In essence, *accountability* denotes some designated supervisory entity critically appraising the effort by a subordinate body to demonstrate responsible behaviour. I would thus urge that accountability be approached via the related yet antecedent idea of duty or responsibility.[17] At core, *responsibility* in public affairs involves the direct or indirect assignment and the consequent acceptance of particular tasks. Accountability focuses on the evaluation of those tasks: assessing the manner in which they have been executed over a particular time period. While the two concepts speak to overlapping concerns, they are, in my formulation, quite definitely distinct.

With this in mind, scholars and policy-makers might advance towards the ultimate goal of fashioning policy proposals useful within the UN context by first working through a set of analytical questions.

- In what ways have duties, either declared or implied, evolved within the United Nations?[18]
- How, in quantitative and qualitative terms, has each part of the United Nations been carrying out its duties?
- How and to whom does each part attempt to demonstrate that it has, in fact, been behaving responsibly?
- How has the supervisory entity, if any, assessed the actions of those who report to it and communicated the results of that assessment?
- To what extent has the part of the United Nations being brought to account reacted to the appraisal in rational and useful ways?
- Finally, how large is the gulf between the manner in which such a system aimed at effective accountability should operate and the manner in which the current system has, in fact, operated?

As one moves down this list of questions, international organization discourse shifts away from the sphere of responsibility and into the neighbouring realm of accountability.

For an entity to be seen as properly accountable, duties must be defined, a clear and effective hierarchy must be established in which one entity brings another to account, an adequate accounting to an appropriate body must occur, the results of the external evaluation must be communicated effectively to the entity being evaluated and the assessment must then be absorbed and, ideally, acted upon[19] in some productive manner. And, I maintain, these fundamental principles are applicable to both *managerial accountability*, that is, the intra-organizational responsibility to manage effectively the administrative affairs of a governmental body, and *political accountability*, that is, a political organization's intra- and extra-organizational efforts to explain and stand behind its behaviour. In each of these cases attention ought to focus both on what the government body has chosen to do and not to do, and the manner in which it has acted, including its effort to learn from its failures and revise its future actions accordingly.

Which United Nations? Disaggregating the pieces of the Organization

If effective analysis hinges in part on arriving at a common understanding of how accountability should be conceived of in the international organization context, I would contend that a precise definition of just what is meant by *United Nations* is in order as well. In the decades since the framing of the UN Charter, "United Nations" has been used quite differently depending on the circumstances in which the phrase was employed. Some will say that the United Nations has various faces or dimensions. For purposes of international relations analysis I prefer to underscore the distinctive nature of its multiple spheres of action by describing them as different United Nations.[20]

Perhaps the narrowest use of the term "United Nations" has focused on the part of the Organization centred on the Secretariat,[21] led by the Secretary-General.[22] In this sense the United Nations is an organization separate from the states that comprise its membership roster. The ideal of this *United Nations of the Secretariat* is impartial internationalism. Its energies are usually absorbed by actions aimed at the issues of development and social and humanitarian affairs,[23] first pointed to in article 1(3) of the Charter.[24] When one says that the United Nations lacks armed forces or military expertise, this is the sense in which the term is being employed, as it is when one says that the Organization is deeply involved in helping to build better lives for people around the world.

However, other common and valid uses of *United Nations* exist as well. The founders who met in San Francisco in 1945 focused chiefly on the task of how states might become united in order to deal with the crucially important problems of world order that had brought two world wars in three decades.[25] These initial discussions launched what might be thought of as the state-centric United Nations.[26] The Charter opens with the declaration that the purposes of the United Nations are "to maintain international peace and security" via "effective collective measures".[27] Such statements principally involve the *United Nations of the Member States*, not the United Nations of the Secretariat. Indeed, throughout the provisions of Chapter II regarding membership in the Organization, the phrase "United Nations" is quite clearly used in this second sense of the term.[28] The ever-larger body of states that have signed the Charter – the United Nations in this venerable usage – is not really headed by the Secretary-General, who is, according to article 97 of the Charter, "the chief administrative officer of the Organization", much less by the other staff of the Secretariat. Both might more accurately be portrayed as working for the United Nations of the Member States.

One might also observe that the United Nations of the Member States can be divided into component parts, separate though overlapping. When international crises come before the Organization, leadership is to be exercised by the Security Council, which is also authorized "to speak and act in the name of the UN".[29] This *executive United Nations*, which might be thought of as one core decision-making group of the United Nations of the Member States, functions "with the assistance of an international staff",[30] and often addresses its instructions to the Secretary-General.[31]

With respect to this particular usage, international relations scholars might argue that this United Nations most certainly does not lack armed forces. To the contrary, its Member States boast the vast bulk of the world's military power, with a significant percentage of that capacity lodged within the militaries of the permanent members of the Security Council.[32] Just how united the Security Council is with respect to the handling of any particular crisis very largely determines the action, or inaction, of this United Nations. However, when powerful states provide troops for peacekeeping and peace-enforcement actions undertaken in the name of the United Nations, they do not typically give up command of their forces.[33] In these circumstances, the authority of the United Nations over the troops acting in the organization's name is problematic, to say the least. And international society is still grappling with the issue of whether the United Nations might be held internationally responsible if a state acting pursuant to Security Council authorization then acts wrongfully[34] – a problem that might arise in various contexts, including the use of national military forces.

When still others employ the term *United Nations*, they have in mind not so much the Organization of the Secretariat, led by the Secretary-General, or the crisis-management institution, centred on the Security Council, but instead what might be thought of as the *plenary United Nations*. Here the focus is on the "verbal function" of the United Nations of the Member States – that is, the heart of modern multilateral diplomacy, "the all-encompassing General Assembly ... the talk-shop, the resolution-passing, declaration-proclaiming, judgment-pronouncing center of the Organization".[35] This is the organ to which are directed a host of studies and annual and special reports,[36] much of the fodder of accountability in a modern bureaucracy. In addition, the *plenary United Nations* approves budgets, which might be thought of as one important though indirect route towards holding the *executive United Nations* accountable.[37] And this particular United Nations has also evolved in significant ways over time, being transformed from what was once frequently a diplomatic instrument of the United States and its allies to one largely dominated by the so-called third world states.

To this list I would add that within international relations discourse the United Nations is also frequently used in shorthand for the broader phrases "UN system"[38] or "UN family of organizations". That is, the term can encompass all those institutions that, over 60 years, have found some place under the aegis of this immense global organization. The specialized agencies are one vital focal point within this *umbrella United Nations*, but the Organization has also spawned a formidable array of other entities, including units and task forces, programmes and conferences, commissions and committees, and expert groups and blue-ribbon panels. (A number of these are alluded to in the chapters that follow.)

In identifying and underscoring analytical distinctions among the *United Nations of the Secretariat*, the *United Nations of the Member States*, its two principal subdivisions – the *executive United Nations* and the *plenary United Nations* – and the *umbrella United Nations*, I do not mean to suggest that these United Nations have in any sense evolved into mutually exclusive bodies.[39] Naturally, the services provided by the Secretariat are critically important to the other organs.[40] Certainly, the Member States regularly influence, if they do not always control, the Secretariat, which depends upon them for vital resources. At the same time, the Secretary-General often has a bearing on Security Council affairs, even enjoying the power to summon that body when he perceives a threat to the peace.[41] In these sorts of ways the multiple United Nations are often connected, intertwined, even interlocked, though I would dispute the notion that they must therefore themselves be very united.

To disentangle issues of accountability, it may be helpful to think about how the various United Nations are or are not, might or might not be, brought to account. This is particularly important since, when it is said that through the years the United Nations has lacked accountability, one could be advancing quite different criticisms:

- that the *United Nations of the Secretariat* is not sufficiently accountable to the Member States in its use of certain funds or its implementation of certain projects
- that the *United Nations of the Member States* is not sufficiently accountable to national constituencies or to the world's people
- that the *executive United Nations*, in undertaking crisis management, is not sufficiently accountable to the plenary United Nations or to "we the peoples of the United Nations"
- that the *plenary United Nations* is not sufficiently accountable to the global public or the rest of the Organization as it makes declarations in its resolutions or fulfils its other duties, including its budgetary work and review of reports
- that the *umbrella United Nations* is not sufficiently accountable to the principal UN organs, the Member States or the general public, as each component part goes about its business in what often seems an emphatically decentralized and autonomous manner.

These possible criticisms suggest a wide array of fields of enquiry for scholars examining UN accountability. Upon which of the United

Nations is the main thrust of the effort to enhance accountability to be focused? One might also carefully consider to whom that accountability might flow. Should it be conceived as flowing to the global public, or might it also flow from one United Nations, such as the Secretariat, to another, such as the Member States?

The "accountability gap" at the United Nations

Why exactly do troubling issues continue to arise with respect to the accountability of each of the United Nations identified above? What is the source of the deficit, or gap, in UN accountability that is both deeply worrisome and quite widespread? Here is an organization that has seldom been accused of shirking paperwork, that employs legions of accountants and auditors, lawyers and administrators, and that has long been committed to publishing and then disseminating extraordinary amounts of material related to its operations. Why does there remain the widespread view, among insiders and outsiders, that the United Nations is insufficiently accountable for its activities?

One conceivable reason is that the public, even fairly knowledgeable observers, may be unaware of the efforts by the various United Nations to be accountable. While certain of the different United Nations no doubt perceive more of an obligation to account for their actions than do others, none has particularly distinguished itself in publicizing its past efforts to be accountable. Thus people may not be sufficiently aware of many of the activities of such institutions as the Ethics Office, the Joint Inspection Unit or the Office of Internal Oversight Services, or of independent inquiry committees, much less such recent advances as whistleblower protection, financial disclosure requirements and post-employment restrictions on UN staffers.[42]

And yet the continuing serious accountability issues that have riveted the attention of so many in countries around the world strongly suggest that something more deeply rooted than a public relations problem is at work. While various explanations might be suggested for the accountability gap, let me identify a handful of exacerbating factors and suggest that they tend to play off one another, each contributing to the gap.

The lack of constitutional guidance

On a philosophical plane, few would quarrel with the assertion that each of the United Nations described above, in policies and projects, statements and decisions, should be true to the constitutional principles upon which the Organization was founded. And, to a notable extent, the UN

Charter does partake of the nature of a constitution. Its words provide a text that is a source of legitimacy and contains certain directives – some clear, some implied, some ambiguous – aimed at organizing a government body, identifying basic principles and distributing and limiting important powers. As a form of constitution, however, the UN Charter is also clouded by various significant problems. For one, the inclination of governments to abide by the Charter may not be as deeply ingrained as is the inclination to abide by their own constitution. Throughout the organization's existence differing ideologies and national interests have regularly pulled the Member States towards pragmatic policies and away from the principled behaviour, the notions of how international politics ought to work, described in the Charter.[43] For instance, as I have argued elsewhere, throughout the Cold War and beyond, the security regime envisioned by the UN founders went largely unrealized on account of a flawed, failed or illusory collective security system.[44]

Furthermore, an international legal regime that might interpret and even enforce the words of the UN Charter remains, at best, fragmentary and underdeveloped. Certainly, the International Court of Justice has never been granted the power to exercise any type of judicial review to ensure that UN legislative organs abide by the words of the Charter. And yet judicial review has been an essential matter in effectively delineating and clarifying the constitutions of so many of the states that adhere reasonably well to the ideal of a rule of law.[45] More broadly, the Charter, as a constitutional document, continues to lack well-developed case law. And the number and variety of potential viewpoints can be perplexing, as now almost 200 sovereign states themselves attempt to interpret the Charter as a living document. This, then, underscores the problems associated with the absence of a body of definitive constitutional judgments issued by a court.

Beyond this systemic difficulty, the UN Charter simply does not speak of accountability frequently or directly. It is true that the Charter spells out certain key tasks envisioned for such vital organs as the General Assembly and the Security Council, and does so much more clearly than the League of Nations Covenant did for the League Assembly and Council. However, a good deal less is said about accountability than responsibility. The Charter designates the "functions and powers" of the General Assembly, Security Council, Economic and Social Council (ECOSOC) and Trusteeship Council, but has no correlative designation for how these organs might be brought to account.

This helps to explain why it has always been unclear to whom various of these organs might be accountable. The preamble to the Charter, with its opening phrase "We the peoples of the United Nations", focuses attention on public accountability. However, the vast majority of UN affairs are too remote for even reasonably well-informed citizens in societies with considerable access to media and scholarship to know or care about, much less painstakingly evaluate. Indeed, if even fairly notable Security Council decisions or General Assembly actions do not garner much attention in the most highly developed countries, there is little chance that the public in most of the Member States will rigorously analyse them, much less try somehow to act in response to them.[46] In any event, it may be futile to expect oversight and action from "We the peoples" in the absence of clear benchmarks against which to measure performance. And here the Charter also fails to provide guidance on the proper standards to invoke when assessing the performance of any of the various United Nations. Instead, usually, a multiplicity of possible standards might be cited when particular parts of the Organization are brought to account.

Just as in the early twentieth century Wesley Newcomb Hohfeld counselled that, in sound legal philosophy, rights ought to be paired with correlative duties,[47] so one might have drafted an international agreement founding a global international organization such that each power was paired with a correlative accountability, including, perhaps, mention of specific standards when appropriate. This, however, was not the manner in which the founders chose to write the Charter.[48] They did not really spell out which different parts of the United Nations were to be brought to account, or how. With a few notable exceptions, such as the General Assembly supervising the work of the Trusteeship Council[49] with respect to non-strategic trust territories, accountability is not clearly designated within the words of the UN Charter. Indeed, only a few Charter provisions so much as use the term *responsibility*,[50] and fewer still speak of *accountability*.[51]

In the final analysis, however, I would argue that such drafting decisions were not fatally defective since political pressures, rather than constitutional processes, are more likely to shape most accountability issues within a global international organization.[52] Thus, with law being somewhat more limited guidance in matters of international accountability than is customary when the accountability of the component parts of domestic governments is analysed, scholars might better explore practice. To date, the conduct of international politics has produced what accountability has been found within the various United Nations. While law certainly has a role to play with respect to criminal matters – one thinks, for instance, of the application of principles of international criminal law to UN agencies and personnel operating in strife-torn areas[53] – in all probability it will be highly political processes, and not so much court cases, much less constitutional changes, that will lie at the heart of future reforms to enhance accountability within international organizations.

One might also note that the United Nations has long been plagued by problems related to the political theory underlying the Organization. The decentralized UN framework was true to that central tenet of classical liberal political philosophy that government is more accountable to the people and less subject to abuse if no individual and no single centre of governmental authority holds ultimate sway. In the case of the United Nations, however, rather than a clear-cut, carefully crafted separation of powers, the Security Council, the General Assembly and the International Court of Justice were expected, with respect to various matters, "to determine the limits of their own jurisdiction".[54] And yet the standard element of democratic governance in which the United Nations was most lacking was the people's ability to bring any of the different organs to account through periodic popular elections.

In the normal functioning of a democracy, accountability for political actions ultimately comes at periodic elections, when the voting public decide whether to reward or punish past decisions, statements and policies. In stark contrast, however, no feature of the United Nations is subject to an electorate's vote. Indeed, it is virtually unheard of for even domestic elections to hinge on the actions that governments take at the United Nations. Thus, while the "We the peoples of the United Nations" phrase is often recited, a wide range of rash, intemperate or foolish decisions at one of the various United Nations may be overlooked or disregarded without any of the discipline provided by upcoming popular elections.

Imprecise standards and objectives

Focusing on standards provides yet another perspective on the accountability gap. In essence, certain United Nations are essentially bureaucratic administrations, while others are chiefly political bodies. However, the standards that ought to be used in bringing this or that United Nations to account are often quite unclear – indeed, they are exceedingly murky with respect to the more politicized dimensions of the Organization. Accountability can be a problem when clear standards are not discernible. Determining what constitutes success or failure when the United Nations somehow acts, or fails to act, in response to situations of violence, human rights abuse or lagging economic development can be vexing, particularly when circumstances change swiftly, when the United Nations is simply one of a significant number of actors or when full resolution of a problem may be beyond human capabilities.

Furthermore, the United Nations at issue may be torn between different, even conflicting, objectives, further clouding the issue of standards. For example, when in 1967 President Gamel Abdel Nasser of Egypt formally requested the withdrawal of the UN Emergency Force (UNEF) from the Suez Canal area preliminary to the onset of the Six-Day War, and when Secretary-General U Thant quickly complied, onlookers differed as to what vital responsibilities had been at issue, what standards the UN actions ought to have been measured against and to whom exactly the Secretary-General ought to have been accountable for his actions. Were the Charter provisions favouring peaceful resolution of disputes most important? What about the views of the Member States that were parties to the dispute, one of which preferred to try to change the status quo? How about the Member States that had supplied the peacekeeping troops? How much deference should have been paid to the original theory of peacekeeping by which the UN force would be positioned to give peace a chance only so long as the rival states both consented to the peacekeepers' presence?

When different responsibilities are at stake and accountability on a given issue might be owed to multiple plausible oversight bodies, and when those responsibilities clash and those bodies might apply different standards to UN actions, the stage is set for political drama. But the charges and counter-charges that are part and parcel of political debate can further shake public faith in an organization's accountability. The lack of clear standards combined with the highly politicized nature of the activities of each of the United Nations contributes to the exceptional difficulties faced in definitively bringing the Organization to account.

The lack of a political tradition of accountability

In attempting to explain the accountability gap, one might also note that, as a historical matter, the various United Nations have not yet developed a strong political tradition of accountability. Within the umbrella United Nations, with the exception of the development banks and especially the World Bank,[55] few institutions or proponents of action have had much enthusiasm for critical evaluation of programmes after the fact. Useful analyses aimed at determining whether a particular programme or operation represented a worthwhile expenditure have been especially scarce.[56]

Again, this is both unfortunate and understandable. In social and economic development projects it is common to have to correct course constantly. One must revise and improvise management decisions to try to meet changing contexts and adapt to local problems and needs and, frequently, the increasing assertion of community input. All this creates the challenge of evaluating a moving target. Wise and effective critical analysis often seems quite difficult to carry out until considerable time has passed. Yet by then attention has usually been diverted to a proliferation of new issues, projects and policies. For these reasons, in the development field that is the focus of so much UN activity, too often the inclination has been at least to postpone rigorous analytical evaluation.

Phrased more sympathetically, one might argue that the accountability of the United Nations of the staff has become controversial in large part because the Secretariat has so often exhausted itself in attempts to respond to complicated problems, determine realistic objectives and then find, craft and implement workable policies. Such forays aimed at progressing towards visions of a better world are themselves such enormous undertakings that, until recent years, one could find scant evidence of pressure from the Secretary-General, or even from the bulk of the Member States, to devote energy and resources to anything but quite basic accountability issues, such as whether approved projects were ever actually carried out or were implemented without gross corruption or mismanagement. More extensive, qualitative and nuanced critiques have not been as common as they should have been.

The other factor that may merit mentioning is that the vast bulk of the membership have paid such small annual dues in terms of a percentage of the UN budget and, as Tadanori Inomata details in chapter 6, so many UN activities now occur through extra-budgetary funding that the Member States have rarely felt deeply that their own vital resources were much at stake when the United Nations carried out its activities. Naturally, one tends to be more cavalier about spending other people's money, particularly sums collected from a large group of others. In addition, I suspect that the UN tendency not to worry unduly about profligate spending has been exacerbated by historical antagonisms between less-developed and more-developed states related to ideological differences and the legacies of colonialism and the Cold War. For some, perhaps, the unspoken subtext has been that, if funds drawn largely from the first world states were not always used wisely, the powerful were simply, in some measure, thereby receiving their just desserts for years of mistreatment of the less powerful. In this sense the UN budget structure and the North–South split have also contributed to the lack of development of a strong political tradition of accountability.

The shortcomings of UN reports

Apart from inadequate constitutional guidance, imprecise standards and objectives and the absence of a political tradition of accountability, one might point to the shortcomings of UN reports as contributing to the accountability gap. Certainly, one window into the accountability that has occurred within the United Nations involves reporting traditions and requirements, both how they have been set up on paper and how they have actually occurred. In a sense, for instance, the International Law Commission is accountable to the General Assembly since it reports to that body. However, to presume that reports necessarily translate into effective accountability would be to misperceive, or at least to exaggerate, their normal role and impact.

By the terms of the definition laid out above, mere reporting does not ensure accountability. Reports may be partial, obscure or perfunctory.[57] For an organization to be properly brought to account, any report must also be critically appraised, an evaluation duly communicated and then action taken to correct shortcomings. Since those latter stages have not always been efficiently and effectively carried out, reporting requirements alone have never ensured control of, or even corrections to, policies and other decisions made within the United Nations. And this has been a problem of longstanding duration.

Consider, for instance, the example of the trusteeship system, which can be viewed, along with the League of Nations mandate scheme that preceded it, as an early effort to instil international accountability in the transitional stage between colonialism and full-fledged sovereignty.[58] While the trustees were obligated to report to the Trusteeship Council on developments in non-strategic trust territories, and while the Council could investigate and even inspect conditions in those territories, it had "no power to enforce its policies, or to compel recalcitrant administering authorities to comply with its regulations".[59] Thus the founders' hope that the Trusteeship Council might become an effective watchdog collided with the difficulties that the United Nations experienced in holding the trustees accountable for their actions, particularly during the bitter ideological disputes of the Cold War.[60]

Beyond this, one might also note that uniformity of reporting across the UN system has never taken root. Supervising entities have not consistently mandated the form and content of reports,[61] much less the manner in which evaluation will occur and be communicated. Since terminating employment is a difficult and thankless process, and since budgetary control is often attenuated, the practical ability of the body that receives the report to compel changes in behaviour has often been quite curtailed. Furthermore, representatives of the Member States rarely feel themselves to be in a strong position to exert pressure on UN entities to discipline their personnel. Not surprisingly, then, reports do not seem to have been notably effective in moulding future actions.

The lack of well-defined and effective hierarchies

One source of continuing difficulty has been that, within this large and complex organization comprising so many competing as well as cooperating units of a multitude of sizes and shapes, a single pyramidal hierarchy fails to exist. This plainly has important consequences for bringing the Organization to account. We have defined accountability in terms of a supervising authority critiquing the efforts of a subordinate body, yet frequently the chain of command within the United Nations is uncertain or blurred, or theoretically present but practically absent. When a Secretary-General presents a plan to reform the bureaucracy and is greeted by an overwhelming vote of no confidence by the UN staff union, as occurred under Kofi Annan's tenure,[62] the normal top-down rules of bureaucratic order and discipline appear to have faced a challenge, to say the least.

Another factor to consider involves organizational hierarchies. Among the different United Nations, it is difficult to discern the orderly hierarchies that people are accustomed to seeing in other complicated human endeavours, from universities to business corporations, from military forces to government agencies. The presumption, then, is that organizations without clearly defined hierarchies also lack accountability. Such a theory is buttressed by such events as the 1994 genocide in Rwanda in which a later UN independent inquiry singled out the Secretary-General, the Secretariat, the Security Council, the UN Assistance Mission for Rwanda (UNAMIR) and the broader membership of the Organization for contributing to the failure of the UN system as a whole.[63] Events in Rwanda and the subsequent efforts to avoid blame underscore the lack of a single clear hierarchy at the United Nations.

Not only is it often unclear to whom accountability is owed, but governments often perceive political ramifications in even potential hierarchies. Hence these become the subject of political battles, which do not necessarily result in definitive winners but instead become ongoing political struggles.[64] In this sense what has been termed the "administrative jungle"[65] of the United Nations differs markedly from the governments of states and, even more so, from the organizational structures of such business entities as corporations – fields of endeavour in which accountability within the Organization, while periodically lacking, is nonetheless more evident than one finds within most international organizations.[66]

Compare, for instance, the role of the UN Secretary-General to that of a prime minister, a university president or a corporate chief executive officer. It is true that, as a matter of principle, the UN Charter contemplates the Secretary-General, as the organization's chief administrative officer, implementing policies established by the Security Council and General Assembly.[67] And yet this vision has collided with the view, held by many and not simply the occupants of the office, that the UN Secretary-General should be an international statesman, the embodiment of the UN Organization in the eyes of the world, and not simply an administrator carrying out whatever initiatives the legislative organs place before him. As a result, in practice the Secretary-General has, and is fully expected to have, his own agenda, and he and the Secretariat have complex relationships with the General Assembly and the Security Council, with each entity influencing, or attempting to influence, the other. Here, the push and pull of international politics frequently trumps any top-down chain of command.

Furthermore, as a legal matter, the Secretary-General enjoys privileges and immunities similar to those accorded to diplomats.[68] And yet even the leading national diplomat, a foreign minister or secretary of state, remains subject not simply to a president or prime minister, but to the jurisdiction of national courts for actions that contravene the constitution or other illegal misdeeds. In the case of a Secretary-General, however, international courts would rarely have and exercise jurisdiction, and national prosecutors and courts would be likely to hesitate to pursue and exert jurisdiction over the epitome of an international diplomat. Just as the legal constraints on the Secretary-General in conducting daily business are uncertain, so there is no procedure laid out in the Charter to remove the Secretary-General from office. The Charter simply observes that the Secretary-General is "responsible only to the Organization", whatever exactly that phrase might mean, and the only Charter provision that clearly relates to the Secretary-General's accountability is the mandate that he report annually to the General Assembly.[69] The Charter is thus conspicuously silent on the issue of how exactly the Secretary-General might be brought to account.

Since constitutional provisions tend to be imperfectly correlated with real-life development,[70] it is certainly important to focus attention on practices as well as legal provisions. But here we find that there is no very revealing historical record of how Secretaries-General have been effectively brought to account. It is true that representatives of the state-centric United Nations have felt obliged, on occasion, to remind the Secretary-General and the Secretariat that the United Nations ought not to be a free-wheeling free agent in international politics, but instead ought to be accountable to the Member States that created it and continue to contribute its funding, employees and at least a degree of policy-making guidance.[71] And in that spirit various Member States have attempted to exert some discipline over Secretaries-General, including, for instance, Trygve Lie[72] and Dag Hammarskjöld[73] in the first decades of the Organization. However, even the permanent members have not always been so satisfied that their efforts to rein in Secretaries-General have succeeded as thoroughly and expeditiously as they would have liked. Indeed, what might be viewed as the ultimate sanction employed to date – denying the Secretary-General the expected second term in office – has been used on only a single, now often-criticized, occasion.[74]

As for the Secretary-General's annual reports, not only have these more regularly extolled UN achievements than illuminated its shortcomings, but various Secretaries-General have used them to lecture recalcitrant Member States on the obligations of membership[75] and chastise those that seemed to have fallen short of their responsibilities.[76] Thus we see the United Nations of the Secretariat occasionally accusing that of the Member States of failing to carry out its duties, just as the reverse has occurred. And yet, other than his "bully pulpit",[77] such as it is, the Secretary-General has few means for holding the Member States at all accountable.

Nor do the Member States have a better record of regularly and effectively bringing each other to account in the United Nations than they do in other intergovernmental organizations. Thus Member States that fail to heed Security Council resolutions, do not live up to day-to-day responsibilities, including the payment of dues (notwithstanding article 19,[78] which does not always serve as an adequate disincentive), or otherwise act contrary to their responsibilities as UN members may not be effectively brought to account. As Anne-Marie Slaughter observed, "representatives of different countries are reluctant actually to censure one another. Examples of this phenomenon in international institutions are legion; it is precisely the reason that it is so hard to mobilize an international institution to condemn a member's actions. Principles of sovereign respect, live and let live, and reciprocity, meaning fear of retaliation, all militate against censure and sanction."[79] Plainly, no orderly, accepted hierarchy exists within the United Nations of the Member States.

As for the accountability of the United Nations of the Secretariat to the Member States, in practical terms what can it mean for a staff overseeing an extensive and far-flung bureaucracy to be accountable to nearly 200 supervisors? Adding further complexity is the fact that while these overseers are theoretically equal, they are, in fact, highly unequal on the various practical scales that determine a state's influence in international relations. As these nominal supervisors proliferate, especially when they are themselves deeply engaged in the multiple games of multilateral politics, those being supervised may be able to skirt being brought to account or at least pick and choose among directives and assessments.

Similarly, the practical control of the Secretary-General over the Organization, indeed even over the Secretariat, may be easily exaggerated, particularly for the many activities that do not occupy his immediate attention, or that of his closest aides. How can the Secretary-General, amid the variegated and often frenetic activities of his office, bring to account a bureaucracy that has grown by leaps and bounds over time and that is stationed around the world undertaking a bewildering variety of projects and programmes? Complexity, which has been termed "the enemy of accountability",[80] can be a highly effective tool in the hands of independent-minded civil servants.[81] Items may be buried in a budget or a lengthy report, yet then be used as an important precedent for future activity. In such ways is independence fostered and accountability weakened.

The extent of the Secretariat's *de facto* freedom from the Secretary-General's control might better be viewed as a perennial thorny issue, sprouting up periodically in different guises. For instance, the initial, rather idealistic, view of the UN Secretariat was that it would function independent from the national governments providing the staff members.[82] A disinterested international civil service was envisioned, accountable to the Secretary-General alone. Although one after another of the early holders of the office publicly endorsed these ideas – some, like Dag Hammarskjöld, with great vigour – various Member States challenged their application in practice. Indeed, each of the superpowers did so during the Cold War.[83] While it may thus be convenient to picture the Secretary-General perched atop the Secretariat, for historical and institutional reasons the actual control of the Secretary-General over the organization's staff has long been both variable and uncertain. The day-to-day influence that any Secretary-General exerts under most circumstances might best be characterized as more theoretical than real. And yet, if the Secretariat is not sufficiently accountable to the Member States or to the Secretary-General, to whom is it accountable?

For its part, significant accountability issues have dogged the Security Council as well, in terms of both its action and its inaction. These, in turn, have raised serious questions about the legitimacy of its resolutions and, more broadly still, of its role in the UN system. This has been particularly troublesome both in those periods when the Council has chosen not to act in any decisive manner, whether in the Balkans, Rwanda, Iraq or Darfur, and when it has seemed to be in an activist mode, such as the recent phase in which it greatly extended the organization's peacekeeping endeavours.[84] Here one might note that countries that are absent from the Security Council and yet supply peacekeepers have not traditionally exerted much effective influence over how their soldiers were used, the rules of engagement or even the decision to modify the mission in mid-stream.[85] How and to whom the Security Council might be brought to account, to answer charges of malfeasance and non-feasance, have been unclear, contributing to a lack of confidence in its decisions and its role in international politics.

Indeed, with respect to this crisis-oriented executive United Nations, thoughts of reforms to enhance accountability immediately collide with weighty aspects of Security Council structure and procedures. In particular, the veto might be viewed as the founders' recognition that in sensitive security matters the great powers might be coaxed into a collective-action framework only if an escape valve, one that could be utilized whenever national interests so dictated, tempered international responsibilities.[86] The founders reconciled themselves to the fact that the permanent members would frequently act in matters of war and peace with an eye cocked to their own foreign policies, domestic constituencies and conceptions of national interests. In order to promote a serious role for the United Nations in global security matters, they felt obliged to create an institution that included an unfortunately rigid, artificial and self-perpetuating power structure. Despite the obvious fact that relative military capabilities are a fluid element in international politics, five designated states were specially privileged on the basis of perceptions of national power in 1945. Furthermore, each gained the ability to veto any effort by other Member States to alter the existing arrangement.[87]

The founders' decision to structure the Security Council in this way – while in my view a realistic and essential one at that time – clouds the accountability of the crisis-oriented United Nations since the permanent members have the capacity to veto matters viewed as incompatible with their national interests. The Security Council can thus be brought to account for its behaviour, if at all, only via rhetorical condemnation. To date the only realistic, though limited, manner to bring to account the executive United Nations (and, on occasion, the plenary United Nations as well) has been via collective legitimization[88] – that is, "politically significant approval and disapproval of the claims, policies, and actions of states".[89]

Thus one of the United Nations sometimes brings another to account in some manner by resorting to political, and often rhetorical, measures. Indeed, not only diplomatic activity by Member States but reactions by influential NGOs, broadly publicized polls and other readings of public opinion and pronouncements by national politicians and within influential media outlets can operate to clothe a particular action with legitimacy or to strip legitimacy from it. This process of collective legitimization, however, does not always proceed in obvious or clearly visible ways. It can encompass matters of tradition as well as of law, and it is regularly obscured by complexities of national and international political culture. If power is conceived in terms of the ability to influence others, legitimacy is an asset for political actions and a form of power. If something becomes widely viewed internationally as illegitimate, this in turn can create problems for any state, including a permanent member.[90] As a consequence, collective legitimization within the United Nations, while a slow process,[91] is one neither wholly satisfactory nor wholly insignificant way in which political bodies are brought to account. And given the fact that sweeping changes in the UN Charter are highly unlikely to occur, perhaps such political processes, aimed at labelling actions by a component part of the United Nations as legitimate or illegitimate, are the most appropriate medicine for this particular political body.

Turning next to what I have been calling the *umbrella United Nations*, let me now suggest that a somewhat more precise metaphor might picture the UN system as something like a large metropolitan area.[92] Downtown would be comprised of the six principle article 7 organs.[93] Within the city limits one also finds an array of organizational "bits and pieces" created by the central organs. Further out, in the suburbs if you will, are the specialized agencies. Distinct in many respects yet related in others, these might be likened to independent townships. They cluster about the nearby city, and in certain respects are deeply affected by it, yet they operate under their own charters and with their own administrations and governing bodies.

For purposes of accountability, the cardinal point is that the UN founders consciously limited the accountability of the outlying units to the central city. Various of the agencies actually pre-date establishment of the United Nations, contributing to a historic independence. And they are related to the United Nations by treaties, by no means of identical content. Moreover, each of the specialized agencies has its own constitution. The typical approach of the agencies is thus to undertake activities while looking first to their own charters and longstanding administrative practices, and only secondarily to such "downtown authorities" as the Secretary-General or the General Assembly. Article 17(3) of the UN Charter calls on the General Assembly to examine the administrative budgets of the specialized agencies, but only with a view to making *recommendations* to them.[94] Under these circumstances they may, but are not compelled to, take advantage of the efforts of the Secretariat or Economic and Social Council (ECOSOC) to coordinate their activities and enhance cooperation with what is going on elsewhere in the metropolitan area.[95] As for the Secretary-General, while he may be the head of all UN agencies in a symbolic sense, and does, for instance, chair the semi-annual meetings of the heads of specialized agencies, his authority, *de jure* and *de facto*, is limited. Thus, once again, a tight, orderly and effective hierarchy is not readily apparent. Conducting reviews and offering recommendations fail to comprise a recipe for adequate accountability, at least as I have defined it above.

In international organization circles, if one side of the coin is charges of lack of accountability, the flip side is charges of undue pressure. From the start, the specialized agencies were purposefully granted considerable administrative discretion, not only to encourage creative innovation but to prevent Member States, perhaps envisioned as routinely implementing their own narrow and selfish foreign policies, from constantly pressuring them.[96] Those who founded the specialized agencies tried to ensure considerable independence of action for their chief executives. The central motivation was to protect them from improper influence by governments that international society could not easily hold to account. Thus longtime independence in policy-making and policy implementation, entrenched via constitutions, treaties and practices, has been and will continue to be exceedingly difficult to scale back in order to enhance accountability within the umbrella United Nations.

The shortcomings of further "democratization"

Some observers have presumed that inadequate accountability is a consequence of the lack of democratic decision-making in the United Nations, and that enhanced democratization of the policy-making process would be a promising route to increased accountability. While the lack of any periodic elections has contributed to the accountability gap, I see this as inherent in the essential nature of an organization created by and for states, one aimed chiefly at helping governments to cooperate to achieve their international objectives. Particularly since the United Nations was not conceived as a path towards world government, nor has it evolved in that direction, I am sceptical that democratic reforms, in the sense of having the votes of all the states determine more matters or in the sense of having the general public determine policy issues, are the answer to the problems identified above.[97]

In addition, given widely divergent views of democracy within the Member States, I doubt whether forming a consensus would be possible on what the concept of democratization might entail in this context. At times, "democratizing the United Nations system" has been used as a kind of shorthand for reforming Security Council operations, and, in particular, changing the composition or role of the permanent members.[98] However, this is not a necessary use or interpretation of the phrase. Should diplomats from a wide range of states advocate enhancing democratic policy-making processes within the United Nations, it is not at all clear that they share the same views as to just what democratization might entail.

As a matter of political philosophy, democracy can be thought of, narrowly, in terms of the types of political selection processes used. Or it can be conceived much more broadly, in terms of a political culture that is conducive to decision-making by an informed populace that is given a choice between political programmes and in which most adult citizens, in fact, exercise a widespread right to vote. To some, democracy connotes broadly distributed, rather than centralized, political power. To others, it suggests that powers are separated among different branches of government. Some people focus upon whether a legitimate, competitive choice exists among political contenders competing on a level playing field, for instance, sharing reasonably equal access to the media and the voting population. And still others concentrate upon the ends of politics. A truly democratic system promotes certain outcomes, such as liberty, equality and freedom. The divergent meanings and connotations of democracy suggest how difficult the task would be to arrive at a consensus among the nearly 200 UN Member States.

Democracy is also a word with considerable positive rhetorical power that many regimes have wanted to coopt, or draw on, in order to augment their own legitimacy. In the United Nations of the General Assembly, for instance, a vast spectrum of states, ranging from Costa Rica to the United States, Japan, Singapore, Mexico, Laos, Yemen, Cuba and North Korea, have claimed to govern themselves by democratic principles, variously defined. The fact that some have much stronger claims to democratic governance than others has not stopped a wide range of states from attempting to associate their regimes with the term *democracy.* What has been termed "the democratic pretensions of undemocratic regimes"[99] further underscores the elasticity of notions of democracy in modern political discourse.

In terms of policy, if "democracy" is reduced to the bare essential of decision-making by voting processes, what might be truly democratic, in the sense of better responding to the desires of "we the peoples of the United Nations", would be to institute weighted voting within various UN organs using the standard of the size of the population of each Member State.[100] One need hardly hasten to add that this would be a most unpopular suggestion. With the possible exception of the governments of such immense developing states as China, India and Brazil, which would gain tremendous influence in such a reformed voting arrangement, such a "democratization" proposal would inflame the vast bulk of an organization in which large numbers of small and micro states view the principle of sovereign equality as key to their exercise of some influence on international affairs. Nevertheless, this whimsical example may illustrate that, just as accountability can suggest quite different things to different people at different times, so the same is true of democratization.

It might also be observed that, in terms of past practice within the United Nations, calls for further democratization have often been associated with initiatives aimed at increasing representation within various units and subunits. However, the question immediately arises: which Member States will be invited to join a particular unit in the bid to enhance representation? The path of least resistance here is simply to allocate seats by blocs, and yet it is difficult to see how exactly bloc politics of this sort fulfils democratic principles.

In any event, any realistic proposal to democratize the United Nations strongly implies the involvement of more decision-makers, or at least more influences upon decision-makers. And yet whether this is a natural route to better accountability is highly questionable. Only exceedingly rarely do the members of a large global organization speak in one voice. I am sceptical that adding multitudes of more and less conflicting voices to those who now conceive or implement policies will improve the efficiency of the policy-making process or its final product. The same might be said of subjecting administration to constant or even periodic votes. Too many cooks might indeed further "spoil the broth". Nor is it immediately obvious that policy becomes wiser and more effective the more heads are involved in devising or implementing it.[101] To date, the greatest number of voices have typically been raised within the plenary United Nations, and yet the General Assembly has never been known as a strong proponent of organizational reform. Indeed, to the contrary, it has more often tried to block proposed changes in administrative practices.[102]

In the light of such experiences, what seems quite likely is that the more voices are added, the greater is the potential for gridlock or for bodies taking only those actions to which no one objects – a lowest-common-denominator approach to policy-making. And so, rather than countering the shortcomings of the United Nations, reforms of this sort might well exacerbate them. As Inis Claude has written, "A massively multilateral body is likely to be plagued by mountainous immobility; its tendency is to be cumbersome, indecisive, and dithering."[103] Democratization can be expected to add more mass to an organization whose administration is already criticized for being flat-footed, if not immovable, with respect to various issues of international politics.

Furthermore, a potential disjunction looms when one suggests that the policy-making process be democratized, but when most reasonable observers would conclude that a sizeable percentage of the states that belong to the United Nations are not themselves democracies.[104] What the government of a Member State might press for and what the people ruled by that government may want, if adequately informed, might be expected to diverge sharply the less democratic is the regime. Thus if there is a marked democracy deficit within the states that make up the membership, moving to majority-rule voting procedures in more aspects of UN activities is not such a logical path to becoming more accountable to "we the peoples of the United Nations".

Some have suggested that non-governmental organizations might be used in some capacity to help to reflect the will of the people in non-democratic states. It is true that various international organizations, both non-governmental and intergovernmental, have served the function of monitoring "state behavior, producing credible neutral information necessary for effective enforcement".[105] However, not only can it be difficult to determine which NGOs to include and which to exclude, but NGOs have their own problems of accountability that cannot be lightly dismissed. What precisely are their responsibilities? To whom must they report? And how are their performances critically evaluated? The enhanced participation of NGOs may well be able to assist in closing the accountability gap to some extent, yet it is neither a panacea nor a synonym for "democratization".

Finally, it might be observed that the states making up the majority viewpoint on particular issues often feel that the Organization should act in accordance with their wishes. As the UN membership roster added scores of newly independent third world states during the lengthy process of decolonization, the agenda of this new majority emphasized economic development, and it vastly increased UN activities in that field.[106] These proponents and beneficiaries of UN programmes, however, have not usually been the voices advocating that the Organization be strictly accountable.[107] Instead of attention to accountability coming from these advocates for more UN action, those states that provide most of the resources for UN operations have most frequently sounded the accountability theme.

Virtually all intergovernmental organizations are constrained by the practical political reality that certain states control the most important financial contributions and thus exercise a disproportionate influence on many issues, including leadership appointments.[108] Ultimately, disgruntled states can withdraw their support from projects, programmes, particular personnel or even from the Organization as a whole. In the United Nations those states that pay the largest budget assessments,[109] as well as the many contributions other than annual dues,[110] have been able to capitalize on this leverage.[111] Thus, naturally enough, these resource providers have promoted accountability, but accountability in the particular sense of the Organization becoming more accountable to them.

For purposes of conceiving of possible reforms to enhance accountability, the cardinal point is that if democratization were to dilute the voices of the resource-providing states, it might very well not serve to enhance accountability within the Organization. Rather, it might hinder it. For all these reasons, the merits of promoting democratization as the answer to accountability problems seem quite debatable.

Conclusion

"In human affairs," it has been said, "the solution of old problems has an unfortunate way of creating new ones or exacerbating dormant ones."[112] So it has been with problems related to accountability. Some will find it ironic that during the First World War various concerned onlookers felt that extensive secret diplomacy had kept governments from being accountable to their peoples, and the hope was that more open diplomacy within a global international organization might help to keep the peace through better accountability; whereas today concerned onlookers question whether our global international organization is at all publicly accountable as it embarks upon its huge array of international activities. Certainly, more than six decades after the founding of the Organization, there remains exceedingly important work to be done in the accountability field.

What brings urgency to the task is the fact that we are contending with a situation that is so unsatisfactory in many respects. Both legal provisions and historical traditions relating to accountability are sorely lacking. The independence of decision-makers is hard to dislodge, even in much less enterprising political organizations. Within the United Nations, with its veto-wielding permanent members, autonomous directors of specialized agencies and independent-minded civil servants intent on running their own projects and programmes, it is extraordinarily challenging. While it would be, as a practical matter, impossible to reform a sprawling political organization like the United Nations such that its multiple competing power centres were transformed into a tight top-down chain of command, we might also acknowledge that the closer we approach everyone being marginally or peripherally accountable to everyone, the more likely it is that no one will be very accountable at all. In conclusion, let me advance a handful of suggestions concerning how accountability might be enhanced.

Given the myriad UN activities, the decentralized nature of the UN system and the lack of any direct connection between so many of them and so many people around the world, public opinion is too unfocused and too difficult to read to bring the United Nations effectively to account. Nevertheless, various United Nations could take steps to become more accountable to public opinion – national and international but especially local opinions. How might UN actions be made most relevant and most useful to local communities? How might the United Nations then be made answerable to localities affected by its actions and programmes? I would suggest that this be termed *popular accountability* to distinguish it from *democratic accountability*. And here the international development banks have made strides forward, as detailed in part IV of this book, and the United Nations would do well to learn from their examples. For instance, the European Union's principle of subsidiarity might provide guidance; that is, the "principle of locating governance at the lowest possible level – that closest to individuals and groups affected by the rules and decisions adopted and enforced".[113]

Apart from the useful ideas and best practices found in other organizations, one plain conclusion can be distilled from the specific UN experience, which, I have argued, features a lack of constitutional guidance, imprecision of standards and objectives, lack of a political tradition of accountability, shortcomings of reports and a lack of orderly and effective hierarchies among the different United Nations. In practice, accountability within the UN system has more often been absent, or sporadic and episodic, than systematic. Rather than a tidy, carefully planned, systematic and legalistic approach, the push and pull of international politics, as concerns discrete issues, has usually determined the extent to which particular parts of the United Nations were – or more frequently were not – brought to account. To my mind, this suggests that the most promising avenues of reform will be sensitive to and indeed will capitalize upon the existing UN political processes, searching for ways to improve, enhance and sharpen an accountability focus within UN politics. One might think of reform of the executive United Nations in terms of further developing, or better sharpening, already existing collective legitimization processes. For instance, if the accountability of the Security Council might be enhanced through collective legitimization (or one might coin the more precise phrase "collective delegitimization"), then reforms to make Security Council deliberations more transparent would be very much in order.[114]

My next suggestion would be that, given the nature of UN activities, accountability deemed satisfactory by the public must include managerial and political dimensions. Increasing the effectiveness of reporting within the United Nations – particularly enhancing the visibility and consequences of those reports – is an area in which further progress might be made. And to bring properly to account individual UN staff members, poor performance, serious errors in judgement and irresponsible behaviour of various stripes must be followed by the credible prospect of non-promotion, reprimand, disgrace or firing.[115] And yet this is far easier said than done since, apart from the most egregious cases, setting and then adhering to high standards without bias and arbitrariness infecting the process can be difficult to implement,[116] especially in a highly political organization like the United Nations. Nevertheless, additional efforts to delineate standards, hold UN employees to them and penalize those who fall short are a vitally necessary dimension of improving managerial accountability.

At the same time, enhancing accountability at the United Nations ought not simply be thought of as a matter of filing promised reports in timely fashion, tracking trails of paper through the administrative labyrinth, identifying the presence or absence of pertinent regulations or administrative processes, or hiring competent bookkeepers who abide by proper accounting practices. Important as these matters are for satisfactory managerial accountability, to renew public faith in the Organization they must go hand in hand with improved political accountability. And yet political accountability of the Organization – perhaps most strikingly the ability to influence the United Nations to change course, to rein it in or to urge it towards different tasks – has long appeared to be lacking, or at least to occur in indirect, uncertain and hazy half-measures.

I would also suggest that, just as more can be done, more transparently, to improve UN accountability in ways that are publicly recognizable, so more can be done behind the scenes as well. In the light of the positive record of government networks in inculcating professional norms in their members and using social pressures and incentives to induce compliance with network norms, even occasionally sanctioning those caught violating those norms,[117] the accountability of individual UN employees might be enhanced if they were participating in networks of like officials from other parts of the United Nations as well as from other international organizations that perform similar functions or try to solve similar problems. In this way even the decentralized and disaggregated nature of the United Nations might be put towards a positive end.

Perhaps most important, I would urge that attention be paid to the definition of accountability laid out at the beginning of this chapter. In general terms the United Nations is insufficiently accountable since only some, but not all, of the essential steps of being properly brought to account are being satisfactorily completed. In particular, even when one of the United Nations does attempt to demonstrate its responsible behaviour, it is not clear that any superior body is carefully assessing what has occurred and communicating a comprehensible critique, much less that the evaluation is conscientiously absorbed and acted upon. Hence, one route to enhanced accountability is for each of the different United Nations to study which of the aspects of being properly brought to account are being duly fulfilled and which are falling short of expectations. Tailored reforms may then be focused on problem areas.

As part of this effort more attention might be paid to how the different United Nations might become more accountable to one another, and how such enhanced accountability might be effectively publicized. How does one create a system of accountability within a huge organization that, historically, has been emphatically non-hierarchical? First, this key question of who should be accountable to whom under what circumstances needs to be further explored with respect to each of the United Nations. I would also suggest not only that much work needs to be done in defining duties, clarifying hierarchies and mandating adequate accounting to appropriate bodies, but that a new emphasis ought to be placed on the results of evaluations being communicated to the entity being evaluated, which should then be expected to demonstrate how the assessment was acted upon in a productive manner. When each of these steps is understood to be part of the organization's regular administrative processes, duly carried out in a timely and conscientious manner, the public is much more likely to view the Organization as satisfactorily accountable.

It is important both for UN accountability to be enhanced and then for accurate public perceptions to be fostered. The Secretary-General and others ought to redouble the current effort to articulate clearly the priority placed on improving accountability – the specific measures that have been taken, the ongoing problems, the matters still to be accomplished and the plans for future reforms. Alongside broad proposals and initiatives, particular tangible problems ought to be identified and addressed. For instance, given the privileges and immunities accorded not simply to the Secretary-General but to many serving the United Nations, if UN staff abuse their power, by what means and to whom should they be accountable? While the answers may not be simple, this nonetheless strikes me as the type of manageable problem that contributes to the accountability gap and that intelligent people ought to be able to attend to and make progress towards resolving.

Despite the various formidable obstacles noted above, the subject with which we are contending is vitally important. As one critic noted of the United Nations: "organizations that are unaccountable finish up by being irresponsible if not corrupt, unresponsive to opportunities, and unintelligible to the public".[118] Accountability issues are closely related to perceptions of UN efficiency and effectiveness. And perceptions are an important aspect of the issue of whether the United Nations, variously defined, will receive the resources and be assigned the tasks that will place it somewhere at the centre of international relations in the twenty-first century, rather than off on the sidelines. Hence improving accountability, a subject too long neglected by scholars, politicians and UN officials alike, is a vital step towards creating a more vibrant future United Nations.

Acknowledgements

The author thanks Professor Julie Bunck of the University of Louisville, Professor Mark Drumbl of Washington and Lee University, Professor Sumihiro Kuyama of the United Nations University and Professor Emeritus Inis L. Claude Jr of the University of Virginia for their comments on drafts of this chapter.

Notes

1. Lynch, Colum (2007) "UN Finds Fraud, Mismanagement in Peacekeeping", *Washington Post*, 18 December, p. A6.
2. UN Independent Inquiry Committee (1999) "Report of the Independent Inquiry into the Actions of the United Nations during the 1994 Genocide in Rwanda", UN Doc. S/1999/1257, 15 December. Chesterman, Franck and Malone noted: "Bill Clinton is alone among the leaders of the permanent five members of the Security Council in having made a serious effort to apologize for the disastrous inaction during Rwanda's genocide." Chesterman, Simon, Thomas M. Franck and David M. Malone (2008) *Law and Practice of the United Nations: Documents and Commentary*, New York: Oxford University Press, p. 541. These authors have compiled a useful collection of documents relating to UN accountability issues; see ibid.: 541–545.
3. UN Office of the Secretary-General (1999) "Summary of the Report of the Secretary-General Pursuant to General Assembly Resolution 53/35: The Fall of Srebrenica, UN Year Book 1999", UN Doc. A/54/549.
4. Ku, Charlotte and Harold K. Jacobson, eds (2003) *Democratic Accountability and the Use of Force in International Law*, New York: Cambridge University Press, p. 372.
5. Chesterman, Franck and Malone, note 2 above, p. 548.
6. See Meyer, Jeffrey A. and Mark G. Califano, eds (2006) *Good Intentions Corrupted: The Oil-for-Food Scandal and the Threat to the United Nations*, New York: Public Affairs. For the reports of the UN commission that investigated the programme see UN Independent Inquiry Commission (2005a) "Interim Report", 3 February; (2005b) "Report on the Manipulation of the Oil-for-Food Programme"; (2005c) "Report on the Management of the Oil-for-Food Programme"; (2005d) "Second Interim Report", 29 March; (2005e) "Third Interim Report", 8 August – all these reports are available at www.iic-offp.org. See also Sachs, Susan and Judith Miller (2004) "Under Eye of U.N., Billions for Hussein in Oil-for-Food Program", *New York Times*, 13 August, p. 1A; Deen, Thalif (2006) "Newly Transparent UN Enters the Future", *Mail & Guardian Observer Online*, 17 November, available at www.mg.co.za/articlePage.aspx?articleid=290078 ("The oil-for-food investigations found more than $10 billion in illicit funds and kickbacks funneled to Iraqi officials by companies bidding for UN contracts, for the supply of food and medicine to Iraqis subjected to UN economic sanctions").
7. Lynch, note 1 above.
8. Lynch, Colum (2008) "Ex-Prosecutor Targets Corruption at UN", *Washington Post*, 20 January, p. A8.
9. Lynch, Colum (2008) "Audit of UN's Sudan Mission Finds Tens of Millions in Waste", *Washington Post*, 10 February, p. A16.
10. Ved Nanda later wrote: "In Bosnia the UN civilian police have been accused of participation in the trafficking of women – buying and selling women, conspiring with criminal groups to recruit and smuggle women into brothels, and patronizing brothels in which trafficked women were abused... There was no accountability for these human rights violations on the part of individual peacekeepers, peacekeeper-contributing states, or the United Nations itself." Nanda, Ved (2005) "Accountability of International Organizations: Some Observations", *Denver Journal of International Law and Policy* 33, pp. 379–390, at p. 383. See also Murray, Jennifer (2003) "Note: Who Will Police Peace-Builders? The Failure to Establish Accountability for the Participation of UN Civilian Police in the Trafficking of Women in Post-Conflict Bosnia and Herzegovina", *Columbia Human Rights Law Review* 34, pp. 475–527, at p. 477.

11. United Nations (2005) "A Comprehensive Strategy to Eliminate Future Sexual Exploitation and Abuse in United Nations Peacekeeping Operations", UN Doc. A/59/710, 24 March.
12. Extensive anecdotal evidence, rather than court cases, formed the basis for this assertion. The report, which included field research involving 341 people living in emergency situations in three countries and 30 humanitarian, peace and security professionals, declared: "Troops associated with the UN Department of Peacekeeping Operations (DPKO) were identified as a particular source of abuse in some of our fieldwork locations, particularly in Haiti and Côte d'Ivoire." Csáky, Corinna (2008) "No One to Turn To: The Under-reporting of Child Sexual Exploitation and Abuse by Aid Workers and Peacekeepers", available at www.savethechildren.org.jk/en/docs/No__One_to_Turn_To.pdf, p. 8. UN statistics likewise suggest that peacekeeping forces are the targets of more allegations of sexual abuse than any other UN staff (United Nations, note 11 above). See also UN Office of the Secretary-General (2005) "Special Measures for Protection from Sexual Exploitation and Sexual Abuse", UN Doc. A/59/782, 15 April; (2006) "Special Measures for Protection from Sexual Exploitation and Sexual Abuse", UN Doc. A/60/861, 24 May; (2007) "Special Measures for Protection from Sexual Exploitation and Sexual Abuse", UN Doc. A/61/957, 15 June.
13. Csáky, ibid., p. 10.
14. Ibid., p. 20.
15. See the evidence cited by Edward Luck in chapter 1. See also Jones, Jeffrey M. (2006) "Americans' Ratings of United Nations Among Worst Ever", Gallup Poll, available at www.galluppoll.com/content/?ci=21871.
16. Since my emphasis will be directed more towards issues of international relations than public administration, I will leave to others the detailed discussion of how to institute procedures and systems that might encourage proper fiscal and organizational management within this or that part of the United Nations.
17. I do not attempt to distinguish between the ideas of *duty* and *responsibility*, but instead, for the purposes of this chapter, consider them to be synonyms.
18. In this regard, it would also be useful to examine the extent to which the responsibilities of each part of the United Nations are delineated from those of others, thus becoming matters of sole or joint responsibility.
19. At the least, when an organization is effectively brought to account, one might expect to see a resolve not to repeat past errors.
20. Inis L. Claude Jr, Professor Emeritus of Foreign Affairs at the University of Virginia, has also elaborated on the multiple uses of "United Nations" in various of his writings and lectures, including "Prospective Peace and Security Roles for the United Nations: Impossible Dreams and Reasonable Possibilities", delivered at the United Nations University Global Seminar in Shonan Village, Japan, in 1995. This paper was later published as Claude, Inis L. Jr (1996) "Peace and Security: Prospective Roles for the Two United Nations", *Global Governance* 2(3), pp. 289–298. See also Claude, Inis L. Jr (1999a) "A Scholar's Beginnings: A Study of the San Francisco Charter", *Virginia Journal of International Law* 40, pp. 311–329, especially pp. 328–329; (1999b) "The United Nations and Kosovo", paper presented at White Burkett Miller Center of Public Affairs, University of Virginia, Charlottesville, VA, 15 October, unpublished.
21. Here Claude noted: "beyond the realm of high politics, we enter a field of activity... directly and primarily involved with the provision of services to states, singly or collectively; to human beings, with or without regard for their nationality; and to the human family and its habitat, without regard for internal boundaries. In this functional zone, the United Nations is best conceived not as a collection of states employing a staff, but as a staff supported by a collection of states." Claude, Inis L. Jr (1993) "Reflections on

the Role of the UN Secretary-General", in Benjamin Rivlin and Leon Gordenker, eds, *The Challenging Role of the UN Secretary-General*, Westport, CT: Praeger, pp. 249–260, at p. 259.

22. Notwithstanding the words of article 7, just what constitutes an organ of the United Nations is subject to some disagreement. Secretary-General Pérez de Cuéllar, for instance, argued that the Secretary-General, by virtue of articles 98 and 99 of the UN Charter, is more than merely a chief administrative officer but himself has "the independent responsibilities of 'a principal organ'". See Goulding, Marrack (2004) "The UN Secretary-General", in David M. Malone, ed., *The UN Security Council*, Boulder, CO: Lynne Rienner Publishers, pp. 267–279, at p. 268.
23. Under the label "humanitarian affairs" one might include "human rights, democracy promotion, and humanitarian intervention". See Malone, David M. (2003) "US-UN Relations in the UN Security Council in the Post-Cold War Era", in Rosemary Foot, Neil MacFarlane and Michael Mastanduno, eds, *US Hegemony and International Organizations*, New York: Oxford University Press, pp. 73–91, at p. 73.
24. This article lays out as a purpose of the United Nations: "To achieve international cooperation in solving international problems of an economic, social, cultural, or humanitarian character, and in promoting and encouraging respect for human rights and for fundamental freedoms without distinction as to race, sex, language, or religion…". Article 1(3), UN Charter.
25. Claude (1999b), note 20 above, p. 12.
26. See, for instance, article 3, declaring: "The original members of the United Nations shall be the states which, having participated in the United Nations Conference on International Organization at San Francisco or having previously signed the Declaration by United Nations of 1 January 1942, sign the present Charter and ratify it in accordance with Article 110."
27. Article 1(1), UN Charter.
28. One might note that in this usage the term ought properly to be considered a plural noun, not a singular one.
29. Claude (1996), note 20 above.
30. Claude (1999a), note 20 above, p. 328. Elsewhere Claude argued, "UN activities are, broadly speaking, of two kinds: those in which states carry out the undertaking, with Secretariat support, and those in which the Secretariat performs the task, with the support of states." Claude, note 21 above, p. 256.
31. Keohane, Robert O. (2003) "The Concept of Accountability in World Politics and the Use of Force", *Michigan Journal of International Law* 24, pp. 1121–1141, at p. 1136.
32. Claude (1999b), note 20 above, p. 11.
33. Keohane, note 31 above, p. 1136, citing Ku and Jacobson, note 4 above, p. 371.
34. See Chesterman, Franck and Malone, note 2 above, p. 539; Sarooshi, Dan (2005) *International Organizations and Their Exercise of Sovereign Powers*, New York: Oxford University Press.
35. Claude (1999a), note 20 above, p. 328.
36. See articles 13 and 15, UN Charter.
37. Keohane, note 31 above, p. 1137.
38. Rosemary Righter has argued that while routinely, and perhaps generously, labelled a *system*, the United Nations might just as fairly be considered a "collection of bureaucracies that developed under autonomous management". Righter, Rosemary (1995) *Utopia Lost: The United Nations and World Order*, New York: Twentieth Century Fund, p. 38.
39. The executive United Nations and the plenary United Nations could be viewed as different manifestations of the United Nations of the Member States.

40. As Inis Claude has observed, "Both the United Nations of a select few of the states and the United Nations of all the states, with their very different roles, are heavily dependent upon the services of the United Nations of the secretariat." Claude (1999a), note 20 above, p. 328.
41. Article 99, UN Charter.
42. Deen, note 6 above.
43. See generally Claude, Inis L. Jr (1993) "The Tension Between Principle and Pragmatism in International Relations", *Review of International Studies* 19, pp. 215–226. See also Franck, Thomas (1985) *Nation Against Nation: What Happened to the U.N. Dream and What the U.S. Can Do About It*, New York: Oxford University Press, pp. 60–93.
44. See generally Fowler, Michael R. and Jessica Fryrear (2003) "Collective Security and the Fighting in the Balkans", *Northern Kentucky Law Review* 30, pp. 299–345.
45. For a description of the ideal of a rule of law see Fowler, Michael R. (1998) *With Justice For All? The Nature of the American Legal System*, Upper Saddle River, NJ: Prentice-Hall, pp. 7–8.
46. Point raised in a letter to author from Inis L. Claude Jr, 28 September 2006.
47. See generally Hohfeld, Wesley Newcomb (1919) *Fundamental Legal Conceptions, As Applied in Judicial Reasoning and Other Legal Essays*, Walter Wheeler Cook, ed., New Haven, CT: Yale University Press.
48. One might add that this constitutional framework is entirely consistent with the long-standing emphasis within international law to focus on "thou shalt not" provisions, rather than "thou shalt" provisions – that is, to focus not on what sovereign states are obliged to do, but on what they are legally proscribed from doing. Letter to author from Inis L. Claude Jr, 7 October 2006. The duties or responsibilities of sovereign states are a subject I have considered in more depth elsewhere. See, for instance, Fowler, Michael R. and Julie M. Bunck (1995) *Law, Power, and the Sovereign State: The Evolution and Application of the Concept of Sovereignty*, University Park, PA: Pennsylvania State University Press, especially pp. x, 12–16, 43 and 156; Fowler, Michael R. and Julie M. Bunck (2001) "The Nation Neglected: The Organization of International Life in the Classical State Sovereignty Period", in Robert J. Beck and Thomas Ambrosio, eds, *International Law and the Rise of Nations: The State System and the Challenge of Ethnic Groups*, New York: Chatham House, pp. 38–60.
49. In 1994 the Trusteeship Council suspended its operations. For implications of this for current issues see Chesterman, Simon (2004) "Virtual Trusteeship", in David M. Malone, ed., *The U.N. Security Council*, Boulder, CO: Lynne Rienner Publishers, pp. 219–233, at p. 222.
50. See, for instance, under Chapter IX on international economic and social cooperation, article 60 of the UN Charter, which reads: "Responsibility for the discharge of the functions of the Organization set forth in this Chapter shall be vested in the General Assembly and, under the authority of the General Assembly, in the Economic and Social Council, which shall have for this purpose the powers set forth in Chapter X."
51. One might note the words of article 15 ("The General Assembly shall receive and consider annual and special reports from the Security Council; these reports shall include an *account* of the measures that the Security Council has decided upon or taken to maintain international peace and security" – emphasis added), and yet doubt that this provision was designed to bring the Security Council *to account* at the hands of the General Assembly.
52. Inis Claude coined the phrase "documentary determinism" to denote the faulty assumption "that constitutional provisions govern the evolution of multilateral agencies". Claude, Inis L. Jr (1986) *The Record of International Organizations in the*

Twentieth Century, Taipei: Tamkang University Press, p. 47. See also Claude (1999a), note 20 above, p. 312.

53. I was initially directed towards this line of reasoning by Professor Mark Drumbl of Washington and Lee University (letter to the author, 12 October 2006). I would also direct the reader's attention to the edited work by Thakur, Ramesh and Peter Malcontent, eds (2004) *From Sovereign Impunity to International Accountability: The Search for Justice in a World of States*, Tokyo: United Nations University Press, especially the chapters by Ahtisaari, Biddis, Lauren and Schabas: Ahtisaari, Martti (2004) "Preface – Justice and Accountability: Local or International?", in ibid., pp. xii–xvi; Biddis, Michael D. (2004) "From the Nuremberg Charter to the Rome Statute: A Historical Analysis of the Limits of International Criminal Accountability", in ibid., pp. 42–60; Lauren, Paul G. (2004) "From Impunity to Accountability: Forces of Transformation and the Changing International Human Rights Context", in ibid., pp. 15–41; Schabas, William A. (2004) "Balancing the Rights of the Accused with the Imperatives of Accountability", in ibid., pp. 154–168.
54. Chesterman, Franck and Malone, note 2 above, p. 540.
55. Among the various World Bank bodies devoted to accountability issues are the Independent Evaluation Group, which critically analyses the Bank's programmes for the board of directors, and the Inspection Panel, which responds to complaints by those who believe a World Bank project may harm them.
56. Rosemary Righter observed: "Scrutiny of the agencies' activities is rudimentary. External auditors verify that money has been spent, that the books square, but conduct few value-for-money evaluations. Most assessment of the effectiveness and impact of programs is internal. With the notable exception of the World Bank, the only organization to take evaluation seriously, the relevant reports go to the director-general, not the governing bodies, for decision, and the findings may see the light of day years late or not at all." Righter, note 38 above, p. 55.
57. Charlotte Ku and Harold Jacobson, in their study of accountability and the Security Council, termed "perfunctory" many of the reports by individual states that the Council had authorized to take military action in the name of the United Nations. Ku and Jacobson, note 4 above, p. 360.
58. Luard, Evan (1982) *A History of the United Nations*, New York: St Martin's Press, p. 13.
59. Claude (1999a), note 20 above, pp. 316–317.
60. See, for instance, Thomas Franck's review of the General Assembly's rhetorical struggles over the US trust territories in the Pacific and elsewhere during the Cold War. Franck, note 43 above, pp. 187–204.
61. Righter, note 38 above, p. 54.
62. See Lederer, Edith M. (2006) "U.N. Staff Union Votes 'No Confidence' in Annan over Proposed Management Reforms", *Associated Press Worldstream*, 10 March.
63. UN Independent Inquiry Committee, note 2 above.
64. In this regard Robert Keohane wrote: "In world politics . . . existing authorizations are typically fragile, and often contested . . . Who gets the ability to influence the power-wielder? . . . After the authorization of a set of accountability relationships, actors engaged in the process will evaluate how these relationships are working from their standpoints. Actors that perceive themselves as disadvantaged by these arrangements, and that think they have sufficient political resources to alter or overturn them, will devise strategies to do so. If successful, some form of reauthorization will take place, and the cycle begins anew." Keohane, note 31 above, pp. 1126–1127.
65. Righter, note 38 above, p. 165.

66. Of course, corporations, while internally accountable to their boards of directors, and ultimately their shareholders, may wholly lack external accountability to those affected by the corporation's activities.
67. See articles 97 and 98.
68. Article 19, Convention on the Privileges and Immunities of the United Nations, 13 February 1946, 21 UST 1418, 1 UNTS 16. Note that the privileges and immunities of UN officials are limited to those "necessary for the independent exercise of their functions in connection with the Organization". Article 29.
69. Article 98 of the UN Charter states: "The Secretary-General shall make an annual report to the General Assembly on the work of the Organization."
70. Here I paraphrase Claude, note 21 above, p. 250.
71. This is underscored by the fact that Member States could be thought legally responsible for the acts of an international organization that acts as their agent. For differences of opinion among international lawyers on this point see Yee, Sienho (2005) "The Responsibility of States Members of an International Organization for its Conduct as a Result of Membership or Their Normal Conduct Associated with Membership", in Maurizio Ragazzi, ed., *International Responsibility*, Leiden: Koninklijke Brill, pp. 435–454.
72. See Luard, note 58 above, pp. 344–351.
73. See James, Alan (1985) "The Secretary-General: A Comparative Analysis", in G. R. Berridge and A. Jennings, eds, *Diplomacy at the U.N.*, New York: St Martin's Press, pp. 31–47, at pp. 43–44; Murphy, John F. (1982) *The United Nations and the Control of International Violence*, Totowa, NJ: Allenheld, Osmun Publishers, pp. 99–100.
74. The United States was instrumental in denying Boutros Boutros-Ghali a second term in office.
75. Simply by signing the Charter, new Member States agree to settle disputes peacefully, maintain friendly relations with other members and cooperate in development issues. UN Member States are also expected to contribute their assessed dues to the Organization, and to follow the directives of the Security Council, particularly when it acts under the powers of Chapter VII of the Charter. Moreover, as peacekeeping has developed into a major UN function, those Member States with the capacity to fund missions or provide troops are increasingly expected to do so.
76. Fowler, Michael R. (1997) "The U.N. Executive, Communication, and the International Public: Toward a Trusted International Executive", *Virginia Papers on the Presidency* 30, pp. 81–93, at p. 82.
77. Certainly, from the UN administration led by Secretary-General U Thant forward, UN Secretaries-General have envisioned their role in terms of addressing a global audience on certain vital issues, and not simply speaking to the Member States and their diplomatic representatives. See Fowler, ibid., p. 87, and "The 'Bully Pulpit'" in Franck, note 43 above, pp. 129–133.
78. Article 19 reads: "A member of the United Nations which is in arrears in the payment of its financial contribution to the Organization shall have no vote in the General Assembly if the amount of its arrears equals or exceeds the amount of the contributions due from it for the preceding two full years. The General Assembly may, nevertheless, permit such a Member to vote if it is satisfied that the failure to pay is due to conditions beyond the control of the Member."
79. Slaughter, Anne-Marie (2004) *A New World Order*, Princeton, NJ: Princeton University Press, pp. 200–201.
80. Righter, note 38 above, p. 38.
81. Ibid.

82. This view is echoed in article 100 of the UN Charter, which reads:
    1. In the performance of their duties the Secretary-General and the staff shall not seek or receive instructions from any government or from any other authority external to the Organization. They shall refrain from any action which might reflect on their position as international officials responsible only to the Organization.
    2. Each member of the United Nations undertakes to respect the exclusively international character of the responsibilities of the Secretary-General and the staff and not to seek to influence them in the discharge of their responsibilities.
83. In light of the statements by Nikita Khrushchev during the Congo crisis and American politicians during the McCarthy-era searches for American communists on the UN staff, I would characterize the position of the Soviet Union on this issue as being that its citizens working at the United Nations should be agents of the Soviet government, while the position of the United States was that Americans staffing the United Nations should not be serving the interests of communist states. For more detailed work on these points see "McCarthyism and the UN Secretariat" and "The Socialists and the Secretariat" in Franck, note 43 above, pp. 100–110. See also "The Secretary-General and the Secretariat" in Luard, note 58 above, especially pp. 353–357.
84. Security Council members authorize and set the mandates for peacekeeping missions, and as early as 1992 the costs of such operations had more than doubled the organization's regular budget; see Goulding, note 22 above, p. 267. From 2000 to 2008 peacekeeping expenses tripled to about $7 billion; see Lynch, Colum (2008) "Expenses at U.N. Balloon 25 Percent", *Washington Post*, 21 March, p. A1. Thus critics like David Malone observed of the Security Council's record in the 1990s: "Wishful thinking on resources, increasing risk, poor planning, the dilution of responsibility inevitable in committee decision-making, and the absence of a powerful and consistently engaged leader among its members... all contributed to the Council's subsequent decline into recrimination, risk-aversion, and flight from reality." Malone, note 23 above, p. 88.
85. Ku and Jacobson, note 4 above, pp. 358–359; Keohane, note 31 above, pp. 1137–1138.
86. For a classic account of the veto, including an appraisal of its advantages as well as disadvantages, see Claude, Inis L. Jr (1964) *Swords Into Plowshares: The Problems and Progress of International Organization*, 3rd edn, New York: Random House, pp. 133–146.
87. Claude, Inis L. Jr (1966) "The Security Council", in Evan Luard, ed., *The Evolution of International Organizations*, New York: Praeger, pp. 68–90, at p. 73. Claude wrote: "As students of world politics, the founding fathers must have known how transient is the glory of great-power status, how essential it is that a list of the major states be subject to addition and deletion. As students of international organization, they must have realized how damaging it is to prospects for the progressive development of institutions to equip the beneficiaries with the capacity to perpetuate those privileges. But, as practitioners of the political craft of organization-building, they had to acknowledge the necessity of giving the major powers a basis for confidence that their strongly demanded and hard-won special status within the [Security] Council would not be shortly stripped away by the majority that conceded this status to them with such obvious reluctance and resentment."
88. Claude, Inis L. Jr (1966) "Collective Legitimization as a Political Function of the United Nations", *International Organization* 20, pp. 367–379.
89. Claude, Inis L. Jr (1988) *States and the Global System*, New York: St Martin's Press, p. 145.
90. Note that this accords with Robert Keohane's notion of "public reputational accountability". See Keohane, note 31 above, pp. 1133–1134.

91. For an example of the considerable time the process of collective legitimization can take, consider the fact that the General Assembly resolution that Zionism should be considered a form of racism was passed in November 1975 and repealed more than 16 years later. See General Assembly resolution 3379 of 10 November 1975 and General Assembly resolution A/46/86 of 16 December 1991.
92. I am indebted for this metaphor to Inis L. Claude Jr, elucidated in a letter to me, 7 October 2006.
93. Article 7(1) of the UN Charter reads: "There are established as the principal organs of the United Nations: a General Assembly, a Security Council, an Economic and Social Council, a Trusteeship Council, an International Court of Justice and a Secretariat."
94. Article 17(3), UN Charter. See also article 58 of the Charter, which reads "The Organization shall make recommendations for the coordination of the policies and activities of the specialized agencies."
95. In this regard both ECOSOC and the General Assembly seem to have been envisioned more as coordinating bodies that might assist in such matters as setting priorities for the specialized agencies, rather than as strict taskmasters with effective means for compelling the agencies to attend closely to their views. Righter, note 38 above, pp. 36–37. Righter noted that the roles of the General Assembly and ECOSOC were so loosely defined that "each could, and did, make recommendations to each other in a circular ritual".
96. As Rosemary Righter observed of the specialized agencies, "in 1945 ... it was recognized that governments might, in practice, use these forums to advance their short-term and not necessarily enlightened national goals rather than to pursue peace, development, and the promotion of human rights. The secretariats were intended ... to make these organizations 'work' even when governments were reluctant to assume their responsibilities." Ibid., p. 39; see also ibid., p. 54.
97. Here I concur with Robert Keohane, who wrote: "Anyone who understands international interdependence and globalization recognizes that sustained cooperation in world politics requires international institutions ... Yet, international institutions will never be democratic, even on standards applicable to very large states. There is no coherent public with a public space, individuals do not have sufficient incentives to pay attention to policy issues at the level of international institutions, and opportunities for participation by ordinary citizens are very limited." Keohane, note 31 above, p. 1122.
98. This, for instance, was the meaning of democratization employed by Secretary-General Boutros Boutros-Ghali in his Cyril Foster lecture at Oxford University entitled "The Diplomatic Role of the Secretary-General". See Goulding, note 22 above, p. 269.
99. Claude, note 89 above, p. 147.
100. Letter to author from Inis L. Claude Jr, 7 October 2006.
101. Claude, note 89 above, p. 142.
102. As Edward Luck has observed, "Too often, the more extreme and confrontational voices in the nonaligned and G-77 caucuses ... seem to be the loudest, blocking forward movement on feasible reform steps and bolstering maximalist positions." Luck, Edward C. (1999) *Mixed Messages: American Politics and International Organization 1919–1999*, Washington, DC: Brookings Institution Press.
103. Claude, note 21 above, p. 257.
104. In 2000, though without offering his definition of democracy, Takashi Inoguchi suggested that more than 100 countries might be regarded as democratic, implying that somewhat more than one-half of UN Member States were democracies, but leaving a substantial number that were not. Inoguchi, Takashi (2000) "Pacific Settlement

of Conflict: The Role of the United Nations", in Mohammed Bedjaoui, ed., *Conflict Resolution: New Approaches and Methods*, Paris: UNESCO, p. 51.

105. Abbott, Kenneth W. and Duncan Snidal (2004) "Why States Act Through Formal International Organizations", in Paul F. Diehl, ed., *The Politics of Global Governance: International Organizations in an Interdependent World*, 2nd edn, Boulder, CO: Lynne Rienner Publishers, pp. 9–43, at p. 35.
106. See Claude, Inis L. Jr (1995) "The United Nations of the Cold War: Contributions to the Post-Cold War Situation", *Fordham International Law Journal* 18, pp. 789–793, at p. 790.
107. Righter observed that by the mid-1980s even the desirability of ensuring that UN money was well spent had become a controversial proposition precisely because of the connotation of accountability. Righter, note 38 above, p. 160.
108. Abbott and Snidal, note 105 above, p. 29.
109. For the assessment equation see UN resolution A/RES/55/5B-F.
110. Here, along with funding peacekeeping operations, the wealthiest states provide disproportionate support for such special programmes as the UN Children's Fund (UNICEF), the UN Development Programme and the World Food Programme.
111. This was made clear in the so-called "Taxpayers Revolt" of the 1980s. See Righter, note 38 above, p. 183.
112. Claude, note 21 above, p. 253.
113. Slaughter, note 79 above, p. 30.
114. Keohane, note 31 above, p. 1138; Ku and Jacobson, note 4 above, p. 368.
115. See the similar statement made by Richard Betts with respect to a different set of circumstances, that of curbing self-serving intelligence estimates, in Betts, Richard K. (2007) *Enemies of Intelligence: Knowledge and Power in American National Security*, New York: Columbia University Press, p. 44.
116. Ibid.
117. See Slaughter, note 79 above, p. 197. See also Reinicke, Wolfgang H. and Francis Deng (2000) *Critical Choices: The United Nations, Networks, and the Future of Global Governance*, Ottawa: International Development Research Centre.
118. Righter, note 38 above, p. 281.

3

Conceptual analysis of accountability: The structure of accountability in the process of responsibility

Hirohide Takikawa

The concept of accountability

Why accountability?

The former UN Secretary-General Kofi Annan once reported that "we need new mechanisms to ensure accountability. Where there is accountability we will progress; where there is none we will underperform." In order to strengthen the United Nations, "we must continue to improve the transparency and accountability of the Secretariat".[1] The United Nations is now under the pressure of accountability.

In general, we live in an age of accountability. Public demand for accountability has been increasing in many areas. Indeed, the insistence upon accountability can consume considerable time, money and effort. Processes of accountability are usually exhausting and burdensome. Making reports on activities often calls for more energy than the activities themselves. Preparing and giving elaborate answers to questions usually require much effort and sensitivity. The quest for greater accountability sometimes obstructs the proper aims of professional practice.[2] The question then arises: why do we believe that accountability is so important?

The justification for accountability lies in three values: compliance, efficiency and legitimacy. First, accountability mechanisms may ensure that those exercising power comply with authorized rules, guarding against the abuse of power. The process of giving an account can check the activities and decisions of those in power. More importantly, merely

Envisioning reform: Enhancing UN accountability in the twenty-first century, Kuyama and Fowler (eds), United Nations University Press, 2009, ISBN 978-92-808-1170-4

anticipating giving an account can help prevent the abuse of power.[3] To prevent the abuse of power is the ultimate goal of accountability arrangements.[4]

Secondly, accountability mechanisms may improve the quality of performance by requiring agents to justify their actions. By improving the flow and the quality of information, accountability can "make an important contribution to the efficient conduct of government".[5]

Thirdly, accountability mechanisms may enhance the legitimacy of decisions. The legitimacy of institutions can rely on tradition, symbols or legality. Decision-making through procedures that ensure accountability may acquire legitimacy based on legality. Accountability as procedural justice may reasonably be expected to yield the right results. Furthermore, giving an account of one's activities can promote legitimacy by assigning reasons to actions. Organizations without accountability can become corrupted and then lose legitimacy.

An elusive idea

Accountability is important, but its definition is elusive and often a source of controversy. Many attempts have been made to elucidate the concept of accountability by compiling a catalogue of adjectives that may modify "accountability". The catalogue includes managerial, democratic, horizontal/vertical, financial, internal/external, formal/informal, political, legal, professional, bureaucratic, military, societal and moral. In an era of accountability, the list continues to become only longer and less clear.

The goal here is not to add other items to this already long list, but to analyse the concept of accountability. The lexicon of accountability includes such terms as responsibility, liability, sanction, answerability, transparency and obligation. This conceptual analysis of accountability helps to clarify the relations between accountability and the affiliated terms.

Before we proceed to a conceptual analysis of accountability, three brief remarks on terminology should be made: the distinction between the word and the concept; a definition of accountability; and the relationship between responsibility and accountability.

Word and concept

Accountability is an English word. Many other languages (French, Spanish, Chinese, Italian, Japanese, etc.) have no synonym for the word.[6] This does not mean, however, that the concept of accountability has no significance in non-English-speaking countries or in international organizations. Rather, non-English-speaking people need to use the term "accountability" when they talk about many types of governance, though they often have difficulty translating "accountability" into their language. Accountability has been becoming an indispensable word for anyone concerned with governance. As Carol Harlow observed, "The new approach, which prioritizes 'good governance', inevitably places accountability high on the list of governance values."[7]

The fact that accountability is an English word does not diminish its global significance. It is important to notice, however, that the word and the concept differ. Different words can indicate the same concept, and one word can indicate multiple concepts. The concept of accountability may have the proper sense even in those languages that have no word equivalent to accountability. We must simply elucidate and analyse the concept.

Definition

We can find the core notion of accountability in any English dictionary. Many dictionaries agree upon the definition of accountability (*Oxford Dictionary of English*, *Longman Dictionary of Contemporary English*, Merriam Webster Online Dictionary, *Cambridge Advanced Learner's Dictionary*, Collins COBUILD, etc.). To be accountable is to be required to explain and justify one's actions. Hence, we can define the term as follows:

> Accountability is the obligation to explain and justify one's actions to others.

This is the core concept of accountability, from which many other meanings are derived. This chapter takes this dictionary definition as a starting point for analysing the concept of accountability.

Responsibility and accountability

The term "accountability" is increasingly being used in place of the term "responsibility". Richard Mulgan reports that while accountability was once seen as the external aspect of the broader concept of responsibility, responsibility is now taken as the internal aspect of the broader concept of accountability.[8] There seems to be no definite and invariable usage of the two terms; dictionaries often list the words as synonyms of each other, and usage seems to reflect just this trend. It would not be fruitful, therefore, to elaborate and articulate definitions of accountability and responsibility to discern a few slight differences between them.

Some claim that we should distinguish between accountability and responsibility because "the difference between accountability and responsibility is culpability".[9] It might then seem that accountability lacks the element of blame, while responsibility does not. However, culpability is not an essential element of responsibility, as the phrases "our responsibility to the future generations" and "the war responsibility of the post-war generations" show.

Rather, etymology confirms the ordinary interchangeable usage of both words. Responsibility can be traced back to the Latin *respondere*, to give an answer. It is not the answer to a request for information, but "an answer in the sense of giving account, justifying oneself, or defending oneself against an accusation".[10] On the other hand, accountability can be traced back through old French *aconter* to Latin *computare*, to count. Counting includes reporting financial expenditures; an account is an answer that provides numbers. Therefore, both responsibility and accountability include the provision of answers to questions; the original sense of each word is "answerability".

My proposal is to use accountability and responsibility in the following manner. Accountability is a narrower concept of responsibility. Accountability focuses on the central processes of responsibility. The two terms are neither coextensive nor opposite, but address different facets of our concern with the control of power. This chapter limits the sphere of accountability to the call and account structure. This is because limitation provides clarity. The second section explores the structure and extracts five components of accountability; the third section situates the structure of accountability in the whole process of responsibility; and the final section draws several fundamental principles of accountability from the conceptual analysis.

The structure of accountability

How can we clarify the concept of accountability? This chapter focuses on the *structure* of accountability, and then situates the structure within the process of responsibility. A paradigm of accountability can be illustrated as follows:

> X asks Y to explain and justify Y's actions. Y then has the obligation to explain and justify his or her actions to X.

This paradigm shows that the structure of accountability consists of five components:

- obligation
- X (account caller)
- Y (account giver)
- action
- explanation and justification.

These five components lead us to five fundamental questions on accountability.

- Obligations are drawn from rules. Question 1 is: on what ground is Y required to give an account? The character and mechanism of accountability vary according to the governing rule.
- Accountability mechanisms postulate two categories of people: those who call to account, and those who give an account. Thus question 2 is: who has the right to call to explain and justify? In other words, to whom is Y required to give an account? Question 3 is: who must provide an account?
- Y is required to account for Y's actions. Question 4 is: with which aspect of the action is an accountability mechanism concerned?
- To be accountable is to explain and justify one's actions. Question 5 is: what must be done to explain and justify? Are there any differences between explanation and justification, and, if so, what are they?

It is often said that there are three basic questions about a theory of accountability: who should be accountable, for what and to whom? Our structural analysis of accountability enables us to identify two other basic questions: why (on what rule) is someone accountable, and how does he or she explain and justify? Figure 3.1 indicates the structure of accountability. Each of these is discussed in sequence.

Rule

Accountable entities have an obligation to account for their behaviour because rules stipulate for them to do so. Rules are the most fundamental

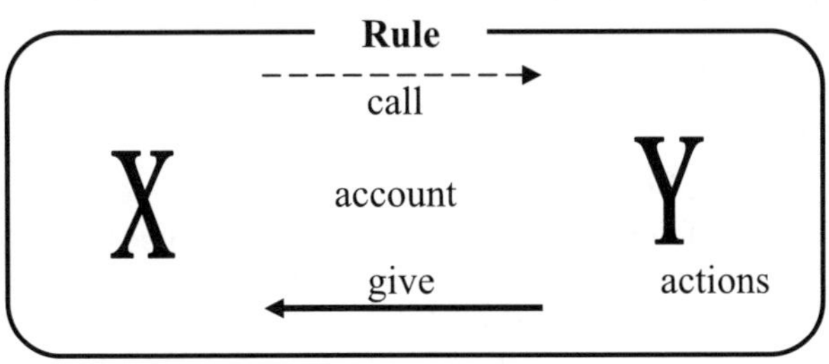

Figure 3.1 The structure of accountability

component in the structure of accountability because they stipulate all the other components: who should account, to whom, for what and how. Rules include some standards that apply to the account, as well as other standards that relate to the quality of the activity being accounted for.[11]

Rules of accountability are not restricted to positive law. Accountability sometimes evolves over time and involves interaction among participants.[12] Positive law, as well as social customs, moral laws, institutional practices and political culture, may constitute the rules of accountability.

Take the example of a parliamentary system. Under constitutional law a prime minister must explain and justify her policies to the parliament. She has no legal obligation to explain and justify her policy to foreign people, although she may have a moral obligation to justify it to them and/or a political obligation to explain it to their governments when it seriously affects them.

All the questions concerning accountability (who, to whom, for what and how) can be considered questions about rules of accountability. Since rules of accountability are often vague or amorphous, disputes over interpretation often arise. The legitimate interpretation of rules urges us to take into consideration principles of accountability, some of which are discussed in the final section of this chapter.

To whom

To whom do decision-makers have to provide an account? In other words, who has the right to ask them to explain or justify? As Robert Keohane claims, "Much of the politics of accountability involves struggles over who should be accepted as a principal."[13]

"Transparency for whom" has been a pressing issue at the global economic multilaterals such as the International Monetary Fund (IMF), the World Bank and the World Trade Organization (WTO).[14] The question "transparency for whom" overlaps the question "accountability to whom".

Stakeholders

An idea of accountability requires entities to give an account to all stakeholders. A stakeholder is formally defined as "any group or individual who can affect or is affected by" the decision of an entity.[15] However, it still remains to be decided who "those groups and individuals who can affect or are affected by the decision" are. They can be classified into three main groups: the superiors, the general public and the experts.

To the superiors

When officers are required to justify their actions to their superiors, their accountability is called managerial accountability or hierarchical accountability. Managerial accountability is an officer's duty to explain and justify his or her actions to his or her superiors.

Why must subordinates account to their superiors? The reason is that superiors have authority over them. This consideration leads to a general principle of accountability, which says: X is accountable to those who delegate authority to X. The flow of accountability corresponds to the flow of delegation. Those who are delegated to are accountable to those who delegate. We will call this the principle of delegation. Managerial accountability is about "making those with delegated authority answerable for carrying out agreed tasks according to agreed criteria of performance".[16]

Managerial accountability and managerial control are sometimes used interchangeably. Patricia Day and Rudolf Klein suggest that the doctrine of ministerial accountability has two aspects. The first is political accountability: ministers are responsible *to* parliament for what their departments do. The second aspect is managerial accountability: ministers are responsible *for* the actions of all their departmental officials.[17] The distinction between political and managerial accountability matches the distinction between two different questions: accountability to whom and accountability for what. Managerial accountability is used as managerial control when it is about "the way in which ministers control the actions and performance of their subordinates".[18]

The conceptual analysis of managerial accountability shows that it should be carefully distinguished from managerial control. First, when A controls B completely, B has no discretion. Without discretion, there is no accountability. Complete control eliminates accountability.[19] When B has an obligation to A, and B has n options (from q_1 to q_n) to discharge it, B also has the obligation to explain and justify to A why B chose q_1 among n options. Accountability thus presupposes discretion. One cannot be accountable to anyone unless one also has discretion and responsibility. Secondly, the flows of operation are also different. Control flows from A to B, whereas accountability flows from B to A. Indeed, holding entities accountable may function as a mechanism for controlling them. The core purpose of accountability is control.[20] However, the concepts of accountability and control are different.

Accountability through hierarchical control may work well where a shared hierarchy of authority exists. Because superiors usually hold institutionalized authority over their subordinates, the subordinates may well discharge their obligation to explain and justify their actions to their superiors. Managerial accountability is an effective and useful mechanism.

To the people

The principle of delegation implies another type of accountability. In democratic societies, all authority is drawn from the people. Social contract theories claim that people establish government and delegate authority to leave the state of nature. Democracy, with the principle of delegation, requires that those in political power be accountable to the general public. These entities must account for their activities "to a much broader group of stakeholders than simply those who have formal authority over [them]".[21]

This type of accountability is called democratic accountability. Democracy is etymologically the rule by the demos (people). Democratic accountability, required for the rule by the demos, can be drawn from another principle of accountability: the principle of impact. The principle of impact proclaims that those who are affected by decisions have a right to demand an account. Government must explain and justify its activities to citizens because its decisions, more or less, affect them.

The principle of impact invites an interesting question concerning the scope of the demos. Who should be counted as "those who are affected by the decisions"? Do foreigners have a right to demand accountability from the President of the United States because they are affected by his decisions? Since democratic accountability is arranged on different levels, national democratic accountability does not necessarily assure global or local democratic accountability. Rather, they often compete with each other. It is often difficult to draw the line between those who are affected and those who are not. A pragmatic version of the principle would be this: decision-makers have to give an account to all but those who are clearly not affected by their decisions.

Accountability does not always go hand in hand with democracy.[22] The relation between accountability and democracy is much more complicated than is typically supposed. On the one hand, accountable governance does not necessarily presuppose democracy. "Accountable monarchy" is not a contradictory concept, just as accountable democracy is not. Rather, accountability has been emphasized because of the so-called democratic deficit. Democratic governance cannot be fully achieved in transnational companies, non-governmental organizations (NGOs) and international organizations because most people cannot participate, directly or indirectly, in the decision process. Democratic accountability is necessary in a democratic deficit and perhaps unnecessary in a democratic surplus.

On the other hand, accountability does rely on the idea of democracy. Democracy is a system in which political legitimacy flows from the people. To acquire legitimacy, any public decisions must ultimately be justified to the people. As discussed earlier, accountability may enhance the legitimacy of decisions. Democracy as the legitimacy principle requires accountability. In other words, we can say that democratic accountability is drawn from the principle of legitimacy. The more that people bring to account their decision-makers, the more legitimate the decisions become. We can summarize the relation between accountability and democracy as follows: accountability is required by democracy as the legitimacy principle, but not by democracy as the participation principle.

To the experts

Democratic governments are accountable to the people for their activities. Democracy ultimately requires office holders to explain and justify their decisions to the general public. However, the extent to which the people can exercise the power to hold officials accountable is limited for at least two reasons.

First, the populace can exercise its checking power only through periodic elections. As Fidelma White and Kathryn Hollingsworth stated, "between elections, the electorate has to rely on surrogates to act on its behalf and hold government to account".[23] The most important surrogate is the parliament. Because the people typically cannot directly hold government accountable, the parliament holds the government accountable on behalf of the people. The government thus accounts to the people for its activities indirectly. In general, the separate powers of government are expected to render accounts to one another.

Secondly, the people do not usually have the time or means to examine the government's account thoroughly, especially in an age of specialization. Because the account often contains terms so professional and technical that ordinary people are befuddled, experts frequently audit the account on behalf of the people. Thus Barbara Romzek and Melvyn Dubnick concluded that "professional accountability occurs with greater frequency as governments deal increasingly with technically difficult and complex problems".[24]

These two considerations make accountability indirect. Indirect democratic accountability can work well only when the surrogate or the expert reflects the will of the people. When those who should call for an account on behalf of the people collude with the account giver, democratic accountability fails. To avert and prevent the failure, we must carefully separate the account demander from the account giver; we must insist upon the independence and performance of the former. Both mechanisms are discussed in the final section.

Internal/external accountability

Accountability is to give an account to others. "Others" are an essential component in the concept of accountability. The fact that X gives an account to itself does not mean that X discharges the obligation to account. X is required to account to someone else. In this sense, accountability is essentially external.

A decision-maker is surrounded by many others. We can divide "others" into two groups: internal and external. Internal others are members of the same organization as the individual making the account. The requirement of externality can be met in the weak sense that one accounts to another person within the same organization. From the standpoint of a particular individual, internal accountability involves justification to someone else, such as a superior or peer in the same organization, and in that sense is external.[25] Since no organization can be entirely manageable from the outside, internal accountability is an important requirement of management.[26] By contrast, external others are those outside the Organization. The requirement of externality is fulfilled in the strong sense that one accounts to a person who is not a member of the same organization.

The distinction between internal and external accountability may be relative, not rigid. Suppose that Y accounts to X, who is not a member of Y's organization. This is external accountability. When X and Y have a close relationship, however, they may appear to Z, an outsider, to belong to the same association. The relationship is considered internal accountability. As examples of the relativity of the distinction, while ministerial accountability to parliament is external for ministers, it can be internal for the citizens; while democratic accountability is external for one government, it is internal for foreign governments.

The question then arises: which is more important, internal or external accountability? Which holds administrative power more accountable? This has been a core problem of administrative responsibility, as shown by the well-known exchange between Carl Friedrich and Herman Finer.[27] Although both internal and external accountability have their own merits and demerits, any accountability mechanism, whether internal or external, must ensure the independence of the account caller (X) from the account giver (Y). When X is dependent on Y, there is no "other" to whom Y should account, and thus there is no accountability relationship at all. The requirement of independence is discussed later.

Democratic government involves two types of delegated power. First, power is delegated to the government by the people. Second, power is delegated among the government. Although some may call the former "external" and the latter "internal", the distinction between external and internal accountability is more relative.

Who

Who should be accountable? Do international organizations such as the United Nations and the World Bank have accountability? Do transnational corporations and NGOs? Keohane mentions six sets of entities that should be, but are not conventionally held to be, accountable: multinational corporations, transgovernmental and private sector networks, the Roman Catholic Church, mass religious movements, covert terrorist networks and powerful states. Keohane excludes NGOs because they are relatively weak.[28]

Basically, rules give an answer to the question of "who?" However, we also often need to interpret social or legal practices to confirm whether an entity is accountable. It is important to note that evasion of accountability is in essence impossible. When someone demands an account, evasion itself is taken as a certain kind of account. That individual would be called to explain and justify his or her refusal to account. When we take accountability as a fundamental requirement for governance, all individuals and organizations that execute power, at least potentially, have the obligation to account.

For what

One action has many aspects. We can judge an action from the viewpoints of efficiency, legality, morality or political legitimacy. This chapter focuses on three kinds of accountability: finance, regularity and performance accountability.

Finance

The original sense of "account" in accountability is "the financial 'account' in which revenue and expenditure decisions are reported to the authorising body, typically Parliament".[29] There is an obvious reason why financial accountability, or auditing, has been the focus of accountability. Financial accountability is about "the verification of financial accounts to check on whether the appropriate funds have come in and whether the outgoing money has been spent properly".[30] Financial accountability of the public sectors is often called fiscal accountability.

Both accounting and auditing focus on a financial aspect of actions. Accounting is recording the financial transactions of an organization on the books, although non-financial reports are becoming more common in the public sector. Auditing, the examination of the account, is the second and separate stage in the accountability process.[31]

Accountability now covers a wider range of reports beyond financial accounts. "To give an account of something" means to provide not only a financial report but a wider range of information as well.

Regularity

Accountability for regularity ensures that actions are performed according to the authorized rules. Those rules include standards on due process of execution and substantial requirements such as fairness and equality, as well as financial standards. When the authorized rules include financial standards, financial accountability is situated as a subset of regularity accountability. Regularity accountability can be called legality accountability because regularity and legality have the same connotation.

Regularity accountability is necessary, but is not by itself sufficient. As E. L. Normanton wrote, "an audit which concerns itself with nothing but 'regularity' is a narrow routine, totally unhelpful to the operations of government in any constructive sense".[32] We require other positive standards to assess the performance of administrative organizations.

Performance

Regularity accountability is concerned with *how* government does what it does. However, we have come to care about *what* government does – what it actually accomplishes.[33] This is called accountability for performance.

This distinction between regularity and performance accountability corresponds to a philosophical distinction between deontology and consequentialism. Deontology asserts that an action is right if a person acts according to duties. The rightness or wrongness of a particular action is not determined by the goodness or badness of its consequences. Consequentialism, on the other hand, asserts that an action is right if its consequences are good. It is highly difficult to resolve the dispute because the dichotomy reflects the two essential aspects of an action: intentions and consequences.

We now observe a basic trend towards results-based accountability. Increasing importance is being placed on value-for-money (VFM) audit.[34] VFM is about three Es: *economy* (minimizing the cost of resources used or required – i.e. spending less), *efficiency* (the relationship between the outputs from goods or services and the resources used to produce them – i.e. spending well) and *effectiveness* (the relationship between the intended and actual results of public spending – i.e. spending wisely) (see the UK National Audit Office webpage: www.nao.org.uk). VFM audit thus focuses on the results of activities. Results-based budgeting (RBB) is another example of this trend.

Robert D. Behn points out "the accountability dilemma" – that is, the trade-off between accountability for finances and fairness (or regularity) and accountability for performance.[35] This dilemma comes from "the accountability bias", which occurs when account demanders focus their attention on finance and regularity, rather than performance, and "the deterrent effect" of government that accompanies the bias. Behn recommends 360° accountability to solve the dilemma.[36] In most organizations, people are usually evaluated by their superiors based on accountability for finances and regularity because of the deterrent effect; 360° accountability requires them to be evaluated by "their subordinates, peers, team members, customers, and suppliers". Behn's argument indicates the important point that accountability *for what* is closely linked to accountability *to whom*. The more people to whom a person is accountable, the more aspects for which he or she is accountable.

To explain and justify

Accountable entities explain and justify their actions. The following questions then arise.

- What are explanation and justification?
- How can we determine whether individuals actually "explain and justify" their actions?
- Should we accept "I do not recall" as an appropriate explanation or justification?
- Is explanation the same as justification?
- If not, what is the difference, and to which is accountability essentially related?

We can distinguish between explanation and justification as follows. To explain one's action is to place it in an intelligible context so that it can be understood. On the other hand, to justify one's action is to give reasons so that it can be accepted. Both explaining and justifying refer to giving reasons. We can thus distinguish between explanation and justification based on the character of the reasons provided by the account giver. In short, to explain is to give *understandable* reasons; to justify is to give *acceptable* reasons. To make an action understandable is to show it to be rational from the standpoint of the agent. Explanatory reasons may refer to the agent's aim, motive or belief. On the other hand, to make an action acceptable is to show it to be reasonable from the standpoint of some other person. Justificatory reasons may refer to the regularity or consequences of the action.[37] To take but one example, an agent explains his action when he says "I did it because I believed it would help them"; he justifies his action when he says "I did it because it would probably help them".

To explain one's actions is a minimum requirement of accountability. To make others understand one's actions is the starting point of accountability. Accountability mechanisms, however, usually require more than that. This is because accountability mechanisms are in place to control the agents. Therefore, accountability is the obligation to explain *and* justify but not to explain *or* justify one's actions.

Accountability may take multiple forms because we can explain and justify our actions in various ways. As shown above, a typical form is call and account: X demands Y to account, and Y answers X's questions. Other basic forms include disclosure (X demands some information from Y, and Y discloses it), and reporting (Y makes a report on Y's activities). Sometimes reporting is not sufficient as accountability. When a government voluntarily issues an annual report, it may not be considered full accountability because it can control the content of the report and exclude poor performance.[38] Therefore, the rights to inspect and have access to information are essential to accountability mechanisms.

The process of responsibility

Thus far, we have explored accountability. We are now in a position to analyse responsibility and clarify its relationship to accountability. Responsibility is also an elusive idea. To illuminate the concept of responsibility, we can examine two representative views: those of Hans Kelsen and H. L. A. Hart.

Kelsen characterizes sanction, offence, obligation (or duty) and liability (or responsibility) as follows.[39] A sanction is a reaction against an action or omission determined by the legal order.[40] Sanctions can be legal, religious or social. Legal sanctions consist of punishments and civil executions. When a definite action or omission is connected with a sanction, it is called an offence. The offence is not the negation but the condition of the norm.[41] An obligation or duty is the norm that commands a certain behaviour.[42] An individual has the obligation to behave in a certain way when this behaviour is commanded by a norm. Kelsen warns against confusion among the concepts of obligation, sanction and liability:

> A sanction itself is not an obligation – it can, but need not be stipulated as such – but it is a coercive act which a norm connects to a certain behavior, whose opposite is therefore legally commanded, that is, the content of a legal obligation. We can also express this by saying: the sanction is the coercive act that constitutes the legal obligation. Liability is no obligation either, but rather the relation between an individual against whom a sanction is directed and the offense committed by him or someone else. Obligation is the omission of offenses by individuals whose behavior forms the offense.[43]

Figure 3.2 The process of responsibility

Hart, on the other hand, classifies responsibility into four senses: role-responsibility, causal-responsibility, liability-responsibility and capacity-responsibility.[44] The first three senses are related to our analysis of responsibility. Concerning role-responsibility, Hart says that "whenever a person occupies a distinctive place or office in a social organization, to which specific duties are attached... he is properly said to be responsible for the performance of their duties... Such duties are a person's responsibilities."[45] "Role" can be extended to include a task or an obligation assigned to any person by rules and customs. "Responsibility" is used as causal-responsibility, when the expression "was responsible for" can be substituted with the word "caused". With liability-responsibility, an individual is liable to be punished (criminally responsible), forced to pay compensation or morally blamed.

Kelsen and Hart share the three main components of responsibility: obligation, action and liability. These three components, associated with accountability, constitute the process of responsibility. Figure 3.2 shows the process.

Responsibility is not different from accountability in the core sense. J. R. Lucas claims that "the central core of the concept of responsibility is that I can be asked the question 'Why did you do it?' and be obliged to give an answer".[46] In short, at the central core of responsibility stands accountability as defined in this chapter. Accountability must, therefore, be centrally situated in the process of responsibility.

Obligation

Many dictionaries tell us that responsibility has two meanings: to have a duty to deal with something, and to blame for something. The former corresponds to an obligation (Kelsen) or role-responsibility (Hart); the latter to responsibility (Kelsen) or liability-responsibility (Hart). These two meanings can be taken as the two stages or mechanisms to make entities accountable in the whole process of responsibility. Obligations can be called *ex ante* (or prospective) accountability mechanisms, and sanctions *ex post* (or retrospective) accountability mechanisms.

The obligation is the first stage in the process of responsibility. Obligations as *ex ante* mechanisms include moral, religious, social and legal obligations or duties. As we have seen, rules stipulate an obligation to act in a certain way and to provide an account when requested. Thus people have a moral, religious or legal obligation to act and account in a stipulated way.

Obligations are only weak mechanisms; effective accountability systems usually contain formal enforcement mechanisms. Obligations, however, can work not only when they can be formally enforced but also when they enhance a sense of obligation or offer incentives.

Action

The term "action" is used here in a broad sense in that omission is also included. People perform actions in order to discharge obligations. When an agent did *p*, she was responsible for *p*. An agent was responsible for both the action and some subsequent events. Strictly speaking, the conditions of responsibility may include causality, intentionality and capacity-responsibility (Hart). Accountability does not require subjective conditions to ascribe responsibility to agents. In other words, when entities fail to discharge obligations, they are not allowed to make excuses for their actions. In this sense, accountability is similar to strict liability.

Accountability

When entities fail to discharge the obligation to act in accordance with authorized rules, they are required to explain and justify their actions. As earlier, this is the core concept of accountability. Accountability connects actions with sanctions in the process of responsibility. If agents fail to justify their actions when they act against rules, they face sanctions.

Furthermore, accountability *per se* may improve the quality of activities. First, the process of giving an account can check decisions and actions retrospectively. Scrutinizing activities may reveal hidden faults. Secondly, anticipating accountability may prevent the abuse of power. In other words, accountability can have an *ex ante* effect. Accountability mechanisms may influence agents to make decisions in an explainable and justifiable way. The realization that one might be held to account stimulates a person to behave responsibly.[47] Accountability mechanisms can thus function in both retrospective and prospective ways.[48]

Sanction

When entities fail to discharge the obligation to explain and justify their actions, or when they fabricate excuses or reports, sanction mechanisms hold them responsible. Sanctions include both negative sanctions to punish irregular or poor performance and positive sanctions to reward good performance. Sanctions themselves are sometimes called responsibility or accountability.

Elections can be considered political sanction mechanisms. The term "democratic accountability" is often used to show the principle according to which it is possible to replace the holders of political office through general elections.[49] Because our terminology confines accountability to its core notion, this mechanism should be called democratic responsibility. The periodic election may be a key mechanism of the responsibility process in democracy.[50] There is, however, no logical reason why elections should be seen as a responsibility mechanism because elections may serve to select good policies, not to sanction bad politicians.[51]

Legal sanction mechanisms include criminal punishment (fine or imprisonment), civil liability (compensation or restitution) and disciplinary measures such as suspension or dismissal from office. Institutionalized legal sanctions are usually more effective than informal social sanctions such as social reputation, censure or movement. With no formal sanction mechanisms, social sanctions may be the last resort. Social sanctions can work only when some people or groups have a strong interest in the entities' activities and an effective tool to reach the general public. NGOs and the media are expected to play an important role in the social process.

Sanction mechanisms as *ex post* responsibility processes ensure that mistakes will not be made in the future by transforming irregular entities or by deterring other entities. Both executed and anticipated sanctions may function as preventive mechanisms. This feedback links sanctions to actions. Other feedback connects accountability to actions, as we saw earlier. Both accountability itself and sanctions after accountability help to improve the quality of activities. Figure 3.2 should be redrawn as figure 3.3 to highlight both these feedback mechanisms and the rules that stipulate obligations and sanctions.

The relation between accountability and sanction has been disputed.[52] Some claim that a sanction is an essential element of accountability.

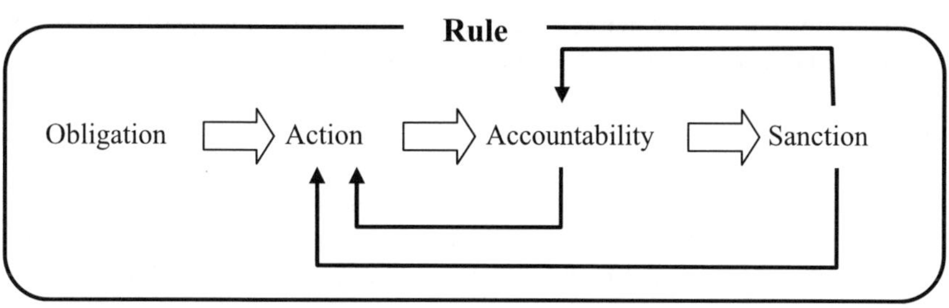

Figure 3.3 The process of responsibility (revised version)

Bernard Manin, Adam Prezeworski and Susan Stokes define accountability as follows: "Governments are 'accountable' if citizens can discern representative from unrepresentative governments and can sanction them appropriately, retaining in office those incumbents who perform well and ousting from office those who do not."[53] Accountability is thus defined as the relation between outcomes and sanctions.

We exclude the element of sanctions from the "definition" of accountability because we should carefully distinguish between the definition and the effective mechanisms. Indeed, accountability mechanisms often do not work well without any sanctions. Some accountability mechanisms, however, may well work with no punitive elements. Extremely powerful countries, such as the United States, often seem immune from accountability because there is no institutionalized sanction mechanism in international relations.[54] It is not unreasonable, however, to claim that even they should be accountable to other states or the global public, and that they really are.

There is no conceptual contradiction in accountability mechanisms without any sanctions, regardless of their effectiveness. It is not essential to the concept of accountability that X has any power along the lines of the power to dismiss or impose fines or sanctions on Y.[55] Accountability for decision-making as the call-and-response mechanism can hold decision-makers accountable almost as much as the electoral and punitive processes. Figure 3.3 shows that the accountability process itself has a feedback effect on decisions and activities.

Accountability mechanisms

There are many types of accountability mechanisms. An accountability mechanism that works well in one area may not work in others.[56] There is little evidence to indicate that there is a universally applicable accountability mechanism. Conceptual analysis, however, enables us to identify some fundamental institutional requirements for accountability mechanisms. These basic principles help us to organize the institutional arrangements in order to enhance UN accountability.

Independence

Accountability is the obligation to explain and justify one's activities to "others". In other words, to account to "oneself" is never considered accountability. An account caller must be separate from an account giver. This analysis leads us to the principle of independence: the reviewer must be independent of the decision-maker. Accountability mechanisms demand some tension between the scrutinizer and the decision-maker. If the reviewer is not independent of the decision-maker, processes of accountability are almost useless; they can promote neither quality nor legitimacy. As White and Hollingsworth observed, "The independence of an *external* auditor is vital to enable the auditor to perform his functions properly" (emphasis added).[57]

E. L. Normanton claims that a new dimension of financial accountability has been established by the separation of powers.[58] Separation of powers divides power among several branches, and controls power by requiring each branch to explain and justify its actions to other branches. Accountability presupposes a division of power which assures independence of each branch from others. There are many types of independence: financial, personal, organizational and operational.[59] The presidential system and the parliamentary system have their own independence arrangements. We need to find and create an optimal institutional arrangement to make each entity accountable.

Global democracy

International organizations present us with another difficult question. To whom should they discharge the obligation to explain and justify their activities: to the member states, to the majority of the member states or to all the people in the world? Democracy is a political system in which every person is supposed to be a stakeholder. Global democracy requires international organizations to account not only to their member states but to absolutely everyone. The provision of information only to the member states' governments is not sufficient from the viewpoint of global democracy.

We have already noticed at least three reasons for global democratic accountability: delegation, impact and legitimacy. First, international organizations are delegated their power from the global demos through the member states. Second, globalization is a series of worldwide interdependencies and exchanges through which major international organizations affect, to some degree, all the people in the world. Third, international organizations may acquire legitimacy when they represent and reflect the world public. On these three grounds, they are theoretically required to account to everyone on earth.

Distribution

While global accountability requires accountability to all entities, Simon Burall and Caroline Neligan highlight the reality that many international organizations are more accountable to some members than to others.[60]

We then face a distributional problem of accountability.[61] Accountability consumes time, money and effort. Too much accountability can become managerially and economically inefficient; accountability is then more likely to be traded off against other values.[62] Accountability mechanisms are expensive and scarce, and must thus be distributed wisely and fairly. The principle of impact dictates that the acting entity should be accountable to the set of people affected. We may need to revise this principle because of the scarcity of accountability. As Keohane suggests, if merely being affected were enough to create a valid claim, "virtually nothing could ever be done".[63]

This distributional problem urges us to construct another type of accountability mechanism that does not include the actual call-and-response process: transparency.

Transparency

Immanuel Kant articulates in his *Perpetual Peace* the transcendental formula of public law: "all actions which relate to the rights of other human beings are wrong if their maxim is not compatible with publicity".[64] Hannah Arendt expands Kant's insight and underlines the significance of spectators in her *Lectures on Kant's Political Philosophy*: "only the spectator occupies a position that enables him to see the whole; the actor, because he is part of the play, must enact his part". In addition, "the actor is dependent on the opinion of the spectator".[65] Therefore, "the public realm is constituted by the critics and the spectators, not by the actors or the makers".[66] Actions do not acquire legitimacy unless they are visible.

To make actions visible and transparent is to expose them to the public eye. An individual or a group of people feels obliged to explain and justify actions when other people are watching. The term "accountability" is a conjunction of account and ability. Accountability thus implies a moment of potentiality.[67] In other words, to be accountable is to be ready to give an account. Transparency has the same value as accountability, in the sense that to become transparent is to disclose one's activities and to be prepared to explain and justify them. Transparency functions in the same way as accountability; transparency can be seen as a potential accountability.

This insight highlights the contrast between transparency and democracy. Democracy controls power by *voice*; transparency controls power by *sight*. Transparency does not require people to participate in decision processes, only to watch over them. Transparency is especially important where neither voice nor exit can be an effective or feasible option.

Indeed, some policies and practices cannot succeed without secrecy. Timing should be secret for an effective examination. Even deliberation and bargaining sometimes rely on secrecy. It is certain that publicity has its limits, but "those limits themselves must be publicly affirmed".[68] We can call this "the paradox of publicity": the limits of publicity are public.

The protection of whistleblowers is another important accountability mechanism that enhances transparency. Outsiders usually cannot access information about the abuse of power by an organization if active steps are taken to hide the evidence. Whistleblowers may make organizations more transparent. The protection of whistleblowers is a clear step to increase the accountability of international organizations.[69]

Network of accountability

Accountability is an essential mechanism for governance. No entity, therefore, should be beyond accountability. "Absolute power" in Lord Acton's famous warning that "power corrupts, and absolute power corrupts absolutely" should be interpreted as "power beyond accountability". Power beyond accountability tends to corrupt absolutely.

We have been informed that not only corporations but also their auditing firms were responsible for many corporate accounting scandals. Here an important question arises: who audits an auditor? The answer is another auditor. Then the next question comes: who audits the second auditor? The answer would probably be a third auditor. We thus face an infinite regress: A is audited by B, B is audited by C and C is audited by D. If we try to achieve terminality, we face a vicious circle: A is audited by B, B is audited by C and C is audited by A. However, we should not call this circle "vicious" if each audit is regularly and effectively performed. All that is required is a network of accountability, rather than a small circle of accountability. No entity is allowed to exit from this network. All entities are accountable to each other. This is the ultimate form of accountability we are now pursuing in international relations.

Notes

1. Annan, Kofi (2005) "In Larger Freedom: Towards Development, Security and Human Rights for All", Secretary-General's Report, Doc. A/59/2005, 21 March.
2. O'Neill, Onora (2002) *A Question of Trust*, New York: Cambridge University Press, ch. 3.
3. Roche, Declan (2003) *Accountability in Restorative Justice*, New York: Oxford University Press, pp. 46–47.
4. Thomas, Paul G. (1998) "The Changing Nature of Accountability", in B. Guy Peters and Donald J. Savoie, eds, *Taking Stock: Assessing Public Sector Reforms*, Buffalo, NY: McGill-Queen's University Press, pp. 348–393, at p. 348.

5. Normanton, E. Leslie (1966) *The Accountability and Audit of Governments: A Comparative Study*, New York: Praeger, p. 338.
6. Harlow, Carol (2002) *Accountability in the European Union*, New York: Oxford University Press, pp. 13–16.
7. Ibid., p. 190.
8. Mulgan, Richard (2000) "'Accountability': An Ever-Expanding Concept?", *Public Administration* 78, pp. 555–573, at p. 558.
9. Flinders, Matthew (2001) *The Politics of Accountability in the Modern State*, Brookfield: Ashgate, p. 11. Cf. Day, Patricia and Rudolf Klein (1987) *Accountabilities: Five Public Services*, New York: Tavistock, p. 229.
10. Bovens, Mark (1998) *The Quest for Responsibility: Accountability and Citizenship in Complex Organizations*, Cambridge: Cambridge University Press, p. 23.
11. Davies, A. C. (2001) *Accountability: A Public Law Analysis of Government by Contract*, New York: Oxford University Press, p. 82.
12. Brown, L. David and Jonathan A. Fox (1998) "Accountability within Transnational Coalitions", in Jonathan A. Fox and L. David Brown, eds, *The Struggle for Accountability: The World Bank, NGOs, and Grassroots Movements*, Cambridge, MA: MIT Press, pp. 439–483, at p. 441.
13. Keohane, Robert O. (2003) "Global Governance and Democratic Accountability", in David Held and Mathias Koenig-Archibugi, eds, *Global Governance and Public Accountability*, Malden, MA: Blackwell, pp. 130–159, at p. 140.
14. Kahler, Miles (2005) "Defining Accountability Up: The Global Economic Multilaterals", in David Held and Mathias Koenig-Archibugi, eds, *Global Governance and Public Accountability*, Malden, MA: Blackwell, pp. 8–34.
15. Freeman, R. Edward (1984) *Strategic Management: A Stakeholder Approach*, Boston, MA: Pitman, p. 46.
16. Day and Klein, note 9 above, p. 27.
17. Ibid., p. 33.
18. Ibid.
19. White, Fidelma and Kathryn Hollingsworth (1999) *Audit, Accountability and Government*, New York: Oxford University Press, p. 8.
20. Mulgan, Richard and John Uhr (2001) "Accountability and Governance", in Glyn Davis and Patrick Weller, eds, *Are You Being Served? State, Citizens, and Governance*, St Leonard, NSW: Allen & Unwin, pp. 152–174, at p. 153.
21. Burall, S. and C. Neligan (2005) "The Accountability of International Organizations", GPPi Research Paper Series No. 2, available at www.globalpublicpolicy.net/fileadmin/gppi/IO_Acct_Burall_05012005.pdf, p. 7.
22. Keohane, Robert O. and Joseph S. Nye Jr (2003) "Redefining Accountability for Global Governance", in Miles Kahler and David A. Lake, eds, *Governance in a Global Economy: Political Authorities in Transition*, Princeton, NJ: Princeton University Press, pp. 386–411, at p. 398.
23. White and Hollingsworth, note 19 above, p. 7.
24. Romzek, Barbara S. and Melvin J. Dubnick (1987) "Accountability in the Public Sector: Lessons from the Challenger Tragedy", *Public Administration Review* 47, pp. 227–238, at p. 229.
25. Mulgan, note 8 above, p. 559.
26. Brodeur, Jean-Paul (1999) "Accountability: The Search for a Theoretical Framework", in Errol P. Mendes, Joaquin Zuckerberg, Susan Lecorre, Anne Gabriel and Jeffrey A. Clark, eds, *Democratic Policing and Accountability: Global Perspectives*, Brookfield: Ashgate, pp. 125–164, at p. 158.
27. See Friedrich, Carl Joachim (1940) "Public Policy and the Nature of Administrative Re-

sponsibility", in Carl Joachim Friedrich and Edward S. Mason, eds, *Public Policy*, Cambridge, MA: Harvard University Press, pp. 3–24; Finer, Herman (1941) "Administrative Responsibility in Democratic Government", *Public Administration Review* 1, pp. 335–350.

28. Keohane, note 13 above, pp. 146–148.
29. Mulgan and Uhr, note 20 above, p. 1.
30. Day and Klein, note 9 above, p. 8.
31. White and Hollingsworth, note 19 above, ch. 2.
32. Normanton, note 5 above, pp. 22–23.
33. Behn, Robert D. (2001) *Rethinking Democratic Accountability*, Washington, DC: Brookings Institution Press, p. 9.
34. White and Hollingsworth, note 19 above, p. 74.
35. Behn, note 33 above, p. 11.
36. Ibid., ch. 11.
37. Cf. Rawls, John (2000) *Lectures on the History of Moral Philosophy*, Barbara Herman, ed., Cambridge, MA: Harvard University Press, p. 166.
38. Davies, note 11 above, p. 84.
39. Kelsen, Hans (1949) *General Theory of Law and State*, trans. Anders Wedberg, Cambridge, MA: Harvard University Press, pp. 50–71; Kelsen, Hans ([1960] 1992) *Reine Rechtslehre, 2. Aufl.*, Vienna: Österreichische Staatsdruckerei, pp. 114–130; Kelsen, Hans (1967) *Pure Theory of Law*, trans. Max Knight, Berkeley, CA: University of California Press, pp. 108–125.
40. Kelsen ([1960] 1992), ibid., p. 114.
41. Ibid., p. 116.
42. Ibid., p. 121.
43. Ibid., p. 129.
44. Hart, H. L. A. (1968) *Responsibility and Punishment: Essays in the Philosophy of Law*, New York: Oxford University Press, p. 211.
45. Ibid., p. 212.
46. Lucas, J. R. (1993) *Responsibility*, New York: Oxford University Press, p. 5.
47. Bovens, note 10 above, p. 39.
48. Harlow, note 6 above, p. 10.
49. Ibid., p. 8.
50. Davies, note 11 above, p. 77.
51. Manin, Bernard, Adam Prezeworski and Susan C. Stokes (1999) "Elections and Representation", in Adam Prezeworski, Susan C. Stokes and Bernard Manin, eds, *Democracy, Accountability, and Representation*, New York: Cambridge University Press, pp. 29–54; Fearon, James D. (1999) "Electoral Accountability and the Control of Politicians: Selecting Good Types versus Sanctioning Poor Performance", in Adam Prezeworski, Susan C. Stokes and Bernard Manin, eds, *Democracy, Accountability, and Representation*, New York: Cambridge University Press, pp. 55–97.
52. Brodeur, note 26 above, p. 143.
53. Manin, Bernard, Adam Prezeworski and Susan C. Stokes (1999) "Introduction", in Adam Prezeworski, Susan C. Stokes and Bernard Manin, eds, *Democracy, Accountability, and Representation*, New York: Cambridge University Press, pp. 1–26, at p. 10.
54. Keohane, note 13 above, p. 148.
55. White and Hollingsworth, note 19 above, p. 6.
56. Burall and Neligan, note 21 above, p. 7.
57. White and Hollingsworth, note 19 above, p. 91.
58. Normanton, note 5 above, p. 5.
59. White and Hollingsworth, note 19 above, ch. 5.

60. Burall and Neligan, note 21 above.
61. Keohane, note 13 above, p. 145.
62. Keohane and Nye, note 22 above, p. 391.
63. Keohane, note 13 above, p. 141.
64. Kant, Immanuel ([1795] 1977) *Zum Ewigen Frieden*, in *Immanuel Kant Werkausgabe XI*, Frankfurt am Main: Suhrkamp, p. 245.
65. Arendt, Hannah (1982) *Lectures on Kant's Political Philosophy*, Chicago, IL: University of Chicago Press, p. 55.
66. Ibid., p. 63.
67. Mulgan, note 8 above, p. 560.
68. Gutmann, Amy and Dennis Thompson (1996) *Democracy and Disagreement*, Cambridge, MA: Harvard University Press, p. 96.
69. Burall and Neligan, note 21 above, p. 19.

4

Legitimacy and accountability of the United Nations

Jochen Prantl

> "When *I* use a word," Humpty Dumpty said in a rather scornful tone, "it means just what I choose it to mean – neither more nor less."
>
> "The question is," said Alice, "whether you *can* make words mean so many different things."
>
> "The question is," said Humpty Dumpty, "which is to be master – that's all." (Lewis Carroll, *Through the Looking Glass*, 1871)

Enhancing the legitimacy and accountability of the UN system has become a key concern in the discussion of how to adapt the world organization to the challenges of the twenty-first century. It is also part and parcel of a wider debate about the development of international norms and procedures for the good governance of globalization.[1] Closing the "democracy gap" in policy-making processes and holding multilateral institutions more accountable to the people of international society seem to be the order of the day. Yet how can we establish norms, beliefs and common procedures to be shared by members of international society in the apparent absence of a strong sense of political community at the global level? How can we secure compliance?

This chapter discusses central aspects of UN legitimacy and accountability. It argues that the norms of "democracy" and "participation" have become touchstones of and yardsticks for international legitimacy. However, if Member States want to improve the problem-solving capacity of the UN system, they need to find a productive trade-off between

Envisioning reform: Enhancing UN accountability in the twenty-first century, Kuyama and Fowler (eds), United Nations University Press, 2009, ISBN 978-92-808-1170-4

the competing demands of inclusiveness, efficiency, informality, transparency and accountability. Short of a one-size-fits-all strategy, there is a striking need to take better advantage of flexible mechanisms and multiple forms of legitimacy and accountability that we can see already in modern democracies.

The chapter is divided into two parts. The first section discusses the question of UN legitimacy and accountability from a wider conceptual and contextual perspective. It argues that the concepts of legitimacy and accountability are closely associated with the notion of authority.[2] Authority needs to be legitimate and accountable in order to gain broad acceptance by international society. At the same time, authority cannot be exercised within a power vacuum. The question of how to reconcile power on the one hand and legitimacy and accountability on the other hand has to come under scrutiny. The second section tests the propositions of the first part by applying them to the specific case of the UN Security Council. The chapter concludes with some lessons learned, including policy implications and recommendations.

Context and concept

Discussing legitimacy and accountability at the beginning of the twenty-first century raises the question of why these have not been a bigger issue before and what factors have contributed to their increased importance. By legitimacy, I refer primarily to the justification of legal and political authority exercised by an international institution through its procedures (or input) and output.[3] By accountability, I simply mean an institution's liability to be called to account.[4] This section looks at the contextual and conceptual sides of legitimacy and accountability. It develops the main argument that any discussion of how to enhance UN legitimacy and accountability must take into account the limits of applying democratic standards and best practices in the absence of a strong sense of political community.

Foreign policy and democratic control

Foreign policy belongs to the most difficult areas where democratic control, and with it legitimacy and accountability, can be achieved at the national level. Alexis de Tocqueville analysed long ago the inherent difficulties of democratic control in the conduct of foreign affairs: "Foreign politics demand scarcely any of those qualities which are peculiar to a democracy; they require, on the contrary, the perfect use of almost all those in which it is deficient."[5] In the early 1920s Walter Lippmann suggested that "democracies in their foreign policies had generally to choose between splendid isolation and a diplomacy that violated their ideals. The most successful democracies, in fact, Switzerland, Denmark, Australia, New Zealand, and America until recently, have had no foreign policy in the European sense of that phrase. Even a rule like the Monroe Doctrine arose from the desire to supplement the two oceans by a glacis of states that were sufficiently republican to have no foreign policy."[6] From today's perspective, such policy would be hard to maintain. Yet the question of how to control foreign policy by democratic means still looms large, as Robert Dahl, perhaps the leading theorist of democracy, argues: "In democratic countries where democratic institutions and practices have been long and well established and where . . . a fairly strong democratic political culture exists, it is notoriously difficult for citizens to exercise effective control over many key decisions on foreign affairs."[7]

The problem of democratic control becomes even more acute in international organizations such as the United Nations. If one accepts the proposition that the influence of citizens in and their control over foreign policy decision-making is rather limited at the domestic level, we can hardly expect some greater role at the international level. UN politics remains essentially unaccounted by "we the peoples of the United Nations". Although the first seven words of the UN Charter, inspired by the preamble of the US Constitution, seem to underline the democratic foundations of the Organization, reflecting the collective will of mankind, a brief look into the proceedings of the San Francisco Conference tells us otherwise. In fact, the majority of Commission I rejected the interpretation that the principles of democracy and cooperation constituted minimum standards which must be respected by all Member States.[8]

It does not come as a great surprise that, in terms of popular control over policies and procedures, international organizations tend to be highly undemocratic. According to Robert Dahl, "international systems will lie below any reasonable threshold of democracy".[9] Especially among realist students of international relations, multilateral institutions are primarily seen as instruments for the pursuance of states' vested interests, as Robert Keohane and Joseph Nye have succinctly argued: "It makes no more sense to ask whether an inter-state organization is 'democratic' than it does to ask if a broom has a nice personality. One should ask merely if the instrument works well."[10] Nevertheless, then we are confronted with the question of why discussions about legitimacy and accountability have re-emerged in the post–Cold War era and how multilateral institutions can meet certain standards of legitimacy and accountability without being "democratic". Those questions will be further pondered in the following subsections.

Why legitimacy and accountability?

Legitimacy and accountability have become touchstones for the effective management of globalization and the regulation of conflicts arising out of the asymmetries of power and influence and the global distribution of wealth and welfare. They help to establish a wider perception of justice and fairness in international society. Looked at from a realist perspective, the willingness of states to commit to effective international institutions originates in the Hobbesian world view that the comparative advantage of cooperation may be greater than the gains of unconstrained conflict.[11] Yet Hobbes was extremely pessimistic about the potential of human beings to commit to voluntary cooperation. While many scholars would not necessarily agree with his conclusions, we should accept the Hobbesian challenge that the effectiveness of institutions not only depends on their effectiveness to solve collective-action problems but also on mutually agreed norms and principles with which members of international society need to comply. In addition, without shared perceptions of justice and fairness, institutional authority is likely to erode.

Why has the issue of institutional authority grown in importance, and with it the debate about institutional legitimacy and accountability? Until recently, scholars of international relations have tended to dismiss questions related to the legitimacy of multilateral organizations, focusing instead on the causes and effects of institutions. Such lack of interest originated to a large extent in the relatively weak authority international institutions exercised. This changed, however, with the breakdown of the bipolar system. Globalization has become the key driving force that impacts on the workings of global, regional, subregional and domestic institutions; the challenge of addressing problems collectively and effectively has significantly increased. The intrusiveness of international norms, adopted at the global level, affects domestic debates on how societies should organize themselves. At the same time, globalization mobilizes growing resistance, especially at the level of developing countries. Such resistance originates in the great asymmetry of power and influence in the international system that relegates the majority of developing countries to the role of "rule takers", with the powerful Organisation for Economic Co-operation and Development (OECD) countries setting the agenda and monopolizing the roles of "rule creators" and "rule enforcers". In this context, unconstrained hegemonic power is of particular concern, as Andrew Hurrell has rightly observed:

> If you want to solve problems in a globalized world, you cannot simply persuade or bully governments into signing treaties and are therefore inevitably drawn to become involved with how other people organize their own societies. This trend has been reinforced by the transformation of the security agenda and this is one of the most important factors that has reshaped the debate about legitimacy and, once more, complicated the exercise of hegemonic power.[12]

Globalization, therefore, seems to foster the creation of a normative sphere of influence. This is important especially for four reasons. Firstly, those members of international society that are able to set the normative agenda and define the dos and don'ts of world politics significantly reduce the political costs for achieving their preferred policy outcomes, as the result is likely to enjoy broader international acceptance. Secondly, the challenges of managing globalization have not only led to a diffusion of power and problem-solving mechanisms but also to a diffusion of the circle of participants in the normative debate, which may include a diverse group of actors such as international non-governmental organizations, transnational corporations and the international media. Thirdly, states and institutions become deeply penetrated by increased normative demands and consequently cannot escape from this debate. They may provide platforms for intensive debate about the content, the justification and the implementation of norms, acting as agents for norm diffusion and socialization.[13] Legitimacy depends a great deal on the ability of stakeholders to win the normative discourse over a specific course of action. This potential needs to be explored much further, as Keohane and Nye have pointed out:

> The problem of accountability for governance at the international level is not the complete absence of mechanisms of accountability. The problem is that the mechanisms are *disarticulated*. In a well-functioning domestic democracy, political inputs – popular activity, media attention, interest group lobbying, parties, elections, and formal legislation – are articulated together. There is a clear pathway by which laws can be created; and when laws are enacted, regular procedures and organizations exist to implement, amend, and change those laws. This is the procedural basis for democratic legitimacy. Internationally, however, the link between popular activity and policy is severely attenuated.[14]

Fourthly, the intrusiveness of globalization has blurred the borderline between domestic and foreign policies, which has consequences for the role of citizens and their involvement in what used to be an "external affair":

> although citizens in democratic countries are usually less interested in foreign affairs than in domestic issues, in some circumstances they can become activated and play an influential or even decisive role in key foreign policy decisions. A policy is likely to activate citizens if it causes or threatens to cause such severe harm to the interests, goals, and well-being of a large minority, or even a majority, of citizens that they become aroused in opposition, political activists arise to champion their cause, and political leaders are themselves split.[15]

Globalization, and with it the intrusiveness of international norms and transnational laws and regulations, has indeed started to concern and activate citizens. The legitimacy and accountability of those institutions that adopt wide-ranging rules and norms have become a serious issue that cannot be ignored, as it might endanger the wider acceptance of the constitutional framework of our international system. The question then becomes: how can we achieve this? Democracy as a source of legitimacy becomes deeply problematic in global institutions where a significant part of the constituency can hardly be described as democratic. To whom is the United Nations accountable? While the preamble of the UN Charter seems to assume the existence of a global demos, that is "we the peoples", the United Nations essentially is a global institution composed of Member States. Any discussion of how to enhance the legitimacy and accountability of the United Nations must take into account the limits of applying democratic standards and best practices in the absence of a strong sense of political community at the global level. Nevertheless, there is a demand for basic standards that international institutions should meet in order to achieve a wider perception of institutional policies and procedures as being just and fair.

The shadow of hierarchy

Multilateral institutions reflect the hierarchical structure of international order. Asymmetries in the distribution of relative power generate a high degree of inequality in institutional decision-making, which may negatively impact on the problem-solving capacity of states and institutions.[16] The principle of sovereign equality of states is severely eroded in a hegemonic system.[17] Yet international organizations may "flatten" the hierarchical order by constraining the powerful and empowering the weak. G. John Ikenberry has developed one of the clearest accounts of how strategic restraint and institutional self-binding may help to maintain hegemonic pre-eminence.[18] Such logic depends, however, on the assumption that international organizations have the legitimacy, authority and capacity to solve problems.

Achieving legitimacy and accountability: Five hypotheses

This section hypothesizes five guiding principles providing an overarching framework for achieving legitimacy and accountability of the United Nations.

Hypothesis 1: Multiple forms of legitimation and accountability

Legitimacy and accountability should not be treated as absolute goods. They rather constitute instrumental values that UN Member States need to trade off against competing demands such as efficiency or informality. The balance between those demands is fluid and context-driven. It needs to be struck on a case-by-case basis. There is a strong case for softening overly rigid principles of international law in order to enhance the effectiveness of international organizations.

Hypothesis 2: Institutional authority

Legitimacy and accountability are directly linked to the political and legal authority of the United Nations. Although separable, they are hard to separate from institutional effectiveness and the underlying distribution of relative power between Member States. Authority appears as a function of legitimacy, accountability and effectiveness.

Hypothesis 3: Process and substance

Institutions of global governance must be able to solve collective-action problems. Ideally, the outcome will be perceived as just and fair by members of international society.[19] Processes without accountability run the danger of becoming corrupt. Yet processes that do not produce substance will lack output legitimacy and are unlikely to generate broad public support. Niklas Luhmann has argued, for example, that organizational procedures help to generate broad public acceptance, a level of general tolerance, which is distinct from agreement with the specific decision at hand.[20] In consequence, although formal international organizations tend to be ineffective, the primacy of procedures seems to make them indispensable. Formal processes may help to achieve international acceptance of policies by generating a wider perception of justice and fairness, which is the *sine qua non* of legitimacy.[21] Broader acceptance is facilitated through a kind of Rawlsian "veil of ignorance", generating a level of tolerance towards institutional decisions but without in-depth knowledge of their future effects. The veil of ignorance constitutes a key element in ultimately achieving what Robert Dahl has called the common good: "Our common good, then – the good and interests we share with others – rarely consists of specific objects, activities, and relations; ordinarily it consists of the practices, arrangements, institutions, and processes that promote the well-being of ourselves and others – not, to be sure, of 'everyone' but of enough persons to make the practices, arrangements, etc. acceptable and even cherished."[22]

Hypothesis 4: Discourse and persuasion

UN legitimacy and accountability can be achieved only as part of a major discourse between stakeholders. In this context, the world organization must create a more productive space for norm diffusion and socialization. Building stronger links between civil society and UN policy-making is of particular concern. Here, international institutions must provide opportunities for the expression of voice.

Hypothesis 5: Accountability starts at home

At the domestic level, accountability is achieved most prominently through the holding of regular elections. International institutions lack this essential feature. While the demand to enhance the transparency of international institutions seems to be obvious, this should not obfuscate the circumstance that accountability in fact starts at home: strengthening domestic procedures such as the enhanced involvement of national parliaments in foreign policy-making. However, efforts to apply accountability standards that can be found in modern democracies are bound to remain piecemeal at the global level. Nevertheless, the analysis of domestic procedures to enhance accountability may help us to develop at least a sense of direction.

Practice: The UN Security Council

This section looks at the practice of the UN Security Council by testing the working hypotheses as developed earlier. It illustrates the relationship between systemic change and increased demands on the legitimacy and accountability of Security Council working methods and procedures. Here I will focus on three aspects: first, the emergence of the Council's informal consultations, the so-called consultations of the whole; second, the article 24 crisis that unfolded as a result of the Council's inability to respond to major security challenges of the post–Cold War security environment; and third, the role and impact of informal groupings of states – contact groups, core groups, groups of friends – which proliferated in response to this crisis. UN Member States adopted a wide range of other, more direct, measures in the post–Cold War era that aimed at enhancing UN legitimacy, transparency and accountability. As those developments have already been very well covered and analysed elsewhere, I will not repeat them here.[23] In particular, I will highlight the impact of informal groups of states on Security Council decision-making. The section argues that informal groups of states bear the potential to enhance the legitimacy and accountability of the Council.[24] Informal groupings epitomize a softening of overly rigid principles of international law. They may ultimately increase the effectiveness of the Security Council and enhance its institutional authority by decoupling the processes of diplomatic problem-solving and its legitimation. In addition, informal groups may provide platforms for the exercise of "voice", allowing a discourse between major stakeholders that do not have necessarily a seat on the Council proper.

Informal consultations of the UN Security Council

Changes in the structural conditions of the international system have forced international institutions to adapt policies and procedures in order to maintain their problem-solving capacity. In essence, the breakdown of the bipolar system exacerbated structural limitations of the UN Security Council that had originated much earlier when the United Nations had to adapt to changes resulting from decolonization. With the increase of UN membership from 51 to 117 Member States between 1945 and 1965, the balance of power in the Western-dominated General Assembly shifted in favour of the post-colonial states. At the same time, the pressure on the Security Council increased to achieve a more balanced geographical representation of countries on that body: enlarging Council membership should help to enhance the legitimacy and accountability of its decision-making.

The enlargement of the Security Council in 1965 impacted on the intra-institutional distribution of influence and power and resulted in a decrease of Western dominance within the Organization.[25] On a few occasions the Council turned into a mini-General Assembly, degenerating into a platform for the ideological battles between North and South. The frequent recourse to article 31 of the UN Charter that allowed non-members of the Council to participate in its formal meetings reinforced such development.[26] Related requests increased from the 1960s onwards.[27] Informal consultations of the Security Council developed in direct response to the growing ineffectiveness of formal meetings. The procedure is mentioned neither in the UN Charter nor in the Security Council Provisional Rules of Procedure. This innovation developed out of practice. Figures 4.1 and 4.2 illustrate the sharp increase in informal consultations between 1972 and 1982 and between 1988 and 2002 respectively.[28] In 1978 the number of informal consultations tripled from 38 to 113 meetings (fig. 4.1). This increase has to be seen in context, with the completion of a separate room built for the sole purpose of holding

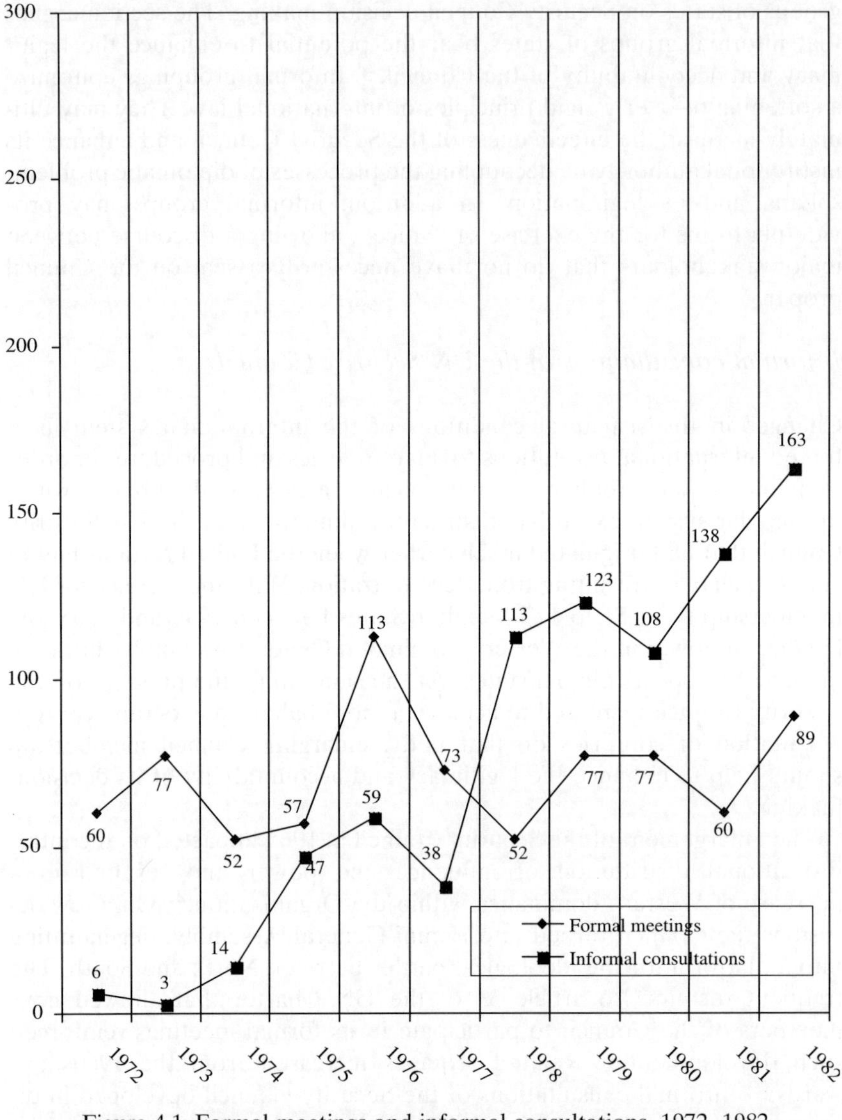

Figure 4.1 Formal meetings and informal consultations, 1972–1982

informal consultations. This formalization of informal processes contributed to the significant increase of the consultations of the whole. The increase in formal meetings since the end of the 1990s (fig. 4.2) is indicative of the growing pressure on the Council to increase the legitimacy, accountability and transparency of its decision-making. Public and thematic meetings of the Council, which are open to the wider UN membership,

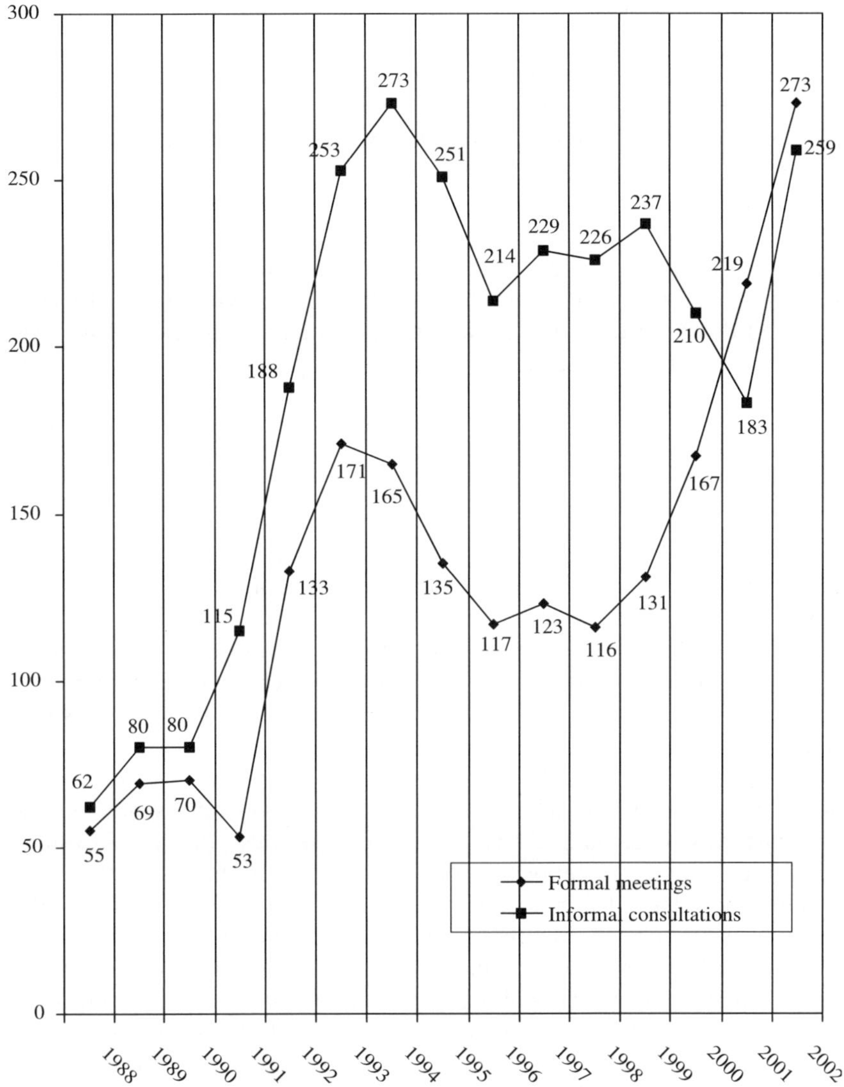

Figure 4.2 Formal meetings and informal consultations, 1988–2002

provide space for public discourse, norm diffusion and socialization. Although the retreat to informal consultations aimed at making Security Council decision-making more effective, the downside of such consultations had already become obvious by the early 1980s. Various diplomats and officials of the UN Secretariat repeatedly pointed to the "deliberate stalling, inaction, watered-down resolutions, secrecy, over-formalization of an informal process, and lack of outside input".[29]

In conclusion, the narrative of the UN Security Council helps to develop a better understanding of the difficulties in making decisions that are legitimate, accountable and effective at the same time. Security Council decision-making is characterized by the constant challenge to strike a balance between the competing demands of legitimacy, accountability, informality, transparency and effectiveness. Such a process is further complicated by the circumstance that the Council is a political body serving as an instrument for the conduct of international diplomacy. Watered-down resolutions, containing extremely ambivalent language, are often the result of a fragile political compromise between Council members. The legitimacy and accountability of the Security Council therefore need to be discussed against the wider background of international politics.

Article 24 crisis

The structural deficiencies of the UN Security Council worsened in the post–Cold War era, which generated a permissive political context that allowed the Organization to deal with more and more complex conflict settings. At the same time the Council has been challenged by increased normative ambitions of UN Member States and a lack of means (as well as a lack of political will by some of its members) to deliver accordingly. This could be well described as an article 24 crisis that essentially comprises three dimensions. The first relates to a crisis of representativeness. The current debate on Security Council reform illustrates the prevailing perception that the composition of the Security Council is neither geographically balanced nor does it reflect the current distribution of relative power among UN Member States. The second dimension relates to a crisis of effectiveness, which illustrates a growing mismatch in the Security Council between the willingness to take decisions and the allocation of resources for their implementation. Those problems had been most prominent in the cases of Srebrenica and Rwanda. The third dimension relates to a crisis of decision-making, which is most prominent in the Council's selectivity in addressing some conflicts while ignoring others. The article 24 crisis, and with it the structural constraints of the Security Council, has in fact deepened against the background of the growing engagement of the United Nations in worldwide peacekeeping operations.[30]

Figure 4.3 illustrates the causal relationship between systemic change and challenges for institutional adaptation, which generated a gap not only in the Council's legitimacy, accountability and transparency but also in its effectiveness. The proliferation of informal groupings of states

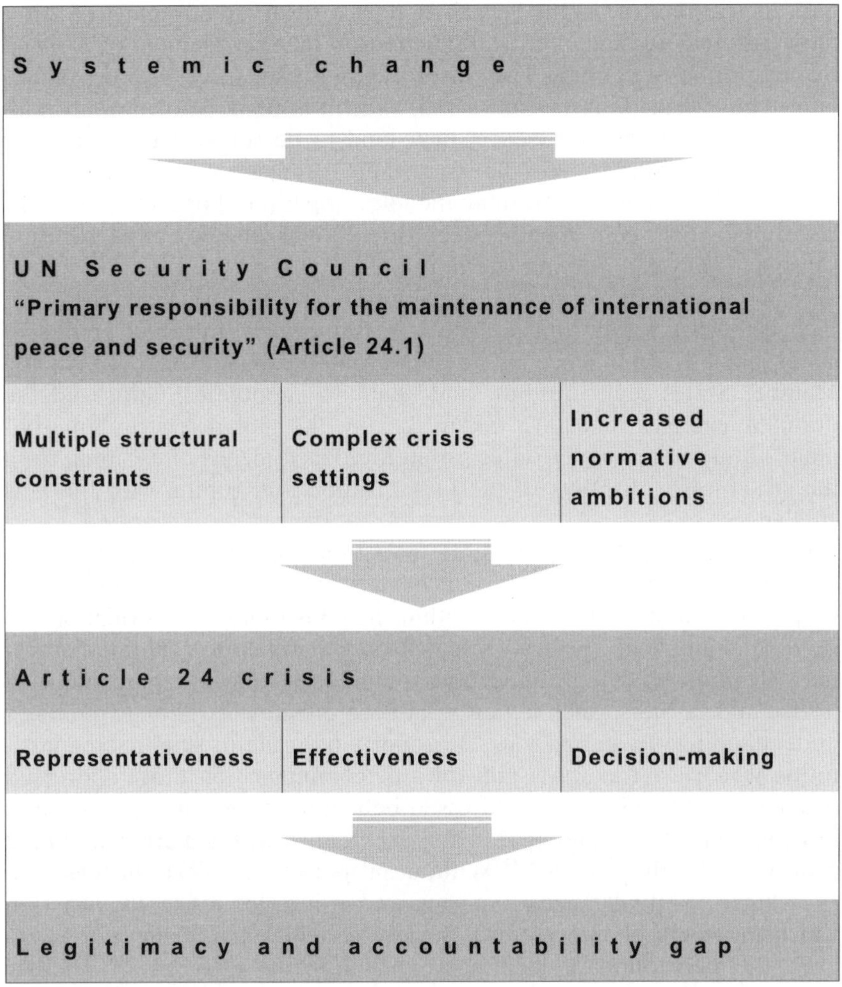

Figure 4.3 Legitimacy and accountability gap of the Security Council: Causes

in the post–Cold War era can be explained as one important response to the tension resulting from those competing demands, as I will further illustrate in the remainder of this section.

Informal groups of states

Why is it important to look at the dynamics between informal groups of states and the UN Security Council?[31] In order to answer this question, we need to analyse first the reasons why those mechanisms emerged, and look then at the role of the Security Council. Informal groupings of states have assumed a range of critical functions in the management of risk and the resolution of conflict. They also occupy a vital space between multilateral governance, on the one hand, and traditional major power diplomacy, on the other. In essence, they tend to be self-selected groupings that develop around a specific issue; their formation occurs *ad hoc* and the meeting structure is informal; they develop a set of operational norms governing, *inter alia*, membership, operational practices and decision rules; and they can operate within the objectives of a resolution or mandate adopted by the Security Council but outside its formal structures, or they can exist wholly outside the UN framework. Informal groups of states gained prominence as an important means through which UN Member States seek to adjust and adapt to geopolitical shifts and the dramatic changes that have taken place in the global security environment. Informal groups of states proliferated as a means of escaping from the structural constraints of the Organization and coping with the new challenges.

How do informal groups of states affect the role of the Security Council? In a nutshell, while informal groups may help to generate some output that cannot be achieved within the constraints of a formal organizational framework, Security Council decision-making generates procedural legitimacy that is important for creating a wider perception of justice and fairness. Such a view is in accordance with Thomas Franck's understanding of legitimacy as "a property of a rule or rule-making institution which itself exerts a pull towards compliance on those addressed normatively because those addressed believe that the rule or institution has come into being and operates in accordance with generally accepted principles of right process".[32] Without proper process, legitimacy is hard to achieve. Mutually agreed norms and principles guide the ways in which members of international society should act or behave.[33] However, the perception of legitimacy, including the question of whether state action should be legitimized by a Security Council mandate or not, may differ significantly from one country to another. Consequently, legitimacy will ultimately depend on who is gaining the monopoly of interpreting a given action as just and procedurally fair.[34] Discourse and persuasion are part and parcel of the legitimation process.

The structural conditions of the post-bipolar era have fostered devolution of crisis management to informal groups of states, with the UN Security Council delivering the right process – that is, the legitimation for state action. While the decoupling of crisis management from the process of its legitimation is far from being new, it has been a significant pattern from the mid-1990s onwards. This pattern was most visible when North Atlantic Treaty Organization (NATO) member states intervened in

Kosovo without authorization of the Security Council. The functions of diplomatic problem-solving and legitimation are separable, though not separate. Despite its structural deficiencies, the Security Council carries a large degree of symbolic power that helps to create a perception of legitimacy, as Ian Hurd has underlined.[35] The article 24 crisis of the Security Council makes this international institution "ineffective but indispensable".[36]

In consequence, decentralizing core functions of the Security Council may, in fact, enlarge the ownership of its decision-making. As Ngaire Woods has observed, "the longer-term considerations of effectiveness require a more active and participatory membership than the traditional hierarchical vision, and herein lies a powerful reason for applying lessons of good governance to international institutions".[37] If one applies three core principles of good governance – participation, accountability and fairness – enlarging the number of participants in Council decision-making may lead to a wider perception of the Security Council being more accountable and legitimate. Those complementary functions of informal groups of states are, however, contingent upon whether these groups of states operate within the objectives of the United Nations or whether they act on their own account.

In conclusion, the dynamics between informal groups of states and the UN Security Council may produce double-edged legitimacy and accountability in terms of procedure and output. Provided the Security Council and informal groups of states act in complementary fashion, legitimacy and accountability as the common good may be achieved.

Conclusions: Institutional authority and its discontents

This chapter has analysed the question of UN legitimacy and accountability from the perspective of the academic discipline of international relations. While international institutions must adhere to minimum standards of accountability and participation, there is a strong demand for enhancing mechanisms that allow for better persuasion rather than coercion. In addition, there is no one-size-fits-all strategy to make UN politics more legitimate and accountable. UN legitimacy and accountability tend to be the result of a rather complicated decision-making process that needs to find a trade-off between competing demands such as informality, transparency and effectiveness. Only a world organization that is able to provide effective solutions for collective-action problems will generate the public support needed to adapt to and deal with the challenges of the early twenty-first century. Without effectiveness the institutional authority of the United Nations will ultimately be undermined. Oxford don and novelist Lewis Carroll taught us long ago about the discontents of authority. His famous character of Humpty Dumpty, the talking egg in a cravat sitting on top of a wall and talking down to little Alice, epitomizes a satirical and ultimately dystopian view of authority that is pretentious and without substance. Consequently, the episode of Humpty Dumpty ends with his fall from the wall, depicting the great fall of false authority.

What does this imply for UN legitimacy and accountability? In order to reinstall the authority of the United Nations, institutional procedures should allow for flexible participation of stakeholders to the greatest possible extent. The narrative of the Security Council in the 1990s suggests already a change in the way the Council meets responsibilities under article 24 to maintain international peace and security. The processes of diplomatic problem-solving and its legitimation have become increasingly decoupled. This development is naturally not without tensions. We should study in greater detail how the dynamics between flexible *ad hoc* mechanisms and formal institutions can be made mutually reinforcing, and learn from those examples. They may provide answers to the question of how to reconcile power and legitimacy in the conduct of global affairs. Yet power must be exercised in a responsible way. The powerful must consider the consequences for the weak whose lives may be transformed by their decisions. The case for developing a common sense of global ethics seems to be particularly strong.

Given the considerable structural constraints of the United Nations in adapting its formal institutions, informal groups have the potential to play a complementary role in enhancing the UN's capacity as problem-solver. Legitimacy and accountability are no absolutes, but may appear in multiple forms. Adopting less rigid rules and more flexible procedures is the avenue the United Nations and its Member States should pursue to make UN politics more legitimate and accountable.

Notes

1. Governance comprises the whole spectrum of both formal and informal processes and institutions that define the activities of members of international society. Globalization shall be defined here as processes that create a net of (inter)dependencies between members of international society on a global scale. However, especially in those cases where huge discrepancies in the distribution of relative power exist, it may be more appropriate to label those relationships as "asymmetric dependencies". See Strange, Susan (1996) *The Retreat of the State: The Diffusion of Power in the World Economy*, Cambridge: Cambridge University Press, p. xiii. See also the various contributions in Held, David and Anthony McGrew, eds ([2000] 2003) *Global Transformation Reader: An Introduction to the Globalization Debate*, 2nd edn, Cambridge: Polity Press.

2. On authority as a central concept of social science and the diverse motives of compliance, see Weber, Max (1978) *Economy and Society: An Outline of Interpretive Sociology*, Guenther Roth and Claus Wittich, eds, Berkeley, CA: University of California Press, especially vol. 1, part 1, ch. III.
3. On the problems of input- and output-oriented legitimization, see Scharpf, Fritz W. (1999) *Governing in Europe: Effective and Democratic?*, Oxford: Oxford University Press, especially ch. 1.
4. In this context, I distinguish between institutional effectiveness and accountability. Effectiveness shall be defined here as the ability of international organizations to accomplish their mandates.
5. De Tocqueville, Alexis (1945) *Democracy in America*, vol. I, New York: Vintage Books, p. 243.
6. Lippmann, Walter ([1922] 1997) *Public Opinion*, foreword by Ronald Steel, New York: Simon & Schuster, p. 171 et seq.
7. Dahl, Robert A. (1999) "Can International Organizations Be Democratic?: A Skeptic's View", in Ian Shapiro and Casiano Hacker-Cardon, eds, *Democracy Edges*, New York: Cambridge University Press, pp. 19–36, at p. 23. See also Almond, Gabriel (1950) *The American People and Foreign Policy*, New York: Harcourt Brace.
8. See Simma, Bruno, ed. (1995) *The Charter of the United Nations: A Commentary*, Munich: C. H. Beck Verlag, p. 46, n. 6.
9. Dahl, note 7 above, p. 21.
10. Keohane, Robert O. and Joseph S. Nye Jr (2003) "Redefining Accountability for Global Governance", in Miles Kahler and David A. Lake, eds, *Governance in a Global Economy: Political Authority in Transition*, Princeton, NJ: Princeton University Press, p. 387.
11. See Hobbes, Thomas ([1651] 1904) *Leviathan; Or, The Matter, Forme & Power of a Commonwealth, Ecclesiasticall and Civil*, A. R. Waller, ed., Cambridge: Cambridge University Press.
12. Hurrell, Andrew (2005) "Pax Americana or the Empire of Insecurity?", *International Relations of the Asia-Pacific* 5(2), pp. 153–176, at p. 163.
13. See Hurrell, Andrew (2001) "Global Inequality and International Institutions", in Thomas W. Pogge, ed., *Global Justice*, Oxford: Blackwell Publishing, pp. 32–54. A very useful empirical study on norm socialization is provided by Gheciu, Alexandra (2005) *NATO in the "New Europe": The Politics of International Socialization after the Cold War*, Stanford, CA: Stanford University Press.
14. Keohane, Robert O. and Joseph S. Nye Jr (2001) "The Club Model of Multilateral Cooperation and Problems of Democratic Legitimacy", in Roger B. Porter, Pierre Sauvé, Arvind Subramanian and Americo Beviglia Zampetti, eds, *Efficiency, Equity, and Legitimacy: The Multilateral Trading System at the Millennium*, Washington, DC: Brookings Institution Press, pp. 264–294, at p. 285.
15. Dahl, note 7 above, p. 30.
16. See Hurrell, Andrew and Ngaire Woods, eds (1999) *Inequality, Globalization, and World Politics*, Oxford: Oxford University Press.
17. See Krisch, Nico (2005) "International Law in Times of Hegemony: Unequal Power and the Shaping of the International Legal Order", *European Journal of International Law* 16(3), pp. 369–408.
18. See Ikenberry, G. John (2001) *After Victory: Institutions, Strategic Restraint, and the Rebuilding of Order after Major Wars*, Princeton, NJ: Princeton University Press.
19. See Olson, Mancur Jr (1965) *The Logic of Collective Action*, Cambridge, MA: Harvard University Press. See also Ostrom, Elinor (1990) *Governing the Commons: The Evolution of Institutions for Collective Action*, Cambridge: Cambridge University Press.

20. Luhmann, Niklas (1983) *Legitimation durch Verfahren*, Frankfurt am Main: Suhrkamp.
21. See Rawls, John (1985) "Justice as Fairness: Political not Metaphysical", *Philosophy and Public Affairs* 14(3), pp. 223–251. Yet the formalization of processes still remains of great importance in global governance. On this point see Stinchcombe, Arthur L. (2001) *When Formality Works: Authority and Abstraction in Law and Organizations*, Chicago, IL: University of Chicago Press.
22. Dahl, Robert A. (1989) *Democracy and Its Critics*, New Haven, CT: Yale University Press, p. 307.
23. See, for example, Bailey, Sydney and Sam Daws ([1975] 1998) *The Procedure of the UN Security Council*, 3rd edn, Oxford: Clarendon Press. For more recent developments see Luck, Edward C. (2003) "Reforming the United Nations: Lessons from a History in Progress", Occasional Paper Series, Academic Council on the United Nations System, especially pp. 13–14, ns 35 and 36; Luck, Edward C. (2006) *The United Nations Security Council: A Primer*, New York: Routledge. Most recently, the UN Security Council Informal Working Group on Documentation and Other Procedural Matters, chaired by the Japanese permanent representative to the United Nations, Kenzo Oshima, has been very active to improve the Council working methods further. On 19 July 2006 the Security Council adopted a "Note by the President" that included several measures to increase the Council's transparency and openness to non-members. For example, the note clarified who is actually entitled to participate in each type of Council meeting and when non-members are allowed to speak. It also clarified the rules of procedure for the so-called Arria-Formula meetings, an informal arrangement that allows the Council greater flexibility to be briefed about international peace and security issues by non-members, including individuals. See Security Council (2006) Update Report No. 4, 19 July, available at www.securitycouncilreport.org.
24. On the dynamics between informal groups and the Security Council in specific conflict settings such as Namibia, El Salvador and Kosovo see Prantl, Jochen (2006) *The UN Security Council and Informal Groups of States: Complementing or Competing for Governance?*, Oxford: Oxford University Press.
25. See Hiscocks, Richard (1973) *The Security Council: A Study in Adolescence*, London: Longman, p. 99.
26. Article 31 of the UN Charter reads: "Any Member of the United Nations which is not a member of the Security Council may participate, without a vote, in the discussion of any question brought before the Security Council whenever the latter considers that the interests of that Member are specially affected."
27. Bailey and Daws, note 23 above, p. 155. At peak times, especially when the Security Council discussed matters related to decolonization and apartheid, as much as 50 per cent of the total UN membership participated in its formal meetings. For example, on 1 June 1983 a total number of 64 delegations, not being members on the Council, participated in this meeting; S/PV.2451.
28. Figures 4.1 and 4.2 are reprinted from Prantl, note 24 above, pp. 109 and 77 respectively.
29. Cited in Feuerle, Loie (1985) "Informal Consultation: A Mechanism in Security Council Decision-making", *New York University Journal of International Law and Politics* 18(1), pp. 267–308, at p. 294.
30. As of 31 August 2006 there were 16 peacekeeping operations ongoing, with 89,955 peacekeeping personnel deployed in the field. See Informational Note, available at www.un.org/Depts/dpko/dpko/bnote.htm.
31. The following paragraphs draw heavily on Prantl, Jochen (2005) "Informal Groups of States and the UN Security Council", *International Organization* 59(3), pp. 559–592.

32. See Franck, Thomas (1990) *The Power of Legitimacy among Nations*, Oxford: Oxford University Press, p. 24.
33. See Ostrom, note 19 above, p. 139.
34. Claude, Inis L. Jr (1966) "Collective Legitimization as a Political Function of the United Nations", *International Organization* 20, pp. 367–379, at p. 369.
35. He argues that "The symbolic power of the Security Council is evident in the energy states expend on having the Council pay attention to issues of concern to them..." Hurd, Ian (2002) "Legitimacy, Power, and the Symbolic Life of the UN Security Council", *Global Governance* 8(1), pp. 35–52, at p. 39.
36. Berdal, Mats (2003) "The UN Security Council: Ineffective But Indispensable", *Survival* 45(2), pp. 7–30.
37. Woods, Ngaire (1999) "Good Governance in International Organizations", *Global Governance* 5(1), pp. 39–61, at p. 43.

5

Accountability of the United Nations from the perspective of international law

Kyoji Kawasaki

Introduction

Accountability seems always to accompany the attribution or delegation of power from one person or entity to another. The delegated person is accountable for his exercise of power towards the delegating person. International organizations, including the United Nations, have competence conferred on them by the states which founded them, and their powers are strictly limited to whatever is necessary to perform the functions which their constitutive charters have defined.[1] It seems, consequently, quite natural for us to talk about accountability of the United Nations at least towards Member States.

In this chapter, I will discuss the accountability of the United Nations from an international law perspective. As appositely remarked by the Committee on Accountability of International Organizations of the International Law Association (ILA), the accountability of international organizations is a multifaceted phenomenon, and the forms under which accountability will arise may be legal, political, administrative or financial.[2] It follows that our examination will touch upon only one facet of the entire picture of UN accountability. It must also be added that such internal order of the United Nations as staff regulations and employment relations is beyond the scope of this chapter. Although it certainly involves legal aspects, international or not, it seems to be better discussed from the perspective not so much of international law as international administrative law. On the other hand, in the context of UN accountability I

Envisioning reform: Enhancing UN accountability in the twenty-first century, Kuyama and Fowler (eds), United Nations University Press, 2009, ISBN 978-92-808-1170-4

will also discuss the responsibility of the United Nations. For the purpose of international law, responsibility of an entity arises from the violation of an obligation owed by the entity.

The United Nations is an international organization whose objects, functions and powers are endowed by the UN Charter, i.e. a multilateral treaty. In addition, the United Nations is a subject of international law, and as such it holds international rights and obligations towards other subjects of international law, including states and international institutions. It follows from these that the United Nations and its organs are continually requested to show that their daily activities are consistent with the requirements and conditions set forth by the relevant conventional and customary international law rules.

Apart from the physiological aspect just mentioned above, there may be a pathological situation in which UN activities are manifestly contrary to international law requirements. In such a case, the relevant UN organs are required to rectify the decisions at issue or should take responsibility for their breach of international obligations towards other international law subjects.

Against this background, table 5.1 shows the whole scenario of UN accountability from the perspective of international law.

In the first section of this table, international law, especially the UN Charter, sets a framework for a variety of activities of the UN organs. In this sense they are requested to explain, not only to the Member States but also to the peoples of the United Nations, that their functions and powers are exercised properly within the mandate of the Charter as well as being based upon the requirement of fairness and justice. In this context, I make a short reference to the emerging need for the transparency of the sanctions regimes established by the Security Council (SC).

The second section concedes that it is not easy, both substantively and procedurally, to confirm definitively the *ultra vires* acts of a UN organ. This is because, substantially, UN organs, especially the Security Council, have large discretion in exercising their powers; it is also

Table 5.1 Basic aspects behind UN accountability from the perspective of international law

	Physiological aspect	Pathological aspect
United Nations as an organization	(1) Proper exercise of its functions and powers	(2) *Ultra vires* acts = nullity
United Nations as a subject	(3) Enjoyment of the rights and implementation of its obligations	(4) Breach of obligations = responsibility

because, procedurally, each UN organ has a primary power to assess the legality of its activities in light of the Charter, and there is no established review procedure for the alleged *ultra vires* activities of UN organs. Notwithstanding that point, it is generally recognized that even the Security Council cannot derogate from *jus cogens* rules of international law.

The third section leads us to the fundamental question of whether and to what extent international organizations, including the United Nations, are similar to or different from states in terms of the extent and nature of obligations to be owed. After examining this question I will discuss, by way of example, the applicability of international humanitarian law rules to UN peacekeeping operations.

The fourth section of table 5.1 deals with the responsibility of the United Nations. This responsibility arises when a UN organ breaches an international obligation towards some other subject of international law. In this sense, responsibility is certainly narrower than accountability if the latter does not necessarily presuppose the breach of an obligation. Whether or not accountability includes responsibility will rest on the definition of accountability. I will discuss some salient characteristics of the responsibility of the United Nations in contrast with that of states, mainly referring to the ongoing work of the International Law Commission on the subject of the "responsibility of international organizations".

Before entering into the discussion, let me turn back to the notion of accountability. Starting from the assertion that accountability constitutes saying something or doing something, complementarily or accessorily, in relation to the exercise of power delegated to you from someone else, I think accountability is composed of three distinctive elements: first, a subjective element, i.e. who is accountable to whom?; secondly, an objective element, i.e. on what matter should one be held accountable, and what must be done or said in order to accomplish, or to be relieved of, one's accountability?; thirdly, a procedural element, i.e. does accountability occur with or without third-party intervention?

The United Nations as an organization of the international community

Proper exercise of the powers endowed by the Charter

A variety of activities of the organs of the United Nations can be classified into three distinctive categories.[3] The first is organizational or self-organizational work. In this category we find, among other items, the election of members of the main councils, the appointment of the Secretary-General and the creation of subsidiary organs. With regard to the Security Council, articles 23 (composition), 27 (voting) and 28–32 (procedure) of the Charter are all dedicated to (self-)organizational activities.[4]

Secondly, the General Assembly and the councils issue resolutions to ask Member States to do, or not to do, something. These resolutions can be legally binding or not for the addressed Member States. Under article 41 of the Charter, by way of example, the Security Council may call upon the members of the United Nations to take economic sanctions against a state that the Council has determined to have threatened or breached the peace or committed aggression.[5] Resolutions under article 41 may be a legally binding "decision" for the Member States, as in the case of resolution 661 (Iraq) in 1990,[6] or they may remain a "recommendation" without binding force, as in the case of resolution 217 (Southern Rhodesia) in 1965.[7] Irrespective of their legal nature, resolutions under this category set forth rules of conduct to be obeyed by the Member States.[8] In this sense, we can term these normative or directive resolutions.

Thirdly, the organs of the United Nations, especially through their subsidiary organs, take their own action in certain situations. Peacekeeping operations are a typical example. We can term these as operational activity, as distinct from the normative activity seen above.

To the extent that the UN organs duly exercise their power under the established procedures in the three fields of activity, there appears to be nothing to blame the UN Organization for. In terms of the accountability of international organizations, this state of affairs can be explained by the principle of constitutionality.[9] According to this principle, each organization is under a legal obligation to carry out its functions and exercise its powers in accordance with the rules of the Organization. Moreover, organs and agents of the Organization must ensure that they do not exceed the scope of their function.

As I mentioned at the outset, accountability may play a complementary role to the mainstream exercise of powers of each UN organ. In this context, along with the principle of constitutionality, several other accountability principles can be pointed out. One is related to access to information.[10] Documents of the United Nations should be available to all concerned people as well as all Member States. In this context, it is reported that an integrated one-volume report on UN activity, including financial matters, was published in September 2006 for the first time in the history of the United Nations.[11]

The following principles are also pertinent. International law recognizes:

- the principle of supervision and control: i.e. parent organs have a duty to exercise a degree of control and supervision over subsidiary organs which corresponds to the functional autonomy granted

- the principle of stating the reasons for decisions or a particular course of action
- the principle of objectivity and impartiality.

Special mention must also be made of the principle of a participatory decision-making process. Under this principle, according to the ILA's Accountability Committee, when taking or reviewing decisions on coercive measures, organs should enable Member States whose interests are specifically affected to express their view.[12] According to a report by Professor Bardo Fassbender, eight of the 10 sanction regimes now working were established with the purpose of designating individuals and entities as targets of sanctions. Targeted individuals are not informed prior to being listed. The current delisting procedures place emphasis on the states particularly involved. Whether the Security Council grants a delisting request is entirely at the Council's discretion, without legal rules on the conditions for the grant.[13] Against this background, there is a growing concern for the introduction of a procedure ensuring just and fair treatment for the targeted persons in the UN sanction regimes. In December 2006 the Security Council adopted resolution 1730[14] with a view to addressing this concern. The resolution establishes new "delisting procedures" as well as a focal point within the Secretariat to serve as liaison with the designated countries and receive delisting requests. According to an observation by the UN High Commissioner for Human Rights, although this constitutes a first step towards ensuring fair and clear procedures for placing individuals and entities on Security Council sanctions lists and for removing them, the measures taken so far remain far from being a comprehensive solution to the problem.[15]

Ultra vires acts and their legal consequences

Needless to say, the organs of the United Nations should act within the mandates and procedures provided by the Charter. In addition, as a matter of principle, it is undeniable that an act beyond the power given in the Charter or with irregular procedures must be regarded as being without legal effect. Nevertheless, the UN Organization, from the beginning, has been confronted with situations not envisaged by the Charter. To cope with such situations, a flexible approach has been inevitable for the United Nations. In other words, a strait-jacket approach based on the written Charter might hamper the effective functioning of the UN Organization. The bottom line of the flexible approach was well described by the famous advisory opinion of the International Court of Justice (ICJ) in the *Certain Expenses* case:

when the Organization takes action which warrants the assertion that it was appropriate for the fulfillment of one of the stated purposes of the United Nations, the presumption is that such an action is not *ultra vires* the Organization.

In the legal system of States, there is often some procedure for determining the validity of even a legislative or governmental act, but no analogous procedure is to be found in the structure of the United Nations. Proposals made during the drafting of the Charter to place the ultimate authority to interpret the Charter in the International Court of Justice were not accepted; the opinion which the Court is in course of rendering is an *advisory* opinion. As anticipated in 1945, therefore, each organ must, in the first place at least, determine its own jurisdiction. (Emphasis in original.)[16]

In the final analysis, the UN activities not in conformity with the Charter provisions have been either crystallized into settled practice without objection or abandoned by the relevant organ in response to objections by Member States. So the attitude of Member States has been crucial in this respect. The following two examples will illustrate this in the field of the organizational activity of the Security Council and the General Assembly.

In the *Namibia* case[17] before the ICJ, South Africa contended that resolution 284 (1970) of the Security Council,[18] which requested the advisory opinion of the Court, was invalid, and therefore the Court was not competent to deliver the opinion. In voting on the resolution two permanent members, the Soviet Union and the United Kingdom, had abstained. South Africa presented an objection to the effect that the resolution was consequently not adopted by an affirmative vote of nine members, including the concurring votes of the permanent members, as required by article 27, paragraph 3 of the Charter. The Court responded to this objection as follows:

the proceedings of the Security Council extending over a long period supply abundant evidence that presidential rulings and the positions taken by members of the Council, in particular its permanent members, have consistently and uniformly interpreted the practice of voluntary abstention by a permanent member as not constituting a bar to the adoption of resolutions This procedure followed by the Security Council, which has continued unchanged after the amendment in 1965 of Article 27 of the Charter, has been generally accepted by Members of the United Nations and evidences a general practice of that Organization.[19]

The UN Emergency Force (UNEF) I, which was established under resolution 998 (ES-1) of the General Assembly[20] and dispatched to the Suez region in 1956, was problematic in light of the condition set out in article 11, paragraph 2 of the Charter: "any such question on which action is necessary shall be referred to the Security Council by the General Assembly". It is true that the International Court of Justice, in the *Certain Expenses* case in 1962,[21] intended to justify the peacekeeping operations based on the GA resolutions by limiting the action referred to in article 11(2) to coercive or enforcement action. But the list of UN peacekeeping operations to date, which includes only two exceptional operations under GA resolutions, i.e. UNEF I and UNSF (West Irian),[22] out of a total over 60 missions, eloquently tells us that the General Assembly itself has come to consider that peacekeeping operations are out of its competence.

Turning to the normative and operational activities of the Security Council, we can discern three salient developments after the end of the Cold War.

From normative to operational

Under article 41 of the Charter, the Security Council may call upon the Member States to apply measures not involving the use of armed force. As we have seen above, article 41 thus enables the Security Council to deliver normative or directive resolutions demanding Member States to take certain courses of action. The Security Council, by its resolution 827 (1993),[23] established the International Criminal Tribunal for the Former Yugoslavia (ICTY). In so doing it was "acting under Chapter VII", but it did not specify a particular article as a basis for this action. Before the appeals chamber of the ICTY (interlocutory appeal on jurisdiction) in the case of *Tadic*,[24] appellant attacked the legality of the SC decision, contending that the establishment of such a tribunal was never contemplated by the framers of the Charter as one of the measures to be taken under that Charter, particularly in articles 41 and 42. In responding to this objection, the chamber stated that the international tribunal matched perfectly the description in article 41 of "measures not involving the use of force". It then went on to say that "Logically, if the Organization can undertake measures which have to be implemented through the intermediary of its Members, it can *a fortiori* undertake measures which it can implement directly via its organs, if it happens to have the resources to do so." It would follow that, according to the decision of the chamber, the Security Council can deliver operational as well as normative resolutions under article 41 of the Charter.

From operational to normative

It is interesting to note that, in contrast with article 41, article 42 appears to have come to accommodate not only the originally envisaged operational activity of the UN Organization but also the normative resolutions of the Security Council. Article 42 stipulates that the Security Council may take such action by air, sea or land forces as may be necessary to maintain or restore international peace and security.[25] Thus article 42 originally envisaged operational activity of the Security Council through a UN force. On 29 November 1990 the Security Council adopted resolution 678[26] to authorize Member States to use all necessary means to restore international peace and security in the Gulf area. At the time of the adoption of the resolution, it was commonly understood that all necessary means included the use of force. Since then, the legality of authorization under resolution 678 has been much discussed. But, following resolution 678, the Security Council has adopted a series of similar resolutions authorizing Member States to use force in a variety of situations. So now it will be safe to say that resolutions authorizing the use of force constitute *acquis* of the Organization and may fall under article 42.

From obligation of solidarity to global legislator?

People nowadays appear to conceive roughly that, in employing Chapter VII, the Security Council may take legally binding decisions towards any state and on any issue. It must be said, however, that "Chapter VII" is not a magic phrase to warrant such a conclusion. Apart from the fact that SC decisions may not legally bind non-Member States of the United Nations, in order to access the binding or obligatory force of the SC resolutions under Chapter VII, one has to distinguish three different types of obligations in terms of the addressee.

First, when the Security Council adopts a legally binding decision to take economic sanctions under article 41, the obligation to take sanction measures will be owed by all the Member States *except the targeted state*. In other words, every Member State other than the wrongdoing state has the obligation to take measures against the latter state. In this sense, one can call this type of obligation an "obligation of solidarity". This is a basic obligation firmly rooted in the collective-security regime of the UN Charter. It must be added in this context that the obligation of solidarity under the UN Charter does not extend to measures involving the use of force.

In contrast, the second type of obligation is alleged to be owed by the wrongdoing state for which sanction measures are planned. In this context it must be recalled that the Security Council, in its resolution 748 (1992) concerning the Lockerbie incident,[27] acting under Chapter VII of the Charter, decided that the Libyan government must comply, without any further delay, with paragraph 3 of resolution 731 (1992)[28] regarding the requests to hand over two persons suspected by France, the United Kingdom and the United States. Resolution 748 thus appears to impose a legal obligation on Libya to hand over the suspected persons to the requesting states. However, with regard to the substance of the dispute, the Security Council may only make *recommendations* on the terms of settlement under article 37, paragraph 2 of Chapter VI and article 39 of Chapter VII. Against this background, in my opinion it would be difficult to argue that resolution 748, in spite of its appearance, created a legal obligation upon Libya to obey the requests made by the concerned states.[29]

More problematic will be the third type of obligation that is alleged to be imposed upon all the Member States without discrimination. In response to the terrorist attacks of 9/11, the Security Council adopted resolution 1373 (2001),[30] in which, acting under Chapter VII, it decided that all States shall take a variety of measures to prevent and suppress terrorist acts. Moreover, resolution 1373 established a committee of the Security Council, consisting of all the members of the Council, to monitor implementation of this resolution.[31]

If we turn next to targeted sanctions regimes, to which I have alluded above, mention must be made of the 2005 *Yusuf* judgment of the European Court of First Instance.[32] In this case the Court declared that it was empowered to check, indirectly, the lawfulness of the resolutions of the Security Council with regard to *jus cogens*. After examining the right to property, the right to a fair hearing and the right of access to a court, the Court reached the conclusion that the relevant SC decisions did not set limitations to these rights in a manner contrary to *jus cogens*. This judgment has at least three implications for international law: the extension of the effect of *jus cogens* to SC resolutions; the recognition of the Court's power to judge on the legality of the resolutions; and the expanded possibility for such human rights rules as the right to property to become *jus cogens*. While the first point should be accepted,[33] the third point is problematic inasmuch as the right to property is generally considered as a right susceptible to derogation in the case of public emergency. With regard to the second point, it remains to be seen in the jurisprudence of the EC courts in the future.[34]

The United Nations as a subject of international law

International obligations incumbent upon the United Nations

The International Court of Justice, in the *WHO and Egypt* case in 1980, stated: "International organizations are subjects of international law and, as such, are bound by any obligation incumbent upon them under general rules of international law, under their constitutions or under international agreements to which they are parties."[35] This section will discuss the applicability of rights and obligations under the UN Charter, under treaties to which the United Nations is a party and under general international law rules.[36]

First, with respect to the UN Charter, it is evident that the UN Organization should be subject to the Charter, i.e. the constituent instrument of the United Nations. However, if we look in detail into the Charter provisions, we find that the rights and obligations enumerated there are, *in grosso modo*, directed to the Member States. In contrast, what the Charter endows to the organs of the United Nations are functions and powers. Accordingly, in spite of the opinion of the ICJ cited above, respectfully, it will not be easy to assume that rights and obligations under the Charter will in fact be applied to the conduct of UN organs. The following episode illustrates the difficulty of direct application of rights and obligations under the Charter to the UN Organization.

In the course of peacekeeping operations, UN missions may confront a situation in which they are obliged to use force against an armed attack by third parties. It must be said that, in such a case, they can employ self-defence to justify their action. Thus the UN Office of Legal Affairs unequivocally stated: "the use of force in self-defence is an inherent right of United Nations forces exercised to preserve a collective and individual defence".[37] However, if we turn to look at article 51 of the Charter, we find that it refers to self-defence only with regard to an armed attack on a Member State. In the course of the codification of the rules on "Responsibility of International Organizations", Special Rapporteur Giorgio Gaja, in his third report, first introduced a draft article on self-defence just the same as that for state responsibility: article 18 (self-defence) "The wrongfulness of an act of an international organization is precluded if the act constitutes a lawful measure of self-defence taken in conformity with the Charter of the United Nations."[38] But the first reading text of the article, which was adopted later by the International Law Commission, was slightly different: "The wrongfulness of an act of an international organization is precluded if the act constitutes a lawful measure of self-defence taken in conformity with *the principles of international law embodied in the Charter of the United Nations*" (emphasis added).[39] The ILC, in its commentary on article 18, went on to state, without reservation, to the UN Organization: "In view of the fact that international organizations are not members of the United Nations, the reference to the Charter of the United Nations has been replaced here with [the phrase italicized above]."

Secondly, with respect to international agreements to which the United Nations is a party, there is no doubt that the United Nations is bound by any obligation under an international agreement to which it is a party.

Article 26 of the Vienna Convention on the Law of Treaties between States and International Organizations or between International Organizations (1986) stated: "Every treaty in force is binding upon the parties to it and must be performed by them in good faith."[40] Looking through several international agreements to which the United Nations is a party, we get an impression that most agreements would relate to the operational or organizational activities of the UN Organization.

Thirdly, whether or not, and to what extent, general customary international law rules may also apply to international organizations, including the United Nations, is a matter to be scrutinized because most of these rules have been created and developed among states. Generally speaking, it seems that if the UN Organization exercises some "governmental" activities similar to those of states, relevant general international law rules will, with necessary changes, also apply to the UN activities. In this regard, operational activities of the United Nations, especially such activities carried out on a country's territory, such as peacekeeping operations or interim administration, will be the first candidates to be subject to relevant general international law rules, together with international agreements between concerned parties.

More specifically, what must be recalled in this context is the "Secretary-General's Bulletin: Observance by United Nations Forces of International Humanitarian Law" issued in 1999.[41] This bulletin contains several basic humanitarian law rules concerning protection of the civilian population, means and methods of combat, treatment of detained persons and protection of the wounded, the sick, medical and relief personnel, etc. Although technically speaking this bulletin remains an internal document addressed to the UN staff, it is safe to say that it reflects general international humanitarian law rules applicable to the UN Organization in relation to other states and international organizations.

Lastly, again in the context of the targeted sanctions regimes of the Security Council, Professor Fassbender presents the following observation:

> At present, customary international law does not provide for sufficiently clear rules which would oblige international (intergovernmental) organizations to observe standards of due process *vis-à-vis* individuals. To the extent that rules of customary law exist with respect to such standards, they address obligations of States in the sphere of domestic law, and not obligations of international organizations. However, a trend can be perceived widening the scope of customary law in regard to due process to include direct "governmental" action of international organizations *vis-à-vis* individuals. To this development, the law of the European Community (European Union) has strongly contributed. The due process rights of individuals recognized as general principles of law are also applicable to international organizations as subjects of international law when they exercise "governmental" authority over individuals.[42]

Breaches of obligations by the United Nations and their legal consequences

If a state breaches an international obligation, that state should accept international responsibility. According to the Articles on State Responsibility,[43] adopted by the ILC and endorsed by the General Assembly in 2001, state responsibilities comprise three main principles. First, the wrongful state should cease the wrongful act. Secondly, the wrongful state should make full reparation for the injury caused by the wrongful act by such means as restitution, monetary compensation and satisfaction. Thirdly, if circumstances so require, the wrongful state should offer appropriate assurances and guarantees of non-repetition. Moreover, if the wrongful state does not cease the breach of the obligation or does not provide reparation through appropriate means, the injured state may take countermeasures against the wrongful state. Countermeasures mean, for the purposes of international law, the non-performance, for the time being, of international obligations of the state taking the measures towards the wrongful state. The legal effect of countermeasures is to preclude the wrongfulness of the non-performance of international obligations by the state taking such measures. In the following paragraphs, I will pick up and discuss several peculiar points in the responsibility of international organizations, including the United Nations, in comparison with the state responsibility regime as summarized above.

First, the most likely case in which the UN Organization may incur international responsibility for a breach of obligations will be one in which it engages in operational activity on a certain state's territory. Having said this, in practice this possibility will not be much expected. The reason is that, according to the model status-forces agreement for peacekeeping operations enacted by the Secretary-General in 1990, even if the operations may cause some damage to private persons, claims will be treated as those of private law to be settled by a standing claims commission.[44] In addition, so-called "operational necessity" may function as an exception to the rule of tortuous liability. According to this concept, the United Nations incurs no liability for damage caused by the necessary actions taken by a peacekeeping force in pursuance of its mandate.[45] This observation shows a marked difference from inter-state claims based upon the regime of diplomatic protection. The reason for the difference is that, while in the case of diplomatic protection two states are located horizontally, side by side, in the case of UN peacekeeping or interim administration the UN missions are exercising their powers, vertically, on the territory of the host country with the consent of the latter.

Secondly, let me turn to the normative or directive activity of the UN Organization. The ILC is now halfway through the codification work on

"Responsibility of International Organizations", finalizing in 2006 its first reading on articles 1–30 that constitute part I of the draft articles: "the international wrongful act of an international organization". For our purposes here, one of the most interesting articles, which has no counterpart in the state responsibility articles, is article 15 adopted in 2005.

Article 15: Decisions, recommendations and authorizations addressed to Member States and international organizations

1. An international organization incurs international responsibility if it adopts a decision binding a Member State or international organization to commit an act that would be internationally wrongful if committed by the former organization and would circumvent an international obligation of the former organization.
2. An international organization incurs international responsibility if: (*a*) It authorizes a Member State or international organization to commit an act that would be internationally wrongful if committed by the former organization and would circumvent an international obligation of the former organization, or recommends that a Member State or international organization commit such an act; and (*b*) That State or international organization commits the act in question in reliance on that authorization or recommendation.
3. Paragraphs 1 and 2 apply whether or not the act in question is internationally wrongful for the Member State or international organization to which the decision, authorization or recommendation is directed.[46]

Although the drafting of the text must be further elaborated and the implication of this article and its relation to other articles calls for further study, the underlying idea is clear. The normative or directive activity of international organizations, including the United Nations, may incur their international responsibility to a state or an international organization whose rights were disregarded.

Thirdly, with respect to the countermeasures mentioned at the outset of this section, the UN Organization is also able to make recourse to them if its international right is continuing to be infringed or adequate remedy was not provided by the wrongdoing state or international organization. However, compared with a case where states are trying to take countermeasures, the United Nations does not seem to have comparable resources to be used for the purpose of countermeasures. It is true that, as seen above, the United Nations must obey general international law rules on human rights and humanitarian law. But these rules are not to be derogated as a tool for countermeasures. Thus article 50 of the state responsibility text enumerates, among obligations not affected by countermeasures, obligations for the protection of fundamental human rights as well as obligations of a humanitarian character prohibiting reprisals. Moreover, it is also true that the United Nations sends its permanent or *ad hoc* missions to Member States, and they usually enjoy privileges and immunities in host countries. But, unlike inter-state diplomatic relations, its relations with the host states lack reciprocity. So if a host state violates an obligation concerning privileges and immunities of a UN mission, the United Nations cannot react reciprocally, violating the same or similar obligations towards the host state. In the final analysis, what remains to the United Nations as a resource for countermeasures is limited to temporary suspension of bilateral agreements with the wrongful state or international organization concerning, for example, technical assistance.

Fourthly, according to article 41 of the 2001 state responsibility text, if a state makes a serious breach of an obligation under peremptory norms of general international law, all other states shall cooperate to bring such breach to an end through lawful means and shall not recognize as lawful a situation created by the serious breach.[47] But the role which the UN Organization is expected to play in such a situation seems not so much to assume the same obligations of non-cooperation and non-recognition as to ask or demand all other states to do so. In this context, one can remember the fact that, after the Iraq invasion of Kuwait, the Security Council, in resolution 662 (1990),[48] after deciding that the annexation of Kuwait by Iraq was null and void, called upon all states not to recognize the annexation. In this case the Security Council was acting not as a subject of international law on the inter-subjective plane but as an (*de facto*) organization of the international community.

Conclusion

In contrast to the accountability and responsibility of (independent) states in international law, those of the United Nations are not free from the shadow of the Member States. Member States are, as a matter of course, structurally integrated in the decision-making process of the UN Organization. It would follow that, in order to get the whole picture of the accountability and responsibility of the United Nations, we should also look at the other side of the coin: the accountability and responsibility of the Member States to the peoples of the United Nations as well as their responsibility to the United Nations.[49]

Notes

1. Cf. Separate opinion of Judge Gros in International Court of Justice (1980) *Interpretation of the Agreement of 25 March 1951 between the WHO and Egypt*, Advisory Opinion, 20 December, 1980 ICJ 87, p. 103.

2. International Law Association (2004) "Final Report", Committee on Accountability of International Organizations, available at www.ila-hq.org/html/main_listofcomm accountability.html, p. 168. For a critical analysis of the report see Dekker, Ige F. (2005) "Making Sense of Accountability in International Institutional Law: An Analysis of the Final Report of the ILA Committee on Accountability of International Organizations from a Conceptual Legal Perspective", *Netherlands Yearbook of International Law* 36, pp. 83–118, especially pp. 102–117.
3. Conforti, Benedetto (2005) *The Law and Practice of the United Nations*, 3rd edn, The Hague: Martinus Nijhoff Publishers, p. 291 et seq.
4. See articles 23 and 27–32 of the UN Charter. In fact the ICJ, in connection with the establishment of subsidiary organs, employed the expression "organizational activities" in the opinion on the *Certain Expenses* case in 1962. International Court of Justice (1962) *Certain Expenses of the United Nations (1961–1962)*, Advisory Opinion, 20 July, 1962 ICJ 151, p. 165.
5. Article 41 of the UN Charter states: "The Security Council may decide what measures not involving the use of armed force are to be employed to give effect to its decisions, and it may call upon the Members of the United Nations to apply such measures. These may include complete or partial interruption of economic relations and of rail, sea, air, postal, telegraphic, radio, and other means of communication, and the severance of diplomatic relations."
6. SC Res. 661, UN SCOR, 45th Sess., UN Doc. S/RES/661 (1990), reprinted in *International Legal Materials* 29 (1990), p. 1325.
7. SC Res. 217, UN SCOR, 20th Sess., UN Doc. S/RES/217 (1965).
8. For the relevance of legally non-binding rules in terms of the accountability of international organizations, the following observation seems pertinent: the situations in which the accountability of international organizations may arise always concern situations in which an international organization does not comply with a legally valid, but not necessarily also legally binding, rule of international law. Dekker, note 2 above, p. 111.
9. International Law Association, note 2 above, p. 179.
10. Ibid., p. 174.
11. United Nations (2006) "United Nations Secretariat First Consolidated Report 2005", UN Doc. A/61/434, 25 September, Center for UN Reform Education, available at www.centerforunreform.org/node/210.
12. International Law Association, note 2 above, p. 173.
13. Fassbender, Bardo (2006) "Targeted Sanctions and Due Process", Report for the UN Office of Legal Affairs, 20 March, Humboldt-Universität zu Berlin, p. 4.
14. SC Res. 1730, UN SCOR, 61st Sess., UN Doc. S/RES/1730 (2006).
15. UN High Commissioner for Human Rights (2007) "Report of the United Nations High Commissioner for Human Rights on the Protection of Human Rights and Fundamental Freedoms while Countering Terrorism", UN Doc. A/HRC/4/88, 9 March, para. 28. For an analysis of the newly introduced procedure under resolution 1730 see Arcari, Maurizio (2007) "Sviluppi in tema di tutela dei diritti di individui iscritti nelle liste dei comitati dell sanzioni del consiglio di sicu rezza", *Rivista di diritto internazionale* 90(3), pp. 656–680.
16. International Court of Justice, note 4 above, p. 151.
17. International Court of Justice (1971) *Legal Consequences for States of the Continued Presence of South Africa in Namibia (South West Africa) notwithstanding Security Council Resolution 276*, Advisory Opinion, 21 June, 1971 ICJ 12, p. 12.
18. SC Res. 284, UN SCOR, 25th Sess., UN Doc. S/RES/284 (1970).
19. International Court of Justice, note 17 above.
20. GA Res. 998 (ES-1), UN GAOR, A/RES/998 (ES-1), 4 November 1956.

21. International Court of Justice, note 4 above.
22. GA Res. 1752, UN GAOR, A/RES/1752 (XVII), 21 September 1962.
23. SC Res. 827, UN SCOR, 48th Sess., UN Doc. S/RES/827 (1993).
24. International Criminal Tribunal for the Former Yugoslavia, Appeals Chamber (1995) *Prosecutor v. Tadic*, Defence Motion for Interlocutory Appeal on Jurisdiction, Case No. ICTY IT-94-1-AR72, 2 October.
25. In its entirety article 42 of the UN Charter states: "Should the Security Council consider that measures provided for in Article 41 would be inadequate or have proved to be inadequate, it may take such action by air, sea, or land forces as may be necessary to maintain or restore international peace and security. Such action may include demonstrations, blockade, and other operations by air, sea, or land forces of Members of the United Nations."
26. SC Res. 678, UN SCOR, 45th Sess., UN Doc. S/RES/678 (1990).
27. SC Res. 748, UN SCOR, 47th Sess., UN Doc. S/RES/748 (1992).
28. SC Res. 731, UN SCOR, 47th Sess., UN Doc. S/RES/731 (1992).
29. Having said this, there may be another possibility to argue that Libya should have made a legally positive response to the requests by the concerned states, based on the fact that, in its letter dated 14 May 1992 to the Secretary-General, Libya expressly accepted resolution 731. UN Office of the Secretary-General (1992) "Further Report by the Secretary-General Pursuant to Paragraph 4 of Security Council Resolution 731 (1992)", UN Doc. S/23672, 3 March, reprinted in *International Legal Materials* 31, pp. 735–743, Annex, pp. 742–743.
30. SC Res. 1373, UN SCOR, 56th Sess., UN Doc. S/RES/1373 (2001).
31. For critical comment on this development see Elberling, Björn (2005) "The *Ultra Vires* Character of Legislative Action by the Security Council", *International Organizations Law Review* 2, pp. 337–360. For the affirmative view see Rosand, Eric (2005) "The Security Council as 'Global Legislator': *Ultra Vires* or Ultra Innovative?", *Fordham International Law Journal* 28(3), pp. 542–590.
32. Court of First Instance (2005) *Yusuf and Al Barakaat International Foundation v. Council and Commission*, Judgment of 21 September, Case T-306/01.
33. On this point see Kawasaki, Kyoji (2006) "A Brief Note on the Legal Effects of *Jus Cogens* in International Law", *Hitotsubashi Journal of Law and Politics* 34, pp. 34–35.
34. For a thorough analysis on the *jus cogens* limitations on the Security Council activities see Orakhelashvili, Alexander (2006) *Peremptory Norms in International Law*, Oxford: Oxford University Press, pp. 411–485.
35. International Court of Justice, note 1 above.
36. For an overview of the sources of international law applicable to international organizations, see Rey Aneiros, Adela (2006) *Una aproximación a la responsibilidad internacional de las organizaciones internacionales*, Valencia: Tirant lo Blanch, pp. 81–117.
37. UN Office of the Secretary-General (1993) "Memorandum to the Senior Political Adviser to the Secretary-General", 19 July, reprinted in *United Nations Juridical Yearbook 1993*, New York: United Nations, 2001, pp. 371–372.
38. A/CN.4/564, 28 February 2006, p. 8.
39. A/61/10, 2006, pp. 265–267. See also A/CN.4/L.687, 31 May 2006, p. 1.
40. Vienna Convention on the Law of Treaties between States and International Organization or between International Organizations (1986) UN Doc. A/Conf. 129/15. Although this convention is not yet in force, it is generally understood that it reflects customary international law rules on the Law of Treaties involving international organizations. In addition, the United Nations itself made its formal confirmation, which is the organization's equivalent of the process of ratification by a state, on 21 December 1998.

41. UN Office of the Secretary-General (1999) "Secretary-General's Bulletin: Observance by United Nations Forces of International Humanitarian Law", UN Doc. ST/SGB/1999/13, 6 August.
42. Fassbender, note 13 above, p. 19.
43. Crawford, James (2002) *International Law Commission's Articles on State Responsibility: Introduction, Text and Commentaries*, Cambridge and New York: Cambridge University Press.
44. A/45/594, 7 October 1990, p. 13. It is also reported that, in reality, in place of the standing commission UN-based claims review boards have been established to settle private third-party claims. Shiraga, Daphna (2000) "UN Peacekeeping Operations: Applicability of International Humanitarian Law and Responsibility for Operation-Related Damage", *American Journal of International Law* 94(2), pp. 406–412, at p. 409.
45. Ibid., p. 410. In terms of UN accountability, effectiveness and transparency of the procedure will be required for the third-party claims settlement. For the conditions to be met for employing operational necessity see ibid., p. 411.
46. UN International Law Commission (2005) *Responsibility of International Organizations*, available at http:untreaty.un.org/ilc/summaries911.htm, sec. A/60/10, pp. 100–105.
47. Crawford, note 43 above.
48. SC Res. 662, UN SCOR, 45th Sess., UN Doc. S/RES/662 (1990).
49. From this perspective, it is understandable that the first reading text of the ILC's codification of the responsibility of international organizations contains several articles dedicated to "responsibility of a State in connection with the act of an international organization". See United Nations (2006) "Report of the International Law Commission (58th Session)", UN Doc. A/61/10, pp. 277–292.

Part II

Managerial accountability

6

Managerial accountability and the UN system

Tadanori Inomata

The purpose of the UNU Tokyo Symposium on Accountability held on 16–17 October 2006 at UN House, Tokyo, consisted in making policy proposals for improving the efficiency and effectiveness of the UN system organizations as a precondition for the organizations to play a leading role in meeting the global challenges of the twenty-first century. As stated in the terms of reference of the symposium, this process aims ultimately at providing the global community, Member States and their peoples with public accountability of the UN system's management with a view to basic objectives entrusted to it. The process deals with two aspects: *managerial accountability* within the UN system and *democratic accountability* of the UN system. The first aspect relates to objectives and policy setting, and management of resources within the UN intergovernmental forums. And the second aspect concerns the delivery of output to the global community, including public scrutiny aimed at making the objectives and policy of the UN system conform to global public interests.

This chapter[1] presents a preliminary analytical framework of how the organizations of the UN system demonstrate their accountability in their management and governance. It also attempts to identify lacunae in the UN management and oversight mechanisms in the light of experiences in such fields as humanitarian assistance and environmental governance where system-wide coordination and governance are required.

Envisioning reform: Enhancing UN accountability in the twenty-first century, Kuyama and Fowler (eds), United Nations University Press, 2009, ISBN 978-92-808-1170-4

Current management and governance framework

Generally speaking, any organization should have in place a clearly defined governance framework for decision-making and a mechanism for setting its agenda and its objectives, goals and policy, as well as a management framework for the implementation of the decisions taken with the necessary resources made available to its administration. In the context of domestic organizations, either governmental or private, there exists a single constitution, a body of law, by-laws, regulations and rules that are relevant to their governance, organization, management and administration. Therefore, it is easier to identify in the domestic context what parameters should apply in performance evaluation of the organization, who should be accountable to whom and for what the executive head should be accountable in the discharge of his or her responsibilities.

The situation radically differs in the case of international organizations, particularly those in the UN system. In view of their intergovernmental nature and composition, not only their objective setting but also the execution and delivery by the administration of organizational decisions are subject to the will of intergovernmental governing bodies composed of Member States. Therefore, in order for an organization to sustain any meaningful work, there should be a common mechanism to identify and agree on concrete and clear objectives and on the benefit of multilateral initiatives for Member States. Obviously, those who meet the expenses of the Organization are reluctant to accept any open-ended commitment to the activities of the Organization without being assured of the best effective use of resources by pre-established oversight and evaluation procedures.

However, it would be wrong to believe that governments take arbitrary decisions on the management of international organizations on account of the sovereign nature of their competence. On the contrary, they have continued to seek to establish an elaborate system of procedures for the governing body to approve collectively the programmes of the organizations, allocate appropriate funds for them and monitor the use and effects of the programmes implemented, as well as providing delegated authority to their executive heads and administrations, in return for the provision of transparency and accountability to them. This reflects the real needs of Member States in tackling the common problems and issues they identify. This sense of realism motivates States to define agendas and adopt a set of goals, objectives and values within a framework of cooperation concomitant with their national interests as well as with their willingness to make resource commitments to agreed programmes.

It is obvious that what is called regime formation in international relations has been motivated by the realism of States to find *in situ* solutions to inter-state problems in which their interdependent interests are at stake. However, the solutions that they have resorted to have been far from complete and durable, rather *ad hoc* and short term and often duplicative in the long run. The result was that, as and when a new global issue sprang up, an independent regime came into life, and the proliferation of international regimes over time increased the burden on Member States to administer and manage complex institutions. This has imposed on States the burden not only of making additional efforts to manage individual regimes better, but also providing effective governance to ensure coherence and coordination among them.

Salient features of management and oversight lacunae

Fragmentation and proliferation in the decentralized UN system institutions prevent the system from setting up a single governance and management framework. On the one hand, a number of salient features in management methods and approach prohibit such a framework at the intergovernmental level. Partly, these features are a corollary of the reluctance of Member States to make long-term policy and resource commitments to durable and far-reaching systematic solutions to the multilateral issues they confront. Also attributable to that reluctance is increased use of voluntary contributions relative to the declining role of assessed contributions, as well as Member States' preference for zero-growth budgeting. Part of this problem concerns a facility of the UN funds and programmes to bear the cost of activities of a normative nature out of their voluntary contributions, which tends to create confusion between normative and operational activities in the UN institutions. On the other hand, there are built-in deficiencies in the methods and approach employed in the management of the secretariats of the organizations. These include a dichotomy between programming and budgeting, the inadequacy of system-wide management frameworks and the lack of a mandatory framework for joint programming and financial appropriation among the organizations.

Let us examine these features in the following paragraphs.

No single governance and management framework

There are diverse independent entities within the UN system, each of which has its own governing body for setting objectives and making management decisions. Therefore, no single management and governance framework exists within the system. This is inherent in the decentralized nature of the structure of international institutions.

Lack of coherent follow-up and implementation

Improvements in setting objectives and governance within the UN system have yet to achieve all that could be desired. Various attempts have been made from the inception of the United Nations through more than six decades, ranging from the adoption of global platforms and action programmes common to all institutions within the UN system through UN-sponsored world conferences to the establishment of new funds, programmes and organizations. Very often, a new organization has been established when coordinated follow-up was required to ensure the implementation of an adopted programme. But monitoring and implementation of the agreed actions were hortatory, relying upon the will of stakeholders and constituencies in the sectors concerned.

Dichotomy between programming and budgeting

There is a dichotomy between programming and budgeting in almost all normative bodies. Policy decisions are taken in isolation from resource considerations, or vice versa. Member States are reticent to accept additional financial obligations as a direct consequence of their programmatic decisions on the work of the Organization. Therefore, extra-budgetary and voluntary contributions in money, goods and services are predominant in the economic, social and humanitarian sectors. The demarcation between voluntary contributions and regular core resources is blurred. In fact, the concept of expenses of the Organization in the meaning of article 17 of the UN Charter, which shall be borne by Member States as apportioned by the General Assembly, seems no longer existent. Funding of the UN system organizations is assured according to the convenience of Member States and donors.

Under the circumstances, the ability of the organizations to deliver programmes depends heavily on the ability of the programme managers to interact with contributors and donors for fundraising. This situation is detrimental to the public mission of ensuring transparency and accountability of UN organizations for mobilizing the necessary regular resources against the objectives and mandated programmes in which they are officially engaged.

Confusion between normative activities and operational activities

The demarcation between normative activities and operational activities has also been blurred. For example, the regular core budget programmes of the UN Development Programme (UNDP), the UN Children's Fund (UNICEF), the UN High Commissioner for Refugees (UNHCR) and other UN funds and programmes cover research and policy development components whose output is very similar to research and policy-formulation activities that should be financed by the regular budget of the United Nations and specialized agencies. Although activities of this type are germane to the development of technical guidelines for the operations of the former category of organizations, the duplication with the normative regular work in policy-making institutions is obvious.

Zero-growth-budget principle

The so-called zero-growth principle has been practised in the formulation of the regular budgets of the organizations to accommodate the concerns of the major contributors among industrialized Member States. However, significant real growth and quantum jumps took place outside the regular programmes of these established institutions. New needs of the world community have been accommodated through the creation of separate bodies, funds and programmes, peacekeeping operations, treaty bodies such as the Comprehensive Nuclear-Test-Ban Treaty Organization, international criminal courts and tribunals and new multilateral environmental conventions.

Lack of system-wide management tools

There are no reliable data and statistics to inform the public of how much money is being spent by the UN system as a whole. This information is fundamental to any systematic planning and management of international organizations. The available data compiled by the Joint Inspection Unit (JIU) indicate the UN system mobilized roughly $15.9 billion (exclusive of the Bretton Woods institutions) in 2003 (see table 6.1[2]). If the expenses of the Oil-for-Food Programme are counted, the total resources amounted to $22.1 billion. More recent data from the UN Chief Executives Board for Coordination (CEB), although not covering the Oil-for-Food Programme and peacekeeping operations, indicate that the UN system spent $21 billion of regular budget and extra-budgetary resources inclusive of in-kind contributions in 2005.[3] In addition, the expenditures on peacekeeping amounted to $4.6 billion in year 2005/2006.[4] If the expenses of $341 million in 2005 on international criminal tribunals for Rwanda and the former Yugoslavia and the International Criminal Court[5] are added, the total expenditures of the UN system amount to $26 billion.

But, so far, the UN system has never been able to establish an accounting framework for measuring total available resources, nor has it attempted to establish a process for common resource planning and allocation. There used to be a reliable interagency report providing more accurate breakdowns of resources spent by programmes, established by programme sectors and subsectors based on the agreed Administrative Committee on Coordination (ACC)[6] Programme Classification

Table 6.1 Total budget of the UN system

Budgets of the UN system organizations				
US$ million	2000	2001	2002	2003
1. UN system organizations				
Regular budgets	3,046.6	3,051.5	3,318.5	3,334.4
Voluntary contributions	6,098.8	7,871.1	7,041.0	9,828.7
2. PKO (ending 30 June of the year from July of previous year)*	1,765.1	2,383.2	2,751.6	2,499.8
3. ICTs				
Rwanda	86.2	94	96.8	111.7
(A/57/5/Add. 11, p. 41 and A/59/5/Add. 1, p. 44)				
Former Yugoslavia	106.1	108.5	125.9	162.4
(A/57/5/Add. 12, p. 41 and A/59/Add. 12, p. 30) (57/288 and 58/254)				
4. Total resources	11,102.8	13,508.3	13,333.8	15,937.0
[plus Oil-for Food Programme]	[22,285.9]	[24,687.3]	[19,539.5]	[22,091.3]
Memorandum items				
Operational activities for development**				
(a) All sectors	6,777.5	7,429.9	7,610.6	9,966.6
(b) Humanitarian assistance	1,755.4	2,102.7	1,545.0	3,019.9
Oil-for-Food Programme***	11,179.0	11,179.0	6,203.0	6,203.0

Sources: A/57/265 and A/59/515, unless otherwise stated.
Notes: ICTs = international criminal tribunals; PKO = peacekeeping operations.
* A/58/5 (vol. II) and A59/5 (vol. II).
** Comprehensive statistical data on operational activities for development for 2003: "Report of the Secretary-General", A/60/74, tables 13 and B.1.
*** Report of the Board of Auditors.

of programmes and resources in the system.[7] But that has been discontinued since 1995 for "unknown reasons", according to ACC senior officers, notwithstanding confirmation of the resumption given to the JIU in 1999 and the active and favourable appraisal received from the Committee for Programme and Coordination and the General Assembly.[8]

The results-based budgeting and management (RBBM) approach in force for the last three biennia since 2002 is a successor concept to the programme budgeting adopted in 1974 within the UN system. It has been instrumental in visualizing specific, measurable, achievable, relevant and time-bound (SMART) objectives in the budgeting in the United Nations.[9] On the recommendations of the Committee for Programme and Coordination,[10] the General Assembly, in a resolution[11] adopted at its resumed sixtieth session in May 2006, approved the benchmarking framework for results-based management (RBM) proposed by the JIU as a concept applicable to the United Nations and recommended consideration of its application in other UN system organizations.

However, it has not been possible to establish a system-wide RBBM resource management framework in the absence of commonly agreed intergovernmental objectives among all organizations within the UN system. Without such a global governance framework, the results-based management approach simply exacerbated fragmentation and compartmentalization of the activities of the organizations, although it contributed to sharpening objectives and output of individual organizations dealing with specific sectors concerned with ensuring linkages between objectives and resources.

Persistence of archaic interagency coordination concept

The traditional concept of so-called interagency coordination is still prevailing; namely, Member States believe that the administrations of UN agencies tend to duplicate their activities despite the will of Member States. To them, the only panacea has appeared to be a call for better interagency coordination at the administrative level. Obviously, there is an inherent limit to such coordination. Unless the governing bodies' decisions are coherent and clear in resource allocation on common ventures among agencies, there is no chance for effective coordination. The current coordination framework of the UN CEB, composed of executive heads of agencies, is run mostly on a *post factum* basis, respecting the *fait accompli* committed by their governing bodies with respect to their own programmatic and financial decisions. There is no mandatory framework to enable the administrations to negotiate and agree *ex ante* in a proactive way on system-wide programmes and projects.

Management and oversight lacunae in play

Examples of the above lacunae can be identified in such sectors as humanitarian assistance and environmental governance.

Lacunae in the humanitarian assistance system

The fundamental principles governing UN humanitarian assistance are contained in the guiding principles in the annex to the landmark UN General Assembly resolution 46/182 of 19 December 1991.[12] The Assembly decided that humanitarian assistance should be provided on the principles of humanity, neutrality, impartiality and independence. Recognizing the central role of the United Nations in international humanitarian assistance, these principles are designed to facilitate delivery of humanitarian assistance in international public goods in a non-excludable and non-rivalrous way, on time, to all victims, without discrimination and regardless of gender, race and nationality.

On the basis of these principles and the Guiding Principles on Internal Displacement,[13] the Inter-Agency Standing Committee (IASC)[14] has developed some 25 policies, principles and guidelines for humanitarian assistance (see table 6.2[15]). These documents are produced essentially for the use of the humanitarian assistance organizations participating in the work of the IASC.

Lessons learned from the Indian Ocean tsunami disaster

However, the UN humanitarian system has continued to face inveterate lacunae in implementing these principles and rules, as evidenced by the Joint Inspection Unit in its review of lessons learned from the Indian Ocean tsunami disaster.[16] The tsunami of 26 December 2004 triggered one of the deadliest and most devastating disasters in living memory. While the international community displayed unprecedented solidarity in providing financial, technical and logistical support to the region, including the largest modern peacetime deployment of military assets in the history of the United Nations, the unprecedented scale of the catastrophe, its transboundary nature and the magnitude of the resources involved in the international response to the disaster entailed enormously complex operations and shed light on the shortcomings of the existing global humanitarian system, as summarized below:

- there are lacunae in principles and policies applied in international humanitarian assistance, which are predominantly of an interagency nature with little ownership of the affected countries and communities over these principles and policies
- the system is fragmented among too many actors involved on the ground
- dichotomies and disjointedness exist between relief and recovery through mitigation stages
- the system has no governance and management framework to cope with large-scale disasters
- resources mobilized in the humanitarian field accounted for the largest part of resources of the UN system devoted to development, but with little accountability and coordination over their use.

Let us examine these shortcomings in some detail.

Lacunae in principles and policies applied in international humanitarian assistance

First, although the principles and policies applied in international humanitarian assistance were developed internationally and received political blessing from the UN General Assembly, they have not been formally approved by it.

Table 6.2 Policies, principles and guidelines developed by the Inter-Agency Standing Committee

The Inter-Agency Standing Committee has developed various policies, principles and guidelines on humanitarian assistance; the UN Humanitarian Coordinator is supposed to promote these and monitor their implementation.* These include the existing policies listed below as well as new ones as they are developed, adopted and issued by the IASC.**

- Consolidated Appeal Process Guidelines (1994)
- IASC Plan of Action for Strengthening the Consolidated Appeals Process (CAP) (2002)
- IASC Appeal and Strategy Documents (2003)
- Guidelines on the Use of Military and Civil Defence Assets in Disaster Relief (1994)
- Guiding and Operating Principles for the Use of Military and Civil Defence Assets in Support of Humanitarian Operations (1995)
- Guidelines on the Use of Military and Civil Defence Assets to Support United Nations Humanitarian Activities in Complex Emergencies (March 2003)
- Exit Strategy from Relief to Development (1995)
- Respect for Humanitarian Mandates in Conflict Situations (1995)
- Guidelines for HIV/AIDS Interventions in Emergency Settings (1996)
- Revised Guidelines for HIV/AIDS in Emergency Settings (2003)
- Exit Strategy for Humanitarian Actors in the Context of Complex Emergencies (1997)
- Policy Statement for the Integration of a Gender Perspective in Humanitarian Assistance (1999)
- Guiding Principles on Internal Displacement (1999)
- Policy Paper for Protection for IDPs (1999)
- Guidelines for Field Staff Promoting Reintegration (Golden Rules) (2000)
- Inter-Agency Contingency Planning Guidelines for Humanitarian Assistance (2001)
- Recommendations on UN/Non-UN Field Security Collaboration (2001)
- Plan of Action on Protection from Sexual Exploitation in Humanitarian Crises (2002)
- Growing the Sheltering Tree: Protecting Rights Through Humanitarian Action (2002)
- Frequently Asked Questions on International Humanitarian, Human Rights and Refugee Law in the Context of Armed Conflict (2004)

Source: IASC website, available at www.humanitarianinfo.org/iasc/content/products/default.asp, except where otherwise stated.
* *Source*: Revised Terms of Reference for the Humanitarian Coordinator, 2003.
** Since the adoption of the Revised Terms of Reference for the Humanitarian Coordinator in 2003, new policies, principles and guidelines have been issued by the IASC. Additions developed since 2003 include:

- Technical Guidelines for the CAP 2006 (2005)
- Guidelines for Flash Appeals (2005)
- Guidelines for Gender-based Violence Interventions in Humanitarian Settings (2005)
- IASC Package on Internal Displacement (2004)
- Operational Guidelines of Human Rights in Natural Disasters (2006)
- Guidelines for the Use of the Self-Assessment Tool (2005)
- Field Guidelines for Assessing the Humanitarian Implications of Sanctions (2004)
- Exit Strategy for Humanitarian Actors in Conflict Situations (2003)

Despite this weakness, the agencies working in the IASC claim that these instruments should be used by the member organizations as if they had the legal status of international conventions governing the operations of the international humanitarian community. They have displayed their internal agreement that one of the primary objectives of the IASC was to "advocate common humanitarian principles to parties outside the IASC".[17] The Inter-agency Task Force for Disaster Reduction (IATF) has also tried to externalize its internal platform that seeks to promote disaster reduction in a concerted manner, particularly through dialogue and "consensus-building among sectors both within and outside the United Nations system". In general, the IASC and IATF presuppose that the affected countries and the bilateral donors are parties to their policies and procedures framework.

But, in reality, the experience of the large-scale disaster on the occasion of the December 2004 Indian Ocean tsunami demonstrated that most of these policies and principles remained unknown to operators in the field and had not been incorporated in the national regulatory frameworks for disaster management. Moreover, there exist no clear and coherent regulatory agreements on disaster management and humanitarian assistance, except for the Tampere Convention on the Provision of Telecommunications Resources for Disaster Mitigation and Relief Operations of 1998.[18]

Institutional deficiencies in the UN humanitarian system

The current UN humanitarian system is characterized by the fragmentation of tasks and responsibilities split among too many institutions and actors involved on the ground. This is illustrated in figure 6.1.

There are also many players and lead agencies active at the respective stages of disaster management transition (see fig. 6.2). Despite its imperative need, there is no central intergovernmental forum providing governance and intergovernmental directives for the overall operations of humanitarian assistance and disaster reduction throughout the entire risk management process.

Dichotomies and disjointedness are prevalent between relief and recovery through mitigation stages despite repeated calls by the General Assembly for integrated management of the disaster cycle. In fact, one of the UN's fundamental tenets of emergency humanitarian assistance, contained in General Assembly resolution 46/182, states that the assistance "must be provided in ways that will be supportive of recovery and long-term development" and requires that "development assistance organizations should be involved at an early stage" to "collaborate with those responsible for emergency relief and recovery". The UN humanitarian assistance system still lacks a transition mechanism that enables

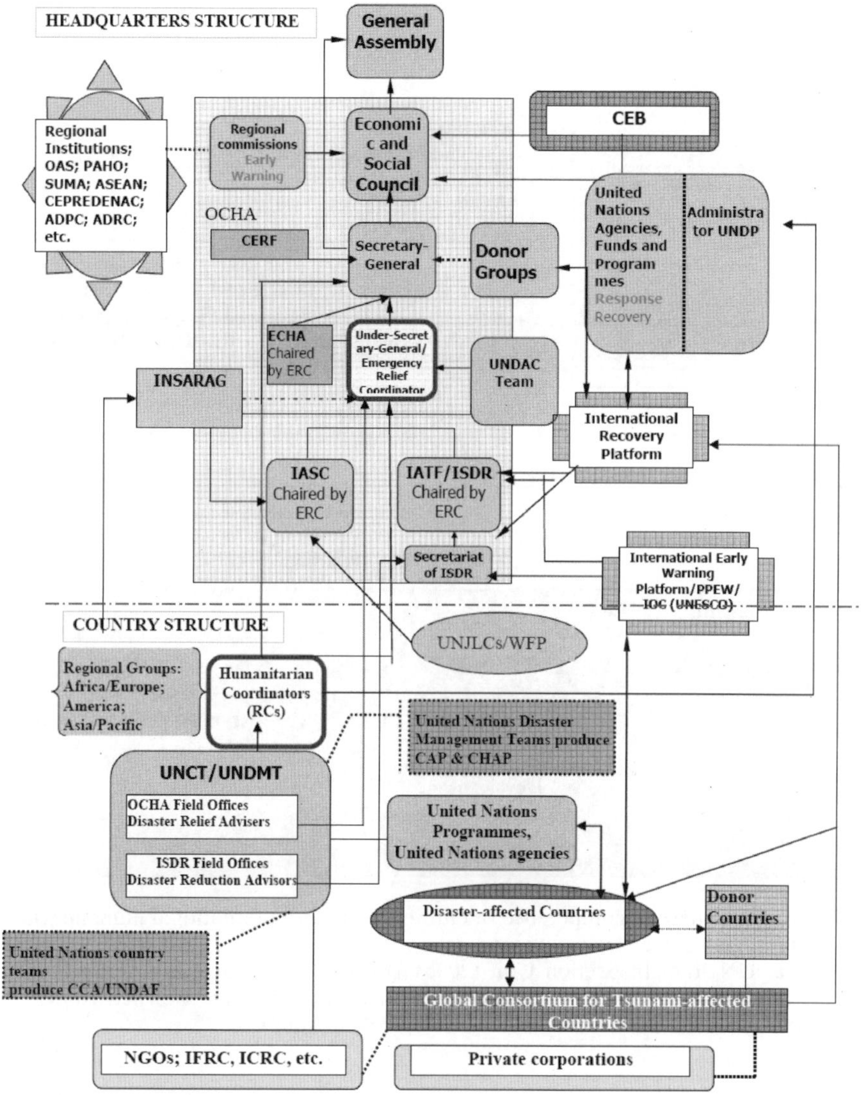

Figure 6.1 Current institutional scheme of disaster reduction and response

Key:

CERF Central Emergency Response Fund
CEPREDENAC Centre for Disaster Prevention in Central America
CHAP Common Humanitarian Action Plan
ECHA Executive Committee on Humanitarian Affairs
ISDR International Strategy for Disaster Reduction
INSARAG International Search and Rescue Advisory Group
PPEW Platform for the Promotion of Early Warning
SUMA Humanitarian Supply Management System

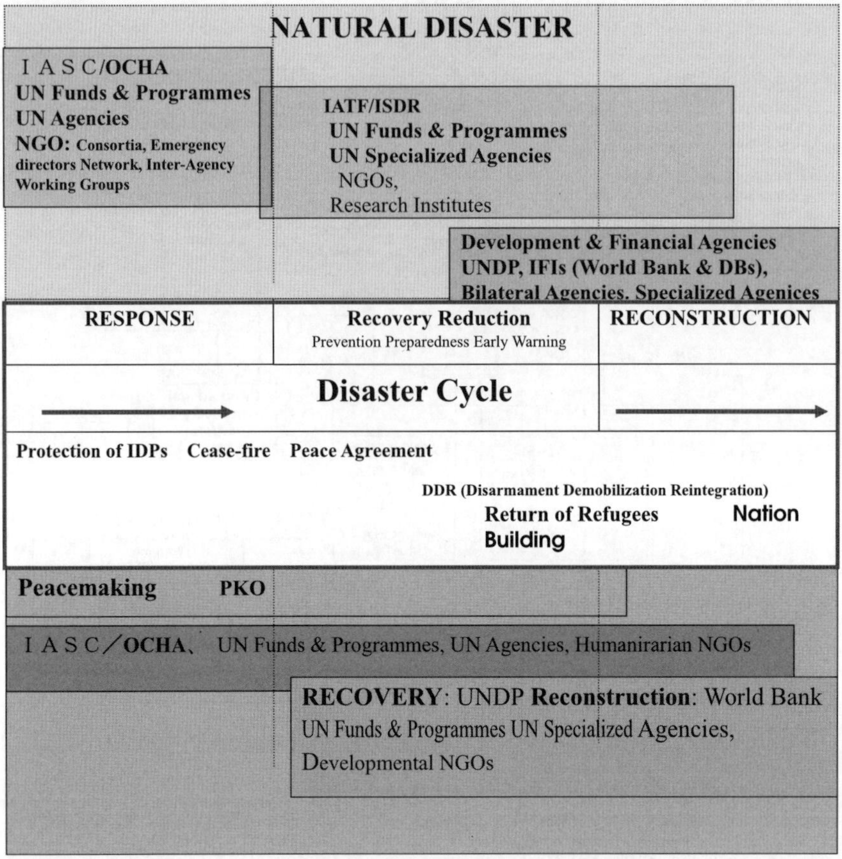

Figure 6.2 Sphere of competence of entities related to international humanitarian assistance at disaster management stages
Source: UN Joint Inspection Unit (2006) *Towards a United Nations Humanitarian Assistance for Disaster Response and Reduction: Lessons Learned from the Indian Ocean Tsunami Disaster*, JIU/REP/2006/5, Annex V.

all the humanitarian organizations related to disaster management and risk reduction as well as development to provide a continuum of seamless and smooth coordinated assistance to disaster-affected countries throughout the entire disaster management process.

There is an alarming institutional divide between disaster response and reduction embodied in two system-wide coordinating mechanisms on disaster management: one for international emergency humanitarian assistance undertaken by the UN humanitarian organizations, and another for disaster risk reduction under the International Strategy for Disaster Reduction. This dichotomy has been an impediment to the strategic management of relief leading to rehabilitation and development.[19]

The successive stages of disaster management are handled by different coordinating agencies without a coherent system of transition from one stage to another. Most international emergency assistance in cases of major disasters is organized and coordinated under the aegis of the Office for the Coordination of Humanitarian Affairs in accordance with the policies established by the IASC within the UN system. The OCHA coordinates and promotes emergency humanitarian assistance through such mechanisms as its consolidated appeal process and flash appeals, the Central Emergency Response Fund and its assistance and advocacy tools, such as the Humanitarian Information Centres, ReliefWeb and Integrated Regional Information Networks (IRIN). When it comes to the recovery stage, where developmental agencies such as the UNDP and the World Bank take charge of the disaster-affected countries, the infrastructure that was built up by the OCHA for humanitarian assistance in local communities at the emergency stage can rarely be handed over to them, as its presence has already been phased out.

On the other hand, disaster risk reduction and mitigation efforts are managed within the framework of the International Strategy for Disaster Reduction (ISDR), created in 2006 by the Global Platform for Disaster Risk Reduction (established in 2006), a Secretariat-sponsored high-level gathering of government officials, Secretariat experts and representatives of NGOs: a successor body to the IATF for the coordination of system-wide activities on the implementation of the strategy. However, the initiatives developed under the ISDR, such as disaster prevention, mitigation and preparedness, are yet to be mainstreamed in the recovery and development stages.

Quest for governance and management framework to cope with large-scale disasters

In the wake of the tsunami disaster the World Conference on Disaster Reduction, convened by the United Nations in Kobe, Japan, in January 2005, adopted the Hyogo Framework for Action 2005–2015, subtitled "Building the Resilience of Nations and Communities to Disasters",[20] which represented intergovernmental consensus on the modalities for integrating all phases of humanitarian assistance in disaster reduction and response, including early warning and emphasizing the needs of the most vulnerable groups in society. The General Assembly at its sixtieth session in December 2005 endorsed this consensus. It remains to be seen whether the consensus thus established can make a breakthrough to overcome the impediment to the strategic management of the transition deriving from the institutional dichotomy mentioned above.

The lessons learned from the Indian Ocean tsunami disaster indicated the need for more adequate principles and guidelines for humanitarian assistance and their application to be developed through an intergovernmental mechanism that would provide a robust system-wide governance and strategic management framework in this sector. Lack of such a framework within the UN system organizations – despite the call of the Secretary-General for consolidating and grouping humanitarian and humanitarian-related matters under a single "humanitarian umbrella" agenda – could negatively affect the mobilization, management and allocation of resources for international humanitarian assistance within and outside the UN system.

In other words, the current governance mechanism, led by the General Assembly and the Economic and Social Council, has been handicapped by the absence of specialized intergovernmental support bodies for system-wide coordination. Under the circumstances, the UN system has little scope for demonstrating democratic accountability.

Management and financial accountability

There are no readily available data and statistics for the entire UN system to assess mobilization and use of resources in the field of humanitarian assistance accurately. Despite the effort of the OCHA to elaborate its financial tracking system, compiling global commitments and expenditures on disaster assistance, the UN system still lacks a system-wide strategic resources planning and management framework that provides financial and administrative accountability.

According to compilations by the JIU, the UN system spent annually US$2.1–4.8 billion on humanitarian assistance over the first six years in the 2000s.[21] Faced with exponential growth in the number of disasters, assistance by the system continued to grow faster than in any other sector from 1999 to 2003 and amounted to US$3 billion in 2003, accounting for roughly 30 per cent, the largest share, of the expenditure of the UN system on operational activities for development. The magnitude of the financial resources devoted to this sector in the UN system is significant (see fig 6.3).

However, unearmarked general resources that the system received amounted to about US$1 billion, representing barely 15 per cent of the US$7 billion aggregate humanitarian assistance made available by the international community. Such a modest share does not provide the UN system with resources commensurate with its central coordinating role in international humanitarian assistance.

As regards management and financial accountability of the human operations, one should note from the experience of the Indian Ocean earthquake tsunami that only half of the required commitments to emer-

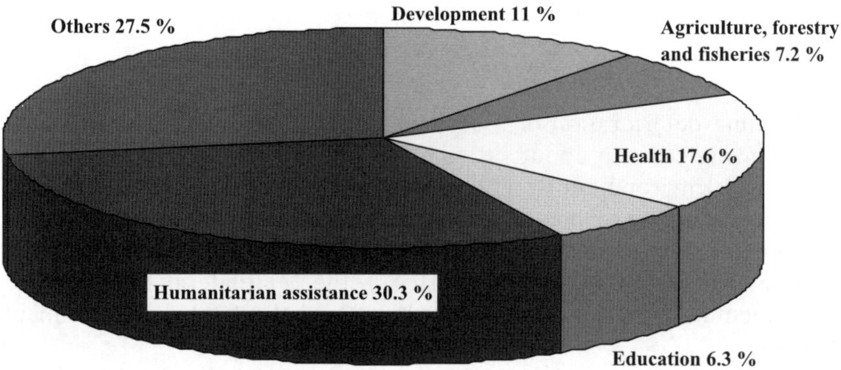

Figure 6.3 Share of expenditures on operational activities of the UN system by sector, 2003
Source: UN Joint Inspection Unit (2006) *Towards a United Nations Humanitarian Assistance for Disaster Response and Reduction: Lessons Learned from the Indian Ocean Tsunami Disaster*, UN Doc. JIU/REP/2006/5, p. 4.

gency and early-recovery assistance were disbursed one year after the disaster. Most of the $14 billion in commitments to long-term recovery, made on the occasion of the flash appeals for assistance to tsunami-stricken countries, were yet to be disbursed after two years. The OCHA's financial tracking system does not provide the public and Member States with adequate information on the use of the resources raised through the consolidated appeal process and its flash appeals, nor the status of the projects for which the funds were raised. The UN system organizations have paid little attention to monitoring the actual use of these huge contributions.

Nevertheless, the views of Member States expressed in General Assembly resolutions 62/91[22] and 62/94[23] of 17 December 2007 indicate incipient signs of their *prise de conscience* that deserve being closely monitored. They consisted in calling upon "the relevant organizations of the UN system to pursue efforts to improve the humanitarian response to natural and man-made disasters and complex emergencies by further enhancing transparency, performance and accountability". These efforts would consist, in particular, of "enhancing financial transparency and accountability with respect to the channeling and utilization of resources, including, as appropriate, through the involvement of international public auditors", and "donors and recipient countries by means of a unified financial and sectoral information online tracking system" in order to "highlight the importance of timely and accurate information on assessed needs and the sources and uses of funds".

Lacunae in environmental governance

Proliferation of environment-related initiatives

Continuing deterioration of the overall state of the global environment and growing concern about sustainable development led to the creation of the UN Environment Programme (UNEP) in 1972. This was followed by the establishment of other environment-related institutions, such as the Commission on Sustainable Development (CSD), numerous multilateral environmental agreements (MEAs), the Multilateral Fund for the Implementation of the Montreal Protocol and the Global Environment Facility.

The environmental sector is characterized not only by the diversity of these environmental institutions but also by the overlapping of activities between these institutions and global and regional cooperative programmes and frameworks that are involved more or less actively in some environment-related activities. Furthermore, it has been accompanied by the existence of multiple intergovernmental and inter-secretariat coordinating bodies (see fig. 6.4).

As the environment is a very popular subject, every organization in the UN system has some environmental activities and projects to attract voluntary contributions from donors, thus perpetuating their survival. Similar to the humanitarian sector, this sector is also subject to confusion between normative and operational activities, and between the modalities of funding these activities.

Towards governance of sustainable development

Adding to the institutional fragmentation is the lack of a *modus operandi* to govern and manage the relationship between sustainable development and environmental protection. In the context of agreements at the Rio Earth Summit and the Johannesburg World Summit on Sustainable Development, sustainable development is meant to be a development process to meet the needs of the present generation without compromising the ability of future generations to meet their own needs. And integrating its three components – economic development, social equity and environmental protection – as interdependent and mutually reinforcing pillars should achieve sustainable development.[24]

A variety of General Assembly and ECOSOC resolutions, notably GA resolution S-19/2 of 28 June 1997,[25] stated that good governance for sustainable development consists in properly constructed strategies to enhance prospects for economic growth and employment and at the same time protect the environment. On the other hand, the UNEP Governing Council/Global Ministerial Environment Forum (GC/GMEF) held in

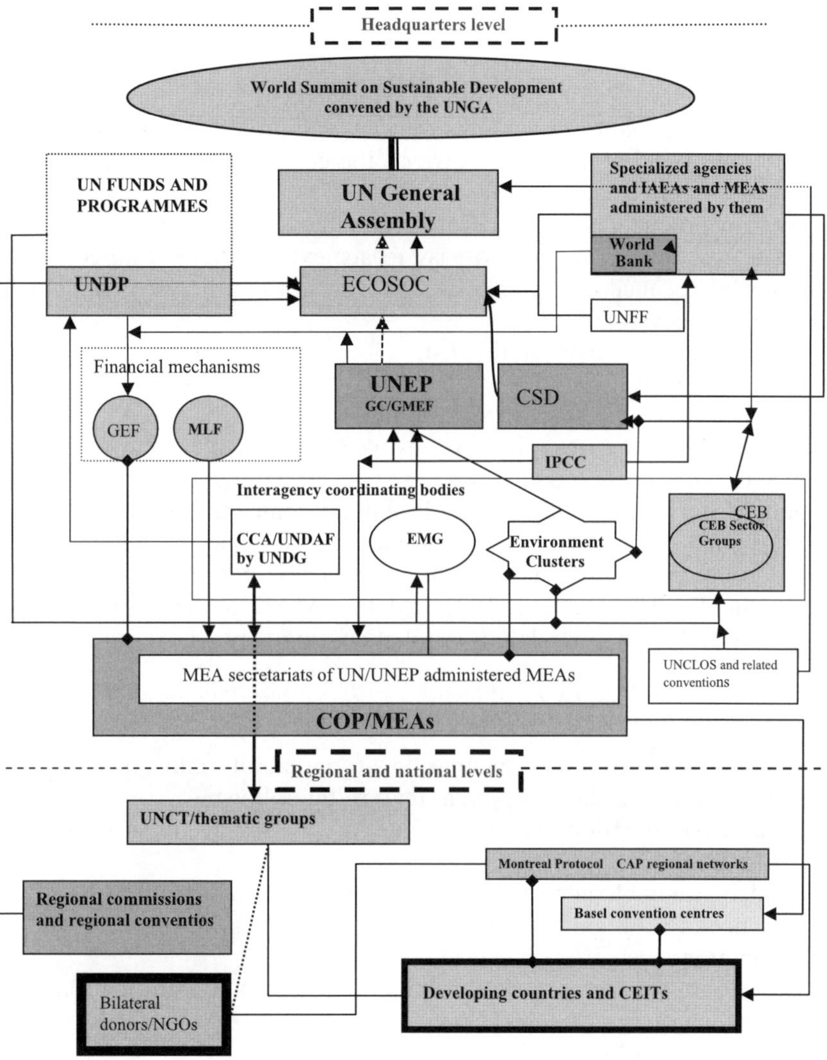

Figure 6.4 Fragmented landscape of environmental governance within the UN system

Key:

↔ or → Management and/or operational reporting channels

– Cooperative relations/consultations

. . . *Ad hoc* relations

CAP – compliance assistance programmes of UNEP

Cartagena in 2002 adopted the "Cartagena Package" on international environmental governance,[26] according to which environmental governance consists of mainstreaming environmental protection into developmental and economic policies through the development of a system-wide coherent policy, as well as resources management for its implementation. Theoretically, a consensus seems to exist within the UN system as to the definition of and relationship between the concepts of sustainable development and environmental protection.

But, in practice, governance of sustainable development and environmental governance are not so easy to achieve, as there is no consensus on how to reconcile the competing priorities of the three components of sustainable development.

At the national level there exists a long-term approach and a mechanism to reconcile the interests in play.[27] However, the UN system has never been able to establish such a process, nor has it had a mechanism to ensure it. As addressed above, ever-growing involvement of international organizations and bilateral donors in strengthening norms, capacity building, networking and funding in the environmental field exacerbated institutional fragmentation and duplication of policies and operations of international environmental initiatives. These initiatives, springing up after the Earth Summit in 1992 and the WSSD in 2002, have eroded UNEP's embracing mandate for global environmental governance.

Salient features deriving from lacunae in UN accountability and environmental governance

Under the circumstances, lacunae in accountability and environmental governance within the UN system feature the following:

- lack of coordination, coherence and cooperation at global level (fragmentation)
- inadequate implementation and coordination at national level
- absence of programmatic and planning instrument for system-wide coordination
- lack of intergovernmental ownership in interagency coordination
- need for synergy of control measures among MEAs, such as between the Kyoto and Montreal Protocols
- inadequate implementation, compliance and enforcement (developing countries)
- lack of harmonization in reporting requirements
- gaps in scientific assessment and information
- absence of environmentally sound procurement policy in international organizations
- inefficient management of resources (competition for funds).

Let us address these features in some depth.

Coordination mechanism

The UN system secretariats established the Environmental Management Group (EMG), with the support of the General Assembly in its resolution 53/242 of 1999,[28] for the purpose of enhancing interagency coordination among the UN agencies, funds and programmes and the secretariats of MEAs in the field of environment and human settlements. It meets under the chair of the UNEP Executive Director, who reports on its activities to the UNEP GC/GMEF. The most important goal of the EMG was to promote a so-called issue management approach to key areas of environmental and human settlements concern. That is aimed at achieving, on an issue-by-issue basis, effective management, coordination, joint action, rational and cost-effective use of capacities and resources and facilitating linkages among MEAs, and between the activities under the MEAs and relevant activities elsewhere in the international environmental governance system.

On the other hand, from 1993 until 2001 the Inter-Agency Committee on Sustainable Development (IACSD) existed for interagency coordination in the area of sustainable development. Its role was to identify major policy issues relating to the follow-up by the UN system and to advise the ACC on ways and means of addressing them so as to ensure effective system-wide cooperation and coordination in the implementation of Agenda 21, the Programme of Action for the Sustainable Development of Small Island Developing States (SIDS) and other UN Conference on Environment and Development (UNCED) outcomes. It provided coordinated policy positions as input to the Commission on Sustainable Development. In 1988 the CEB disbanded it and took steps through its High-level Committee on Programmes to establish or strengthen interagency collaborative arrangements in the key areas of freshwater, water and sanitation, energy, oceans and coastal areas, and consumption and production patterns. Specific actions taken included the establishment of various sector groups: UN-Water, UN-Oceans, the International Strategy for Disaster Reduction, the Marrakesh Process on sustainable consumption and production patterns and UN-Energy.

From the above, it is obvious that there are two sets of coordinating mechanisms building up: one in UNEP on environmental protection and another in the CEB purview on sustainable development. Irrespective of any theoretical or juridical explanation of their relationships, one cannot deny considerable overlapping of their tasks.

At the country level, the UN agencies are yet to generalize the use of the Common Country Assessment and UN Development Assistance Framework (CCA/UNDAF) processes to mainstream environmental protection in development policy. Although compliance with MEAs should take place at the country level as the responsibility of the contracting parties concerned, the UN resident coordinators and the secretariats of the MEAs have made few efforts to promote the implementation of MEAs in the CCA/UNDAF processes.

Programmatic and planning instrument for system-wide coordination

The UN system is still to develop a common fundamental programmatic instrument spelling out who does what and how their commonalities of interests can be enhanced.

Under the implementation frameworks of the Millennium Development Goals, the CEB has identified 27 mechanisms for international cooperation to ensure environmental sustainability, such as the GEF, UN-Water, the Water Assessment Programme, the Global Environment Monitoring System (GEMS), Cities Alliance, the ISDR, UN-Oceans, the Global Programme of Action for the Protection of the Marine Environment from Land-based Activities (GPA), Millennium Ecosystem Assessment, etc.[29]

On the other hand, UNEP has compiled a list of joint projects and programmes undertaken with other UN system organizations relevant for the activities of MEAs in the areas of world climate impacts assessment, biodiversity, protection of regional seas, marine pollution, chemicals and waste control, customs and illegal trade, harmonization of reporting under MEAs, health and environmental initiatives and education for sustainable development and advocacy. As of September 2007 there were 49 of them in partnerships with a number of specialized agencies (the FAO, UNESCO, IMO, World Bank, WMO, IFC, ILO, WHO), with UN funds and programmes (the UNDP, WFP, UNITAR, UNU-IAS, UNOPS, UNCTAD, UN-HABITAT, UNFPA) and with MEAs secretariats such as the UNFCCC and UNCCD.

In the light of the foregoing, it is still not clear how the UN system should integrate these networks and a series of joint programmes as a programmatic and planning instrument for system-wide coordination.

Lack of intergovernmental ownership in interagency coordination

Most environmental management issues have been left to the discretion of the secretariats, probably because of the technical and scientific nature of environmental protection. Most coordination issues have been perceived at the administrative level and dealt with among the secretariats of international organizations. The issue of synergies among the various MEAs has also been approached with the aim of achieving coherence between the operations of the conventions' secretariats. The Environment Management Group and the CEB environmental sector groups are essentially secretariat bodies and subject to the "principles of subsidiarity" for decision-making among them. That means these interagency bodies should make their decisions at the lowest level, but obviously cannot take decisions contrary to the interest of any of their organizations.

In the absence of explicit directives from Member States, the organizations have not established even a basic administrative discipline to implement environmentally sound procurement. For example, none of the UN system organizations except for the United Nations University and the International Atomic Energy Agency implements ISO 14001 standards.

Need for synergy of control measures among multilateral environmental agreements

The international community is not equipped with a regular mechanism to solve substantive contradictions in control measures between the environmental conventions, for example between the Kyoto Protocol and the Montreal Protocol regarding the use of alternative substances and technology to replace chlorofluorocarbons and other ozone-depleting substances by hydrochlorofluorocarbons and its by-product hydrofluorocarbons with high global warming effects. Successive efforts within the Montreal Protocol at applying an environmentally responsible approach to its primary-rule system for the control of ozone-depleting substances, i.e. to use alternative substances taking into account environmental effects such as global warming, are yet to succeed in ensuring integrated implementation of that protocol and the Kyoto Protocol on climate change.[30]

This lack of coherence in governance is due to the inadequate development of common criteria for environmentally responsible principles, and more fundamentally due to the absence of an overriding legal framework applicable to all environmental conventions ensuring environmentally sound and responsible policy and behaviours in the implementation of MEAs.

Such a framework, which would be based on a world convention on the law of environmental treaties, has yet to be developed. Development of a *jus cogens* in this field might include the principle that actions under multilateral environmental programmes and conventions must be harmonized to ensure that perceived benefits under one are not achieved at the expense of deleterious consequences for another.[31] This means that no multilateral environmental convention shall solve its problems at the expense of other conventions.

Such a law of treaties should consist of identifying and harmonizing horizontally principles and rules applicable to MEAs with respect to environmentally responsible principles, precautionary approaches, sharing of scientific assessments, mutual information and monitoring transboundary hazards, compliance procedures and mechanisms of coordination of normative and operational actions. Without these principles and rules, a full and integrated accountability could not be rendered to meet human demands on the environment, recognizing that environmental issues are inextricably linked through the multiple drives stemming from these demands.

Notwithstanding the increasing trend to call for more conventions and legally binding frameworks for environmental protection, there are serious and paradoxical lacunae in the rule of law that should govern the coherent application of different provisions of control measures under the MEAs.

Table 6.3 Multilateral resources available for environment activities, 2006

Organization	US$ million
UNEP	136.5 (core and non-core budget)
Global MEAs	146.5
9 global MEAs* administered by UNEP	62.3
4 global MEAs administered by United Nations (UNFCCC, UNCCD, UNCLOS and Fish Stocks Agreement)	55.0
Other global MEAs (Convention on Protection of World Cultural Heritage/UNESCO, ITPGRFA**/FAO and Ramsar Convention)	29.2
Multilateral Fund for the Implementation of the Montreal Protocol	179.9
Global Environment Facility	600.0 (2006, based on donor commitments of US$3 billion for the period 2002–2006)
Other UN system organizations***	592.4
Total	1,655.3

Source: Unless otherwise stated, based on the Joint Inspection Unit's compilation of core and non-core programme budgets of the UN system organizations contained in "Management Review of Environmental Governance within the United Nations System", JIU/REP/2008/3, Annex II.

* Vienna Convention for the Protection of the Ozone Layer; Montreal Protocol on Substances that Deplete the Ozone Layer; Convention on Biological Diversity; Cartagena Protocol on Biosafety; Convention on International Trade in Endangered Species of Wild Fauna and Flora (CITES); Convention on Migratory Species (CMS); Basel Convention on the Control of Trans-boundary Movements of Hazardous Wastes and Their Disposal; Stockholm Convention on Persistent Organic Pollutants; Rotterdam Convention on Prior Informed Consent Procedure for Certain Hazardous Chemicals and Pesticides in International Trade.

** International Treaty on Plant Genetic Resources for Food and Agriculture.

*** UNDP, UNICEF, UNITAR, UNRWA, UNWTO, WHO, UNU, ESCAP, ESCWA and ECE, including ECE regional environmental conventions.

Management of resources

The resources mobilized in the environmental sector within the UN system amounted to annual expenses of $1.6 billion in 2006 (see table 6.3). This should be compared with $1.44 billion committed to general environmental protection in 2006 by 22 member states of the OECD Development Assistance Committee in their bilateral official development assistance to developing countries.[32] Underfunding persists as a source of weakness in the UN system, as is often claimed by its bureaucrats. But if funds were strategically used with better coherence, an amount of $1.6 billion would enable the system to play a more significant catalytic role in ensuring global governance in the environmental sector than in the humanitarian sector.

Again, what prevents the UN system from managing resources efficiently is the competition and confusion of mandates between the environmental institutions and development organizations undertaking environment-related activities. Table 6.4 indicates a clear trend that

Table 6.4 Expenditures on normative and operational environmental activities within the UN system

	US$ million		
	1993	2000	2006
Normative activities			
Environmental protection activities by UNEP funds	89.8	139.8 (6.5%)**	132.5 (−0.9%)**
Total expenditures for UN/UNEP-administered MEAs***	6.8	45.0 (31.0%)	78.3 (9.7%)
Operational activities			
Non-UNEP operational activities for development devoted to environment*	149.4	176.7 (2.4%)	332.7 (10.6%)
UN system operational activities for development	5,153.3	6,494 (3.4%)	16,368.4 (16.7%)

Sources: Operational activities: UN Doc. A/61/77-E/2006/59 (2006) and A/63/71-E/2008/46 (2008). Normative activities: In 1993 and 2000, financial reports and audited statements in Reports of the Board of Auditors (e.g. UN Doc. A/49/5/Add. 6 to A/63/5/Add. 6) (1994–2008) and A/61/203 (2006) on UNFCCC; in 2006, budget performance reports of organizations concerned.

* Undertaken by UNDP, UNICEF and specialized agencies

** The percentage in parentheses indicates growth per annum over the previous period.

*** Core activities.

during the 1990s normative activities promoted by UNEP and the multilateral agreements for environmental protection grew much faster than operational activities for development devoted to the environment. But in the early 2000s that trend was reversed in favour of operational activities. Nowadays the first growers are developmental agencies such as the UNDP, UNICEF and specialized agencies undertaking environmental-related activities as part of their work on sustainable development. In recent years the MEAs' core budgets have stagnated. This suggests that much of the MEAs' additional financial needs for normative activities had to be met by voluntary contributions under their non-core programmes.

Conclusions

The review of the management and governance in humanitarian assistance and environmental protection indicates that the UN system organizations have been provided with considerable autonomy and discretion to ensure system-wide cooperation and coordination. Most of the system-wide initiatives have been launched by the secretariats, but with little evaluation of the follow-up actions made. Even if an evaluation is made, it is often done by individual agencies on their own activities, largely serving as an instrument to account for the use of money they get from bilateral donors. Entire Member States do not feel ownership over the actions they finance. This gives rise to concerns about the difficulties of ensuring the democratic accountability of the UN system.

The guiding principles, rules and policies that the UN system secretariats have established for their operations should be thoroughly reviewed and streamlined by Member States so that they serve their peoples and governments.

Accountability in global environmental governance is difficult to render unless a law of environmental treaties is established. To this end, synergies among MEAs should be increased through the coherent application of environmentally responsible principles, precautionary approaches, use of independent scientific assessments and mutual information, reporting and monitoring of transboundary hazards among contracting parties, as well as through the development of common compliance procedures and mechanisms to coordinate normative and operational actions.

At the headquarters level, the secretariats should not create further permanent interagency coordinating bodies nor perpetuate the existing ones established among them. Rather, a bottom-up process of compiling needs in the field at the country level should be strengthened. To this end, active use should be made of the CCA/UN Development Assistance

Framework processes to identify common country needs in sustainable development and environmental protection and map national and regional ecosystem problems, including compliance with the MEAs as well as needs for disaster management and disaster risk reduction. Such bottom-up processes will keep momentum for multilateral cooperation in the respective areas of environmental protection and disaster response and reduction efforts. Based on these processes, the global legislative forums, such as the UN General Assembly and the Economic and Social Council, should develop at field and headquarters levels a system-wide planning process for managing resources for results.

Results-based management has yet to take effect for ensuring accountability of the secretariats to Member States. In view of the fragmented and decentralized nature of the UN system structure, RBM would not ensure system-wide strategic planning and resource management unless the governing bodies adopt common objectives applicable throughout the UN system.

Last but not least, the organizations have to develop a common fundamental programmatic and administrative planning instrument containing a catalogue of initiatives and stakeholders spelling out who does what and how commonalities of interests can be enhanced among them. In such an instrument, the purposes of normative activities and operational activities should be clearly spelled out, together with financial bases of the types of activities to be met by both core and non-core funding.

Notes

1. The views expressed in this chapter are those of the author and do not reflect those of the Joint Inspection Unit of the UN system.
2. This table is taken from UN Joint Inspection Unit (2006) "Towards a United Nations Humanitarian Assistance for Disaster Response and Reduction: Lessons Learned from the Indian Ocean Tsumnami Disatser", JIU/REP/2006/5, Geneva, prepared by Tadanori Inomata.
3. UN Chief Executives Board for Coordination (2006) "Budgetary and Financial Situation of Organizations of the United Nations System, Note by the Secretary-General Transmitting the Statistical Report of the United Nations System Chief Executives Board for Coordination on the Budgetary and Financial Situation of the Organizations of the United Nations System", UN Doc. A/61/203, Corr. 1-2, p. 46.
4. UN Board of Auditors (2006) "Report of the Board of Auditors, Financial Report and Audited Financial Statements for the 12-month Period from 1 July 2005 to 30 June 2006", A/61/5, vol. II on UN peacekeeping operations.
5. International Criminal Court, A/61/5/Add. 11, p. 39; International Criminal Court, A/61/5/Add. 12, p. 16; International Criminal Court, ICC-ASP/6/5, p. 28.
6. The ACC is a predecessor body to the CEB, established by the Secretary-General in response to ECOSOC resolution 13(III) of 23 September 1946.

7. UN Administrative Committee on Coordination (1991) "Addendum to the Annual Overview Report of the Administrative Committee on Coordination, Programme and Resources of the United Nations System", UN Doc. E/1991/42/Add. 1., table 1; UN Administrative Committee on Coordination (1993) "Programme and Resources of the United Nations System for the Biennium 1992–1993", UN Doc. E/1993/84, table 1; UN Administrative Committee on Coordination (1995) "Programme and Resources of the United Nations System for the Biennium 1994–1995", UN Doc. E/1995/64, table 4, sector 160.
8. The ACC Consultative Committee on Programme and Operational Questions and ACC Consultative Committee on Administrative Questions addressed the issue for the last time in 1998 and 1999, respectively. See ACC/1998/7 and ACC 1999/6 as well as CEB Management Handbook, section 17-6, "Inter-organization Financial Reporting", para. C.4.
9. UN Joint Inspection Unit (2004) "Implementation of Results-based Management in the United Nations Organizations", JIU/REP/2004/6, available at www.unjiu.org/data/reports/2004/en2004_6.pdf.
10. UN General Assembly (2005) "Report of the Committee for Programme and Coordination", UN Doc. A/60/16, 1 July, Corr. 1, para. 248.
11. UN General Assembly (2006) "Programme Planning", UN Doc. A/RES/60/257, 8 May, para. 2.
12. UN General Assembly (1991) "Strengthening the Coordination of Humanitarian Emergency Assistance of the United Nations", UN Doc. A/RES/46/182.
13. The guiding principles were submitted by the representative of the Secretary-General on internal displacement and taken note of by the Commission on Human Rights in 1998. UN Commission on Human Rights (1998) "Guiding Principles on Internal Displacement", UN Doc. E/CN.4/1998/53/Add.2, noted in Comm. Hum. Rt. res. 1998/50.
14. Established in June 1992 in response to General Assembly resolution 46/182 as the primary mechanism for interagency coordination relating to humanitarian assistance in response to complex and major emergencies, under the leadership of the Emergency Relief Coordinator, the IASC is composed of eight full members – UNICEF, UNDP, UNHCR, the Food and Agricultural Organization (FAO), the Office for the Coordination of Humanitarian Affairs (OCHA), the UN Population Fund (UNFPA), the World Food Programme (WFP) and the World Health Organization (WHO) – and nine standing invitees – InterAction, the International Committee of the Red Cross (ICRC), the International Council of Voluntary Agencies, the International Federation of Red Cross and Red Crescent Societies, the International Organization for Migration, the Steering Committee for Humanitarian Response, the Office of the High Commissioner for Human Rights, the Office of the Special Representative of the Secretary General on Internally Displaced People and the World Bank.
15. This table is taken from UN Joint Inspection Unit, note 2 above.
16. Ibid.
17. UN Inter-Agency Standing Committee and Inter-Agency Standing Committee Working Group (1998) "Concise Terms of Reference and Action Procedures", revised and abridged.
18. Tampere Convention on the Provision of Telecommunications Resources for Disaster Mitigation and Relief Operations (1998), opened for signature 18 June 1998, entered into force 8 January 2005, available at www.itu.int/ITU-D/emergencytelecoms/tampere.html.
19. UN Joint Inspection Unit, note 2 above.
20. UN World Conference on Disaster Reduction (2005) "Hyogo Framework for Action 2005–2015: Building the Resilience of Nations and Communities to Disasters", UN Doc. A/Conf. 206/6, 18–22 January.

21. UN Joint Inspection Unit, note 2 above, Annexes I and II.
22. UN General Assembly (2007) "Strengthening Emergency Relief, Rehabilitation, Reconstruction and Prevention in the Aftermath of the Indian Ocean Tsunami Disaster", UN Doc. 62/91, 17 December.
23. UN General Assembly (2007) "Strengthening of the Coordination of Emergency Humanitarian Assistance of the United Nations", UN Doc. 62/94, 17 December.
24. UN General Assembly (1987) "Our Common Future: Report of the World Commission on Environment and Development", UN Doc. A/42/427.
25. UN General Assembly (1997) "Programme for the Further Implementation of Agenda 21", UN Doc. S-19/2, 28 June.
26. UN Environment Programme (2002) "Cartagena Package on International Environmental Governance", UNEP GC/GMEF decision SS.VII/1 on international environmental governance.
27. See, for example, Quebec's Sustainable Development Act. Canada [Quebec] (2007) *Sustainable Development Act*, R.S.Q. c. D-8.1.1, available at www.canlii.org/qc/laws/sta/d-8.1.1/20080115/whole.html.
28. UN General Assembly (1999) "Report of the Secretary-General on Environment and Human Settlements", UN Doc. A/RES/53/242, 28 July.
29. UN Chief Executives Board for Coordination (2005) "One United Nations – Catalyst for Progress and Change", Annex, May.
30. Inomata, Tadanori (2001) *Toward Integrating the Implementation of Multilateral Environmental Agreements – Reflection on the Harmonization of Measures to Protect the Ozone Layer and Global Climate System*, Tokyo: Gaimushou Chosa Geppou.
31. UN Office of the Secretary-General (2000) "Protection of the Atmosphere", UN Doc. E.CN.17/2001/2, 13 December, para. 3; Inomata, ibid..
32. Organisation for Economic Co-operation and Development (2008) "OECD Stat Data, Dataset 3: OECD by Sector", 25 February.

7

UN management reform as a basis for enhancing accountability

Hideaki Shiroyama

Introduction

I would like to analyse the management institutions and methods of international organizations in the UN system, and to make several recommendations based on the analysis. The appropriate design and implementation of management institutions and methods are essential for the effective assurance of accountability of organizations.

The attempts of various entities concerning management reform, based on theories such as new public management (NPM), influenced the process when the United Nations restructured its existing organizational arrangements by revamping organizations and relations between the organizations and society. NPM is based on the idea that, on the condition that control by output and outcome through evaluation is strengthened, control of input such as finance and personnel affairs should be decentralized to the field level.[1] Two concrete important elements in the United Nations relating to NPM were a results-based budgeting system and related evaluation mechanism, and introduction of the Millennium Development Goals (MDGs) and attempts to manage the development process using the MDGs as policy goals.

Before going into concrete analysis, I would like to stress two general points here relating to the special character of the system of international organizations. First, the amount of resources being invested in international organizations is limited, and it is therefore dangerous to expect

Envisioning reform: Enhancing UN accountability in the twenty-first century, Kuyama and Fowler (eds), United Nations University Press, 2009, ISBN 978-92-808-1170-4

too much in terms of the role they can play. It is, however, evident that these organizations have an important function in taking up issues which are not dealt with by any other actors, and they should not be underestimated. The limitations of international organizations can be seen in the fact that the expenditure of Member States on UN security operations is very small compared to national defence budgets, and that the importance of investment by international organizations continues to decline in comparison to that of international investment expenditure by the private sector. However, it is apparent from a consideration of UN peacekeeping operations (PKOs) and the humanitarian activities of the UN High Commissioner for Refugees (UNHCR) and the UN Children's Fund (UNICEF) that international organizations have important roles to play in international affairs that would not otherwise be fulfilled. In addition, the ongoing activities of specialized agencies such as the International Telecommunication Union (ITU) and the World Health Organization (WHO) clearly indicate that international organizations fulfil essential international public functions, including the setting of international standards.

Second, it is true that there can be many occasions when evaluations of activities of international organizations from the perspective of the international public interest are different from evaluations of national interests. But there are also many cases in which the pursuit of international public interest coincides with the pursuit of national interests. For example, Japan has offered support to PKOs and UNHCR activities in the Asian region, which is of interest to Japan; Western nations did the same, for the same reasons, in the former Yugoslavia. However, inasmuch as the interests of donor nations have complemented each other, the support provided was consistent with the pursuit of international public interest. The cooperation with UNICEF for the implementation of a Japanese initiative for a grant aid programme targeting children's health is another example of national interest matching the international public interest. Furthermore, Japan's support for an increase in the number of Japanese personnel working in international organizations conforms to the international public interest in that it seeks to ensure that international organizations have a more international character. Clearly, activities which use extra-budgetary resources in pursuit of specific goals often run counter to the international interest, but such activities also frequently prove not to be in the national interest. Therefore, on a practical level, we must determine what forms of management to employ to make national interests coincide more closely with the international public interest.

Managing the activities of the international organizations of the United Nations – Basic issues

Lack of performance indicators

For the management of international organizations, it is necessary to determine outputs and outcomes of their activities as yardsticks to evaluate these activities. However, it is difficult to determine what is output and what is outcome. It is particularly difficult to specify outcomes in areas such as security and development, in which comprehensive goals have been established. This is also the case with respect to the application of evaluation systems, which are being experimented with in numerous international organizations. The determination of indicators is a difficult task for a national administration, but becomes even more complicated in the case of an international organization, where a variety of complex factors are involved. There is no simple solution, but if international organizations are to be managed as systems, then a concerted effort should be made to determine suitable evaluation indicators.

Partnership with private sector organizations

The importance of cooperation or partnership with private sector organizations such as non-governmental organizations (NGOs) or companies has come to be the prevailing view in discussions of the accreditation of NGOs by the UN Economic and Social Council (ECOSOC) or the recent Global Compact (the name for cooperation in UN activities by private enterprises). One fact of great interest is that, for some organizations, private enterprise already has an important role from the perspective of practical management of the provision of funds.

In the case of UNICEF, $0.38 billion of the organization's 2000 income of $1.14 billion, or almost 30 per cent, was provided by its national committees, which are private sector organizations. In Japan annual income from the national committee is well in excess of ¥10 billion, a figure much higher than government contributions. Forty per cent of the extra-budgetary funds and 25 per cent of the entire budget of the WHO in 2000–2001 came from private sector organizations. The ITU is an organization specializing in a marketable technology, and it has historically been equipped with mechanisms enabling direct participation by private sector members. Approximately 12 per cent of the ITU revenue is obtained from these members. The organization's Telecommunication Standardization Sector, in particular, is dependent on private sector members for more than 70 per cent of its annual expenditure. At a time when the ability of the Telecommunication Standardization Sector to survive in competition with private and regional standardization organizations was being frequently questioned, the ITU effectively transformed itself into a private-sector-friendly organization. In addition, the role of private enterprises and NGOs continues to increase as subcontractors and service providers for PKOs and the field activities of the UNHCR.

Given these trends, the question of how to construct continuous partnerships with private sector organizations which are more than one-off events is an issue for every international organization.

Opaque financial systems and their management

The primary reason why the financial systems of international organizations are opaque is their employment of large-scale extra-budgetary resources.[2] The tendency to rely on extra-budgetary resources, which are contributions made for a limited range of purposes, can be observed in various international organizations.

In the field of security, the activities of the UN Department of Political Affairs are chiefly financed by means of a regular budget, but PKO budgets are made up by separate extra-budgetary funds set aside for PKOs and based on a special scale of contribution that is calculated separately. In the development field, Japan provides the World Bank with trust funds such as the Japan Social Development Fund (JSDF) and the Policy and Human Resources Development Fund (PHRDF). The UN Development Programme (UNDP) has, from the beginning, been based on a budget made up almost entirely of voluntary contributions, and the proportion of non-core resources, the range of purposes of which are even more limited, in the total budget is increasing. Concerning human rights, in 1992–1993 the budget for human rights was $31 million (of which extra-budgetary funds represented $7 million), while in 2002–2003 it was $105 million (of which extra-budgetary funds represented $63 million), marking a threefold overall budget increase in 10 years. However, the major part of the increase was financed by an increase in extra-budgetary resources, and the same trend can be observed in many specialized agencies. In the case of the ITU the percentage of extra-budgetary funds is small, but at the WHO, while the regular budget experienced nominal zero growth from 1996–1997 ($840 million/two years), extra-budgetary funds are continuing to expand and now represent approximately 1.5 times the regular budget.

The contribution of extra-budgetary funds by Member States is an important method of enabling those states to use international organizations to pursue their national interests and achieve their own foreign policy objectives. (There are, of course, some cases in which it is doubtful whether the goals actually represent the "genuine" national interest.) The use of international organizations to pursue national interests does not necessarily contradict the pursuit of the international public interest by those organizations. If the areas to which each country contributes extra-budgetary resources are complementary, then the portfolio (the distribution of fields of activity) of the international organization will be balanced.

Furthermore, there are many cases in which the flexible provision of extra-budgetary funds in an emergency has contributed to swift response by the international organizations concerned. However, there are of course also times when there is friction between the goals of the international organization and the country that is providing the extra-budgetary funding, and questions as to what extent dependency on extra-budgetary funds is appropriate and in what situations it emerges as an issue. The answer to such questions varies depending on the type of extra-budgetary funding concerned. To respond to such issues, the WHO holds a meeting of interested parties (MIP) as a forum for debate, including debate on programmes using extra-budgetary funds. The organization has experimented with a mechanism for inputting the opinions of countries other than donors into programmes using extra-budgetary funds by enabling developing countries to participate in the MIPs, but this is currently being scrapped. Again, in the case of UNICEF, although the Organization has access to extra-budgetary funds in the form of a supplementary support fund, because provision of the funds is restricted to programmes based on the plans of individual countries, there are limitations on the specification of purposes by donors.

To date, the issue of extra-budgetary funds has received some discussion, but there is still a lack of transparency and the issue has tended not to be discussed openly. From now on, in addition to increased transparency, debate over systems and procedures will be required.

The second reason for the opacity of the financial systems of international organizations is the lack of transparency regarding transfers of funds between them. For example, the UNDP is an organization providing funds for technical assistance by the UN system, and it has traditionally transferred funds for the implementation of technical assistance programmes to a variety of specialized agencies, both directly and indirectly. The Global Environment Facility (GEF) has recently been conducting global environment programmes using the World Bank, the UNDP and the UN Environment Programme (UNEP) as implementing agencies. It is extremely difficult to grasp the whole picture of the flow of funds transferred to implement these programmes. In cases in which the funds transferred are understood as income of the international organizations carrying out the programmes, there is the danger that these funds will be counted twice as international public sector income: once as income of the donor international organization, and again as income of the receiving international organization.

The trend towards reform of international organizations and evaluation based on the idea of NPM

A variety of trends stressing the importance of evaluating the real activities of international organizations as a method of evaluation can be observed. Among these I will focus on and offer a limited account of the introduction of results-based budgeting (RBB) and the Millennium Development Goals, which have received considerable attention.

The introduction of results-based budgeting

With the inauguration of Secretary-General Kofi Annan in 1997, the United Nations commenced management reforms, against the backdrop of a worldwide wave of reform in management.[3] The major element in these reforms was the trial introduction of RBB into the UN system. Secretary-General Annan proposed a results-based style of budgeting in his report entitled "Renewing the United Nations: A Programme for Reform", presented in July 1997.[4] Consequently, there was a shift from input-based to results-based budgeting, with an emphasis on the transition from micromanagement to macromanagement and the need to measure performance. In a proposal made in October 1999,[5] Annan suggested a gradual approach; he proposed the introduction of performance indicators for the 2002–2003 budget, while indicating that it was not necessary immediately to change financial regulations or the rules and regulations governing programme planning. Finally, the introduction of RBB was decided in a resolution of the UN General Assembly in January 2001, on the conditions that the external factors affecting the results be identified in advance, the level of detail of input data be maintained, the division between personnel expenses and other expenses be contingent on the agreement of the General Assembly and the standards and decisions of the General Assembly be strictly respected when the flexibility of the system was exercised.[6] An important element of the management reforms was the introduction of flexibility in financial affairs in place of the stricter control of the evaluation of results, but the General Assembly, which feared an increase in the Secretariat's powers of discretion, approved the introduction of RBB only once restrictions had been placed on the widening of powers of discretion. The reform was therefore incomplete, but it was decided that results-oriented budgeting would be introduced in each of the UN organizations from the 2002–2003 budget.

Because the system has been in place for only a few years, trial and error is still being used to determine what to employ as indicators for results. There is a strong inclination to set the results in a range enabling the person concerned to take responsibility, so in many cases results remain at the output level. There is still insufficient effort being put into the creation of indicators which conform to a variety of business environments, as was raised earlier as an issue.

The introduction of the Millennium Development Goals

Meanwhile, independently of the changes discussed above, the UN Millennium Declaration was adopted at the UN Millennium Summit held in September 2000, leading to the establishment of the Millennium Development Goals, which brought together objectives agreed on at a variety of global conferences in the 1990s. The goals were to eradicate extreme poverty and hunger; achieve universal primary education; promote gender equality and empower women; reduce child mortality; improve maternal health; combat HIV/AIDS, malaria and other diseases; ensure environmental sustainability; and create a global partnership for development. As far as possible, specific target values were established under these broad headings. For example, with regard to the reduction of the child mortality rate, the target was established as a two-thirds reduction against 1990 figures in the mortality rate of children under five by 2015.

The fact of moving beyond output to establish specific target values relating to outcome was significant. However, as was the case with the targets established by the global conferences quoted by the Millennium Development Goals, the bases for specific numbers were not well elaborated. In addition, it has been announced that there will be a partial examination of progress towards the targets every year, and the first comprehensive review was carried out in 2005, five years after the establishment of the goals.[7] Many issues remain to be resolved with respect to the establishment of a system for evaluating outcomes.

Reform of the financial systems of international organizations

The issue of extra-budgetary funds outlined above has been acknowledged and discussed in numerous forums. For example, following an enquiry by UN Secretary-General Boutros Boutros-Ghali, the Independent Advisory Group on UN Finances (chaired by Paul Volcker and Shijuro Ogata) submitted a report entitled "Financing an Effective United Nations" in February 1993, which recommended enhanced regulation and management of voluntary donations.[8] However, no definite action has been taken on the issue of extra-budgetary funds.

In individual organizations the question of dependence on extra-budgetary funds, and particularly extra-budgetary funds with a very limited purpose, came to the forefront. For example, formally speaking, almost the entire income of the UNHCR is derived from extra-budgetary funds. The issue was that, among them, the ratio of special programmes with a limited purpose had increased against general programmes which can be used to achieve the overall goals of the UNHCR. In 1993, for example, the budget for special programmes, at $818 million, was more than twice the $311 million budget of the general programmes. It was therefore thought that the ratio of the budget going to general programmes should be raised, with the result that in 1999 general programmes had $327 million compared to $585 million for special programmes. In 2000 the accounts system was changed, and the distinction between general programmes and special programmes was eliminated, leaving annual programmes, supplemental programmes and the Junior Professional Officer (JPO) Programme. However, this change in the accounts system was merely nominal and was not accompanied by any real change; funds were earmarked for specific purposes, and the problem of extra-budgetary funding was merely concealed.

In addition, systems for the evaluation of projects conducted by international organizations in the field of development are being introduced. For example, at the World Bank, under James Wolfensohn's presidency, a report entitled "Annual Review of Development Effectiveness" has been published since 1997. This review measures the outcome of projects, their sustainability and their impact on institution building. These various elements are combined to form a comprehensive indicator of project performance. However, there are limitations: it is an internal evaluation, concrete criteria are generally not made clear and, while it purports to discuss outcome, what it shows is closer to output.

At the UNDP, in addition to the standard annual evaluation report, the "Result-Oriented Annual Report" (ROAR), which reflects results-based management, has been submitted since 2000. This report indicates the percentage of projects that achieved their goals. The ROAR offers results on the basis of clear evaluation criteria and procedures, but, of course, the limitation remains that this is a self-evaluation, and the definition of outcome is extremely close to that of output.

Analysis and recommendations concerning management of international organizations as a basis for enhancing accountability[9]

Increased transparency in flow of funds and provision of information that is continuously comparable

The funding of international organizations, including extra-budgetary funds and the transfer of funds between organizations, must be made transparent. In recent years, following the introduction of RBB, changes have been made in a variety of areas, including the formatting of budget documents, but mechanisms are still required to ensure the transparency of the flow of funds.

Furthermore, there is the issue of basic information regarding input and output not being provided in a form that can be compared over time. It has become clear that although budget documents are formulated annually, there are cases in which numerical values cannot be compared over time because of frequent changes in the categories used in budget or programme classification. Ironically, discontinuities in data of this type can often be observed as a result of the changes in budget documents observed following the introduction of RBB in 2002–2003 budgets. On the one hand, it is important to continue to improve information regarding financial programmes to make it easy for citizens and others concerned to understand. On the other hand, because time-series information is indispensable from the point of view of evaluation, the provision of information that can be compared over time is recommended. Moreover, to enable international organizations to be compared, the establishment of a method of rendering accounts information which is consistent from organization to organization is recommended.

Development and application of evaluation indicators applicable to diverse areas of activity

If an international organization is to be managed as a system, conscious and continuous efforts must be made to determine indicators for evaluation. However, indicators are frequently established hastily and without an essential understanding of the activities of the organization, making evaluation ineffective. Indicators need to be established which are applicable to international organizations involved in a diverse range of activities and are based on a comprehensive and explicit analysis and understanding of the management environments in a wide range of international organizations. The first step in this direction would be to attempt to determine performance indicators suited to a diverse range of fields and activities.

The problem of over-emphasis on evaluation: The importance of a variable which is difficult to measure

The establishment of output and outcome indicators and their employment in evaluation wherever possible, as attempted in this research, is essential to the management of international organizations as systems. However, although it may at first sound like a contradiction of what has been stated so far, there is also some danger in pursuing evaluation as an end in itself.

For example, in the field of security the provision of a forum is extremely important from the political perspective – that is, from the perspective of legitimization. This function can be evaluated indirectly in an increase in the number of times the Security Council is convened or the number of resolutions which are passed, but it is difficult to show the outcome of these mechanisms quantitatively. In the development field also, multilateral organizations like the World Bank or the UNDP give the official justification to, that is to say legitimize, general development policy. Although these functions are not compatible with quantitative evaluation, they are nevertheless important.

With respect to normal programmes, there are those which are easy to evaluate clearly and those which are not. For example, as shown by the debate between the vertical approach and the horizontal approach, which became visible in the policy disputes between UNICEF and the WHO, as well as the policy dispute within the WHO, the vertical approach which establishes clear goals from the top down frequently deals with only one side of the issues, and there is the danger that by its very nature it will aim only at the solution of that one side.[10]

Furthermore, the analysis of degree of contribution, which shows how responsible a specific international organization is for a shared outcome, is extremely difficult. Therefore, practically speaking, it probably makes sense to concentrate on evaluation at the output level.

Creation of unified actors for evaluation: Revitalizing general assemblies and councils or boards of directors as the first step

As discussed in the section concerning the Millennium Goals, the process of evaluation is not completed with the establishment of indicators; evaluation must be monitored in a unified manner, and a functioning system must be created on this basis. Because there are times when multiple international organizations contribute towards a single goal (for example, the goals of UNICEF and the WHO with respect to outcomes showed significant overlap in the field of health promotion, and also formed part of the development goals of the UNDP and the World Bank), a system for coordination between the international organizations becomes necessary. In view of this, the executive committee that was established under Secretary-General Kofi Annan is of great interest. The committee is made up of the Executive Committee on Peace and Security, the Executive Committee on Humanitarian Affairs, the UN Development Group and the Executive Committee on Economic and Social Affairs. In the formation of the new executive committee, it was presupposed that these committees would function to coordinate the international organizations that formed their respective fields.

However, as the number of international organizations under these executive committees increases, each one bringing with it a board of directors or a council and the governments of the Member States which dominate it, they cease to function effectively as coordinating committees. There is also an argument to the effect that duplication of the functions of international organizations is useful in inducing competition and thus increasing their level of activity. If this is so, then what is important is activating the general assembly or board of directors or council of each international organization, which are made up of the representatives of each member nation functioning as joint chief managers; this is especially true of the general assemblies or boards of directors or councils of the United Nations and the World Bank, which can conduct debates from a comprehensive perspective. If the boards of directors or councils and general assemblies of international organizations were able to change, many things would be possible. For this reason, it is hoped that schemes which stimulate more substantive debate in general assemblies or on boards of directors or councils are put into effect, at both the institutional and the management levels.

From evaluator to evaluated: The possibility of third-party evaluation of Member States

Member States frequently function in the role of evaluators, and attempt to evaluate international organizations (that is, the Secretariat). However, as has been stated many times, the absolute volume of resources invested in international organizations is low; what is more, the effectiveness of an international organization actually changes according to the manner in which a Member State behaves. To put it another way, when an international organization is evaluated, Member States should not act as external evaluators, but should themselves be evaluated from the perspective of their contributions. However, it is rather difficult for the secretariat of an international organization to say this to a Member State functioning as one of its managers. Therefore, it will be sometimes meaningful to construct a third-party organization that can externally evaluate the contribution of each member to international organizations.

Notes

1. For the basic idea of NPM see Hood, Christopher (1991) "Public Management for All Seasons?", *Public Administration* 69 (Spring), pp. 3–20.
2. See Tadokoro, Masayuki (1996) *Kokuren zaisei* (*UN Finances*), Tokyo: Yuhikaku; Shiroyama, Hideaki (1994) "Kokusai gyoseigaku (International Public Administration)", in Masaru Nishio and Michio Muramatsu, eds, *Koza gyoseigaku, Daiikkan: Gyosei no hatten* (*Course in Public Administration, Vol. 1: The Development of Administration*), Tokyo: Yuhikaku, pp. 252–255, at pp. 254–255.
3. Shiroyama, Hideaki (2002) "Kokuren zaisei shisutemu no genjo to kadai tayo na tekio to manejimento kaikaku no kokoromi (Present Status and Problems of the UN Financial System: An Experiment in Adaptive Strategies and Management Reform)", in *Nihon Kokusai Rengo Gakkai, Kokuren kenkyu daisango: Gurobaru akutaa toshite no kokuren jimukyoku* (*Japan Association for UN Studies, UN Research, No. 3: The UN Secretariat as a Global Actor, Japan Association for UN Studies*), Tokyo: Kokusaishoin, pp. 209–211.
4. Annan, Kofi (1997) "Renewing the United Nations: A Programme for Reform", UN Doc. A/51/950, July
5. Annan, Kofi (1999) "Results-Based Budgeting", UN Doc. A/54/456, October.
6. UN General Assembly (2001) Resolution A/RES/55/231, January.
7. UN General Assembly (2001) "Road Map Towards the Implementation of the United Nations Millennium Declaration", UN Doc. A/56/326, 6 September.
8. Ogata, Shijuro and Paul Volcker (1993) "Financing an Effective United Nations: Report of the Independent Advisory Group on UN Finances", Ford Foundation, New York, April; Ogata, Shijuro (1993) "Kokuren zaisei no kyoka e kaku kuni no kyoryoku o uttaeru (An Appeal for International Cooperation to Strengthen UN Finances)", *Sekai Shuho* (*World Weekly*), 3 August.
9. The analysis and recommendations in this section are based on Tadokoro, Masayuki and Hideaki Shiroyama, eds (2004) *Kokusaikikan to Nihon* (*International Organization and Japan*), Tokyo: Nihonkeizaihyoronsha.
10. Siddiqi, Javed (1995) *World Health and World Politics*, London: Hurst & Co. pp. 126, 166, 190; Beigbeder, Yves (2001) *New Challenges for UNICEF*, New York: Palgrave.

8

A ladder of accountability: Analysis of subconcepts of managerial accountability in the United Nations

Ikuyo Hasuo

Introduction

Why accountability in the United Nations?

Public administration within the United Nations[1] is neither sufficiently transparent nor easily comprehensible. In fact, it is largely influenced by the complexity and technicality of modern administrative structures, by the diversity of international administration and by the confidentiality of international diplomacy.

Despite attempts by the UN Secretariat to expand and transform administrative activities rapidly, throughout the 1990s measures to strengthen internal administrative management and control lagged considerably. In response to repeated requests made by certain countries (most notably the United States, which did not hide its irritation at the situation[2]), in 1994 the United Nations established the Office of Internal Oversight Services with a mandate to strengthen the organization's internal audit function.[3] However, public audit is primarily of an *ex post* nature; hence this effort alone was not sufficient to improve the overall administrative management and effectiveness of the institution. Inaugurated as the UN Secretary-General in 1997, Kofi Annan immediately tried to introduce into the United Nations new public management (NPM),[4] which was a new method of administrative management prevalent in the Organisation for Economic Co-operation and Development (OECD) member countries

Envisioning reform: Enhancing UN accountability in the twenty-first century, Kuyama and Fowler (eds), United Nations University Press, 2009, ISBN 978-92-808-1170-4

at the time. In July 1997 Secretary-General Annan initiated the first comprehensive reform plan in the report "Renewing the United Nations: A Programme for Reform".[5] In it, Annan proposed that, for the first time, the United Nations adopt results-based budgeting (RBB),[6] which was a method based on the technique of "performance measurement".[7] This initiative opened the door for the UN Secretariat gradually to transform its traditional management into results-based management.

In spite of these administrative reform efforts, however, the UN General Assembly summit meeting in September 2005, which celebrated the sixtieth anniversary of the UN foundation, strongly demanded accountability within the Organization.[8] The demand was triggered mainly by the corruption scandals resulting from the Iraq UN Oil-for-Food Programme,[9] which was intended to provide humanitarian relief to the Iraqi people who were affected by the economic sanctions imposed by the UN Security Council. Under resolution 706[10] the Security Council permitted Iraq to export a quota of oil, with the revenue then being used to purchase humanitarian goods such as food and medical supplies, all under UN supervision. However, on account of various scandals related to this programme, not only was the administrative capability of the United Nations questioned, but the credibility of governance *per se* by the United Nations came under suspicion.

Facing such a symbolic incident, one that drove UN credibility into rapid decline, a less-politicized approach from the perspective of sound principles of public administration might be a major step forward. Moreover, a debate is needed not only on what the United Nations can do to promote international peace and security, but also, and equally important, on how the United Nations should promote international peace and security. Put another way, scholars should increasingly focus upon public administration issues, analysing the position of the United Nations as one of the principal agents in global governance.

How to address the issue of accountability

When one examines this issue from this administrative viewpoint, the concept of "accountability" increases in importance. It should be noted as a caveat, however, that accountability is a very elusive concept and is used in diverse contexts.[11] As Edward Luck and others have noted in the preceding chapters, two major ideological strands exist in the notion of modern accountability: "political accountability" and "managerial accountability".[12]

Each of these strands has separately developed from its own historical origin, and although both strands are important, this chapter will focus mainly on clarifying how the concept of managerial accountability applies within the United Nations. Historically this concept has been greatly influenced by the management methods prevalent in each time period. For example, in the domestic public sector the change of administrative management methods in central or local governments largely defined the concept. The same could be true of the United Nations as well. It is thus important to examine how trends in internal management methods within the United Nations, such as budget systems or human resources management systems, shifted at the initiative of the Secretaries-General or the governing bodies.

When one searches for historical analysis of comprehensive administrative-management methods in the United Nations, it is surprising to discover that none exists. This chapter therefore represents an attempt to explore a method of examining UN administration from a historical perspective, by focusing on the changes in the subconcepts of managerial accountability in the United Nations over time.

This chapter assesses this issue in sequence. The first section searches for a fundamental concept of managerial accountability in the United Nations. By applying a general concept of accountability in the public sector to the United Nations, it identifies the principal actors within the concept of managerial accountability in the United Nations and the relationship among these actors. The second section examines the historical transition of the subconcepts of managerial accountability in the United Nations by referring to a hypothesis called the ladder of accountability, proposed by J. D. Stewart.[13] Finally, the UN model of a ladder of accountability is clarified. Recommendations are made about subjects that need to be examined in the future.

The fundamental concept of managerial accountability

The fundamental concept of accountability

Since accountability is a very elusive notion, the fundamental concept must be clarified to create a basis for further discussion. The concept of accountability requires the existence of at least two actors; one actor giving an account to another actor who receives it.[14] In British public auditing theory, Leslie Normanton defined accountability as *liability* to reveal, explain and justify what one does: how one discharges responsibilities, financial or other, whose several origins may be political, constitutional, hierarchical or contractual.[15] In this definition the concepts to reveal, explain and justify were all defined within one notion of liability.

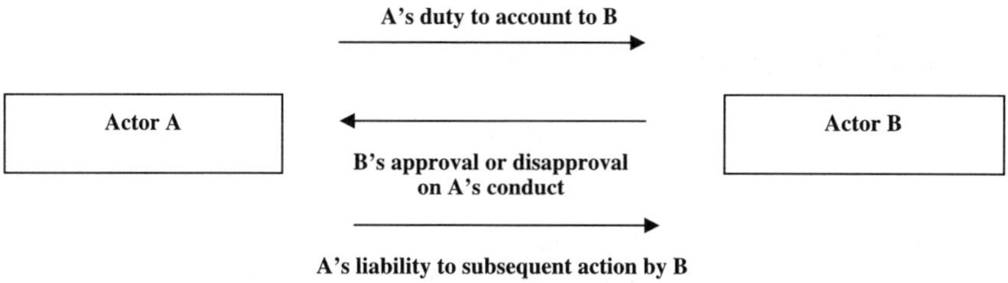

Figure 8.1 The fundamental concept of accountability

Fidelma White and Kathryn Hollingsworth, however, expressed these concepts to disclose, explain and justify within one notion of duty, instead of liability, in the following definition.[16] They analysed the constitutional role of the British public sector audit, and proposed that the fundamental concept of accountability consists of two elements: a person A has a *duty* to render an account to another person B, which discloses, explains and justifies A's conduct; and the *liability* of A to subsequent action by B in the event that B disapproves of A's conduct.[17]

This chapter will principally follow the definition provided by White and Hollingsworth. In a two-party relationship, the fundamental concept of accountability thus consists of *duty* and *liability*, as expressed in figure 8.1.

Two historical strands of the concept of accountability

Two historical strands exist within the modern concept of accountability – political accountability and managerial accountability. Each originated separately, and each followed its own historical development.

The origin of the concept of political accountability is found in ancient Athens, when that city-state was governed by direct democracy during the fifth century BC.[18] Here accountability took its simplest form; it was conducted by means of a face-to-face relationship.[19] However, later, under the medieval feudal system, accountability was not viewed as a means of democratic control of the administration.[20] By the nineteenth century John Stuart Mill at last developed a more modern notion of political accountability in a representative democracy.[21]

As for the concept of managerial accountability, one must look further back in history than for the concept of political accountability – as far back as 4000 BC in ancient Babylonia.[22] The present form of managerial accountability finds its origins in fiscal accountability.[23] Unlike political accountability, the most distinctive feature of managerial accountability is that, as a neutral, technical exercise, it can be found within any kind of political framework.[24]

The fundamental concept of managerial accountability in government

The two ideological strands of the concept of accountability continue to be evident in the present time as political accountability and managerial accountability, respectively. The core consideration of this chapter is managerial accountability. It is a form of accountability internal to organizations, and it involves the delegation of some discretionary decision-making powers.[25] The relationship of delegation of authority exists multidimensionally in any organization. The same point can be applied to the managerial accountability relationship in government. When one analyses managerial accountability in government, therefore, it is important to consider the levels at which the delegation of authority occurs.

White and Hollingsworth focused their attention on the relationship between *government* defined in a narrow sense and *government* defined in a broad sense.[26] They defined *government* in a narrow sense as elected politicians holding office, or, put more simply, ministers. Their broader definition of *government* includes "not only ministers but also the whole range of public organizations such as departments, agencies and non-departmental public bodies, along with the civil servants and other officials who staff them".[27]

Based on these definitions, the fundamental concept of managerial accountability in government is described as follows.[28] The first element consists of the *duty* of government in a broad sense (actor A) to render an account to government in a narrow sense (actor B), which discloses, explains and justifies A's conduct. The second element consists of the *liability* of A to subsequent actions by B, in the event that B disapproves of A's conduct. This relationship of accountability is presented in figure 8.2.

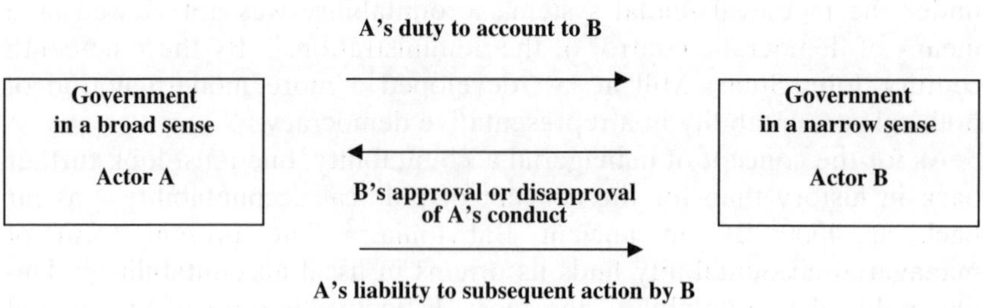

Figure 8.2 The fundamental concept of managerial accountability in government

The fundamental concept of managerial accountability in the United Nations

Managerial accountability in the United Nations is a form of accountability that is internal to the Secretariat. The internal management of any organization, including the United Nations, is usually structured multidimensionally. This chapter, however, focuses on a specific relationship of the delegation of authority within the United Nations. It looks at the most representative example – a relationship in the United Nations between what corresponds to government in a narrow sense and what corresponds to government in a broad sense. First, we must assess which UN actors correspond to government in its narrow and broad senses. Following the definition provided by Fidelma White and Kathryn Hollingsworth, the actor that represents government in a narrow sense in the case of the United Nations is the UN Secretary-General and high-ranking officials, such as the Deputy Secretaries-General, the Under-Secretaries-General and the Assistant Secretaries-General.[29] Further, again following the definition by White and Hollingsworth, government in a broad sense in the United Nations includes not only the UN Secretary-General and high-ranking officials but also the whole range of the United Nations and its subsidiary organs, such as the UNDP and UNFPA, along with the international civil servants and other officials who staff them.

Second, we must examine elements of the fundamental concept of managerial accountability in the United Nations. Here it is useful to apply the managerial concept of the domestic public sector to the United Nations. The fundamental concept of managerial accountability in the United Nations consists of the relationship between government in a broad sense (actor A) and government in a narrow sense (actor B). The first series consists of the *duty* of actor A to render an account to the UN Secretary-General (actor B), which discloses, explains and justifies A's conduct. The second series consists of the *liability* of A to subsequent action by B, in the event that B disapproves of A's conduct (fig. 8.2).

A ladder of accountability in the United Nations

Historically speaking, various dimensions exist in the subconcepts of managerial accountability in the United Nations. As I explore the historical shift of the subconcepts of managerial accountability in UN administration, this section will first analyse a hypothesis that explains the relationship among the subconcepts of accountability.

"A ladder of accountability" by J. D. Stewart

The concept of managerial accountability is internal to organizations, regardless of whether the institution is public or private. At present, scholars typically subdivide the concept of managerial accountability and discuss its many dimensions. Although the methods of classifying these subconcepts are of virtually infinite variety, this chapter adopts four representative subconcepts of managerial accountability.

The first category is *accountability for probity and legality*. Accountability for probity is defined as being "concerned with the avoidance of malfeasance".[30] Accountability for legality is "concerned with ensuring that the powers given by the law are not exceeded".[31] The second category is *process accountability*, which considers "whether the procedures used to perform the research were adequate, in terms of time and effort spent on the work and whether experiments were carried out as promised".[32] The third category is *performance accountability*, which is "concerned with whether a performance achieved meets required standards".[33] The fourth category is *programme accountability*, which is concerned "with the work carried out and whether or not it has met the goals set for it".[34]

In order to understand mutual relationships of these subconcepts of managerial accountability, J. D. Stewart proposed a model called "a ladder of accountability"[35] (see fig. 8.3). Stewart sets out the subconcepts of public sector accountability as a ladder. The first stage at the bottom is *accountability for probity and legality*; the second stage is *process accountability*; the third stage is *performance accountability*; the fourth stage is *programme accountability*; and the fifth stage, at the top of the ladder, is *policy accountability*. Policy accountability assesses whether or not policy activities have effectively achieved policy objectives.

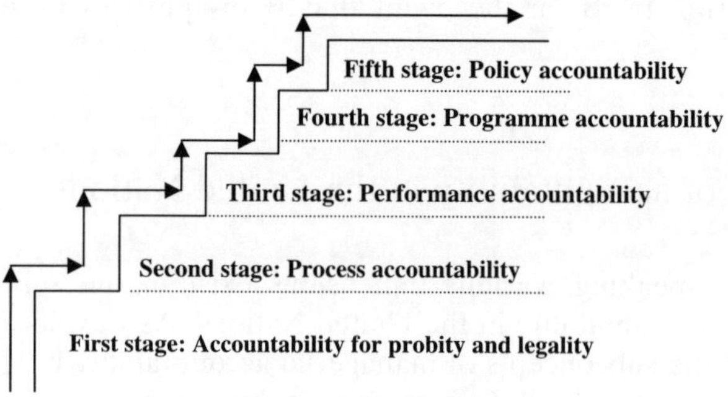

Figure 8.3 Stewart's model

Transition of the subconcepts of managerial accountability in the United Nations

This section represents an attempt to clarify a historical shift of the subconcepts of managerial accountability in the United Nations with regard to Stewart's model. I thus propose to divide the history of the UN administration into three different time periods, 1945–1981, 1981–2002 and 2002–present, and to explore the practice of administrative methods in each period.[36]

First period (1945–1981): Accountability for probity and legality, and process accountability

The key feature of the first period was the predominance of traditional administrative management based on a principle of constitutional government. Accountability for probity and process accountability were sought during this period.

In 1993 the Joint Inspection Unit (JIU) claimed that compliance accountability and process accountability had been dominant to that time.[37] Compliance accountability is a type of accountability that values observance of legality, probity, regulations and rules. In this sense, compliance accountability closely resembles accountability for probity.

In analysing UN administration with reference to Stewart's model, one might have expected to see a shift to performance accountability at the third stage, following process accountability at the second stage (see fig. 8.3). The UN administration, however, did not shift to a third stage which values pursuit of efficiency, but moved directly to programme accountability, which values effectiveness. Why did such a shift fail to occur in the United Nations, while pursuit of efficiency played such an important role in public administration in most developed countries?

First of all, at the time the influence of American administrative values should have strongly affected UN administration. During the Great Depression and the Second World War demand increased for social welfare improvements in the United States, which, in turn, led to scrutiny of the effectiveness of the programmes put into place. Thus, immediately after the Second World War when the United Nations was founded, the search for efficiency in the United States was no longer as dominant as it had been earlier in the twentieth century.

Second, at the time of its creation the United Nations was not expected to perform various large-scale administrative functions, such as peacekeeping operations and development assistance. The founders originally intended it to be a forum offering an opportunity for multilateral diplomatic negotiations.[38] Consequently, the pursuit of efficiency in administration was not emphasized, as it is today. In 1974, towards the end of the first period, programme budgeting was introduced into the United Nations.[39] Programme budgeting aimed to combine the functions of *ex ante* planning/programme analysis and budgetary processing. In the programme budget, for instance, instead of solely indicating objects of expenditure, as in the previous traditional budget, every budget unit had to indicate *outputs*, *objectives* and *accomplishments expected*.

I consider the following internal and external factors to be influential in introducing programme budgeting into the United Nations. First, as an internal factor, the initial financial crisis of the United Nations in the 1960s, resulting from the events in the Suez and Congo, should have triggered a drastic budgetary reform. In those days the budgetary debates turned out to be another battlefield for East/West confrontation. In order to resolve the deadlock, the United Nations established the Ad Hoc Committee of Experts to Examine the Finances of the UN and the Specialized Agencies.[40] In 1966 this committee made various recommendations, including that programme budgeting be introduced.[41]

Second, as an external factor, the roots of UN programme budgeting can be traced back to the "planning-programming-budgeting system" (PPBS), which originated in the United States.[42] In 1961 the Department of Defense under the Kennedy administration first successfully implemented PPBS. Its broader range of adoption in the federal government occurred in 1965 under the Johnson administration. The US government, with its experience with PPBS, pushed for it to be introduced in the United Nations as well.

However, serious resistance occurred not only in the UN Secretariat, which was anxious about an increased administrative burden, but also among the Member States, which feared the loss of vested interests in the budgetary process.[43] In 1974 the United Nations at last successfully introduced programme budgeting with the support of powerful advocates, such as Maurice Bertrand, a former JIU inspector.[44] Ironically, however, as early as 1971 the United States under the Nixon administration, despite the fact that it had been an original advocate, virtually withdrew from PPBS when the United Nations at last adopted it.[45]

Thus in the first time period the United Nations did not shift to performance accountability, with its close attention to the pursuit of efficiency, for various reasons. The United States significantly influenced administration at the United Nations for much of this period, and public administration within the United States was not particularly focused on efficiency at the time. In addition, with certain exceptions, such as the peacekeeping operations in the Congo in the early 1960s, the United Nations was not performing the large-scale administrative functions that it does today, which might have naturally led to scrutiny of the efficiency of the Organization. Instead, the United Nations jumped forward to programme budgeting, drawing on the experience with PPBS in the US government.

Second period (1981–2002): Programme accountability

Reinforcement of an internal programme evaluation system in the United Nations characterized the second period, which was largely focused on programme accountability. Two factors are proposed as the main driving forces which reinforced the evaluation systems in the United Nations at that time.

First, the emergence of the North/South problem in the 1970s in the United Nations caused a division of the Member States. The introduction of programme budgeting in 1974 spotlighted *ex ante* planning at the end of the first period. However, *ex ante* planning required the Member States to be in accord on policy priorities. In the 1970s, however, the North/South problem was becoming a new axis of confrontation, and such a division of Member States posed an obstacle for *ex ante* planning processes.

The second factor which influenced reinforcement of internal evaluation was a shift of administrative values in the US Congress from the end of the 1960s to the early 1970s, from *ex ante* planning to *ex post* evaluation. Although PPBS successfully combined a planning process and a budgetary process, it failed to develop processes such as *ex post* evaluation and subsequent examinations based on such evaluation. Then, as part of its reform initiatives in the 1970s, the US Congress introduced programme evaluation with the purpose of reinforcing the surveillance function of Congress. As one might expect, the United Nations was not excluded from being affected by such a shift of values within the US Congress.[46]

The US Department of State began applying political pressures to the United Nations, with the cooperation of the Joint Inspection Unit. It resulted in various General Assembly resolutions from 1981, requesting the UN Secretary-General to reinforce the evaluation system and strengthen the responsible offices within the Secretariat.[47] Consequently, a series of measures for strengthening internal evaluation were adopted one after another.[48] In 1982 the UN General Assembly at last adopted "Regulations Governing Programme Planning, the Programme Aspects of the Budget, the Monitoring of Implementation and the Methods of Evaluation",[49] and greatly advanced steps towards institutionalizing internal evaluation methods in the Secretariat. The second period thus represented an attempt to improve programme accountability by reinforcing the evaluation system in the United Nations.

Third period (2002–present): Performance-based accountability

The third period represents a gradual introduction of results-based budgeting into the UN Secretariat, which started in 2002 and which I see as indicative of "performance-based accountability".[50] Samuel Paul suggested a useful definition of performance-based accountability: "holding individuals and organizations responsible for performance measured as objectively as possible".[51] Performance-based accountability in the United Nations is thus considered as being aimed at avoiding authoritarian management systems that are based on the traditional concentration of authority in the hands of higher-ranked officials. It instead underlines affirmation of a liberal management based on the delegation of authority and guidance.[52]

Again, J. D. Stewart's "ladder of accountability" model predicts that the UN administration would shift to policy accountability at the fifth stage during the third period, after pursuing programme accountability at the fourth stage during the second period (see fig. 8.3). In fact, however, it shifted to performance-based accountability at the third level. Why did this occur?

Two factors should have affected such a transition of accountability. The first is persistent political pressures by the Member States, calling for curtailing the rapid increase in the UN budget, mainly triggered by the frequent creation of peacekeeping operations.[53] The second factor is that the UN administration of the 1981–2002 period, despite its pursuit, had actually fallen short of achieving programme accountability at the fourth stage (fig. 8.3). The United Nations had failed to institutionalize an evaluation system sufficiently in the second period, which was a prerequisite of achieving programme accountability.[54] The United Nations here laid the groundwork for further institutionalizing programme evaluation, by making it possible to compare an actual output (or outcome) with an expected output (or outcome) on a project base. That is, the United Nations of the third period, through pursuit of performance-based accountability, consolidated a necessary precondition for attaining programme accountability, which the United Nations of the second period had failed to accomplish.

I would suggest that one particular driving force resulted in introducing performance-based accountability into the United Nations. Throughout the 1990s, in response to pressures of new changes such as globalization as well as fiscal and structural problems, OECD countries had to tackle extensive public sector reform.[55] Although methods under this approach varied, the common feature was a focus on achieving results. The approach was thus called "managing for results", later becoming "results-based management", in which the key element was performance measurement.

With respect to development assistance, the phenomenon of aid fatigue had occurred in Western countries throughout the 1980s, caused by issues such as the aggravation of fiscal balance and international balance-of-payment problems. It was further accelerated by the fall of the Berlin Wall at the end of the 1980s that eliminated the East/West confrontation. Under pressure from their taxpayers, OECD governments increasingly became interested in assessing the effectiveness of development aid. The "managing for results" broadly adopted in public sector reform in OECD countries also expanded into other areas, such as bilateral official development assistance (ODA). The pursuit of results put more pressure on ODA outcomes and effectiveness, gradually reinforcing evaluation activities and eventually incorporating them as an integrated part of ODA. This phenomenon spread to multilateral development assistance, carried out by organizations such as the World Bank.[56] Such external pressure served not only to reinforce the evaluation function of programme activities, but also to improve the internal administrative management of multilateral development aid organizations,[57] including the World Bank and the UNDP.[58]

The pressure was felt by the UN Secretariat as well. At the beginning of his term, Secretary-General Annan tried to implement administrative reforms in the United Nations, largely influenced by new public management. In July 1997 Annan presented the first comprehensive reform proposal, which was aimed at introducing results-based budgeting applying performance-measurement techniques.

Demand for managing for results gradually affected the entire UN system, including the UN specialized agencies.[59] As a pioneer in the UN system, the World Intellectual Property Organization (WIPO), a UN specialized agency, decided to introduce results-based budgeting in the 1998–1999 fiscal year.[60] The UN development assistance agencies were also increasingly exposed to the rising demand by OECD countries for concrete results regarding development assistance. In order to respond to these voices, the UNDP decided in 1998 to develop a framework to measure and evaluate results of programmes, and to introduce results-based budgeting in 1999.[61] Similarly, the UNFPA introduced such budgeting in 2000 by the multi-year funding framework.[62]

In January 2001, after three years of debate, the UN General Assembly adopted a resolution that decided to introduce results-based budgeting gradually into the UN Secretariat.[63] The Assembly decided not to modify immediately the various related administrative rules, even though this was in fact needed, and instead gradually introduced the first results-based budget in the 2002–2003 fiscal year.[64]

Conclusion

To sum up the historical transition of the subconcepts of managerial accountability in the United Nations, it is clarified as follows: UN administration period I (1945–1981) was characterized as accountability for

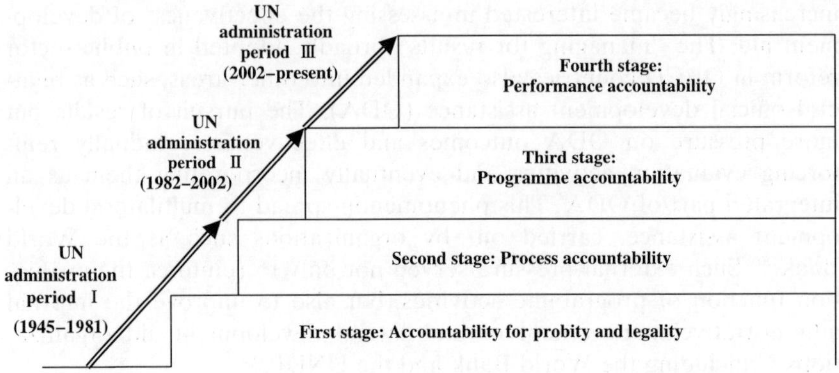

Figure 8.4 Conclusion: UN model of a ladder of accountability

probity and legality as well as process accountability; UN administration period II (1982–2002) corresponded to programme accountability; lastly, UN administration period III (2002–present) is perceived as pursuing performance-based accountability. Such a transition of subconcepts of managerial accountability is expressed as a ladder of accountability in the United Nations, indicated in figure 8.4.[65]

It was also confirmed that at present new public management serves as a basis for the concept of managerial accountability in the United Nations. With further implementation of new public management, what kinds of other subjects will inevitably be brought to the UN administration to be examined in the future?

It must be understood first that results-based management focuses on overall administrative management. This method is not confined to budgeting techniques, as is the case with the United Nations at present, but comprehensively covers the domain of administrative management, including for instance human resources management and the administration of justice. Further promotion of the delegation of authority in human resources management should be a key factor for the effective advancement of results-based management, particularly in such areas as peacekeeping operations.[66] However, it is foreseen that such promotion would most likely be accompanied by a rise in frequency of litigation, which would result in further accumulation of litigation cases as well as further delays in ongoing lawsuits. These examples strongly suggest that reforms of the administration of justice will become essential in the near future.[67] However, it is still too early to examine these issues since specifics have not been formulated yet, and should be left for future consideration.

Acknowledgements

This chapter was originally delivered as a working paper prepared for the United Nations University (UNU) Tokyo Symposium on Accountability on 16–17 October 2006 at UNU House, Tokyo, Japan. It extends the argument found in Ikuyo Hasuo (2006) "The United Nations and Global Governance: The Transition of the Sub-concepts of Managerial Accountability in the United Nations", *Hitotsubashi Journal of Law and International Studies* 5, pp. 179–223.

Notes

1. In this chapter the term *United Nations* does not refer to the UN system at large, which normally includes specialized agencies, but to the UN Organization. Furthermore, although subsidiary organs such as the UN Development Programme (UNDP) are generally included in the concept of the UNO, this chapter focuses solely on the Secretariat of the UN Organization.
2. UN Doc. A/C.5/48/35, 29 November 1993, letter dated 24 November 1993 from the permanent representative of the United States of America to the United Nations addressed to the Secretary-General.
3. GA Res. 48/218 B, 29 July 1994, para. 4.
4. New public management is the term often used in the United Kingdom and New Zealand. It is also used in multilateral organizations such as the OECD, the International Monetary Fund (IMF) and the World Bank. The term public management is used mainly in the United States. In Scandinavian countries and in Germany a term equivalent to public modernization is often used.
5. UN Office of the Secretary-General (1997) "Renewing the United Nations: A Programme for Reform", UN Doc. A/51/950, 14 July.
6. UN Office of the Secretary-General (1999) "Results-based Budgeting, Annex I: Glossary of Relevant Terms", UN Doc. A/54/456, 11 October, pp. 19–20.
7. The arguments of this reform proposal contained three points: carrying out structural reform of leadership and tasks of the United Nations in order to improve administrative management and cost-effectiveness; developing a performance-oriented human resources system; and introducing results-based budgeting in order to measure programme performance.
8. Bolton, John (2005) "Open Letter on the Draft Outcome Document, 30 August 2005", available at www.un.int/usa/reform-un-jrb-ltr-manage-8-05.pdf.
9. For a good account of the Oil-for-Food Programme refer to Chesterman, Simon, Thomas Franck and David Malone (2008) *Law and Practice of the United Nations*, Oxford: Oxford University Press.
10. Security Council Resolution 706 (1991).
11. The fundamental concept of accountability is discussed below.
12. Johnson, N. (1974) "Defining Accountability", *Public Administration Bulletin* 17, pp. 3–13. There may be differences in opinions regarding the definitions of these two concepts. Note, however, that this chapter adopts the more specific definition provided by Patricia Day and Rudolf Klein. Political accountability means those with delegated authority are answerable for their actions to the people, whether directly in simple societies or indirectly in complex societies. Managerial accountability concerns making those with

delegated authority answerable for carrying out agreed tasks according to agreed criteria of performance. See Day, Patricia and Rudolf Klein (1987) *Accountabilities: Five Public Services*, London: Tavistock Publications, pp. 26–27.

13. Stewart, J. D. (1984) "The Role of Information in Public Accountability", in Anthony Hopwood and Cyril Tomkins, eds, *Issues in Public Sector Accounting*, Oxford: Philip Allan Publishers, pp. 16–18.
14. White, Fidelma and Kathryn Hollingsworth (1999) *Audit, Accountability and Government*, Oxford: Clarendon Press, p. 6.
15. Normanton, E. Leslie (1971) "Public Accountability and Audit: A Renaissance", in Bruce L. R. Smith and Douglas Chalmers Hague, eds, *Dilemma of Accountability in Modern Government: Independence versus Control*, London: Macmillan, p. 311.
16. White and Hollingsworth, note 14 above, pp. 6–7.
17. Ibid., p. 6.
18. Day and Klein, note 12 above, p.4.
19. Sinclair, Robert K. (1988) *Democracy and Participation in Athens*, Cambridge: Cambridge University Press, pp. 49–76.
20. Day and Klein, note 12 above, p. 10.
21. Mill, John Stuart ([1859] 1969) *On Liberty, Representative Government, The Subjection of Women*, London: Oxford University Press, pp. 211–212.
22. O'Reilly, Vincent M. ([1957] 1998) *Montgomery Auditing*, 12th edn, New York: John Wiley & Sons.
23. Fiscal accountability is defined by Robinson as focused "almost exclusively on the procedures by which funds are accounted for, and on the actual expenditures of funds". See Robinson, David Z. (1971) "Government Contracting for Academic Research Accountability in the American Experience", in Bruce L. R. Smith and Douglas Chalmers Hague, eds, *Dilemma of Accountability in Modern Government*, London: Macmillan, p. 111.
24. Day and Klein, note 12 above, p. 8.
25. White and Hollingsworth, note 14 above, p. 8.
26. See ibid., p. 4. For a distinction between different senses of the word *government* see Harden, Ian (1995) "Regulating Government", *Political Quarterly* 66, pp. 299–306, at p. 299.
27. White and Hollingsworth, note 14 above, p. 4.
28. Here only one example of the delegation of authority is given for convenience. In practice, the concept of managerial accountability in government is structured multidimensionally.
29. The Secretary-General is appointed by the General Assembly upon the recommendation of the Security Council. See article 97 of the UN Charter.
30. Stewart, note 13 above, p. 16.
31. Ibid., pp. 16–17.
32. Robinson, note 23 above, pp. 110–111.
33. Stewart, note 13 above, p. 17.
34. Robinson, note 23 above, p. 109.
35. Stewart, note 13 above, pp. 17–18.
36. For overall consideration, the recent historical work by Thant and Scott is recommended: Thant, Myint-U and Amy Scott (2007) *The UN Secretariat: A Brief History*, New York: International Peace Academy.
37. UN Joint Inspection Unit (1993) "Accountability and Oversight in the United Nations Secretariat", UN Doc. JIU/REP/1993/5, Geneva: p. 2, para. 9.
38. See "The Evolution of United Nations Structure for Development Assistance" in Jackson, Robert (1969) *A Study of the Capacity of the United Nations Development System*, vols I and II, Geneva: United Nations, vol. II, part II, ch. 2, paras 9–10.

39. UN General Assembly (1972) "Form of Presentation of the United Nations Budget and Duration of the Budget Cycle", GA Res. 3043, UN GAOR, A/RES3043 (XXVII), 19 December; UN General Assembly (1973) "Formulation, Review and Approval of Programmes and Budgets", GA Res. 3199, UN GAOR, A/RES3199 (XXVIII), 18 December.
40. UN General Assembly (1965) "Ad Hoc Committee of Experts to Examine the Finances of the UN and the Specialized Agencies", GA Res. 2049, UN GAOR, A/RES2049 (XX), 13 December. See also Luard, Evan (1979) *The United Nations: How it Works and What it Does*, London: Macmillan, pp. 129–130.
41. UN Doc. A/6343, 19 July 1966, paras 26–67.
42. For a historical overview of PPBS in the United States see Korb, Lawrence (1977) "The Budget Process in the Department of Defense, 1947 to 1977: The Strengths and Weaknesses of Three Systems", *Public Administration Review* 37, pp. 247–264; Wildavsky, Aaron (2003) *The Revolt Against the Masses and Other Essays on Politics and Public Policy*, New Brunswick, NJ and London: Transaction Publishers; Mosher, Frederick C. (1979) *The GAO: The Quest for Accountability in American Government*, Boulder, CO: Westview Press, p. 170.
43. Bertrand, Maurice (1996) "Organisations internationales universelles – planification, programmation, budgétisation et évaluations a l'ONU", *Annuaire Français de Droit International* 32, p. 404.
44. One of the reports produced by Maurice Bertrand may be found at UN Doc. A/7822, 3 December 1969 (JIU/REP/69/7, September).
45. Several explanations could be made for this suspension of PPBS in the United States. One could be the technical complexity and difficulty of PPBS *per se*, and another could be resistance by the US Congress, which constantly feared that its vested rights in the budgetary process might be infringed by PPBS.
46. US General Accounting Office (1987) "United Nations: Progress to Strengthen UN Internal Evaluation Systems Has Been Slow", GAO-NSIAD-87-54, 14 January.
47. Ibid.
48. UN Doc. Res. A/36/228B, 18 December 1981.
49. UN Doc. Res. A/37/234, 21 December 1982, Annex, "Regulations Governing Programme Planning, the Programme Aspects of the Budget, the Monitoring of Implementation and the Methods of Evaluation".
50. In this chapter "performance accountability" and "performance-based accountability" are intentionally distinguished. The former is used in a broader sense in which performance is pursued in diverse ways. The latter is used in a narrow sense in which the technique of performance measurement is specifically required.
51. Paul defined accountability, not performance-based accountability *per se*. Paul, Samuel (1991) "Strengthening Public Service Accountability: A Conceptual Framework", World Bank Discussion Papers, World Bank, Washington, DC, p. 2.
52. UN Joint Inspection Unit (2004) "Delegation of Authority and Accountability", UN Doc. JIU/REP/2004/7, Geneva.
53. See, for example, Hoge, Warren (2005) "The UN Adopts a 2-Year Budget, Averting a Financial Crisis", *New York Times*, 24 December, p. A10. See also US Institute of Peace (2005) *American Interests and UN Reform: Report of the Task Force on the United Nations*, Washington, DC: US Institute of Peace, available at www.usip.org/un/report/usip__un__report.pdf.
54. US General Accounting Office, note 46 above.
55. OECD (2000) *Results-based Management in the Development Cooperation Agencies: A Review of Experience*, Paris: Organisation for Economic Co-operation and Development, pp. 3–4.

56. OECD Development Cooperation Directorate (1996) *Development Cooperation 1996 Report*, Paris: Organisation for Economic Co-operation and Development, p. 107. See also World Bank (1993) *Annual Report*, Washington, DC: World Bank, p. 62.
57. OECD, note 55 above, p. 3.
58. Ibid. See also RBM in United Nations, UN Development Programme (1999) "UNDP Results Framework: Overview", UN Doc. DP/1999/CRP.4, p. 2.
59. UN Joint Inspection Unit (2004b) "Overview of the Series of Reports on Managing for Results in the United Nations System", UN Doc. JIU/REP/2004/5, Geneva, p. 3.
60. World Intellectual Property Organization (2000) "*Program Performance in the 1998–1999 Biennium*", WIPO A/35/2, 7 August, p. 1. A detailed mandate of WIPO is available at www.wipo.int/portal/index.html.en.
61. See UNDP Doc. 98/23 Executive Board Decisions and DP/1999/CRP.4, and UN Development Programme, note 58 above, p. 7.
62. In the UNFPA the Multi-Year Funding Framework was introduced in the 2000–2003 year. See UNFPA Executive Board Decision 2000/9, 2000.
63. UN General Assembly (2001) "Results-based Budgeting", UN GAOR, A/RES/51/231, 23 January.
64. Ibid.
65. This chapter focuses solely on the UN Secretariat. It therefore disregards the fact that other subsidiary organs of the United Nations (such as the UNDP) shifted to performance-based accountability prior to 2002. See UNDP Doc. 98/23, note 61 above, and others.
66. UN Joint Inspection Unit (2006) "Evaluation of Results-based Budgeting in Peacekeeping Operations", UN Doc. JIU/REP/2006/1, Geneva.
67. UN Joint Inspection Unit (2002) "Reform of the Administration of Justice in the United Nations System: Options for Higher Recourse Instances", UN Doc. JIU/REP/2002/5, Geneva; UN Joint Inspection Unit, note 52 above.

Part III

Political accountability

9

Enhancing the political accountability of the United Nations via multi-stakeholder synergy

Tatsuro Kunugi

> We must form coalitions for change, often with partners well beyond the precincts of officialdom. No shift in the way we think or act can be more critical than this: we must put people at the centre of everything we do.
>
> Finally we must spare no effort to make the United Nations a more effective instrument in the hands of the world's peoples for pursuing all three of these priorities – the fight against poverty, ignorance and disease; the fight against violence and terror; and the fight against the degradation and destruction of our common home. (Kofi Annan[1])

Introduction

The above excerpts from Kofi Annan's "Millennium Report" issued in March 2000 succinctly capture the three basic elements of the UN's political accountability: who is accountable, to whom and for what. The introduction to the report from which the first two sentences are quoted makes it clear that "We" means the United Nations as an intergovernmental organization, the Charter of which is written in the name of "we the peoples". Together with the third sentence, excerpted from the concluding paragraph of the report, it is clear that the United Nations is accountable *to* the world's peoples *for* making the United Nations a more effective instrument in their hands for pursuing by themselves all the three priorities. A people-centred participative approach is also implicitly emphasized.

Envisioning reform: Enhancing UN accountability in the twenty-first century, Kuyama and Fowler (eds), United Nations University Press, 2009, ISBN 978-92-808-1170-4

Thus identification of these three elements of accountability may not be difficult, but regarding the main question as to how and/or whether accountability is observed in practice at the United Nations, there can be a variety of views and the issue becomes problematic. Depending on the context, questions may even be raised as to whether more accountability is necessarily better for the effectiveness and legitimacy of the United Nations. Questions may also be asked about the real impacts of enhanced political accountability, as distinct from its rhetoric and normative assumptions.

The thesis of this chapter is that the United Nations will benefit from enhanced political accountability, which I define as an emerging principle of global governance transcending the existing omni-governmental multilateralism of the United Nations. Although political accountability already exists to some extent at the United Nations, far greater effort will be necessary to draw support from its multiple constituencies – member governments, parliaments, local authorities, the private sector, non-governmental organizations (NGOs) and the peoples of the world. Instead of being engulfed in the current global turmoil, the United Nations with enhanced accountability can become an agent of change by envisioning and designing the future of mankind in concert with its constituencies.

The chapter starts with comparative analysis of the concepts of political and democratic accountability as they are utilized in social campaigns and political discourse. The concepts will be further examined in reference to a declaration of accountability and other codes of conduct that facilitate the enhancement of accountability and effectiveness of global governance. Special considerations applicable to responsibility and accountability for peace and security will be addressed, with a view to overcoming some of the difficulties that lie in the pursuit of peace and security. Finally, transformative but non-structural changes proposed for strengthening the United Nations, such as multi-constituency processes and multi-stakeholder initiatives, will be analysed, since such measures would have the effect of enhancing the accountability and legitimacy of the United Nations.

Political accountability and democratic accountability

For several decades following the Second World War, the use of the terms "accountability" and "legitimacy" with reference to contemporary politics was extremely rare. During the 1980s "NGO Working Groups on the World Bank", established under the auspices of the Geneva-based

International Council of Voluntary Agencies (ICVA – one of the oldest consultative umbrella organizations), often used the term "accountability" when they criticized the World Bank for lack of accountability and transparency in its decision-making on structural adjustment lending (SAL) and development projects causing environmental degradation in the South.[2] It is an interesting fact that the frequent use of the terms in political discourse and literature started after the Cold War. As noted by James Rosenau in 1990 and further articulated in 1992,[3] the concept of legitimate authority was undergoing a shift away from the traditional criteria of legitimacy as derived from constitutional and other legal sources. The new criteria seem to share the core characteristics of democratic governance: respect for human rights, popular participation, informed consent, transparency and accountability in the exercise of power.

For the purpose of this chapter, the concept of political accountability is distinguished from that of managerial and financial accountability. Today, democratic governance is a core value and the dominant principle of governance worldwide, with the exception of several countries. In this prevailing circumstance it has become fashionable to discuss the democracy of international organizations, including the United Nations as the universal political institution. Thus scrutiny is sometimes made of the extent to which international organizations and their policy-making are governed by democratic rules. It is also assumed that conscious design for the development of international organizations should be guided by democratic principles.[4] This tendency may help to explain why "democratic accountability" and "democracy deficits" are often discussed regarding public international organizations.

Political accountability is broader than democratic accountability, as the latter, strictly speaking, may not properly apply to some categories of non-state actors, e.g. civil society organizations, associations of business, social movements, the media and academia. As these societal organizations sometimes cooperate with the activities of the United Nations, thereby forming a part of UN work, it may not be appropriate to address the overall UN work from the viewpoint of *demos kratos*, or people rule, meaning that people govern themselves. However, in view of the frequent use shown below, the terms "democratic accountability" and "democracy deficits" will be accepted in this chapter unless such use detracts from the analysis concerned.

Discussions of accountability in global institutions have often centred on the so-called "democracy deficits" or "public accountability deficits" of the World Bank, International Monetary Fund (IMF), UN Security Council and World Trade Organization (WTO). The term "accountability" refers to the right of some actors over others in such a way that the first have the right to hold the latter to a set of standards and impose sanctions if they determine that the latter have not fulfilled their responsibilities in light of those standards. Four core components of accountability are further identified: *transparency*; *answerability* (or *justification*); *compliance*; and *enforcement* (or sanctions for shortfalls in the three other components).

According to another definition, accountability is an institutionalized relationship in which the exercise of power by one set of actors is subject to responsiveness to those over whom their power is exercised. Two functional dimensions are *transparency* in reporting on the exercise and *enforceability* of responsiveness that can be imposed on power holders.[5] Most of the time neither of these two dimensions seems to be available in the case of the Security Council's political sphere. Asymmetry of only five permanent members' power *vis-à-vis* 187 other members of the United Nations apparently makes perennial deficits in democratic accountability.

Without structural reform of the Security Council, some innovative counterpoise practices against oligarchic control might be usefully devised.

- The General Assembly can more fully utilize its broad mandate relating to peace and security under articles 10 and 11 of the Charter, and the Secretary-General can perform broader functions concerning peace and security, upon request by the General Assembly as an organ of authority for conflict prevention and settlement.
- The Security Council can contribute to the broadening of the General Assembly's peace and security functions, for instance by not keeping many matters continuously under review when their emergency phase ceases.
- For enhancing transparency, taking into account the recent tendency for multi-stakeholder engagement in UN peace activities, both the Security Council and the General Assembly can act in accordance with paragraphs 171–175 of the 2005 Outcome Document[6] (concerning co-operation with parliaments, local authorities, the private sector and civil society organizations);
- Demilitarize the dominant influence of the Permanent Five by countering it with the peace-fostering influence of middle and small powers for the policy-making processes of the Security Council.

Arguments in favour of inclusionary politics or cosmopolitics to strengthen international organizations have been advanced by David Held, Robert Keohane and Joseph Nye, and Steve Charnovitz, as well as by former and present Directors-General of the WTO (Mike Moore and Pascal Lamy). Keohane and Nye observe: "Insofar as legitimacy depends on processes, accountability is central. Accountability need not take place exclusively from elected national governments with parliamentary oversight . . . They must balance greater transparency and participation with opportunities for closer ties between public leadership and constituencies."[7]

The meaning of accountability thus differs considerably depending on the context. The case of the Security Council is primarily an internal political question, whereas the WTO problem concerns closer ties between public leadership and constituencies. A great array of interests needs to be aggregated in ways that are democratically acceptable at global institutions such as the World Bank and WTO. With regard to particular issues in the WTO, for instance, constituencies in different member states may form coalitions transcending national boundaries. Thus there may exist global publics even though there is no global community as yet. Political accountability, no matter what it is called, remains purportedly advanced in the case of the International Labour Organization (ILO) due to its tripartite structure, and it has slowly improved at the World Bank and WTO. As for the United Nations, Richard Falk's general assessment may be close to the reality when he observes: "In an important sense, the challenge of the first fifty years was centered on the incorporation of non-Western states. For the next fifty years the challenge will be to incorporate non-state actors."[8]

In this context it may be recalled that Boutros Boutros-Ghali in *An Agenda for Democratization*, which was one of his last reports to the General Assembly before leaving office in December 1996, stressed the importance of promoting democratization within the architecture of the United Nations. He averred *inter alia*:

> If democratization is the most reliable way to legitimize and improve national governance, it is also the most reliable way to legitimize and improve international organization, making it more open and responsive by increasing participation, more efficient by allowing for burden sharing and more effective by allowing for comparative advantage and greater creativity.[9]

In summary, it may be said that fostering an effective and legitimate United Nations is indeed a crucial problem in today's turbulent world, and political accountability holds a key for ensuring closer ties between UN leadership and its global constituencies.

Declaration of Accountability for Global Governance

With regard to the relationship between democracy and global governance, the co-chairs of the Commission on Global Governance state in the foreword to the report *Our Global Neighborhood*:

> Global governance is not global government...We are not proposing movement towards world government, for were we to travel in that direction we could find ourselves in an even less democratic world than we have – one more accommodating to power, more reinforcing of the roles of states and governments rather than the rights of people.[10]

And the final chapter of the report underlines the world's need for enlightened leadership that can inspire people to acknowledge their responsibilities to each other, and to future generations.

These were among the key thoughts that guided those who drafted the Declaration of Accountability for Global Governance in San Francisco on the occasion of the fiftieth anniversary of the signing of the UN Charter. Some 30 NGO representatives plus several lawyers and college professors participated in the drafting of the declaration during the Citizens Conference on NGO-UN Relations, 21–24 June 1995, sponsored by Citizens Network for Sustainable Development, Rainforest Action Network and three other NGOs. Over 350 people took part in the conference, the main theme of which was the role of civil society organizations in the founding history and the future of the United Nations. A number of founders and early leaders in the development of the United Nations as well as the present executive heads and senior officials of the UN system organizations, including Secretary-General Boutros Boutros-Ghali, were invited speakers.

As I participated in the drafting of the declaration, I should like to share some information about the principal ideas embodied in it that deserve attention. It is to be noted that this was probably the first attempt by civil society leaders to identify the elements and principles of accountability applicable to actions of all partners in global governance.

At first, it was proposed that the declaration should set a standard of accountability to hold up to governments and international agencies, including the United Nations, World Bank, IMF and WTO, for developing ecologically sustainable societies. After discussions, it was agreed that the concept of accountability should apply to all actors, including civil society organizations and transnational corporations, not only in relation to sustainable development but also to all sectors of major global issues. It was pointed out that all actors, both public and private, must form a pluralized partnership for global governance. By *pluralized partnership*, as the term is used in the third preambular paragraph of the declaration,[11] is meant plural modes of vertical engagement among various actors according to the subsidiarity principle that problems would best be dealt with at the most appropriate level, from the local to the global, and horizontal engagement aimed at optimum division of labour and synergy among different actors.

The concept of *synergy*, which has often been used in social science and business administration in recent years, was discussed by the drafters of the declaration. It was generally agreed synergy means that the effect obtained from the combined cooperative action of, or interaction between, two or more distinct actors is greater than that obtained from the sum of their independent actions. The effect obtained could be shared by other actors and by the public at large. It is therefore different from symbiotic mutualism, in which two or more actors derive mutual benefit from living or acting together. Likewise, synergistic partnerships are different from business partnerships. The purpose of business partnerships is exclusive sharing of profits or benefits by partners alone, whereas the primary purpose of partnership for global governance should be the inclusive sharing of benefits for the well-being of humanity and other forms of global public goods.

In the fifth preambular paragraph a distinction is drawn between the *responsibility* of all partners to each other and their *accountability* to the global community, both present and future. Responsibility and accountability may both be regarded as obligation *erga omnes*, but by the first is meant the responsible manner in which all partners must act in their relations with each other, taking into account the differences of their respective capacity, role and function in society. Accountability, on the other hand, applies to the consequences which various actions may cause, for instance to the global community and global commons.

It is true that some of the UN system agencies, such as the Bretton Woods institutions, have often been criticized by developing countries and NGOs, but it was noted that this should not detract from appreciation of their overall work in the past and expectations about their contribution to harmonizing pluralized partnership in global governance. As is shown in the text of the operative paragraphs reproduced below, governmental deliberation on accountability for global governance, with a view to adopting a set of principles on the subject by the UN General Assembly, was considered as the most appropriate step for the future.

Declaration of Accountability for Global Governance

We the Peoples of the Earth, assembled in the City of San Francisco on the occasion of the 50th anniversary of the signing of the Charter of the United Nations... [five preambular paragraphs omitted]

Agree to urge the formulation and adoption, by the United Nations General Assembly, of a set of principles of accountability applicable to actions of all partners in global governance,

Agree also that the set of principles of accountability should include, *inter alia*, the following

1. All partners in global governance have responsibility to each other and are accountable to the global community as a whole for their actions that may adversely affect the various types of global commons;
2. In case of uncertainty about the irreversibility of harm to the global commons, the precautionary principle of erring on the side of safety should be observed;
3. All partners in global governance have the right, directly or through appropriate channels, to take part in planning, decision-making and implementing activities that may adversely affect their well-being, environment and development;
4. All of these partners have the right of access to information necessary for pluralized global governance, and they likewise have the duties to ensure transparency and information-sharing;
5. The will of the people shall be the basis of the authority and legitimacy of global governance; and this shall be ensured by appropriate mechanisms to be established and maintained by the United Nations system.[12]

Several principles of crucial importance to global governance are listed in the second operative paragraph. Thus there are brief statements on the *precautionary principle* concerning the global commons; the right and duty concerning *transparency* and *information-sharing*; and the right of all partners to participate in planning, decision-making and implementing such activities that may adversely affect their lives.

The last and definitely most important principle, set forth in the fifth paragraph, concerns the *authority and legitimacy* of the institutional process of global governance, the basis of which shall be *the will of the people*, and this "shall be ensured by appropriate mechanisms to be established and maintained by the United Nations system". This principle is intended to go beyond the mere rule of democratic representation within a state, as embodied in article 21, paragraph 3 of the Universal Declaration of Human Rights. Furthermore, the opinion was widely shared by the drafters of the Declaration of Accountability that acceptance of popular sovereignty, in place of state sovereignty, as the basis of the United Nations would constitute a conceptual breakthrough for the adaptation of the United Nations as a universal political organization for the twenty-first century which should play a pivotal role in global governance.

Codes of conduct facilitating accountability and global governance

With the relative decline in power of the state in many parts of the world, civil society organizations and the private sector have gained greater influence, as they supplement or even partially substitute for the traditional politics of the state. Thence comes a clearer demarcation of three categories of societal organizations as actors, not only in national and international domains but also global domains, concomitant with the tendency for the state to become too small for the big things and too big for the small things.

There has also been a growing interest in the concept of global governance since the publication of *Common Responsibility in the 1990s: The Stockholm Initiative on Global Security and Governance* in April 1991.[13] Global governance – defined as collective and concerted efforts to deal effectively with issues that go beyond the capacities of states or governmental organizations, intergovernmental organizations (IGOs), NGOs, the private sector and other actors to address on their own – needs the cooperation and partnership of all stakeholders to overcome the absence of a central authority. This need, in turn, has given rise to growing interest in various kinds of guidelines and codes for a new type of cooperation/collaboration (also called partnership, synergy, alliance) among different actors that makes a departure from the traditional adversary or competitive relations among them. Indeed, there was a remarkable increase in the number and diversity of codes during the 1990s.

The use of instruments variously called codes, guidelines, standards, sets of principles, declarations, resolutions and so forth is not a new phenomenon in the national scenes of various countries and in the practice of international organizations, such as the ILO, United Nations, Food and Agricultural Organization (FAO), World Health Organization (WHO) and Organisation for Economic Co-operation and Development (OECD). However, the proliferation of what may be called "framework documents" of a similar nature in the form of declarations or plans/programmes of action adopted by major conferences and codes of conduct, codes of ethics, codes of practice and charters adopted by NGOs and business associations is of recent origin. Compilations of codes of conduct which contain full texts or excerpts of documents with commentaries that have a bearing on partnership in governance show only the metaphorical tip of the codes-of-conduct iceberg.[14] There have been many studies on the use of non-binding norms (often called "soft law") and compliance therewith in several topic areas within international law, and a number of reviews have been made of codes of conduct for self-regulation by non-state actors, e.g. business corporations and NGOs, as well as codes of principles governing the relations between business corporations, NGOs and civil society.[15]

Most of the "framework documents" are generally broad in scope and take a long-term perspective, emphasizing the universal principles and ethics pertaining to the attitudinal dimension for all actors in the community of mankind. In most of these documents it is also recognized that rights as the foundation of freedom, peace and justice must be joined with responsibilities and accountability. They likewise propose a policy-oriented agenda to be pursued on the basis of mutual respect and partnership among individuals, groups and organizations of society. Civil society organizations are many times challenged in regard to their representativeness, professionalism and accountability. A study of self-regulatory codes of civil society brings to light many of the collective constructive actions taken by civil society that pre-empt and respond to such criticisms.[16]

The following characteristics of codes may be worth noting as factors making codes of conduct particularly suitable for partnership in governance.

- The *multicentric* and *multilayered* process of the operation of codes is useful for *achieving the communal goals* (e.g. UN Declaration on a Culture of Peace).[17]
- *The voluntary and participatory basis* of codes as norms is conducive to wider and *reciprocal acceptance by each and every partner concerned* (e.g. the Universal Declaration of Human Responsibilities).[18]
- Codes are forward-looking and capable of being infused with an inspiring *ethos* – an important attitudinal dimension (e.g. the Earth Charter).[19]
- Transparency of codes contributes to avoiding cooptation between different actors (e.g. UNHCR-NGO Oslo Declaration and Plan of Action, 1994).[20]
- Codes, particularly those with contents relevant to public affairs, once accepted by partners, create expectations about their conduct that cannot easily be disrupted unilaterally (e.g. Code of Conduct for the International Red Cross and NGOs in Disaster Relief).[21]

It may be added that provisions of codes tend to be general, as they set forth principles to uphold rather than rules which need to be strictly followed. Not in spite of, but because of, this generality, codes for partnership in governance in the world today can be particularly useful for several reasons. Firstly, partnership in governance often involves actors in multiple categories pursuing their respective interests; hence, guiding principles for achieving their common goals could usefully be evoked and emphasized. Secondly, generality that allows differing interpretations and flexible application can prove to be useful for developmental transition from "autonomous to responsive law", as described by Philippe Nonet and Philip Selznick, particularly in rapidly changing times.[22] Thirdly, as codes usually relate to horizontal engagement rather than hierarchical control, they tend to facilitate partnership in governance through the instrumentalities of the UN system and other multilateral institutions, which in turn may gradually undergo desirable transformation from bureaucratic to what Nonet and Selznik call "postbureaucratic" and "mission-oriented" institutions.

It is becoming widely recognized that a multi-stakeholder approach is not an option but a necessity for dealing with important global issues, including peace and security. In light of the occasional use of Arria formula meetings (an informal arrangement that allows the Security Council greater flexibility to be briefed about international peace and security issues) in recent years, where NGO and private sector representatives are invited to the Security Council for policy dialogue, new avenues might be opened for more active participation of non-state actors in UN-mediated conflict prevention, conflict mitigation and post-conflict peacebuilding.[23] Having regard to the exacerbating influence that the private sector often exerts in conflict situations (such as blood diamonds, traffic in arms and exploitation of natural resources), cardinal principles of corporate social responsibility in conflict situations might be added to the existing 10 principles of the Global Compact (GC).[24]

It may appropriately be noted here that a tentative proposal for adding "peace and security" provisions to the Global Compact, formulated by a few Japanese scholars, was introduced at the Second Seminar on Human Security held early in 2008 at Coventry University in England. The draft proposal, reproduced below, received some favourable response, and further work is being planned. The draft proposes the addition of the UN Charter, the Millennium Declaration[25] and the 2005 Summit Outcome Document to the preamble to the Global Compact, and the addition of the following principles.

> *Peace and Security*
>
> *Principle 11*: Businesses should support concerted efforts by the United Nations and other international organizations to build and maintain peace and security; and
>
> *Principle 12*: Support measures for conflict prevention and peace-building, and for protection of people in armed conflict, as well as empowerment of their capacity for human security at all times.

Responsibility and accountability for peace and security

In the aftermath of a series of tragic events (Somalia 1992–1993, Rwanda 1994, Bosnia and Herzegovina 1994–1995 and Kosovo 1999), the work of the International Commission on Intervention and State Sovereignty helped to clarify the dual responsibility of the state: externally to respect the sovereignty of other states, and internally to respect the dignity and basic rights of all the people within the state. A set of core principles on the responsibility to protect (R2P) set forth in the Commission's report issued in September 2001,[26] including a collective international responsibility to protect by military intervention as a last resort, was endorsed by the High-level Panel on Threats, Challenges and Change in its report of November 2004.[27] Its shorter version, retaining the essence of the principles, was subsequently incorporated in the 2005 Summit Outcome Document, paragraphs 138 and 139.

The cardinal principle of R2P was often not recognized or disregarded and violated by many states in the past. And the fact remains that a number of such states continue the same practice of brazen disregard, as if they claim the unlimited power of the state to do whatever it wants to its people. These paragraphs 138 and 139 of the Outcome Document importantly recognize that the international community, through the United Nations, also has the responsibility to act under Chapters VI and VIII, and "to take collective action, in a timely and decisive manner, through the Security Council" under Chapter VII, "should peaceful means be inadequate and national authorities are manifestly failing to protect their populations from genocide, war crimes, ethnic cleansing and crimes against humanity".

In cases where there exists an obvious deficit in the performance of R2P on the part of UN Member States and when the United Nations is unable to deal effectively with the situation by taking adequate collective action, as is the case with Darfur, what can be done? I would argue for several steps to be taken in advance to dispose of future cases, such as the following.

- The Secretary-General should ask Edward Luck, special adviser for the responsibility to protect, to prepare in consultation with Francis Deng, special representative for the prevention of genocide and mass atrocities, a set of operational rules and guidelines for taking "collective action, in a timely and decisive manner, through the Security Council", for consideration and adoption by the General Assembly. From a normative perspective, such rules and guidelines should clearly be formulated so that the exercise of R2P, through the United Nations, would initially be an *ex ante* responsibility to prevent and stop mass atrocities effectively, rather than an *ex post* responsibility.
- To assist decision-making by the United Nations, an emergency standby observer force of an appropriate size under the command of the Secretary-General should be established as soon as possible, and it should be dispatched to assess the situation for reporting to the Secu-

rity Council and to take action as necessary, possibly as part of a forward echelon, under the authority of the Security Council and the command of the Secretary-General.

- To ensure speedy decision and action, an exceptional rule might be adopted by the Security Council that permanent members should voluntarily renounce the veto in favour of a two-thirds vote when humanitarian intervention is urgently at issue. Furthermore, if the Security Council fails to act immediately, an emergency special session of the General Assembly should take up the matter without delay.
- The rule relating to *ex post* R2P should state that international criminal justice will be administered against the perpetrators of mass atrocities by the International Criminal Court, the UN's *ad hoc* international criminal tribunals (e.g. the ICTs for the former Yugoslavia and Rwanda) or "mixed courts" (e.g. those set up in East Timor, Bosnia and Herzegovina, Sierra Leone and Cambodia). Furthermore, the implementation of the rule will demonstrate that impunity is no longer the order of the day and there shall be no prescription for crimes against humanity. The second element of *ex post* R2P will be ensuring peacebuilding by people themselves with time-limited assistance from within and outside the United Nations.
- Furthermore, in extreme cases of a recalcitrant state ("rogue state"), a possibility should perhaps be explored for suspension of the rights and privileges of membership (article 5 of the Charter) or expulsion from the United Nations (article 6). However, generally speaking the twin tasks of protecting the victims and punishing the perpetrators must be assessed and balanced against the consequences for the process of peace enforcement, the need for post-conflict reconciliation and the fragility of international or domestic institutions.

The radical reinterpretation of state sovereignty as a responsibility to protect its people made by the International Commission on Intervention and State Sovereignty was quite remarkable. Yet incorporation of this underlying principle in the 2005 World Summit Outcome Document was epoch-making indeed. Although the Commission achieved this feat, the basic principle has not been translated into action in relation to the situations in several countries. As the Commission rightly defined it, the responsibility to protect has three elements of responsibility: to prevent a conflict, to react to situations of compelling human need and to rebuild after a military intervention. Having regard to the management of action *vis-à-vis* the time factor, it would seem better to utilize the result-oriented accountability concept rather than responsibility which is time-neutral. In fact, the term "accountability" is used several times in the Commission's report, but in a sufficiently discriminating way. For future development of this innovative approach of R2P, in reference to the evolving situations of today and the future, wisdom and guidance from its main architects would be useful.[28]

Transformative but non-structural changes proposed in the Cardoso Report

Recommendations of the report

The Report of the Panel of Eminent Persons on UN-Civil Society Relations (Cardoso Report)[29] contains several proposals that would, when implemented, have a far-reaching transformative effect on the United Nations as a political institution. The paragraphs on one of the Panel's key proposals, namely fostering multi-constituency processes, are particularly worth noting. The Panel states that civil society and other constituencies (including the private sector, parliaments and local authorities) are important to the United Nations because their experience and social connections can help the United Nations to do a better job, improve its legitimacy, identify priorities and connect it with public opinion. Civil society can also raise new issues, focus attention on the moral and ethical dimensions of decisions in the public sphere, expand resources and skills, challenge basic assumptions and priorities and protest unfair decisions. Therefore enhanced engagement, carefully planned, would make the United Nations more effective in its actions and its contributions to global governance. The Panel concludes that there is a synergy here, not a contest, and that the UN's opportunities strengthen civil society, and this in turn empowers the United Nations, enhancing its relevance to the issues of our times.[30]

The Secretary-General's report *In Larger Freedom* emphasizes the role of civil society and the private sector in relation to the "imperative of collective action" against a broad trend in the contemporary world in the following terms:

> Sovereign States are the basic and indispensable building blocks of the international system. It is their job to guarantee the rights of their citizens, to protect them from crime, violence and aggression, and to provide the framework of freedom under law in which individuals can prosper and society develop ... States, however, cannot do the job alone. We need an active civil society and a dynamic private sector. Both occupy an increasingly large and important share of the space formerly reserved for States alone, and it is plain that the goals outlined here will not be achieved without their full engagement...

> In our efforts to strengthen the contributions of States, civil society, the private sector and international institutions to advancing a vision of larger freedom, we must ensure that all involved assume their responsibilities to turn good words into good deeds. We therefore need new mechanisms to ensure accountability – the accountability of States to their citizens, of States to each other, of international institutions to their members and of the present generation to future generations.[31]

Furthermore, recalling that the Millennium Declaration reaffirmed that the General Assembly has a central position as the chief deliberative, policy-making and representative organ of the United Nations, Annan's report states that the General Assembly should engage much more actively with civil society – reflecting the fact that, after a decade of rapidly increasing interaction, civil society is now involved in most UN activities. It notes that "the goals of the United Nations can only be achieved if civil society and Governments are fully engaged, and it proposes that the General Assembly should establish mechanisms enabling it to engage fully and systematically with civil society".[32]

Member States' response to the proposals

Despite all these significant proposals, only a few brief references and endorsement are given to some of them in the 2005 World Summit Outcome Document,[33] as listed below:

- enhancing the contribution of NGOs, civil society organizations, the private sector and other stakeholders in national development as well as in the global partnership for development (para. 22.e)
- channelling private capabilities and resources into stimulating the private sector in developing countries (para. 24.d)
- ensuring that multiple institutions and international partners all work under one agreed framework on health issues (para. 57)
- promoting gender equality and empowerment of women (para. 58)
- integrating a gender perspective and promoting full participation of women in the prevention and resolution of conflicts (para. 116)
- strengthening cooperation between the United Nations and parliaments, in particular through the Inter-Parliamentary Union, for furthering all aspects of the Millennium Declaration in all fields of work of the United Nations (para. 171)
- welcoming the positive contributions of the private sector and civil society, including NGOs, and local authorities in the promotion and implementation of development and human rights (paras. 172–173)
- encouraging responsible business practices such as those promoted by the Global Compact (para. 174)

• welcoming the dialogue between those organizations and Member States in the first informal interactive hearings of the General Assembly (para. 175).

The list is short, and it is difficult to find other passages in the Outcome Document that relate to the engagement of non-state actors with the work of the United Nations. Earlier versions of the draft Outcome Document did not contain specific passages on the last four items in the list, and they are welcome additions. What is sorely missing is recognition of the role and responsibility of non-state actors, particularly in relation to the peace and security function that is crucially central to the United Nations as a global political institution.

To put it bluntly, the basic approach of the Outcome Document to peace and security is outmoded, as it is state-centric with an emphasis on the role of states, particularly major powers, and it fails to take account of the constructive role played by civil society organizations and the social accountability of the private sector in the field of security, including conflict prevention and post-conflict peacebuilding, as discussed in the Security Council meetings with representatives of the private sector and civil society in April and June 2004. Recent studies such as *Parliamentary Oversight of the Security Sector – Principles, Mechanisms and Practices*[34] and *Peace Support Operations, Parliaments and Legislation*[35] indicate greater interest in and increased activities on peace and security on the part of parliaments in many countries. This also should have been taken into account. The Outcome Document likewise fails to deal adequately with one of the key sectors of security, namely planetary security (the environment and resources), and it did not include any recommendation on disarmament and non-proliferation of weapons of mass destruction, apparently as a result of trade-offs between negotiating groups among member governments.

In view of a marked tendency for multiple actors working together to cope with new and evolving issues, it is for consideration whether the concept of "cooperative security" should be re-examined in the new context. Cooperative security as advocated in a prescient manner in studies such as those by Gareth Evans[36] and Janne Nolan[37] encompassed elements that are becoming increasingly more relevant today. It is a broad approach to "multidimensional security" that emphasizes reassurances rather than deterrence, and does not privilege military solutions over non-military ones. The approach is inclusive, accepting non-state actors' role in addition to the role of states as the principal actors, and it stresses the value of creating the habits of multilateral dialogue. A certain adaptation of some of these elements might be particularly useful: for instance, inclusivity of participation of non-state actors for synergistic partnership rather than merely working together, and acceptance of social responsibility and accountability by non-state actors for the prevention of conflict and for post-conflict peacebuilding processes. Furthermore, a combination of the cooperative security approach thus adapted with the operationalization of the concept of human security, i.e. the protection and empowerment of people by way of "redressing specific security deficits" that should be identified and quantified, would help achieve effective and equitable security in a world where there are competing claims for limited resources.[38] Justice requires fairness in procedure and equity in distribution; and cooperative human security is therefore an important means for achieving justice in the community of mankind.

Steps towards multi-stakeholder partnerships for enhancing legitimacy and accountability

The impression is inescapable that member governments have responded to proposals for non-structural transformative changes of the United Nations without much enthusiasm. It is said that the concentration of energy on the Security Council reform issue and "quick-win" solutions to poverty consumed too much oxygen in the final stage of negotiations on the Outcome Document. This is unfortunate, because these reform proposals of a far-reaching nature, if adopted, would greatly help to strengthen the United Nations in the long run by bringing the Organization to work together with wider constituencies of all stakeholders, thereby bringing it closer to the peoples of the world.

Historically and generally, intergovernmental organizations have often followed an evolutionary path: from a *forum of policy consultations* among states, to developing gradually into an institutionalized *framework for cooperation* for member states, to pursuing their own interests and sometimes dealing with their common problems. In order to respond to major global issues which are beyond the control of individual states, the United Nations has now reached the third stage by transforming itself into an *actor* actively promoting the common interests and shared values of the emergent global society. If the UN system as a universal IGO can gradually assume a leadership role in building and managing a quadrilateral partnership of governments, IGOs, NGOs and the private sector, it may eventually reach the fourth evolutionary stage: transforming itself to be the core process of global governance by way of synergistic partnerships.[39]

It can be argued that the policy relevance and effectiveness of the working of the UN system could gradually be enhanced if the synergy-promotion function of the UN system were to be further nurtured. It is emphasized in this connection that the legitimacy of the UN system, to a large extent, hinges upon the enhancement of such a function in two ways.

If any representation system of non-state actors such as a "Second General Assembly" cannot be established soon in the intergovernmental structure of the United Nations, an important progressive step would be for the UN General Assembly to elaborate and adopt a declaration on the principles of accountability in the public sphere of global governance that would help to foster the multi-stakeholder partnerships and multi-constituency processes of the United Nations.

Elaboration of such a declaration in the form of a voluntary code of conduct addressed to all actors, including both state and non-state actors, could be done by the General Assembly with the interactive participation of representatives of member governments, parliaments, civil society and the business sector. For that purpose, the format of the two-day interactive hearings held on 23–24 June 2005 will serve as a procedural model with some improvements. It is parenthetically added that voluntary codes of conduct that often treat states and non-state actors as partners on a co-equal footing (e.g. the Universal Declaration of Human Responsibilities and the UN Declaration on a Culture of Peace) contribute to wider and reciprocal acceptance of communal norms by each partner concerned, due to the multicentric and multilayered process of the operation of the codes. In addition, once accepted by partners, codes create expectations about the conduct of the partners that cannot easily be disrupted unilaterally.

A "Second General Assembly", for which many proposals have been advanced in the past, is always conceived as an assembly of non-governmental actors, i.e. elected parliamentarians and/or representatives of civil society and the private sector. For maximizing the political legitimacy of the interactive process of a Second General Assembly, I would argue that it should be an inclusive public sphere with Member States, non-state actors and representatives of other intergovernmental organizations, including regional organizations, participating as appropriate. It is noted in passing that it has become customary for the General Assembly to hold informal interactive hearings with civil society, NGOs and the private sector a couple of times every year on selected questons. For instance, during 2006 three hearings were held on least-developed countries, international migration and development, and AIDs. Depending on the priority issues to be taken up, selection of representatives could be made in a businesslike manner by applying explicit criteria for e-governance using advanced communication technologies. These steps (i.e. elaboration and adoption of a declaration and setting up an inclusive public sphere) would conform with the broader trend towards human-centred democratic governance around the world, as well as with a shift to partnerships of all major actors in coping with global issues.

It is widely accepted that the resolution of interrelated global issues requires a multisectoral and multi-actor approach, instead of a single-focus alliance of selected actors directly concerned. One of the four purposes of the United Nations as set forth in the Charter is "To be a centre for harmonizing the action of nations in the attainment of these common ends",[40] and in today's world it is necessary for the United Nations to harmonize the action of the private sector and civil society actors as well as "nations". By working with civil society organizations which are capable of influencing how governments and businesses see their own interests in relation to global public goods in a long-term perspective, the UN system can gradually transform itself to be the centre of global governance processes.

By and large, in view of the affinities of visions and the principles that guide the UN system and NGOs, efforts to build and manage a strategic partnership between them should be less difficult than other types of bilateral partnerships. The UN's institutional effectiveness requires leadership to make necessary initiatives, coordinate various actions, facilitate compliance with relevant norms and oversee the implementation of decisions. Partnerships between the United Nations and NGOs have indeed contributed to such leadership, as demonstrated by the formation and functioning of a number of multi-stakeholder schemes that have been set up in the past 10 years or so. The Global Biodiversity Forum, Global Environment Facility, Global Water Partnership, Global Alliance for Vaccines and Immunization and the Joint UN Programme on HIV/AIDS, Tuberculosis and Malaria are a few examples of multiple partnership arrangements that are less formal than traditional intergovernmental organizations and more suitable for inclusive participation of stakeholders concerned. The UN Fund for International Partnerships (UNFIP), which promotes new public-private partnerships and alliances worldwide, had as of 2004 facilitated over 200 project and partnership requests that included 19 UN entities, five academic institutions, 65 companies, 35 foundations, 10 governments and 65 NGOs.[41] It is hoped that public engagement of non-state actors in these numerous organizational arrangements will also be made in due course by the recently established Peacebuilding Commission and the Human Rights Council, as well as by other institutions in the UN system.

Conclusion

The foregoing analysis of recent developments that have a bearing on the accountability and legitimacy of the United Nations points to the need for the UN system to take the role of synergizer, so that positive benefits deriving from horizontal engagement of multi-stakeholders can be appropriately combined with existing vertical modes of governance. Strengthened accountability of the United Nations and its cosmopolitan leadership, imbued with solidarity, would promote much-needed synergy and interface of vertical and horizontal governance of sustainable peace and development. Strong leadership and participative engagement are often mutually exclusive, but most effective when appropriately combined.

Notes

1. Annan, Kofi (2000) *"We the Peoples": The Role of the United Nations in the 21st Century*, UN Doc. DPI/2103, New York: UN Department of Public Information.
2. See the origin and outcome of the NGO dialogue with the World Bank discussed in Yamaguchi, Kenji (1995) *Sekai Ginko* (*World Bank*), Tokyo: Kindai Bungeisha, pp. 416–434. See sections relating to NGO Working Groups on the World Bank in ICVA (1986–1993) *Annual Reports*, Geneva: International Council of Voluntary Agencies; see also Malena, Carmen (1995) *Working with NGOs: Practical Guide to Operational Collaboration*, Washington, DC: World Bank.
3. For extensive discussion of the related background see Rosenau, James (1990) *Turbulence in World Politics: A Theory of Change and Continuity*, Princeton, NJ: Princeton University Press, chs 5 and 15; for further analysis with reference to the United Nations see Rosenau, James (1992) *The United Nations in a Turbulent World*, Occasional Paper of the International Peace Academy, Boulder, CO: Lynne Rienner Publishers, chs 3 and 4.
4. See introduction and ch. 1 of Zweifel, Thomas (2006) *International Organizations and Democracy: Accountability, Politics, and Power*, Boulder, CO: Lynne Rienner Publishers.
5. Ebrahim, Alnoor and Edward Weisband, eds (2007) *Global Accountabilities: Participation, Pluralism, and Public Ethics*, Cambridge: Cambridge University Press, pp. 3–5 and 252–255.
6. UN General Assembly (2005) "2005 World Summit Outcome Document", UN Doc. A/RES/60/L.1, 16 September.
7. Keohane, Robert and Joseph Nye Jr (2001) "The Club Model of Multilateral Cooperation and Problems of Democratic Legitimacy", in Roger Porter, Pierre Sauvé, Arvind Subramanian and Americo Beviglia Zampetti, eds, *Efficiency, Equity, and Legitimacy: The Multilateral Trading System at the Millennium*, Washington, DC: Brookings Institution Press, pp. 264–294, at p. 291. See also arguments for WTO cosmopolitics in Charnovitz, Steve (2002) "WTO Cosmopolitics", *New York University Journal of International Law and Politics* 34(2), pp. 299–353, at pp. 299–344.
8. Falk, Richard (2002) "The United Nations System: Prospects for Renewal", in Deepak Nayyar, ed., *Governing Globalization: Issues and Institutions*, Oxford: Oxford University Press, pp. 177–208, at p. 207.
9. Boutros-Ghali, Boutros (1996) *An Agenda for Democratization*, DPI/1867, New York: UN Department of Public Information, pp. 26–27.
10. Commission on Global Governance (1995) *Our Global Neighbourhood: The Report of the Commission on Global Governance*, New York: Oxford University Press, p. xvi.
11. The text of the declaration as adopted at the conference on 24 June 1995 is reproduced as Doc. 75 together with a commentary in Kunugi, Tatsuro and Martha Schweitz, eds

(1999) *Codes of Conduct for Partnership in Governance: Texts and Commentaries*, Tokyo: United Nations University Press, pp. 302–305.
12. Ibid., pp. 302–303.
13. Stockholm Initiative on Global Security and Governance (1991) *Common Responsibility in the 1990s: The Stockholm Initiative on Global Security and Governance, April 22, 1991*, Stockholm: Prime Minister's Office. The Stockholm Initiative focused on major areas for multilateral cooperation and the ways and means to strengthen international institutions. Thirty-six statesmen and senior officials of the United Nations and other organizations participated in the preparation of the initiative. This was the first international conference document that used the term "global governance".
14. See compilations with commentaries, e.g. Kunugi and Schweitz, note 11 above, which contains 80 documents; Williams, Oliver, ed. (2000) *Global Codes of Conduct: An Idea Whose Time Has Come*, Chicago, IL: University of Notre Dame Press, which contains 27 documents and studies thereof.
15. See the publications in note 14 above; see also Shelton, Dinah, ed. (2000) *Commitment and Compliance: The Role of Non-Binding Norms in the International Legal System*, Oxford: Oxford University Press; UN Non-governmental Liaison Service (2002) *Voluntary Approaches to Corporate Responsibility*, Geneva: UN Non-governmental Liaison Service.
16. Bendell, Jem (2006) *Debating NGO Accountability*, Geneva: UN Non-Governmental Liaison Service (NGLS). For further information on the NGLS see www.un-ngls.org.
17. UN General Assembly (1999) "UN Declaration on a Culture of Peace", UN Doc. A/RES/53/243, 6 October.
18. InterAction Council (1997) *Universal Declaration of Human Responsibilities*, available at www.interactioncouncil.org/udhr/declaration/udhr.pdf.
19. Earth Charter International (2000) *Earth Charter*, available at www.earthcharter.org/, (text of the Earth Charter as proclaimed in 2000).
20. See the text as Doc. 50 with a commentary in Kunugi and Schweitz, note 11 above, pp. 289–299.
21. See the text as Doc. 21 with a commentary, ibid., pp. 96–103. This code was drawn up by major operational humanitarian agencies in 1993. It defines standards in ethics and behaviour for agencies and their staff operating in disasters. But it also contains, in annexes, recommendations to disaster-affected governments, donor governments and intergovernmental organizations. When the code was discussed at the 1995 International Red Cross Conference, where the representatives of all state parties to the Geneva Conventions were present, the conference welcomed the code and encouraged its use, thus conferring a degree of official recognition. Some 200 agencies have registered their support, many donor governments use it as part of their funding criteria and it has become a common tool for evaluators.
22. Nonet, Philippe and Philip Selznick (2001) *Law and Society in Transition*, London: Transaction Publishers, pp. 1–27. See further discussion in Kunugi, Tatsuro (2003) "Challenges Posed by Globalization and Synergistic Responses: Multilateral Institutions in Transition", in Alexandre Kiss, Dinah Shelton and Kanami Ishibashi, eds, *Economic Globalization and Compliance in International Environmental Agreements*, The Hague: Kluwer Law International, pp. 13–34, at pp. 18–21.
23. UN Non-governmental Liaison Service (2004) *Go Between*, No. 103, Geneva: UN Non-governmental Liaison Service, p. 38.
24. See the text and many reports and studies on the Global Compact, available at www.unglobalcompact.org/.
25. UN General Assembly (2000) "United Nations Millennium Declaration", UN Doc. A/RES/55/2, 8 September.

26. International Commission on Intervention and State Sovereignty (2001) *The Responsibility to Protect*, Ottawa: International Development Research Centre. (The report is known as the ICISS Report on R2P.)
27. UN High-level Panel on Threats, Challenges, and Change (2004) *A More Secure World: Our Shared Responsibility*, New York: UN Department of Public Information, paras 203–208.
28. See Thakur, Ramesh (2006) *The United Nations, Peace and Security*, Cambridge: Cambridge University Press, ch. 11; Evans, Gareth (2008) *The Responsibility to Protect: Ending Mass Atrocity Crimes Once and for All*, Washington, DC: Brookings Institution.
29. UN Panel of Eminent Persons on United Nations-Civil Society (2004) "We the Peoples: Civil Society, the United Nations, and Global Governance", UN Doc. A/58/817, 11 June. (The report is known as the Cardoso Report: the panel was chaired by Fernando Henrique Cardoso.)
30. Ibid, ch. X, paras 177–187.
31. Annan, Kofi (2005) *In Larger Freedom: Towards Development, Security, and Human Rights for All*, Report of the Secretary-General, New York: UN Department of Public Information, section C of Introduction, paras 18–22.
32. Ibid., para. 162.
33. UN General Assembly, note 6 above.
34. Born, Hans, Philippi Fluri and Anders Johnsson, eds (2003) *Parliamentary Oversight of the Security Sector: Principles, Mechanisms and Practices*, Lausanne: Geneva Centre for the Democratic Control of Armed Forces/Inter-Parliamentary Union, chs 2, 3, 6, 13, 25 and 29.
35. Nikitin, Alexander, ed. (2004) *Peace Support Operations, Parliaments and Legislation*, Moscow: Aslan, chs 1 and 2.
36. Evans, Gareth (1993) *Cooperating for Peace: The Global Agenda for the 1990s and Beyond*, St Leonards, NSW: Allen & Unwin, ch. 1.
37. Nolan, Janne E., ed. (1994) *Global Engagement: Cooperation and Security in the 21st Century*, Washington, DC: Brookings Institution, chs 1 (on concept), 2 (regime architecture) and 7 (global institutions).
38. See discussion of three methodological merits of "redressing security deficits" in Kunugi, Tatsuro (2005) "Redressing Security Deficits in Our Fragmented World: UN Perspectives and Beyond", in Yoichiro Murakami , Noriko Kawamura and Shin Chiba, eds, *Towards a Peaceable Future: Redefining Peace, Security and Kyosei, from a Multidisciplinary Perspective*, Pullman, WA: Thomas S. Foley Institute for Public Policy and Public Service, Washington State University, pp. 18–22.
39. For analysis of the four evolutional stages of international organizations see Kunugi, note 22 above, ch. 2, sec. IV, pp. 26–29.
40. UN Charter, article 1(4).
41. See a compendium of UN system engagements in UN Non-governmental Liaison Service (2005) *UN System Engagement with NGOs, Civil Society, the Private Sector, and Other Actors: A Compendium*, Geneva: UN Non-governmental Liaison Service.

10

Democratic accountability in UN field operations

Kazuo Takahashi

The governance of post-conflict territories by the United Nations embodies a central policy dilemma: how does one help a population prepare for democratic governance and the rule of law by imposing a form of benevolent autocracy? And to what extent should the transitional administration itself be bound by the principles that it seeks to encourage in the local population?[1]

Inherent difficulty and contradictions

With the end of the Cold War, democracy has become the paramount political ideology in the world community, but diversity in its forms and substance is widely recognized. Even in a country where social conditions and culture may not provide a fertile ground for democracy, there is a widespread belief that democracy should be good for the country and should work well. Reflecting the dominance of liberalist values, democracy has become a global ideology which has been incorporated into the workings of the United Nations as its basic value in recent years. Therefore, when the question of accountability becomes an issue at the United Nations, it has come to include democratic accountability in addition to managerial and financial accountability.

Democratic accountability, which has evolved over time, should include a number of factors irrespective of the interpretation of democracy: popular participation in decision-making, including elections, transparency in governance and rule of law. Beyond the essential characteristics of elections, other factors such as plurality of political parties, a free press

Envisioning reform: Enhancing UN accountability in the twenty-first century, Kuyama and Fowler (eds), United Nations University Press, 2009, ISBN 978-92-808-1170-4

and civil society are all important and helpful for deepening democracy, but they are not necessarily conditions for democracy, particularly in its infancy.

One major difficulty of the term *democratic accountability* arises from the debates between modernists and post-modernists. Modernists tend to believe in liberalist approaches to a political system, putting emphasis on values as expressed in the 1948 Universal Declaration of Human Rights.[2] In the post–Cold War period, this perception tended to be emphasized by the Western alliance in a somewhat triumphant manner. Post-modernists believe in the uniqueness of individual societies, with their own cultures, traditions and histories. They prefer a more neutral term, such as political accountability. However, with the emergence of post-post-modern perception, as expressed by the Millennium Declaration, the Sustainable Development Summit and the 2005 Outcome Document,[3] some of the modernist elements have emerged as common values, including democracy, which has not been rejected even by such countries as Russia, China and other developing countries. It can therefore be reasonably assumed that, while the debate on its use has been real until recently, the term *democratic accountability* may be used for the purposes of the analysis of the issues that are our concern in this work.

The field operations of the UN system in development cooperation, humanitarian emergency, peacekeeping operations (PKOs) and peacebuilding are all essentially of an autocratic nature, however benevolent their intentions. While these categories of operations have widely different levels of hierarchical, and thus undemocratic, character, the central functions of the UN system in promoting democracy are pursued by these autocratic field operations. Namely, democracy is pursued by a non-democratic structure – the field offices of the UN system. There is an inherent contradiction in this relationship. Even if the external actor is not the United Nations, be it a bilateral donor or an international non-governmental organization, the relationship remains basically contradictory. The dilemma for the United Nations is that democracy has now become its core institutional value, so the contradiction has become salient in UN field operations.

Beyond this basic contradiction, the inherent problem is aggravated by such seemingly nominal but real factors as the four-tier structure of incomes in the field, a phenomenon that is common in many countries. For example, it is widely pointed out in Afghanistan that the monthly incomes of UN staff are around $10,000, those for international NGOs around $5,000, for local NGOs $500 and for government officials $50. In this situation, the autocracy of the UN field operation is fortified by plutocracy. To make it worse, the high incomes of the UN field staff tend to generate inflation, with a devastating impact on a local population that is largely unemployed and generally extremely poor. Sexual abuses by UN officials and PKO soldiers have become major problems.[4] Long-term impacts of these factors will become a major negative consequence of well-meaning UN operations.[5] This situation creates, to say the least, a hostile environment for any consideration of democratic accountability of field operations.

Thus, the question of democratic accountability of UN field operations is faced with inherent difficulty and basic contradictions, which are aggravated by practical and real factors including enormous gaps in income and high inflation. This issue will become a major priority concern in the world community in the near future.

Increasing primacy of field operations

The UN Charter did not anticipate any substantial operational activity by UN organs, except military operations under Chapter VII. With the onset of the Cold War the Security Council became basically non-functional, with the consequence that the expected structure for military operations did not materialize.[6] However, the United Nations proved to be a highly practical peace organization. Within the strong constraints of the Cold War, the United Nations invented peace operations that had not been expected by the founders of the Charter, such as the PKO, a seed which has eventually grown so that it has changed the fundamental character of the United Nations.

Operational activities of the UN system emerged from the changing structure of the world community. They responded to such needs as development cooperation, humanitarian emergencies and enlarged PKOs. Peacebuilding will be next on the agenda. By responding practically to the needs of the world community, the Organization has evolved beyond the UN Charter, resulting in significant expansion of field operations.

The operational activity of the UN system began with the shift in the membership structure of the United Nations and its specialized agencies from the dominance of industrial powers towards the increasing majority of newly independent countries. Development became a rallying cry of these countries. Through the resolutions in the UN General Assembly and the general conferences of specialized agencies, development cooperation has become increasingly one of the most prominent functions of the whole UN system. *Developmentalism* spread over the UN system as a whole through the 1950s and 1960s. Operational activities through the Expanded Programme of Technical Assistance (EPTA) and the Special Fund, which were merged into the UN Development Programme (UNDP), as well as through specialized agencies and other subsidiary bodies of the UN General Assembly, such as the UN Children's Fund (UNICEF) and the UN Population Fund (UNFPA), gradually became important features of the United Nations in the course of these years. Backed up by the voting powers of the developing countries at the deliberative bodies,[7] these operational activities have been strengthened over time.

The end of the Cold War brought two new major features to the UN system, although both had been pursued on a smaller scale and with a lower profile during the period of developmentalism: large-scale humanitarian interventions,[8] and PKOs with voluminous UN interim administrations. The end of the Cold War has changed the world structure from the twin axes of East-West and North-South to *globalism*. These large-scale operations have basically been promoted to underpin global solidarity, but national perspectives, unavoidably, are always at work.

While large-scale humanitarian disasters have been constant features in modern history, the post–Cold War period has been characterized by UN agencies intervening in them.[9] In many cases the UN High Commissioner for Refugees (UNHCR) has been leading the way.[10] However, other agencies, such as the World Food Programme (WFP) and the World Health Organization (WHO), have also been heavily involved in these complex emergencies. Through these activities, operations of UN agencies within sovereign states have acquired further legitimacy. Humanitarian interventions, mainly through UN agencies, are now constant features of the international landscape, resulting in increasing recognition of the importance of UN field operations.

Large-scale PKOs and UN interim administrations are now familiar aspects of the post–Cold War period. Well over 20,000 people were involved under the UN Transitional Authority in Cambodia (UNTAC) and more than 40,000 in the UN Mission in Bosnia and Herzegovina (UNMIBH). The PKO budget for 2005 was three times the size of the regular budget of the United Nations ($5 billion and $1.6 billion respectively). While discussion of the possibilities and limits of these large-scale operations abounds, they are becoming a constant and important feature in the world community (estimates for 2008 are $7 billion and $2.6 billion respectively). The relatively quick exit of UNTAC from Cambodia by emphasizing elections contributed significantly to large-scale PKO/interim administrations acquiring legitimacy, although it left a number of problems unresolved in Cambodia.

Development cooperation, humanitarian intervention and large-scale PKO/interim administrations have together changed the nature of the United Nations substantially. The operational character of the UN system, which the founders of the UN Charter did not foresee, has become an important aspect – perhaps the predominant feature when measured in terms of budget and staff.[11] It is essential that the question of accountability of the United Nations should be addressed within this new and emerging structure and within the operation of the UN system as a whole.

Emerging principles of democratic accountability

While the issue of contradictions and dilemmas related to democratic accountability is highlighted most dramatically in the large-scale PKO/interim administrations category, it may also be clearly seen in humanitarian interventions and development cooperation.

Development cooperation

In the field of *development cooperation*, issues of governance have acquired increasing importance since 1989, when two major documents became public. One was the adoption of the work programme of the Development Assistance Committee (DAC) of the Organisation for Economic Co-operation and Development (OECD) for the 1990s at its high-level meeting in December 1989. Governance was highlighted as one of the major issues that would be addressed by the DAC in the coming years. The other was the publication of a report by the World Bank on the constraints for development of African countries.[12] It dealt mainly with poor governance of African countries.

Following the emphasis on structural adjustment in the course of the 1980s, governance became the main feature of development cooperation in the 1990s. This shift of emphasis partly reflected the new concern of major donors who did not have to support dictators, military regimes or corrupt governments any more as part of a zone-of-influence competition with the Soviet Union. The net impact of the consecutive emphasis on highly interventionist approaches of development cooperation, namely structural adjustment policies and governance, has been to bring about tension between field operations and democratization of the recipient governments. UN field operations are pursued by administrative structures which are, of necessity, autocratic. The concept of governance having always a double meaning, namely democracy and responsible and effective administration, democracy is implied when an emphasis is put on governance. Development cooperation of UN agencies has, therefore, been considered as an important component of democratization of the recipient country. Pursuit of democracy in developing countries by benevolent and yet autocratic UN operations is bound to have various implications for democratic accountability of these operations. The three major components of democracy, namely participation including elections, transparency and rule of law, are beginning to have implications (detailed below) in development cooperation operations of UN agencies, so that they enhance democracy in the recipient country while UN field operations maximize democratic characters in spite of their essentially autocratic nature.

Participation

Two forms of participation of the population are widely practised. One is participation of local NGOs in the formulation of a project as well as in its execution. One important task of UN field offices is to find proper local NGOs and cultivate good relations with them. Their participation in the various phases of the project cycle is an increasingly important component in democratic accountability of UN operations in development cooperation. International NGOs, which tend to have stronger delivery capacities, are sometimes viewed as competitors by local NGOs for resources of UN agencies. Implications of this sentiment must always be kept in mind in considering popular participation.

Another is the use of public forums for the purpose of promoting participation of a broad spectrum of the population in various phases of a project. It is important to develop a device through which people whose voices are weak are heard at these forums. People are highly sensitive about the nature of the forum. When it is organized just for an alibi, they immediately feel it. Public forums have to be for listening to the real voices of the people. An effective sociological analysis of the community where the forum is held is an essential requirement for this purpose.

Transparency

Local media such as radio and the press, and also television in some cases, have come to play important roles in enhancing transparency for UN development cooperation operations. In many poorer countries, in which radio is the most important mass medium, producing documents in local languages contributes significantly to strengthening transparency. It is also important to keep key communication persons (rumour mills, rumour channels) informed.

Rule of law

In many developing countries, customary laws prevail in daily life. However, it is essential for UN field operations to pursue activities based on contractual agreements with the government and other local partners as much as possible. Observance of legal obligations should have a demonstration effect on the local community, thus rule of law is an essential requirement in the democratic accountability of UN field operations. Lack of legal expertise in many field offices is a problem in this respect.

In summary

Basic components of democratic accountability are emerging around the above factors in the field of UN development cooperation. However, further elaboration of them is needed to establish a set of principles for democratic accountability. The United Nations is clearly weak in this area.

Humanitarian interventions

In the field of humanitarian interventions, most of the situations in which actions take place are characterized as *complex emergencies*. A number of agencies with different specialities are involved, including a variety of UN agencies such as the UNHCR, WFP and UNICEF. Quick actions are needed in these situations. These actions are carried on in an environment where the security of UN staff has increasingly been undermined. Democratic accountability in complex emergencies has to be considerably different from development cooperation. However, the major components, namely participation, transparency and rule of law, are the same in both.

Participation

Any systematic participation of the local population is impossible in complex emergencies, which are characterized by chaotic situations. However, cooperation of the local population is an essential requirement for successful operations. In such a situation, an evaluation arrangement after an initial phase is a useful approach. An evaluation team might be sent to the emergency spot in a year or so to look into a variety of potential issues, including participation of the local population and the interaction between their participation and interagency coordination. Participation of local people in these difficult situations has to be a major concern in the evaluation from the viewpoint of democratic accountability.

Transparency

In complex emergencies mutual suspicion is the most dangerous factor that tends to aggravate already precarious situations. Transparency plays a critical role in alleviating mutual suspicion. UN agencies' efforts to enhance transparency have to lead the way to avoid deterioration of the emergency situation.

A number of different approaches have been experimented with. The most effective among them has been the use of radio. The literacy rate tends to be low in a country in which a complex emergency takes place. Radios can be bought at an affordable cost or even distributed free of charge. The most delicate matter in most cases is the question of languages.

Rule of law

In a complex emergency the local situation is characterized by lawless chaos. Rule of law tends to be neglected. UN agencies have to act quickly, with a significant amount of improvisation on the spot. Cooperation among various agencies has to be left to the discretion of the officers in charge. Chaos, improvisation and discretion are the dominant reality in complex emergencies.

However, from the viewpoint of democratic accountability, a modicum of rule of law has to be inserted into this situation. This is related to inter-agency agreements and contractual agreements with local NGOs and individuals as they participate in the operations. The agreements do not have to be detailed instruments that are drafted by lawyers from both sides. However, rule of law, rather than pure human relations, should be incorporated into the chaotic situation through the operations of UN agencies. It should be possible to establish certain patterns of agreements that would be proper in those operations. Several models of agreements might be produced, based on recent experiences in the world community.

In summary

If one puts all these considerations together, evaluation mechanisms should be the most important instruments in securing democratic accountability in complex emergencies. Elaboration of these arrangements should be an important task for the Peacebuilding Commission of the United Nations.

PKO/interim administration operations

In *PKO/interim administration* operations, the contradictions between the structure of these operations and promotion of democracy in the country concerned get sharpened. Securing democratic accountability of these operations becomes all the more important.

Participation

Participation of the local population takes many forms. Beyond public policy concerns, the livelihood factor plays a key role in relation to the question of participation. In most countries to which a PKO/interim administration is sent, the private sector is virtually non-existent. Thus the only employment opportunities are in the public sector, which in turn means UN operations. Therefore, it is of vital importance to consider the question of participation from the viewpoint of employment opportunities. Since the sustainability of employment with these operations will be impossible, a transition of employment to domestic sectors has to be kept in view at an early stage. At the same time, since the allocation of employment opportunities has significant implications for the social stability of the country, a set of clear guidelines for employment is an essential requirement.

Transparency

In order to avoid any misunderstanding that the PKO/interim administration might be a new form of occupation by foreign powers, the transparency of the operations is vitally important. Beyond radio, which is a powerful instrument, newspapers should be encouraged. Critical comments by local experts on UN operations should be welcomed, so that information provided through radio and newspapers can be credible in the minds of the local population.

Rule of law

In most cases laws and lawyers are scarce in the countries in which a PKO/interim administration is deployed. Social actions, including employment, tend to be dictated by human relations rather than rule of law. Prevalence of nepotism is seen in most of these countries.

In this situation, it is important for UN operations to make the rule of law its principal code of operation. Application of their own principles and legal instruments to the local situation might have to be considered in some cases, although this kind of imposition should, in principle, be avoided.

A new dimension of the UN reform exercise

The above considerations of the question of democratic accountability make it clear that UN reform attempts should include field operations, which have already become the predominant feature of the United Nations in terms of both budget and staff. While financial/fiscal and managerial accountability may largely be considered as an extension of these concerns at the Secretariat headquarters,[13] democratic accountability of field operations raises different types of issues, as has been discussed above. It is important for the UN community to begin to look into this question now, so that the next round of the reform exercise can deal squarely with this dimension of issues.

Any consideration of reform should start with strengthening the participation of the local population in field operations, enhancing the transparency of these operations and applying the principle of the rule of law to them. While it is encouraging that these factors are beginning to play increasing roles, they are far from being satisfactory. Detailed analysis of concrete cases should reveal important lessons to be learned. The short account of this subject in this chapter indicates that there may probably be substantial common patterns of requirements among different kinds of operations.

A team approach should be pursued to conduct meaningful research. For the next round of the reform exercise, research-based proposals rather than political considerations (the 2005 round for the United Nations at 60 was based on the trend set by the UNGA presidency of 1997–1998) should play important roles in relation to the question of democratic accountability of UN field operations. A credible basis for political negotiations should be established by solid research on the emerging predominant feature of the UN system, the field operations. The report of the Secretary-General's High-level Panel, "Delivering as One", provides a useful starting point for this exercise.[14]

Notes

1. Chesterman, Simon (2004) *You, the People: The United Nations, Transitional Administration, and State-building*, New York: Oxford University Press, p. 127.
2. UN GA Res. 217 (III), 10 December 1948.
3. United Nations (2005) "Outcome Document, 2005 Global Summit Meeting", UN Doc. A/RES/60/1, 16 September.
4. Kent, Vanessa (2007) "Protecting Civilians from UN Peacekeepers and Humanitarian Workers: Sexual Exploitation and Abuse", in Chiyuki Aoi, Cedric de Coning and Ramesh Thakur, eds, *Unintended Consequences of Peacekeeping Operations*, Tokyo: United Nations University Press.
5. Baehr, Peter R. (2007) "How to Come to Terms with the Past", in Edel Hughes, William A. Schabas and Ramesh Thakur, eds, *Atrocities and International Accountability: Beyond Transitional Justice*, Tokyo: United Nations University Press.
6. Kennedy, Paul M. (2006) *The Parliament of Man: Past, Present, and Future of the United Nations*, New York: Random House, p. 42.
7. Peterson, M. J. (2006) *The UN General Assembly*, New York: Routledge.
8. Ogata, Sadako (2005) *Turbulent Decade*, New York: W. W. Norton.
9. UN Office of the Secretary-General (2006) "Delivering as One: Report of the Secretary-General's High-level Panel on UN System-wide Coherence in the Areas of Development, Humanitarian Assistance, and the Environment", 9 November, available at www.un.org/events/panel/resources/pdfs/HLP-SWC-FinalReport.pdf, p. 15.

10. Ogata, note 8 above.
11. Takahashi, Kazuo (2006) "UN in Structural Change", in Tatsuro Kunugi and Takeo Uchida, eds, *UN and the New Horizon of Global Civil Society* (in Japanese), Tokyo: Toshindo.
12. World Bank (1989) *From Crisis to Sustainable Growth – Sub-Saharan Africa: A Long-term Perspective Study*, Washington, DC: World Bank.
13. Gordenker, Leon (2005) *UN Secretary-General and Secretariat*, New York: Routledge.
14. UN Office of the Secretary-General, note 9 above.

Part IV

Case studies of accountability

11

Accountability and NPM reforms in the European Union: Implications for UN reform

Koji Fukuda

Introduction

Accountability is essential for effective government and a precondition for all democratic systems. The use of new public management (NPM) reforms as a means of improving accountability in the United Nations was one of the major topics of debate at the UNU Tokyo Symposium on Accountability in October 2006. Given the importance being attached to this issue by the United Nations, it would be useful to examine similar reforms recently initiated in the European Union to see if there are lessons the United Nations can learn.

Since democracy depends on "both elite and mass commitment to its norms and procedures",[1] it is reasonable to ask to what extent, and to whom, should international organizations such as the United Nations ultimately be held accountable. In the light of the corruption scandal surrounding the UN's largest-ever aid programme, the Oil-for-Food Programme in Iraq, in which the Secretary-General's own son was implicated,[2] it would appear the United Nations is facing enormous problems with accountability. It seems appropriate to ask whether the United Nations will be able to reform itself and what guidelines it will use to do so. One option available to the United Nations is the type of NPM reform which has been enacted in the European Union in the past few years in a reasonably successful attempt to enhance its accountability.

It had long been realized that for the European Union to fulfil its mission of creating a "citizens' Europe", higher levels of transparency and

Envisioning reform: Enhancing UN accountability in the twenty-first century, Kuyama and Fowler (eds), United Nations University Press, 2009, ISBN 978-92-808-1170-4

accountability would be essential. Consequently, the European Council's Laeken Declaration[3] stressed the need for the European Union to create a constitution as a way of achieving greater accountability and legitimacy. The declaration set out the four following requirements:

- to create appropriate division and definition of competence between the European Union and its member states
- to effect simplification and ensure transparency of the EU institutions
- to secure more democracy and efficient decision-making processes in the European Union
- to draft a constitution for European citizens.[4]

It also emphasized the significance of strengthening the accountability and legitimacy of the European Union to its member states and European citizens.

However, when citizens were given the opportunity to vote on the Treaty on the Constitution for Europe in 2005, ratifications were rejected by referendums in France and the Netherlands.[5] Indeed, in the case of the Netherlands ratification was rejected by an overwhelming majority, with 61.6 per cent against and only 38.4 per cent in favour.[6] The underlying reason for these rejections was a belief that the EU institutions were becoming excessively complicated, and its governing powers were becoming increasingly remote from the average EU citizen. EU decision-making processes had increasingly become controlled by technocrats in Brussels, and turnouts in European parliamentary elections had been declining for years.

One of the most frequent and damning criticisms of the European Union is that power is held by European élites or unaccountable Eurocrats, and that democratic processes and the will of the people are often ignored as a result. The European Union has been particularly criticized for its perceived lack of accountability in its mechanisms and policy processes. This lack of accountability represents a long standing problem known as the "democratic deficit"[7] in the European media.

This chapter will discuss how successfully the NPM reforms of the late 1990s and early twenty-first century have enhanced accountability in the European Union, and the implications for UN reform. It will mainly focus on managerial accountability and its relationship with democratic or parliamentary control. The specific objectives of the study are as follows.

Firstly, it will examine the history of the concept of accountability and consider its definitions with regard to comparative politics, international relations and public administration. The evolution of notions of accountability and responsibility needs first to be examined by both theoretical and empirical analyses. This examination will define the nature of accountability in the mechanisms of the administrative reform processes in the European Union and other international organizations.

Secondly, it will look at European governance reforms which have been introduced in the light of NPM thinking. It will analyse and summarize the EU experiences of administrative reforms with regard to NPM, and address the broader issues concerned with accountability, agencies and public management. It will then ask how we can make up for the perceived deficit in political/managerial accountability in the European Union and its member states using NPM guidelines.

Thirdly, it will consider what kind of role is expected of agencies and evaluations in the European Union and the United Nations, and the repercussions for accountability lines and links. It will also examine and attempt to explain the similarities and differences between the frequently confused concepts of responsibility and accountability, with particular emphasis on the field of public administration. It seems essential to ask whether the new agencies and policy evaluation systems actually secure the functioning of democratic processes and the effective administrative management of public governance or not.

Concepts and mechanisms of accountability

Historical evolution and types of accountability

The roots of the concept of accountability are derived from notions of political accountability in the "Athenian politics" of ancient Athens.[8] The primary meaning of accountability is the giving of an account or explanation.

Nowadays the word is more frequently used in its parallel sense as a financial term in budgetary management. We are able to distinguish accountability relating to public financial management, bookkeeping and auditing from political accountability, since the former has become independent from the latter and taken on its contemporary meaning as a technical and financial concept.

In the early nineteenth century Jeremy Bentham and John Stuart Mill started developing the concept of political accountability with regard to parliamentary democracy.[9] By the middle of the nineteenth century the constitutional notion of ministerial responsibility had been firmly established in the United Kingdom. According to the works of Albert Dicey,[10] the idea of a "balanced constitution" depends upon two pillars of political responsibility of ministers to parliament: ministerial accountability to elected members, and bureaucratic accountability to ministers.[11]

In the present context, "democratic accountability" is a term familiar in political science, especially comparative politics. It is frequently used to describe accountability in terms of its relation to suffrage, and is mainly focused on the issue of "parliamentary accountability". It seems that democratic/political accountability borrows from the traditional ministerial responsibilities developed by Bentham and Mill, who argued over whether elected representatives should be able to exert political control over the administrative organs of the bureaucracy or not.

Political and managerial accountability

While responsibility has traditionally been broadly defined as including the moral and ethical values of politicians and bureaucrats, the concept of accountability contains notions of "institutional control" and "sanctions", which can be enforced by means of legal force by external persons or bodies. It is therefore fair to say that accountability is actually a highly rigid and specific notion that can be contrasted with the looser and more general notion of responsibility. Philip C. Schmitter argued that: "Accountability, in short, implies an exchange of responsibilities and potential sanctions between rulers and citizens, made all the more complicated by the fact that a varied and competitive set of representatives typically interposes between the two."[12]

Larry Diamond and Leonardo Marlino defined accountability as "the obligation of elected political leaders to answer for their political decisions when asked by citizen-electors or other constitutional bodies".[13] Academic discussion of public administration tends to distinguish "political accountability", including the representative organizations which are accountable to the people's will, from "managerial accountability", which is related to the implementation of public policies in accordance with the performance standards which have been agreed officially.

In another attempt to divide accountability into two subsections, Guillermo O'Donnell described accountability as consisting of "vertical accountability" and "horizontal accountability". Vertical accountability is concerned with representative democracy and corresponds to the accountability defined by Diamond and Marlino.[14] O'Donnell reserved the term "horizontal accountability" for accountability which is related to the inter-branch relations among the judiciary, the executive and the legislature.[15] In other words, horizontal accountability refers to the checks and balances within governmental organizations.

From the perspective of international relations or political-military relations, accountability poses many problems. It is often necessary to cede elements of political control to chiefs of staff when "military planners are given clear guidelines from elected decision-makers".[16] Furthermore, military operations are often performed under the control of international organizations like the North Atlantic Treaty Organization (NATO) and the United Nations, and since the end of the Cold War these operations have become more frequent. Following the 11 September 2001 terrorist attacks in the United States, the Japanese Self-Defense Forces were authorized to provide support for the US-led military action in Iraq. In Japan, the Anti-Terrorism Special Measures Law was adopted by the Diet in October 2001. With this new legislation in place it became possible for armed Self-Defense Forces to be sent to foreign soil during a time of war. However, questions have been raised concerning the law's constitutionality and implications for accountability, since the Japanese constitution forbids the use of force as a means of resolving international disputes.

Considering the various definitions of accountability, it appears that they all have the "principal-agent relationship" in common. The "principal-agent"[17] theory works something like this. Political accountability demands that those to whom power is delegated ("the agent") have a responsibility to justify their decisions and actions to the citizenry ("the principal"). However, the agent must be accorded some room for manoeuvre in deciding the appropriate timing and level of detail of explanations. If this were not the case, excessive time and effort might be spent on unnecessary explanations, conflicting with another important objective – efficiency.

The setting up of adequate standards and "good practices" for use in regular evaluation of European Community activities to realize public policy goals and secure managerial responsibility also lies within the remit of political responsibility. In the present context of criticism of dysfunctions in the checks-and-balances mechanisms, a new structure for securing accountability has been demanded.

Reforming the European Commission and governance using NPM thinking

NPM had spread not only to Britain but also to other Anglo-Saxon countries by the 1990s. NPM was born of a general decline in "govern-ability" among the governments of nation-states and increased civic distrust of governmental problem-solving capability. In its effort to conquer these problems, NPM thinking was augmented by a series of trends collectively known as neo-liberalism. The chief elements of these neo-liberal trends can be summarized as follows:

- practical use of market mechanisms
- serious consideration of the principle of competition
- deregulation or outsourcing of certain government services
- "agencification" and privatization

- greater focus on competition between public and private organs
- a belief in "small government"
- the enhanced use of performance as a criterion for evaluation.[18]

Christopher Hood and Sandford Borins defined NPM as involving hands-on professional management, standards and performance measures, output measurement and controls, disaggregation of units and operating autonomy, competition, privatization and private-sector-style management, discipline and parsimony, and customer service.[19] Managerial accountability refers to the responsibility which the commissioned authority exercises in accordance with the performance evaluation standards previously agreed at a political level.

Financial responsibility and legal liability are both important factors as far as managerial accountability is concerned, and they must be incorporated into both policy-making and implementation processes. The main points can be outlined as formal, rational, practical use of public financial resources; "value for money",[20] rational, practical use of resources; and programme accountability in attaining policy goals.

In March 1995 the Jacques Santer Commission (1995–1999) launched a programme entitled "Sound and Effective Management 2000" (SEM 2000),[21] shortly followed by a further policy statement on "Modernization of Administration and Personnel Policy" (MAP 2000).[22] In 1996 the European Commission launched a "Communication on Evaluation",[23] which introduced strengthened evaluation systems and shared elements of NPM thinking, such as an emphasis on "decentralization" and "performance". However, scandals involving nepotism and inefficiencies in the Santer Commission would have a profound effect on the process of those reforms. Although the European Commission administrative reforms of the mid-1990s were not directly modelled on NPM thinking, they were affected by their member states' NPM reform practices.

The eventual resignation of the Santer Commission made a radical reform effort virtually inevitable. In 1999 the succeeding President of the European Commission, Romano Prodi, appointed the Vice-President, Neil Kinnock (the UK commissioner), to take charge of "European governance" reform using NPM guidelines, with the intention of achieving administrative reforms and encouraging greater accountability. It should be noted that the reforms initiated under Kinnock were indeed strongly influenced by NPM reforms in the United Kingdom.[24]

Although, generally speaking, important progress was made with the issue of accountability at that time, one area where a deficit seemed inevitable was agencification. This is especially problematic because establishing agencies according to NPM strategies is common not only among the EU member states but also in the EU institutional mechanisms. The goal of achieving greater accountability may conflict with other equally important goals, such as greater efficiency and cost reduction. This is particularly true of Western Europe, where people have learnt to prefer "small government".

Based on the results of Kinnock's activity, in 2000 the Prodi Commission published a white paper, "Reforming the Commission",[25] which stressed major changes in "strategic priority setting and resource allocation" and described a system of "activity-based management (ABM)". The paper outlined a policy of "externalizing" operational tasks and activities so as to be able to refocus on policy priorities. The European Commission was more cohesive in its efforts to import ABM than it had been with SEM 2000, MAP 2000 or Dessiner la Commission de Demain (DECODE – "Designing the Commission of Tomorrow")[26] (1997–1999), and the results were more systematic and successful.

NPM is a highly client/customer-oriented system and extremely effective in dealing with the "red tape" associated with traditional bureaucracies. It is used as a hard-core tool for building efficient European public governance by administrative or managerial reforms in the European Union, and also serves as a means of improving the accountability and efficiency of EU administrative management through its "depoliticizing" of power, i.e. keeping policy implementation organs distant from decision-making organs.

Furthermore, the policy evaluation element of NPM is considered to be another important method of enhancing democratization and efficiency in the policy-making processes of the European Union. In this context Hellmut Wollmann demonstrated three phases in the development of relations between public sector reforms and evaluation, as follows:

- the first wave of evaluation during the 1960s and 1970s in the United States, Sweden and Germany
- the second wave of evaluation beginning in the mid-1970s in the Netherlands and the United Kingdom
- the third wave of evaluation during the late 1980s and 1990s, related to the NPM movement when the European Union introduced programme evaluation.[27]

Policy evaluation has already proved effective at eradicating bid rigging and political corruption, and has helped to restore trust in the European Union among both the nation-states' representative organs and the citizens themselves. The white paper on European governance focused on accountability, which the Prodi Commission saw as one of the most important principles to be considered when reforming governance.[28] The overall purpose of the policy evaluation framework is to help strengthen accountability and legitimacy in the European Union.

Table 11.1 Chronological overview of accountability reforms in the European Union

1953	Publication of general reports on the activities of the European Union and bulletin of the European Coal and Steel Community (ECSC)
1958	Publication of general reports on the activities of the European Union and bulletins of the European Economic Community (EEC) and European Atomic Energy Community (EAEC)
1975	Establishing of new community agencies
1977	Setting up of the European Court of Auditors
1979	Introduction of a system of direct European parliamentary elections
	Power of discharge of EU budgets by European Parliament and parliamentary audit
1989	Creation of Conférence des Organs Spécialisés en Affaires Communautaires (COSAC) system to ensure EU legislative processes are watched over by representatives of European Parliament and national parliaments
1992	Establishment of "EUROPOL" cross-border policing unit
1993	Establishment of Office of European Ombudsman to investigate complaints of maladministration in Eurocracy
1998	Opening up of meetings of certain public bodies and increased public access to administrative information concerning European Union
1999	Creation of Fraud Prevention Office (OLAF)
	Creation of committee of independent experts, consisting of Euro MPs, to scrutinize cases of corruption, nepotism and mismanagement
2002	Introduction of "EUROJUST" cross-border prosecution unit for judicial cooperation in criminal matters
	Incorporation of evaluation systems in European Union

Evolution of accountability mechanisms in the European Union

Public accountability mechanisms have gradually developed throughout the EU administrative and management reform processes (table 11.1[29]). Audit and financial control have been exercised under the financial regulations since the 1970s, and a wide variety of steps have been taken to add to the accountability of EU institutional systems.

All the new instruments for enhancing public accountability share certain key characteristics. The Council of Ministers' responsibilities towards the member states and the European Commission's collective responsibilities have been strengthened as a result of the greater accountability to European citizens. However, the accountability of Council of Ministers' members or commissioners towards the European Parliament is only one aspect of transparency.

Accountability can be viewed as an important method of attaining good governance and ensuring governmental objectives are reached. Managerial accountability can be defined as the accountability of a subordinate to a superior in an organization, and it can be found inside public sector organs as well as outside. In order to enhance accountability, we need an evaluation system that is based on a set of ideal criteria with a certain value system, usually referred to as "benchmarking".

John D. Stewart[30] and Kiyoshi Yamaya[31] classified the evolution of the concept of accountability into five stages, all of which are relevant to the modern understanding of accountability. The arrangements for audit and financial control in the European Union are intended to secure legal accountability, which is a law-based system of EU public administration. Staff regulations[32] and financial regulations provide for compensation with regard to the damage suffered by the European Union as a result of an official's misconduct. The five evolutionary stages are illustrated in table 11.2.[33]

Legal accountability and process accountability are concerned with "input legitimacy", while performance accountability is concerned with "performance measurement" and "output legitimacy".[34] "Benchmarking of the best practices" in the public sector should be exercised at

Table 11.2 Modern understanding of accountability

Level	Accountability stages	Measures and institutions
1 Political	Policy accountability	Direct election of European Parliament, policy evaluation directorates-general of the European Commission
2 Political and administrative/managerial	Programme accountability	Programme evaluation Project evaluation DGs of the European Commission
3 Administrative/managerial	Performance accountability	Performance evaluation Administrative inspection European Court of Auditors DGs of the European Commission
4 Administrative/managerial	Process accountability	European Ombudsman European Court of Auditors OLAF DGs of the European Commission
5 Administrative/managerial	Legal accountability	European Court of Justice, a committee of independent experts consisting of Euro MPs and DGs of the European Commission European Court of Auditors EUROJUST, OLAF

every stage of performance measurement.[35] Programme accountability and policy accountability are concerned with the criteria for making judgements about an outcome; while programme and performance accountability imply stated goals which may not always be attainable, policy accountability cannot be confined within any such pre-set standards.

Constitutional and administrative systems may require transparency to an even greater degree than that demanded from commissioners and members of the Council of Ministers. Thus the European Union has always sought to achieve high levels of accountability and demonstrate its sense of political responsibility to its citizenry. Greater accountability of public policy governance, consistent at both international and domestic levels, will be demanded by citizens in the future. An evaluation system operates in the light of pre-fixed standards, and dissatisfaction leads to demands for greater accountability and new instruments for ensuring accountability. Some reformers seek through "privatization" the accountability of market forces, while others seek through "decentralization" bonds of community control. Each idea seeks to replace a hierarchical control dependent on the European Council's or European Commission's accountability by more direct bonds.

Accountability of the European Commission and the Council of Ministers

Accountability of the European Commission

Christopher Lord proposed an analytical framework for accountability at the core of democracy which divides the concept into four categories, distinguishing between *ex ante* and *ex post* accountability of decisions before and after they are taken; vertical and horizontal accountability; internal and external accountability; and output and input accountability.[36] The European Commission's accountability can be appraised from three different viewpoints.

Though commissioners are formally independent of national governments, there are in fact many ways in which the Commission can be supervised by those governments. The Commission depends on the European Parliament and member states for commissioner appointments, the DG's staffing and the commissioners' cabinet staffing, as well as other resources. It is also accountable to the European Parliament, by which it can be dismissed in extreme cases. Thus the Commission is effectively accountable to both member states and the European Parliament. The European Parliament's power to confirm the Commission in office is concerned with *ex ante* accountability, and its power to dismiss the Commission is the instrument which ensures *ex post* accountability. The Commission should also be directly accountable to European citizens, since it has a duty to provide good administration for individuals or groups, as the white paper on governance pointed out.[37]

On 16 March 1999 the Commission of the European Union, then presided over by Jacques Santer, collectively resigned after reading the first report of the Committee of Independent Experts.[38] The Committee had been created six weeks earlier by the European Parliament in order to investigate documents from commissioners which led to allegations being made by the European Parliament itself, as well as by certain sections of the press, concerning fraud, mismanagement and nepotism by individual commissioners. At the end of its investigation the Committee concluded that as far as fraud was concerned, it had not found any evidence on the part of the Commission. However, it had established, in two of the investigated documents, instances of fraud by a certain number of civil servants working for the Commission and by third persons to whom the Commission had outsourced executive tasks. It also found that individual commissioners, and the Commission as a whole, had not dealt adequately with fraud committed by those persons, and that it was therefore guilty of mismanagement. Moreover, flagrant nepotism was identified on the part of one member of the Commission.

Following the Commission's resignation, the European Parliament mandated that the Committee of Independent Experts prepare a second report formulating recommendations for improving the Commission's practices, particularly procedures for awarding financial contracts and contracts for temporary staff. In a "Second Report on Reform of the Commission", submitted to the European Parliament on 10 September 1999,[39] further recommendations were made to formulate measures to deal with the incidents of fraud, mismanagement and nepotism which had been discovered. The second report pointed out the role of the European Parliament in its relation with the Commission: "As in all parliamentary democracies, the relationship between Parliament and the executive branch is of a dual nature: first, Parliament has a right to be *informed* by the Executive, which gives account of its action (hereafter *accountability*); second, it also *judges* the ultimate political responsibility of the Executive and draws the political consequences (hereafter *political responsibility*)."[40] Many of the recommendations were taken into account by the new Commission, under Romano Prodi, in the preparation of its reform proposals.

As has already been mentioned, a keystone of constitutionalism in a parliamentary system, as it exists in most EU member states, is the accountability and political responsibility of cabinet ministers to an elected parliament. This implies that the head of government, the prime minister, and his cabinet ministers must render an account of their actions to parliament, which may hold them politically responsible for any shortcomings in the performance of their duties of office. If these shortcomings cause parliament to lose confidence in the executive, it has the power to force individual ministers, the prime minister or the whole cabinet to resign through a vote of no confidence.

All this raises the question of how the accountability and political responsibility of the European Commission's President and its members in the European Union can be similarly ensured; and there are, in fact, treaty articles in the European Constitution designed to achieve this. Commissioners are bound to explain their actions to the European Parliament, and they can be held accountable by Parliament when those actions constitute wrongful behaviour.

The first requirement follows from article 197 EC, which gives the European Parliament the right to hear and question commissioners orally and in writing: "The Commission shall reply orally or in writing to questions put to it by the European Parliament or by its Members."[41]

The second requirement follows from article 201 EC, which enables the Parliament, by open vote, to censure the Commission, compelling it to resign "as a body" if the motion is carried by two-thirds of the votes cast. Moreover, as a result of the Santer Commission problems, the political leadership function of the Commission's President has been strengthened by the Nice Treaty, which now grants him or her extensive powers over other commissioners if they transgress the rules. It can be seen from the forgoing of some power of individual commissioners to the Commission President that the principle of the accountability of the Commission to the European Parliament already constitutes a basic element of the European Community's legal framework.

All of the above relates to the Commission, which is the executive branch under the first pillar, and leaves unanswered the question of how the principle of accountability and political responsibility should also apply to the Council of Ministers.

Accountability of the Council of Ministers

One reason for the existence of a democratic deficit in the Council is that, under the first pillar, it is not actually part of the executive branch but instead part of the legislative branch – even though its individual members are, at the level of the member states they represent in the Council, members of executive government, and in that capacity accountable only to a member state's national or regional parliament. The Council is supported by many subordinate committees and working groups (more than 250) staffed by national officials, among them the highly effective Committee of Permanent Representatives (COREPER), the Political Committee on Common Foreign and Security Policy and the K.4 Committee on Justice and Home Affairs.[42] COREPER is an indispensable means of interlocking Community administration with a member nation's administrative processes. In principle, European Community administration relies on national administrative organs to carry out Community policy, although in practice there are some notable exceptions, such as defence and welfare policy.

The European Council, which consists of ministers from the elected governments of member states, was not politically accountable to any European Community institution before the Nice summit. Under the Nice Treaty, accountability of the European Council to the public has been enhanced by obliging it to provide when "acting in its legislative capacity greater access to Council documents".[43]

As in the case of member states, the issue of accountability centres on the duty of executive officers to keep Parliament informed, in the sense of rendering account to Parliament by explaining actions and giving insights into executive decision-making. In that context, the question is often raised whether executive officers (commissioners or ministers) should be disciplined only for knowingly misleading Parliament, or also for giving inaccurate or incomplete information provided by the European Commission. It is also reasonable to ask whether some distinction should be made between personal guilt and managerial accountability. In other words, to what extent should a minister or commissioner be sanctioned for wrongdoing on the part of his subordinates when he has no personal knowledge? In such cases, would it be reasonable to expect the minister or commissioner to resign, or should some less serious sanction be imposed? If a minister were suspected of committing illegal actions, he would ultimately be accountable to his own member state's electorate at the next domestic general election. If the voters had lost confidence in his competence or managerial ability, he would risk paying the penalty with his career at this point.

In the second report of the Committee of Independent Experts, the issue of political responsibility was defined as follows: "Political responsibility concerns the political consequences attached to conduct of holders of public office, or to conduct of civil servants working under them within their sphere of competence, by the institution or person who can hold such holders of public office to account."[44]

Although political responsibility is essential in all democratic legal systems, it exists in different forms and at different levels depending on the constitutional structure of the legal system concerned. The report pointed out that differences exist:

(1) as to the extent of political responsibility: only for individual, personal or functional misconduct or also for misconduct of subordinate civil servants?
(2) as to the nature of the political consequence: dismissal, or other consequences of a lesser nature?; imposed collectively, or also individually?
(3) as to the institution or person called upon to impose the political consequence: Parliament, president or prime minister?"[45]

However, the above provisions relate only to the first, or European Community, pillar of the European Union to which the relevant EC Treaty provisions specifically apply. By contrast, no similar provisions apply to the second and third pillars, in which both the European Commission and the Parliament play only a limited role. Under the terms of the first pillar, the European Council and its individual members are not to be held accountable to any organ of the European Union for action undertaken at EU level.

As for managerial accountability, an important distinction should be made between deliberate and accidental acts of misconduct. On the one hand, a superior might order a subordinate to carry out an action which the subordinate does not realize is illegal; while, on the other hand, a subordinate may carry out illegal acts of which his superior has no knowledge.

Under the governance reforms, an official whose misconduct consists solely of ignorance or procedural errors is sanctioned less severely than an official whose misconduct is premeditated and motivated by private interests. An official guilty only of the former type of offence may receive a salary cut or be forcibly transferred to another department, depending on the seriousness of the case. All civil servants are subject to political control under the vertical structures of accountability. Internal and external accountability mechanisms are interdependent and prerequisite conditions in the European Union.

Enhancing accountability through new agencies and evaluation systems in the European Union

Decision-making systems are required to account for actions in terms of their consequences. The European Commission, the Council and the EU agencies should be accountable to their principal, the European citizens or electorate. Output and input accountability are of great importance, in so far as policy implementation processes should be accountable to the citizens as well as decision-making processes.

The white paper on European governance set out to revise the executive processes in the European Community and reduce its reliance on the sprawling and overcomplicated committee system, sometimes negatively referred to as "comitology",[46] with more robust use of the more transparent and manageable autonomous regulatory agencies. Some such agencies existed before the reforms, mainly as information-gathering entities, though there has been a recent trend towards granting them stronger decision-making authority – examples are the European Food Safety Authority[47] and the European Aviation Safety Agency.[48]

The agencies are distinct from the EU Council, European Parliament and European Commission in the framework of the European Union's "first pillar". These EC agencies have their own legal personality, and they are "set up by an act of secondary legislation in order to accomplish a very specific technical, scientific or managerial task".[49] European regulatory agencies are not intended to reduce the Commission's own executive power but, on the contrary, to enhance its power by providing it with specialist support and essential information that it cannot provide independently (see table 11.3).[50] Most of the EC agencies are created by secondary legislation adopted on the basis of article 308 of the EC Treaty, in which no provision is made with regard to political responsibility for agency acts. In order to remedy that situation, one commentator has rightly proposed improving the accountability of agencies through legal means, mainly through procedural scrutiny.[51]

Accountability derived from law can operate as a valuable substitute for accountability derived from politics in instances where the latter does not exist or operates inefficiently. The device is actually used in the case of the Commission itself, whose regulatory institutions can be seen as prime examples of genuine regulatory agencies.[52] As was emphasized in the second report of the Committee of Independent Experts, executives or implementing agencies should also be submitted to strict "accountability through law" devices. In that report, the use of temporary implementing agencies was advocated as a legal instrument designed to organize and better control the contracting out and funding of European Community tasks carried out by third parties – the agency being responsible only for implementing measures, with the Commission retaining the power to make policy choices and judgements.

According to the first Director of the European Environment Agency, his agency is a new type of network administration, its mission being the provision of timely, targeted and reliable information to policy-making agents and the public. Its role is to supersede for informational purposes the complex network of inaccessible committees and other entities responsible for environmental policy-making and make them more accessible to NGOs and the public.[53] The EU model is easily applicable to

Table 11.3 Agencies of the European Union

	Acronym	Date set up
"First pillar" of the European Union		
European Centre for the Development of Vocational Training	CEDEFOP	1975
European Foundation for the Improvement of Living and Working Conditions	EUROFOUND	1975
European Environment Agency	EEA	1990
European Training Foundation	ETF	1990
European Monitoring Centre for Drugs and Drug Addiction	EMCDDA	1993
European Medicines Agency	EMEA	1993
Office for Harmonisation in the Internal Market (Trade Marks and Designs)	OHIM	1993
European Agency for Safety and Health at Work	OSHA	1994
Community Plant Variety Office	CPVO	1994
Translation Centre for the Bodies of the European Union	CdT	1994
European Monitoring Centre on Racism and Xenophobia	EUMC	1997
European Agency for Reconstruction	EAR	2000
European Food Safety Authority	EFSA	2002
European Maritime Safety Agency	EMSA	2002
European Aviation Safety Agency	EASA	2002
European Network and Information Security Agency	ENISA	2004
European Centre for Disease Prevention and Control	ECDC	2005
European Agency for the Management of Operational Cooperation at the External Borders	FRONTEX	2006
"Second pillar" of the European Union		
European Union Institute for Security Studies	ISS	2001
European Union Satellite Centre	EUSC	2002
European Defence Agency	EDA	2002
"Third pillar" of the European Union		
European Police Office	EUROPOL	1992
European Police College	CEPOL	2000
European Judicial Cooperation Office	EUROJUST	2002

horizontal and vertical forms of accountability (table 11.4) which involve sharing sovereignty between member states, pooling it in Brussels and dividing it among the member state governments.

As mentioned above, the SEM 2000 recommended enhancing the eva-

Table 11.4 Evolution of accountability mechanisms in the European Union: Measures and institutions

Administrative managerial legal/ judicial accountability	Administrative managerial process accountability	Administrative managerial performance accountability	Political administrative managerial programme accountability	Political policy accountability
CJ EUROJUST	European Ombudsman	Performance evaluation	Programme evaluation	Policy evaluation
OLAF	OLAF	Administrative inspection	Project evaluation	Direct election of European Parliament
European Court of Auditors	European Court of Auditors	European Court of Auditors		Committee of Independent Experts consisting of MEPs
DGs of the European Commission	DGs of the European Commission	DGs of the European Commission	DGs of the European Commission	DGs of the European Commission

luation capacity for "sound and efficient management", and the appropriate evaluation systems have been established in most of the major directorates-general. It also argued in favour of expanding its network of evaluators at both member state and EU levels. However, external evaluators pointed out that evaluation was "not yet mature enough to be used systematically for decision support". The focus of the evaluation consequently shifted from project evaluation to programme and policy evaluation. In July 2000 the European Commission published a new communication recommending a more complete evaluation system. Up to that point evaluations had focused only on the results of projects, a system known as output evaluation. It was realized that this was insufficient and the evaluation would be enhanced if it covered all stages of a project, using continual evaluation.[54] This was a means of improving the quality of evaluation inside the European Commission and was aimed at evaluation of wider activities.

By applying such an "activity-based evaluation" system, the quality of evaluation within a committee is raised and it becomes possible to use evaluation as a basis for decision-making. The success of a project or programme can easily be measured by comparing pre-set standards with eventual results using the programme accountability and performance-accountability models. As a result of the NPM reforms, evaluation of personnel, policies and systems is now operational in all EU institutions. To prepare a report detailing the results of a particular evaluation, the activity-based evaluation standard, which can also be considered an evidence-based system, must be combined with the five stages of accountability described in table 11.4 (policy, programme, performance, process and legal accountability).

Accountability and NPM-guided reforms in the United Nations

While the United Nations was a latecomer to NPM-guided reforms, NPM concepts now inspire UN reform measures as far as efficiency and accountability are concerned. The United Nations must be seen "to be a center for harmonizing the actions of nations"[55] if it is "to achieve international cooperation in solving international problems".[56]

The UN Secretariat has the specific function of ensuring accountability with regard to UN administration and actions taken in accordance with budget and legal and accounting standards. This is managerial accountability – that is, vertical or hierarchical accountability and internal to the Organization – and is required in the United Nations in respect of relations such as those between the Secretary-General and officials, including UN Ambassadors, of each Member State, representatives of the permanent members of the Security Council, and between the Secretary-General and UN staff.

The United Nations is also required to provide horizontal and political accountability to stakeholders who are affected by UN actions, such as other international organizations, Member States, NGOs and multinational companies. In other words, in the UN context political or managerial accountability is required depending upon the policy/decision-making process, the implementation process, the evaluation process and other processes.

Proposals for NPM-guided reforms in the United Nations are primarily concerned with the international management of public administration. According to Graham T. Allison Jr, the "function of general management" consists of "strategy", "managing internal components" and "managing external constituencies".[57] In this case, "strategy" means deciding organizational goals and priorities and setting out the implementation plans to achieve them.[58] "Managing internal components" refers to management of UN internal organs, personnel administration and control of performance. "Managing external constituencies" is an organizational response to external outsourcing organs, agencies, pressure groups, private enterprises, the media and civil society. The following four steps can be suggested as an NPM reform approach for the United Nations in the light of the lessons learned during the EU reform process.

Firstly, a benchmark assessment system should be introduced into the internal organs, whereby every objective should be linked to a management assessment system. This is an example of a top-down approach, featuring practical use of an external agency. It is necessary to build a stakeholders' participation and supervision system so that the United Nations and its stakeholders can cooperate together more fully in order to provide global public goods better.

Secondly, a bottom-up process should also be introduced to assist the reform of systematic internal management. This would oversee office administration and the administrative performance evaluation systems, and be indispensable for planning and assessing outcomes as well as setting budgets.

Thirdly, the results of public policy implementation evaluations carried out by Commission staff representing various member states together with the results of audits carried out by the independent European Court of Auditors must both be utilized throughout the policy formulation process. The viability of a prospective project or programme could then be assessed by considering or analysing the information obtained during the two different types of evaluation, namely the qualitative policy evaluation and the quantitative financial evaluation. The resultant "double" evaluation would be more accurate and effective, and reflect the Commission's commitment to the concept of "best practice".

Whenever dubious financial management or instances of fraud occur, not only in member states but also in international organizations such as the United Nations and the European Union, the organizations are criticized for the deficits in transparency and accountability. Furthermore, any organization which offers global public goods in cooperation with international organizations and their member states, NGOs or private enterprises has to secure its accountability towards its constituencies. Some lessons learned from the EU experience will be applicable to UN attempts to improve its "accountability" to the global community, and will also help to enhance the democratization of the policy-making processes of the United Nations and related organizations as well as their accountability to "the peoples of the United Nations".

Conclusion

This chapter has tried to show how NPM-guided public sector governance reforms have been introduced into the European Union and how, during the course of these reforms, the aim has been to enhance accountability throughout the European Union and the United Nations. According to the Commission staff working document, "If it is accepted that democracy in Europe is based on two twin pillars – the accountability of executives to European and national legislative bodies and the effective involvement of citizens in devising and implementing decisions that affect them – then it is clear that the reform of European modes of governance is all about improving democracy in Europe."[59]

This chapter finds that NPM reforms have been inextricably linked with accountability in the European Union, and there are a number of channels through which accountability, under its various definitions, may be achieved. As far as political accountability is concerned, these include democratic elections, by which parliaments are held accountable, and systems of scrutiny and sanctions which can be applied to ministers. With regard to managerial accountability, such channels include the right of the public to consult an ombudsman, to have open access to administrative documents and to have projects or programmes scrutinized by auditing bodies. Although normally considered the principal, citizens should shift to being the agent when obliged to monitor and assess official decisions. If the EU experience of NPM reform is drawn upon, it can be concluded that accountability, both political and managerial, must be institutionalized if it is to work effectively in the United Nations.

The notion of political/democratic accountability differs from that of managerial accountability, in that the latter is hierarchical and internal to the organization, though usually supported by external audit agencies. Recently, due to concern over the imperfect enforcement of EU law, the EU agencies have begun to accrue regulatory and executive functions. Former UN Secretary-General Kofi Annan attempted to reform many of the UN's organs and agencies, starting in 1997, but progress has been slow.

In this context I would like to suggest a few methods by which institutional reform at the United Nations may be advanced:

- the establishment of a clear system of delegation of authority in the Secretariat as a basis for enhancing accountability
- greater transparency and more openness in sharing information and decision-making
- strengthening the monitoring and evaluation systems in the United Nations.

Success or failure of the EU's recent expansion to 27 members may depend on whether it is viewed as being accountable to its citizenry or not, and the United Nations might find itself in a similar situation if the reform initiatives taken by former Secretary-General Kofi Annan are not followed through by Secretary-General Ban Ki-moon.

The United Nations will be able to use the EU's experience with NPM as a framework for its attempts to reform itself and make itself more relevant and, above all, accountable to its citizens in the increasingly globalized and ever-changing world of the twenty-first century.

Notes

1. Institute of Human Rights and Humanitarian Law (2007) "Homepage", available at www.ihrhl-ng.org/aboutus.html, p. 5/9.
2. Zweifel, Thomas D. (2006) *International Organizations and Democracy: Accountability, Politics, and Power*, Boulder, CO: Lynne Rienner, pp. 59–60.
3. Laeken Declaration on the Future of the European Union (2001) European Council Meeting in Laeken, 14–15 December, in Koji Fukuda and Akiba Hiroya, eds (2003) *European Governance After Nice*, London: RoutledgeCurzon, annex, pp. 176–179.
4. Ibid.
5. European Commission (2006) "The European Constitution: Post-referendum Survey in the Netherlands, June 2005," in Koji Fukuda, ed. (2006) *What Is the EU Constitutional Treaty?*, Tokyo: Waseda University Press, pp. 13–15; European Commission (2006) "Flash Eurobarometer, The European Constitution: Post-referendum Survey in France, June 2005", in Koji Fukuda, ed. (2006) *What Is the EU Constitutional Treaty?*, Tokyo: Waseda University Press, pp. 15–17.
6. Ibid.

7. Zweifel, Thomas D. (2002) *Democratic Deficit?*, Lanham, MD: Lexington Books, pp. 13–14.
8. Elster, Jon (1999) "Accountability in Athenian Politics", in Adam Prezeworski, Susan C. Stokes and Bernard Manin, eds, *Democracy, Accountability, and Representation*, New York: Cambridge University Press, pp. 253–278, at pp. 253–254.
9. Przeworski, Adam, Susan C. Stokes and Bernard Manin, eds (1999) *Democracy, Accountability, and Representation*, New York: Cambridge University Press, p. 32.
10. See Harlow, Carol (2002) *Accountability in the European Union*, New York: Oxford University Press, p. 6; Strom, Kaare (2003) "Parliamentary Democracy and Delegation", in Kaare Strom, Wolfgang C. Müller and Torbjörn Bergman, eds, *Delegation and Accountability in Parliamentary Democracies*, New York: Oxford University Press, pp. 55–106, at p. 72.
11. Dunn, Delmer D. (1999) "Mixing Elected and Non-elected Officials in Democratic Policy Making: Fundamentals of Accountability and Responsibility", in Adam Prezeworski, Susan C. Stokes and Bernard Manin, eds, *Democracy, Accountability, and Representation*, New York: Cambridge University Press, pp. 297–326, at pp. 297–299.
12. Schmitter, Philippe C. (2005) "The Ambiguous Virtues of Accountability", in Larry Diamond and Leonardo Marlin, eds, *Assessing the Quality of Democracy*, Baltimore, MD: Johns Hopkins University Press, pp. 18–31, at p. 18.
13. Diamond, Larry and Leonardo Marlino, eds (2005) *Assessing the Quality of Democracy*, Baltimore, MD: Johns Hopkins University Press, p. xix.
14. Ibid.
15. O'Donnell, Guillermo (1998) "Horizontal Accountability in New Democracies", *Journal of Democracy* 9(3), pp. 112–126.
16. Bono, Giovanna (2004) "The European Union as an International Security Actor: Challenges for Democratic Accountability", in Hans Born and Heiner Hänggi, eds, *The "Double Democratic Deficit": Parliamentary Accountability and the Use of Force under International Auspices*, Aldershot and Burlington, VT: Ashgate, pp. 163–181, at p. 175.
17. Hooghe, Liesbet (2001) *The European Commission and the Integration of Europe: Images of Governance*, New York: Cambridge University Press, pp. 153–155.
18. Walzenbach, G. P. E., ed. (2006) *European Governance: Policy Making between Politicization and Control*, Aldershot and Burlington, VT: Ashgate, pp. 74–75.
19. See Kickert, Walter J. M., ed. (1997) *Public Management and Administrative Reform in Western Europe*, Northampton, MA: Edward Elgar, p. 18; Kettle, Donald F. (2005) *The Global Public Management Revolution*, Washington, DC: Brookings Institution Press, pp. 17–18.
20. Levy, Roger (1996) "Managing Value for Money Audit in the European Union: The Challenge of Diversity", *Journal of Common Market Studies* 34(4), pp. 509–529.
21. European Commission (1995) *Sound and Effective Management 2000 (SEM 2000)*, Luxembourg: Office for the Publications of the European Communities.
22. European Commission (1997) "Modernization of Administration and Personnel Policy", MAP 2000, *Bulletin EU*, p. 123, point 1.9.10. It aimed at inventory staff and their functions.
23. European Commission (1996) "Communication on Evaluation", SEC (96)659final.
24. Jenkins, Kate, Karen Caines and Andrew Jackson (1988) *Improving Management in Government: The Next Steps: Report to the Prime Minister*, London: HMSO. This report proved to be highly influential and had far-reaching consequences for the OECD countries.
25. European Commission (2000) *Reforming the Commission: A White Paper*, parts 1 and 2, Luxembourg: Office for the Publications of the European Communities.

26. European Commission (1999) *Designing Tomorrow's Commission: A Review of the Commission's Organization and Operation (Dessiner la Commission de Demain – DECODE)*, 7 July, Brussels: European Commission.
27. Wollmann, C. Hellmut, ed. (2003) *Evaluation in Public Sector Reform*, Northampton, MA: Edward Elgar, pp. 1–2.
28. European Commission (2001) "European Governance – A White Paper", COM(2001)428final, 25 July; Fukuda, Koji (2003) "Institutional Reform and European Governance", in Koji Fukuda and Akiba Hiroya, eds, *European Governance After Nice*, London: RoutledgeCurzon, pp. 41–66, at pp. 62–64.
29. The source is Fukuda, Koji (2006) "Accountability and New Agencies in the European Union", *Waseda Journal of Political Science and Economics* 36(4), p. 8.
30. Stewart, J. D. (1984) "The Role of Information in Public Accountability", in Anthony Hopwood and Cyril Tomkins, eds, *Issues in Public Sector Accounting*, Oxford: Philip Allan Publishers, pp. 15–34, at pp. 17–18.
31. Yamaya, Kiyoshi (2002) "Evaluations and Control in Public Sector", in Koji Fukuda, Masaru Mabuchi and Koichiro Agata, eds, *Gyosei no hyouka to tousei* (*New Aspects of Public Administration: Issues and Perspectives*), Tokyo: Horitsubunkasha, pp. 145–181, at p. 163 (fig. 6.2).
32. European Commission (2004) "Staff Regulations of Officials of the European Communities and the Conditions of Employment of Other Servants in the European Communities", 5 January, available at http://ec.europa.eu/dgs/personnel_administration/statut/tocen 100.pdf.
33. The sources are Stewart, note 30 above, pp. 17–18; Yamaya, note 31 above.
34. Lord, Christopher (2004) *Democratic Audit of the European Parliament*, New York: Palgrave Macmillan, pp. 131–132.
35. European Commission, note 26 above, pp. xii–xiii.
36. Lord, note 34 above, pp. 130–132.
37. European Commission, note 28 above, pp. 19–20, 34–35.
38. Fukuda, Koji (2000) "On the Resignation of the European Commission and European Parliamentary Control", *Waseda Journal of Political Science and Economics* 34(1), pp. 233–263, at pp. 249–250.
39. European Commission, Committee of Independent Experts (1999) *Second Report on Reform of the Commission*, vol. I, 10 September, available at www.europarl.europa.edu/experts/pdf/rep2-1en.pdf.
40. European Commission, Committee of Independent Experts (1999) "Second Report on Reform of the Commission", vol. II, 10 September, available at www.europarl.europa.edu/experts/pdf/rep2-2en.pdf., p. 129 (point 7.14.1).
41. See article 197, EC, paras 2 and 3; OJ No. C 352/116, 24 December 2002.
42. Lord, note 34 above, p. 162.
43. Article 207, EC.
44. Committee of Independent Experts, note 40 above, vol. II, p. 132 (point 7.14.15).
45. Ibid.
46. See Bergström, C. Fredrik (2005) *Comitology: Delegation of Powers in the European Union and the Committee System*, New York: Oxford University Press.
47. Regulation No. 178/2002, 28 January 2002 (OJ L31).
48. Regulation No. 1592/2002, 15 July 2002 (OJ L240).
49. See http://europa.eu/agencies/community agencies/index_en.htm.
50. The source is http://europa.eu/agencies/index_en.htm, 30 September 2006.
51. Dimitrakopoulos, Dionyssis G., ed. (2004) *Changing European Commission*, New York: Manchester University Press, p. 97.
52. Ibid., pp. 101, 160.

53. See http://europa.eu/agencies/community_agencies/eea/indexen.htm; Arnull, Anthony and Daniel Wincott (2002) *Accountability and Legitimacy in the European Union*, New York: Oxford University Press, p. 396.
54. European Commission (2000) "Communication to the Commission from Mrs. Schreyer in Agreement with Mr. Kinnock and the President", SEC (2000)1051, 26 July, p. 3.
55. UN Charter, article 1(4).
56. Ibid., article 1(3).
57. Allison, Graham T. Jr (1982) "Public and Private Management: Are They Fundmentally Alike in All Unimportant Respects?", in Frederick S. Lane, ed., *Current Issues in Public Administration*, New York: St Martin's Press, pp. 13–33, at p. 17.
58. Ibid.
59. Commission Secretariat on the European Communities (2000) "White Paper on European Governance: Enhancing Democracy in the European Union", Work Programme SEC(2000)157/7final, p. 4.

12

Improving accountability and legitimacy in the European Union

Michael Reiterer

Introduction

If you consult the popular Wikipedia[1] online encyclopaedia on "accountability and the European Union" you are greeted by what I would call the "negative" concept of accountability, namely the risk of maladministration of public budgets, the creation of the European Court of Auditors, the European Anti-Fraud Office (OLAF) and the need for transparency and double-entry bookkeeping, and you are reminded of the spectacular fall of the Santer Commission in 1999, orchestrated by the European Parliament.

"Accountability" is part of democratic government, governance and control. There is a (fine) difference between "accountability" and "responsibility": while the former puts more emphasis on the need to explain (transparency), the latter implies a liability to carry out a duty, e.g. to be held liable for the policy goal and its implementation. Thus a decision-maker can be held accountable, as he/she is responsible. Consequently, one can be held personally accountable democratically, legally, politically or financially, depending on the context.

Democratic accountability

In the context of the European Union (EU), *democratic* accountability plays a particular role and has to be assured in a different manner

Envisioning reform: Enhancing UN accountability in the twenty-first century, Kuyama and Fowler (eds), United Nations University Press, 2009, ISBN 978-92-808-1170-4

compared to a nation-state, as the European Union lacks the political institutions and procedures normally associated with democratic control. It lacks an elected government – which the European Commission (EC) is not. It also lacks the usual tension between government and opposition, a function which the European Parliament is not providing, as there is no party "backing" a European government (or the EC). There is no real Europe-wide party system,[2] no real European public and consequently only a nascent European public opinion. The European Parliament, directly elected since 1978, has successfully increased its controlling rights and its oversight over the budget – the right to dismiss the EC over the budget being the strongest means. National parliaments, pressure groups, non-governmental organizations (NGOs) and other emanations of civil society attempt to fill the remaining void. The Treaty of Lisbon (2007)[3] even strengthens the rights of national parliaments of member states in surveying respect for the principles of subsidiarity and proportionality, although they are not European institutions (art. 61B).

The European Commission presented its views on accountability in the context of its white paper on European governance (2001).[4] Accountability is regarded as an instrument to overcome the "disenchantment of many of the Union's citizens" in delineating clearly the responsibilities and competences of each European institution and also the corresponding ones of its member states. Information and communication are the strategic tools to implement accountability, as they would empower interested citizens to exercise control and participate actively, thereby contributing to governance on the European level.

In presenting a special report in 2006 on integrating new EU members, the European Commission reverted to the issue of accountability in the context of measures to ensure the EU's capacity to maintain the momentum of European integration, consisting of three components: institutions, common policies and budget. In relation to institutions, "The Union needs to ensure that its institutions and decision-making processes remain effective and accountable, for the sake of current Member States as well as in view of further enlargement."[5]

Carol Harlow criticizes the EC approach as too process-oriented and claims that the institution should have an obligation to render an account of its doings, e.g. the content of its policies. Furthermore, she advocates a pre-eminence of democratic accountability (through national parliaments) over the judicial one, represented by the European Court of Justice.[6] She refers to a statement of principles developed by the Committee of Independent Experts, set up to investigate the Santer Commission:

> The principles of openness, transparency and accountability are at the heart of democracy and are the very instruments allowing it to function properly. Open-

> ness and transparency imply that the decision making process at all levels is as accessible and accountable as possible to the general public. It means that the reasons for decision making are known and that those taking decisions assume responsibility for them and are ready to accept personal consequences when such decisions are subsequently shown to be wrong.[7]

While I agree that respect for procedures alone is not a sufficient condition – content-wise, disastrous decisions can be taken while meticulously respecting procedures – it is true that within the EU system procedures play a particularly important role as they differ from pillar to pillar (comitology), reflecting for example whether a matter is within Community, mixed or member states' competence.

Legal accountability

Law plays a specially important role in the functioning of the European Union: the Union is based on a treaty which is enforceable; EU law is the same in all member states and has an autonomous character in relation to national law of member states. which it supersedes; and large parts of the law are directly applicable in member states.

Thus the European Court of Justice (ECJ) is the unique manifestation of legal accountability at the European level. The Court may decide disputes among member states, between the European Union and member states, among EU organs and between European citizens and the European Union. Disputes on which the Court may act fit into several categories: infringement actions and preliminary rulings are related to the obligations of member states; annulment proceedings, action for failure to act, action in damages and rulings on international agreements are related to the institutions of the European Community.[8]

European citizens can seek legal proceedings for any dispute involving European law at their national courts, given the supremacy of European law over national law and the direct applicability of the former. National courts may, and sometimes must, submit questions to the European Court of Justice for a preliminary ruling. The ECJ must then give an interpretation or review the legality of a rule of European law, which is of a binding nature for the national court asking the question.

The Court has also recognized the principle of liability: infringements committed by member states are likely to give rise to obligations to pay compensation. Most conspicuously, the development of ECJ case law illustrates the Court's contributions to creating a legal environment for European citizens by protecting the rights which Community legislation confers on them in various areas of daily life, as well as advancing

European integration in some areas by means of so-called judge-made law (e.g. the *Cassis de Dijon* decision[9]).

The Court of First Instance, set up to relieve the ECJ from some case-load, has special competence for actions brought by companies in the field of competition. The latest addition to the European court system is the European Civil Service Tribunal (2005) to adjudicate between the European institutions and their staff.

Political accountability

The revamped Lisbon Strategy of the European Union[10] is an example of political accountability with a "positive" connotation already close to public diplomacy. Heads of state or government committed publicly to take actions to realize agreed policy goals in a verifiable manner, setting up a system of reporting and peer review based on agreed benchmarks allowing for public scrutiny. In devising this strategy, member states committed publicly to implement a programme for which they themselves, and *not* the European Union, are largely responsible. Positive as transparency is, this technique has one important snake: the public can get the impression that "the EU" (and not the member states) has to implement or, as it is presently the case, has largely failed to implement policies in time, thereby rolling over political accountability (inadvertently?) from the member states to "the EU". Thus this example of "positive" political and public accountability (as opposed to the negative one referred to earlier) can also be a double-edged sword in terms of the perception of the European Union by the public.

The European Union and the United Nations: Some parallel developments

While there are obvious differences in the geographical extent, range and depth of integration of policies covered by the United Nations and the European Union, there are some parallels in historical and organizational terms.[11]

Both were born in the aftermath of the Second World War – the United Nations in 1945 and the European Coal and Steel Community, the forerunner of the modern European Union, in 1951, while the EC itself was founded in 1957. Both have expanded enormously since then – the United Nations from 51 to 191 member states and the European Union from six to 27, with a few more to come in the future. The range of activities of each institution has seen similarly radical growth. Each institution has faced the challenge of how to agree and deliver effective policies in spite of the very different political intentions, culture and administrative traditions of their member states and staff. Both are struggling to close the discrepancy between expectations and the legal and financial means with which they are implemented.

Furthermore, the administrative and governance structures created in the 1940s and 1950s were not adapted to deal with the increased complexity expansion generated – nor with the new challenges arising from the need to cooperate internationally in order to have the capacity to solve an ever-growing array of problems whose solutions need to be international in nature to meet new security threats. While there were attempts to deal with these issues in the past, they were piecemeal and made limited progress, hampered not only by bureaucratic inertia but also by a lack of understanding of the genuine need to cooperate and the corresponding lack of political will to cooperate closely on the international level.

Nevertheless, both institutions have achieved much over the years: the United Nations in the areas of sustainable development, refugees, fights against diseases and the promotion of good governance; and the European Union in the creation of a single currency, a functioning single market, enlargement and border-free travel in most of Europe (Schengen area). But both have been badly affected by scandals, worsened by the perception of outsiders that there exists a climate of inefficiency and systemic corruption. The result for both institutions has been a loss of confidence by key stakeholders, and of morale by staff.

It is against this background that both the Commission and the United Nations have committed to far-reaching reforms of internal management and governance.[12] The constitution for Europe would have added clearer institutional reform, which is a necessary complement to efforts to improve management. However, the above-mentioned Treaty of Lisbon (2007), which replaced the constitution after the latter was rejected in referendums in France and the Netherlands, pursues institutional reform, although the structure of the treaty is less transparent than its failed predecessor. Its implementation hinges on a second positive vote in Ireland, in a referendum due in October or November 2009.

While the United Nations and the European Union cooperate extensively in the realm of development policy, they also cooperate in the non-external relations parts of activities, of which "administration" is of particular interest for this study. Both organizations exchange experience and best practices, including staff exchanges and experience in planning, budgeting, human resource management, internal audits and controls and ethics. Because of the many areas of cooperation in the field – the European Union contributed in 2006 €1,400 million to the work of the

United Nations – they undertake joint action in anti-fraud investigations and activities including sharing of experience, participation in investigators' conferences and detachment of staff.[13]

Because of the organizational differences between the European Union and the United Nations, parallels between the two institutions should not be overstated. In the European Union, unlike the United Nations, the internal organization of the European Commission operates with very considerable autonomy from the member states, both organizationally and as regards policy development. As the executive body of the European Union, the Commission is headed by senior politicians. They are appointed collectively and subject to approval by the directly elected European Parliament, still with one per member state. Most importantly, the Treaty of Lisbon imposes a clear obligation requiring them not to accept instructions from anyone, including their country of origin. In turn, member states have agreed not to seek to influence commissioners.

Thus, while the commissioners obviously bring with them an awareness of national issues and sensitivities, they are committed to seeking to develop policies in the collective interests of Europe as a whole, and are genuinely free to do so. Failure to comply with these obligations can result in the European Parliament forcing the College of Commissioners as a whole to resign. However, only the President of the Commission can request the College to discharge a fellow commissioner.[14]

Much of the Commission's power comes from its right of initiative, while the decision-making power remains with the member states organized in the Council of Ministers and the European Parliament. The Commission can try to cajole and shame member states into action by means of the "Community method". Compared to the United Nations, the possibility of taking decisions by majority rather than consensus is an important difference and asset.

The EU reform

The Commission structure allowed for largely separating internal management reform from the wider issues of political control over the organization. Where the member states were involved, however, some were reluctant to accept changes in the Commission's internal systems which conflicted with the approach used in their home civil services, complaining that the reform was too "Anglo-Saxon" or "Nordic". Member states also used EU reform to push their national agendas in trying to set an example for their own internal reforms in reducing the cost of the European administration.

The reform attempted to rebuild trust after the Santer Commission scandal and make sure that responsibility was clearly defined and ascribed. Modernizing the administration by ensuring that the planning, financial control and governance structures were able to deliver policy and manage programmes rapidly and coherently were the key objectives.

The reform concentrated on three essential elements:

- improving financial management and adding personal accountability
- a new strategic plan through better use of limited resources
- investing in personnel.

Key elements of the reform

First, the *financial management and control system* was changed to assign responsibility clearly and specifically to the relevant individuals (decentralization); transparency is assured through annual activity reports and declarations from all the Directors-General, forming a comprehensive management reporting system; and a new financial regulation enabled rapid transition to modern accrual accounting in 2005 – although some overshooting had to be corrected.

The Internal Audit Service (IAS) replaced the old system[15] of central *ex ante* financial control. The idea is to monitor the system rather than individual transactions in giving real responsibility to those authorizing a transaction. The new system assures transparency, especially for procurement awards and procedures, in separating functions of checks and balances. Internal control standards, the corresponding baseline requirements, are implemented and reviewed annually. The introduction of the new system was accompanied by continuous and obligatory training – no transfer of responsibility without previous training.

The European Court of Auditors regularly reports on the financial management of the EU budget in order to inform the European taxpayer. If necessary, the Court of Auditors involves OLAF, the European Anti-Fraud Office, in reporting on fraud or other irregularities. In addition, officials are obliged under the new statute to report suspected irregularities to their superiors, the Secretary-General of the Commission or directly to OLAF. The so-called "whistleblowers" are personally protected and can be assured of a thorough investigation and an effective response.

In order to avoid "EU-bashing", European citizens should be made aware of a recent report by the Court of Auditors highlighting that financial mismanagement of the EU budget predominantly takes place at the *national* level, given that 90 per cent of income and expenditure is managed by national authorities.[16] As a relatively small bureaucracy, the European Union makes use of national bureaucracies to implement European measures nationally (mediatization).

The second pillar of reform was *strategic planning and programming*. This essential component of reform enables the Commission to show, by using activity-based management (ABM), how resources are matched – or in some cases *not* matched – to tasks assigned with much greater precision. It should also allow Commission, Council and Parliament to make informed choices between priorities for the use of limited resources. In other terms, decisions on priorities, policy objectives and activities should be matched with decisions allocating human, administrative, IT and financial resources. Thus the use of resources should become much more policy-driven and promote performance management throughout the Commission,[17] while avoiding the Commission being tasked with actions without having the required means to deliver.

This was vital in order to address what had been a recurring theme in EU affairs: member states or the European Parliament asking the Commission to act in some new, currently topical areas. Always keen to increase its areas of competence and influence, the Commission agreed. Then, finding it had inadequate resources, either the policy was not delivered – or worse, complex structures outside the proper control of the Commission were created to try to stretch the available resources further than they would go. Inevitably, these then sometimes failed. Furthermore, outsourcing to agencies is also accompanied by the danger of loss of democratic and political control.

Ideally, the system will provide a tool to develop effective multi-annual programming, screen Commission activities and identify where resources were underused and could thus be redeployed more productively to other areas. Management must be able to cost, plan and deliver policies and operations on time and on budget – or admit to negative priorities and refuse to undertake these tasks if the required skills or resources are lacking.

Beyond managerial improvements, systemic ones are required: accountability in the Commission's strategic planning is increased by implementing the principles of subsidiarity (whenever there is no exclusive European Community competence) and proportionality. Furthermore, the assessment of the economic, environmental and social impact of a proposed legislative initiative contributes to holding decision-makers accountable. This is not only a principle of administrative technique and distribution of power, but a means to assure a greater degree of democracy: citizens have the possibility of participating in the decision-making process on issues which concern them most, thereby providing real added value to European Community actions.[18]

In the third theme of reform, *modernization of personnel policy*, fundamental changes to the staff structure were introduced. The philosophy underlying these was simple. For many people, and for much of its history, the European "project" has been seen as an exciting and forward-looking task to be part of. Thus many very high-calibre staff were attracted to work for this ideal, forming the "European élite". But that had allowed the institution to become rather lazy about staff development and motivation: many staff were not being empowered to fulfil their potential and often became very frustrated as a result. I shall revert to this issue later.

A new individual personnel appraisal system, merit-driven promotion and a more linear career structure, breaking down the barriers between secretaries, assistants and professional staff, are meant to contribute to motivation and flexibility of staff. Other measures included a major increase in staff and management training and strengthening of the disciplinary system.

Reform also introduced compulsory five-yearly job changes – rotation – for "sensitive jobs", and indeed for all staff with financial responsibilities. The objective was to achieve a balance between experience and bringing new ideas into an area – and also to prevent relations between staff and contractors becoming too close. In the past, some senior management positions were seen – informally – as "flagged" for particular member states: this has changed to some degree. Individual member states are no longer entitled to fill "their" specific positions; merit plays a greater role, creating additional opportunities for the best staff of all nationalities. Of course, achieving a reasonable geographic balance remains vital – and will never be straightforward in an international organization. Presently nationals from new member states are favoured over other EU nationals to facilitate the filling of the informal newcomer quotas. As part of reform, active measures to improve gender balance are being taken – from a starting point where representation of women at professional and especially management levels was deficient. Appointing the first-ever female Secretary-General of the European Commission was a visible sign of this policy commitment.

Taking stock – Managing change

Reform – however vital for the long term – is always a disruptive process and therefore needs clear goals and means, permanent screening and two-way communication.

Reform is thus a process, and requires cultural change. It needs rolling out, and not a big bang overnight. Managing change is an art in itself. In that light it should be noted that staff continuously contribute to incremental improvements of their working methods by means of "ideas banks", where improvements can be proposed and scrutinized.[19]

One of the most difficult issues for both the Commission and the United Nations is to achieve the right balance between empowering staff and managers on the one hand, and retaining control by those at the centre commensurate with their political accountability on the other.

This is a major challenge for any governmental organization: compared to the private sector, there is no equivalent to the simple measure of profitability to determine whether a particular approach should be pursued. In government and governance – particularly at the international level – the interaction between different policies is very complex, so effective coordination and special know-how are vital. The complexity of "things European", mastering the intricacies of the legal and institutional European system, grown over 52 years and showing layers of political compromises and various successful and not-so-successful reforms, while coping with the unique structure of the decision-making process of the European Union (Community level, mixed competences, member states' prerogative) requires a high degree of technical expertise vested in many European officials. The political level, the commissioners, while making use of this expertise, have to add their political analysis, instinct and evaluation in giving political guidance and in making decisions – individually in their respective area of competence or collectively when voting in the College of Commissioners. This is the basis for accountability to the European Parliament, which has the power to censure them.

While this interaction between officials and politicians, between the administrative and political levels, is common to any government structure, the reliance of commissioners on public servants may in some cases or for some time be larger than on the national level because of the described complexity on the European level, with which nationally experienced politicians may not be familiar. It therefore turns into a question of management by the commissioner (politician), supported by a private office (cabinet) of trusted and personally selected officials, and not a question of officials taking control over politicians. Management also means finding the right mix of central control and delegation of power when exercising political guidance. Central, top-down control does not result in effective policy, as it is likely to demoralize staff in the process. It is an ongoing challenge to find an adequate solution; systems need careful fine-tuning. All stakeholders (officials, politicians and the public) need education about the constraints if any system is to have the flexibility to function.

A major element of the EU's reform in terms of the foreign policy-making process was to try to distinguish between policy and programme formation and design, and implementation tasks for the Directorate-General for External Relations (RELEX) and EuropeAid Co-operation Office (AIDCO) respectively. The former were seen as core tasks, linked to the Commission's position as having the sole right to propose policy initiatives. The idea was that if the policy design was clear, the implementation phase could essentially proceed automatically, without further political involvement. Implementation was moved to various offices and agencies, semi-independent of the Commission. The master plan was that the centre would be free to concentrate on the core tasks and important strategic thinking, while agency managers would be empowered to structure their activities in the most efficient manner. The agencies would also be able to employ less-skilled and less-expensive staff.

Practice showed, however, that the boundary between policy-making and implementation is fuzzy, and that it is very difficult to insulate the Commission from the consequences of failings in the agencies. Further, there are inefficiencies: agencies tend to recreate core support services – finance and human resources for example – that were previously provided by the Commission. And their management boards tend to blur the lines of accountability. So, agencies are certainly no panacea.

Honest stock-taking also admits that in the reform process sometimes a new bureaucracy was created in the process, particularly through increases in controls to address inadequacies revealed by past problems. Over-regulation and over-documentation have happened, thereby reducing the implementation capacity; speed in implementation sometimes produced contradictions or poorly designed procedures. Whatever the cause, the result has been somewhat to discredit reform. Therefore a "simplification" campaign was set up, in which staff are invited to submit their ideas for improvements – so far, the response has been very encouraging. E-Commission should reduce the paper flow, redesigning internal procedures for delivery by IT.

Management "plus" reform

While management reform is necessary to restore confidence – if the European Commission and the European Union cannot deliver what they promise in a reasonably efficient and timely fashion, they are not credible – it is not sufficient.

A basic consensus on objectives and policies among member states and a clear division of labour are also of utmost importance, as administrative reform is only one part of the plan to facilitate effective and efficient delivery of actions. It is clear that both the Commission and member states share accountability in the delivery of results.

Efficient and effective implementation of policies and fewer scandals will stem the flow of negative publicity. However, this will not address the underlying basic problem: too few people really understand the work of the institutions and the continuing relevance of a mission established in the 1940s and 1950s. In essence, if something goes wrong in the administration, the damage is substantial; if things go smoothly, this will not be reported – only bad news is news. Therefore the Commission strives to gain approval through results in policy, not in delivery. In that light, the Barroso Commission put renewed emphasis on impact assessment of major legislative and policy-defining proposals in the European Commission's annual work programme, particularly as regards the assessment of key economic impacts. The delivery of items in the work programme has been substantially improved, from under 50 per cent at the start of the last Commission to 70 per cent in 2004.[20]

Further, it should be stressed that increasing and enhancing accountability is not only about administrative reforms, but also consists of a democratic component (see democratic accountability, above). The European Union functions, as explained earlier, on the basis of technocratic policies worked out in endless meetings to find compromises. Decisions are taken by highly experienced persons for the people – the people often being represented by a complex web of lobbies and NGOs as well as traditional government. However, today a growing share of citizens want to know how policy is made and to make their own inputs, not least because trust has been eroded. Therefore, the Lisbon Treaty introduced the Citizens' Initiative: 1 million citizens from a number of member states will have the possibility to call on the Commission to bring forward new policy proposals.

In its "Plan D for Democracy, Debate and Dialogue", the Commission stresses that communication is first and foremost a matter of democracy. For that reason the website Your Voice in Europe was among others launched, allowing members of the public to take part in interactive policy-making by contributing to debates on emerging policy issues and responding to public consultations.[21]

It is not sufficiently clear yet that communicating is not just a Brussels affair, but rather a work that should mobilize all EU institutions and especially member states, local and regional authorities, political parties, civil society and the media. The European Economic and Social Committee and the Committee of the Regions, two advisory organs of the European Union, play an important role here – they form a centre of information and a mouthpiece for organized civil society bridging Europe and its citizens, thereby complementing their political representation by the European Parliament. In addition, voicing ideas and mobilizing people through other channels will be crucial in raising awareness and commitment among European citizens. Furthermore, education on the basics of European integration is essential to provide European citizens with a better understanding and skills to judge information they get in order to create a genuine European public opinion on European affairs.[22] Ending the well-established, because politically in the short-term perspective convenient, blame-game that "Everything good from the national capital, everything bad from Brussels" is no longer either a cheap political joke or a political recipe. It has become a political necessity to re-establish trust and confidence in the European project to ensure its continued acceptance and thus survival.

Democracy requires increased transparency of European activities. For that reason the Commission firstly seeks to simplify and improve the regulatory environment in order to improve understanding and access to EU law for both business and citizens. Better lawmaking also means combating legislative inflation. Striking a balance between appropriate consultation, as more democracy requires more time, and efficiency of legislation is hard.[23] It is equally difficult to strike a balance in selecting areas where Community regulation is more efficient compared to 27 national regulations (political choice in implementing subsidiarity).

Secondly, the European Commission developed a culture of communication with representatives of civil society, a development furthered by the

> relocation of aspects of social activism to the Community level [which] is a complex process with manifold consequences for both the institutional sector and the civil society from which public interest groups arise. Viewed from the multifarious perspectives of different policy areas, evaluation of the reasons for, and the repercussions of, this relocation requires understanding of the consequences of the process of European integration for organised civil society... a complex sector which includes non-governmental organisations, social movements, advocacy groups, charities, representatives of self-help organisations and promotional groups.[24]

The rather symbiotic relationship between civil society and the various European institutions is explained "by these institutions' concerns for legitimacy and the controversial issue of the democratic deficit",[25] a hypothesis which is also applicable to the UN system. However, civil society institutions also have to face quests for representativeness and social and political accountability.

Against this background the European Commission launched a transparency initiative in May 2006, which aims at ensuring transparency on who lobbies[26] for whom or which policy, who gets what money and how it is spent. The initiative will again seek to strengthen ethical standards across the European institutions, in particular concerning declarations of interest. But this will be a difficult discussion – previous experience shows that getting agreement between institutions and across the varying cultural norms even within Europe is hard.[27]

EU accountability also includes, to a certain degree, foreign policy – an area traditionally regarded to a greater extent as a national policy matter compared to other policies,[28] and therefore less open to public scrutiny, a concept familiar in nearly all national states. This became clear when the European Union among others committed to each Millennium Development Goal (MDG). The existence of practical targets and indicators for the MDGs can help to increase the much-needed accountability and transparency of cooperation in general and European aid in particular, and the undertaken reforms already contribute to the effectiveness of European Community aid.[29]

Institutional reforms, envisaged by the European Constitution and largely taken over by the Lisbon Treaty, will also contribute substantially to an increased accountability of the institutions and to diminishing a perceived democratic deficit, as national parliaments' involvement would have been increased by among others their power to send any proposal back to the Commission for reconsideration if they believed the proposal lay outside the EU's competence and the mentioned Citizens' Initiative (obligation of the Commission to consider any proposal for legislation that has the support of 1 million citizens). In a first step to increase accountability, the Council of Ministers decided autonomously to meet in public when legislating, from November 2006 onwards.

Conclusion

European experience shows that reform can increase accountability, but it needs commitment from the highest political and managerial levels if it is to overcome institutional inertia and vested interests, not only within the Commission but also in member states. Therefore *all* stakeholders need to "buy in" to the process, to understand how it will genuinely help their institution deliver better in the future. The particular importance attached to legal accountability is a specific feature of the European Union because of its legal nature. Making use of the "positive" side of accountability could become an incentive to increase participation of the public in the process, thereby avoiding the reinforcement of negative perceptions on the part of the European public. As Harlow and Rawlings demonstrate in their case study, "There is a strong sense already of a self-organising and self-generating network of investigative officials, fortified by shared professional expertise and ethos, who have come together to execute the common purpose of fostering and encouraging good administration, and of holding administrators throughout the EU accountable for acts of maladministration."[30] This is a distinctive feature of the EU system compared to the UN system.

Similarly, and based on an empirical survey of officials working in various European institutions and taking "a sociolinguistic and discourse-analytical perspective – one that shares the viewpoint that the EU, its organizations, and its representatives are largely constructed (and construct themselves) discursively",[31] Ruth Wodak establishes various patterns connected to the question of identity, such as group status, accepting or construing an identity for the European Union, leading to "similarities in the types of definitions of European given by all of those interviewed".[32] Thus, based on a "core of beliefs about what Europe is" in addition to national identity, this contributes the imaging of EU "we groups" in contrast to "out groups" like so-called "third countries" (the United States, Asian and African countries . . .). This attitude, combined with a sense of ownership (e.g. being part of the European role model, including the European social model), responsibility and caring for the success of the European project "dovetails nicely with the Commission being described as carrying the 'European conscience' . . . that is, as promoting specifically European interests",[33] which include in my mind accountability, in line with liberal institutionalists' views.

Thus the administrative cultures of the European Union and the United Nations are quite different: while the various European administrations developed largely on the French administrative model and recruited persons with a similar background (see above), the UN system followed from the outset an Anglo-Saxon approach and, naturally as a universal organization, recruits persons from various cultural, ethnic and geographic backgrounds, which makes the socialization process much more difficult compared to the European Union.

The difference in the very nature of the two institutions under consideration also poses limits to finding parallels: although both serve a "social purpose" in the sense of Weber, the degree of delegated power received from the constituent members is quite different. While the institutions of the European Union hold and continuously increase supranational powers, making it the (in)famous *sui generis* international institution, performing acts on behalf of its present 27 member states previously reserved to national states, the United Nations remains a classic international organization, involved in an endless reform discussion in order to increase efficiency and effectiveness while maintaining the historic legacy of its foundation, including the five permanent members of the Security Council.

"The more international organizations are pushed to the forefront of global governance, the more frequent are the catcalls and criticism – and the more interested are social movements and states keen to question their actions, to limit their powers, and to search for alternatives."[34] The European Union was pushed to deal in its reform process with both aspects of accountability, managerial and political. It is clear that management reform is only part of the story – the technical, albeit difficult, part of it. There must be sufficient common understanding of and a vision on the goals and values of the institution and what they stand for; form and reform cannot substitute for content and vision. Thus the political aspect gained importance and centred on the issue of deepening the European Union, something put in contrast to its widening. *La finalité européenne* had to be redefined after the perceived success of the first one, namely establishing peace between the former arch-enemies, France and Germany. Enlargement in the sense of extending the zone of peace, democracy, rule of law and prosperity, stabilizing the European continent (thereby facing the question of the borders of Europe), became the political challenge, to which new issues like environment, climate change, sustainability, energy and energy security, to name just a few, were added. Institutionally and procedurally, making a union of 27 work on the basic structure of 1957 that had hardly changed is another colossal challenge. Therefore, it does not come as a surprise that "accountability" became a main theme in and for the European Union: the peoples of Europe held their élites, which traditionally have been in the driving seat of European integration, accountable. They advocated more democratic control over the political goals of the process, the process itself and the use of financial means in pursuit of the goals, putting European solidarity to the test. The parallel pursuit of institutional reform in order to render the institutions more effective and accountable, while enlarging at relative high speed the European Union geographically and numerically, and preaching deregulation and liberalization, might have been asking too much from the European public. The quest is on for the hearts of Europeans who feel more and more as stakeholders in the process, in making use of the Treaty of Lisbon; the success remains to be seen, but *accountability* as part of democratic government, governance and control, as well as in its second function of *responsibility*, e.g. to devise and implement European integration, has become a main ingredient in it.

Notes

1. Answers.com (undated) "Accountability in the European Union", available at www.answers.com/topic/accountability-in-the-european-union; EU Lobby.net, available at www.eulobby.net/eng/desktopdefault.aspx.

2. See Harlow, Carol (2002) *Accountability in the European Union*, Oxford: Oxford University Press, p. 216; Harlow, Carol (2002) "Problems of Accountability in the European Union", Technical Report, NEC Paper No. 53, National Europe Center, Australia National University, available at www.anu.edu.au/NEC/harlow.pdf#search=accountabilityintheEuropeanUnion, p. 7.
3. Treaty of Lisbon amending the Treaty on European Union and the Treaty Establishing the European Community, CIG 14/07, 3 December 2007, available at http://europa.eu/lisbon_treaty/index_en.htm.
4. European Commission (2001) "European Governance – A White Paper", COM(01)428 final, July.
5. European Commission (2006) "Enlargement Strategy and Main Challenges 2006–2007", COM(06) 649, 8 November, p. 18.
6. Harlow, "Problems of Accountability", note 2 above, p. 15, n. 3.
7. Ibid.
8. Bradley, Kieran St Clair (2002) "European Court of Justice", in John Peterson and Michael Shackleton, eds, *The Institutions of the European Union*, Oxford: Oxford University Press, pp. 118–138, at p. 123.
9. Case 120/78 Rewe-Zentrel ("Cassis de Dijon"), 1979 ECR 649.
10. European Commission (2006) "First Assessment of Community Lisbon Programme", 26 October, available at http://europa.eu.int/rapid/pressReleasesAction.do?reference=MEMO/06/399&format=HTML&aged=0&language=EN&guiLanguage=en. See also Sapir, André, Philippe Aghion and Giuseppe Bertola (2004) *An Agenda for a Growing Europe: Making the EU Economic System Deliver*, Oxford: Oxford University Press.
11. Kallas, Siim (2006) "Strengthening Multilateral Institutions for the 21st Century – The EU, UN and Management Reform", speech presented at European Union Studies Center, City University of New York, New York, 17 May, available at http://europa.eu/rapid/pressReleasesAction.do?reference=SPEECH/06/317&format=HTML&aged=0&language=EN&guiLanguage=en.
12. King, Tim (2006) "Commission and UN Co-operate on Reform", *European Voice*, 5 October, p. 19.
13. UN Regional Information Centre (2007) "Improving Lives: Results from the Partnership of the United Nations and the European Commission in 2006", available at www.unbrussels.org/improvinglives.pdf, p. 17.
14. See European Parliament (undated) "Oversight over the Commission and Council", available at www.europarl.europa.eu/parliament/public/staticDisplay.do?id=46&pageRank=9&language=EN; European Commission (undated) "Role and Powers: José Manuel Barroso", available at http://ec.europa.eu/commissionbarroso/president/role/index_en.htm.
15. The old *ex ante* financial control system consisted of centralized checking and approval of financial transactions against largely procedural rules laid down in the financial regulations – called the *ex ante* visa – but this has proved inadequate as a way of comprehensively assessing the added value and correctness of financial operations. Consequently, the system gave decision-makers a false sense of security, leading to a culture that e-responsibilizes managers. Finally, being a cumbersome and procedurally complex system, efficient execution of the budget became harder.
16. European Commission (2000) "Reforming the Commission", COM(00) (final/2); European Court of Auditors, available at http://europa.eu/institutions/inst/auditors/index_en.htm.
17. European Commission, ibid.
18. European Commission (undated) "The European Commission at Work", available at http://ec.eu/institutions/inst/auditors/index_en.htm; European Economic and Social Committee (2002) "Opinion on European Governance – A White Paper", CES 357/2002, 20 March.

19. European Commission, note 15 above; European Commission (2005) "Progress Report on the Commission Reform Beyond the Reform Mandate", COM(05)668 final.
20. European Commission (2005) "Progress Report on the Commission Reform beyond the Reform Mandate", COM (2005) 668 final, available at http://eur-lex.europa.eu/LexUriServ/site/en/com/2005/com2005_0668en01.pdf.
21. European Commission (2005) "The Commission's Contribution to the Period of Reflection and Beyond: Plan D for Democracy, Dialogue and Debate", COM(05)494 final.
22. European Commission (2006) "White Paper on a European Communication Policy", COM(06)35 final; European Economic and Social Committee (2005) "Better Lawmaking", INT/265, 2005.
23. European Commission (2005) "Annual Policy Strategy for 2007", COM(06)122 final; European Economic and Social Committee, ibid.
24. Ruzza, Carlo (2004) *Europe and Civil Society: Movement Coalitions and European Governance*, Manchester and New York: Manchester University Press, p. 1.
25. Ibid., p. 22.
26. See EU Lobby.net, available at www.eulobby.net/eng/desktopdefault.aspx.
27. European Commission (undated) "Transparency Initiative and Its Related Green Paper", available at http://ec.europa.eu/commission_barroso/kallas/transparency_en.htm.
28. Reiterer, Michael (2006) "Interregionalism as a New Diplomatic Tool: The EU and East Asia", *European Foreign Affairs Review* 11, pp. 223–243, especially on essential elements clauses, p. 232 et seq.
29. European Economic and Social Committee (2005) "The European Union Development Policy 'The European Consensus'", ECOSOC(05) REX/199.
30. Harlow, Carol and Richard Rawlings (2006) "Promoting Accountability in Multi-Level Governance: A Network Approach", available at www.connex-network.org/eurogov/pdf/egp-connex-C-06-02.pdf, p. 28.
31. Wodak, Ruth (2004) "National and Transnational Identities: European and Other Identities Constructed in Interviews with EU Officials", in Richard K. Herrmann, Thomas Risse and Marilynn B. Brewer, eds, *Transnational Identities: Becoming European in the EU*, Lanham, MD: Rowman & Littlefield, pp. 97–128, at p. 98.
32. Ibid., p. 122.
33. Ibid., p. 123.
34. Barnett, Michael and Martha Finnemore (2005) "The Power of Liberal International Organizations", in Michael Barnett and Raymond Duvall, eds, *Power in Global Governance*, Cambridge: Cambridge University Press, pp. 161–184, at p. 182.

13

The World Bank Inspection Panel: Participation and accountability

Edith Brown Weiss, Peter L. Lallas and Anna S. Herken

There is an urgent global need to address poverty, and in turn to hold accountable those who do so. According to the 2008 World Bank Development Indicators, about 1.4 billion people, or more than one-fifth of the world population, live on less than \$1.25 a day; more than 3 billion people live on less than \$2.50 per day.

The International Bank for Reconstruction and Development (World Bank) was established in 1946 to assist in the reconstruction of countries destroyed or heavily damaged in the Second World War. Since then the World Bank, with 185 member countries, has become a leading financier in promoting development in impoverished and middle-income countries. In recent years it has provided loans and grants totalling about \$18–20 billion per year.

There are increasing concerns about accountability of institutions in all sectors, whether public or private. The World Bank and other multilateral development banks are no exception. It is appropriate, then, to explore how the World Bank is accountable for its work.

Before doing so, it is useful to note the relationship between the legitimacy of institutions and their accountability, and to identify important aspects of accountability. There is broad consensus that institutions need to be legitimate, in the eyes of both those who established them and those whom they serve or affect. Legitimacy is essential if people are to accept the actions of the institutions as valid and entitled to respect. For institutions to be legitimate, they need to be accountable for their actions and the effectiveness of their work. *Webster's English Dictionary* defines

Envisioning reform: Enhancing UN accountability in the twenty-first century, Kuyama and Fowler (eds), United Nations University Press, 2009, ISBN 978-92-808-1170-4

accountable as "being obliged to account for one's actions, i.e. to give satisfactory reasons". Accountability can be distinguished from responsibility, although in languages other than English the two concepts may be joined and translated as "responsibility". One can be responsible for doing something, but not have to account for what is done or how it is done. Accountability adds the important input of "process" into the norm of legitimacy.

We can identify at least five questions related to accountability. Who is accountable? To whom? For what? When? And how? The answers to these questions will vary by institution and by the chosen instrument for implementing accountability. For institutions like the World Bank, one important dimension of accountability is compliance with policies and procedures designed to support its mission and to avoid harm. Different strategies are appropriate for promoting compliance, including "sunshine" or transparency strategies, incentives and sanctions.

This chapter focuses on one instrument for ensuring accountability: the World Bank Inspection Panel. The Panel, which carries out fact-finding and analyses issues of compliance and harm in response to complaints from local communities about World Bank-funded projects, reflects in part a strategy of sunshine or transparency.

When the World Bank established the Inspection Panel in 1993, it created an independent instrument for ensuring that Bank management and staff complied with Bank policies and procedures. It enabled the Panel to be brought in at the design, appraisal or implementation phase of the project or programme cycle, and imbued it with the power to conduct independent, impartial fact-finding investigations, the results of which are conveyed directly to the Bank's board of executive directors. In so doing, the World Bank enhanced the institution's accountability not only to the countries that fund the Bank, but also to the impoverished communities which the Bank serves.

Since the Inspection Panel was established more than 15 years ago, all multilateral development banks and several national export and investment agencies have now established similar instruments, in good part modelled after the Inspection Panel. The UN system itself has become more concerned with issues of accountability and the instruments for enhancing it.

Since the UNU Tokyo Symposium on Accountability was intended to focus on specific case studies of accountability in international financial institutions, this chapter focuses on the World Bank Inspection Panel and its investigation report on the Mumbai Urban Transport Project (MUTP), and developments subsequent to the Panel's report. Many of the requests to the Inspection Panel involve infrastructure projects and consequent resettlement of peoples affected by the construction and location of the infrastructure. Hence it is especially appropriate to use a case study here that involves infrastructure. Questions are sometimes raised about the importance of infrastructure and the Panel's role. Infrastructure projects are essential to development, and the risk-taking involved is part of economic development. The Panel has a crucial role, for it can serve as a means to provide accountability for the institution when it undertakes such projects.

History of the Panel

Developments leading to establishment of the Panel

The Inspection Panel was established at an important – and lively – moment in the field of international cooperation and development. In the late 1980s and early 1990s the international community was engaged in a major debate over how to support development and, at the same time, tackle interrelated social and environmental problems emerging around the world.[1] The 1992 Rio Summit on Environment and Development brought these issues on to the world stage, particularly the need to integrate policy objectives in support of sustainable development.[2] The summit also helped to bring into view a relatively new factor in the equation: the phenomenon we now refer to as "globalization".

During these years the role of international financial institutions, such as the World Bank, emerged as a subject of attention and intense controversy. Since its establishment, the Bank[3] has played a significant role in financing a range of development-related projects in developing countries, including infrastructure projects such as dams, transport systems, energy production and irrigation systems. The Bank has also financed policy and institutional development on matters of social and environmental importance, as for example in the management and protection of natural resources. Along with funding, the Bank provides significant analytical and technical support to borrower countries in the design and implementation of projects. Over time, the Bank adopted operational policies and procedures to help ensure that Bank-funded projects were designed and implemented in a manner that properly addressed, among other things, potential social and environmental impacts.[4] Bank management is required to follow these policies and procedures.

During the 1980s members of civil society, including many grassroots non-governmental organizations (NGOs) and locally affected communities, put a spotlight on Bank-funded projects that were producing major negative social and environmental impacts, notwithstanding the existence of Bank policies designed to anticipate and avoid such potential impacts.

Some projects were seen as "development disasters" which resulted in particularly adverse impacts on local people who were poor, vulnerable and not in a position easily to protect their rights, or even give voice to their concerns.[5] These views were strengthened by the perception that the Bank and other international economic institutions generally operated out of public view.

The Bank decision in 1985 to finance the Sardar Sarovar Dam and canal along the Narmada River in India became a focal point of these criticisms. The decision was made despite major opposition at the village level, and amid claims that the Bank was violating a wide range of its own internal policies.[6] In 1990, following strong protests by civil society, the Bank agreed to establish a commission to conduct an independent review of the Sardar Sarovar project;[7] this became known as the "Morse Commission".

The Morse Commission Report was issued in 1992, the year of the Rio Summit. It found that the Bank had failed to comply with several of its safeguard policies in relation to the project. It then described a more systemic concern: "the problems besetting the Sardar Sarovar Projects are more the rule than the exception to resettlement operations supported by the Bank in India".[8] The Bank, according to the analysis of the report, was not living up to promises in its operational policies and procedures, and local communities were bearing the impacts.

Shortly thereafter, Bank Vice-President Willi Wapenhans conducted an in-house review of Bank investment lending. The Wapenhans Report found that 37.5 per cent of Bank projects that had been recently evaluated were rated "unsatisfactory", and that many projects failed properly to take into account critical problems relating to local capacity and priorities.[9] It found that the Bank had developed a pervasive "culture of approval" which emphasized the ability to move money and gain approval of projects, without adequate attention either to issues of capacity of the borrower or to the potential social and environmental impacts of the projects.

These reports validated many of the concerns raised in those years by civil society, and helped to galvanize action to improve accountability and transparency at the World Bank. In early 1993 civil society organizations worked to develop a basic concept and proposal for this purpose.[10] In February 1993, as indicated in one study, "executive directors from The Netherlands, Germany, Malaysia and Chile, with support from the Swiss executive director, circulated a proposal for a new accountability mechanism".[11] In May 1993 hearings before the US Congress relating to the Tenth Replenishment of the International Development Association (IDA) highlighted concerns over the performance of the World Bank. On 22 September 1993, in the context of these many actions and considerations, the board of executive directors of the World Bank adopted a resolution creating the independent World Bank Inspection Panel.[12]

Purpose of the Panel

The Inspection Panel provides a forum within the World Bank Group for people who believe that they have been, or are likely to be, harmed by World Bank-funded projects or programmes to bring their concerns directly to the Bank's board of executive directors. The board created the Panel to promote accountability at the Bank and ensure that the voices of people who may be adversely affected by Bank-financed projects will be heard.

The Panel carries out this mandate through its work as an impartial fact-finding body, independent of Bank management. In response to requests by affected people, the Panel has the power to review Bank-funded projects and programmes to determine whether management is following its own operational policies and procedures in the design, appraisal and/or implementation of projects.[13] These policies and procedures are designed to ensure that Bank-financed projects provide social and economic benefits, and avoid harm to people or the environment. The Panel reports its findings to the Bank's board of executive directors for consideration and action.

As expressed in its operating procedures:

> The Panel has been established for the purpose of providing people directly and adversely affected by a Bank-financed project with an independent forum through which they can request the Bank to act in accordance with its own policies and procedures...[14]

The Panel and the international legal system

The creation of the Inspection Panel may be viewed as part of a system-wide evolution in recent decades relating to the articulation and practice of international law. By offering a way for locally affected people to have their concerns heard by the Bank's board of executive directors, management and staff, the Inspection Panel provides an innovative means to enable non-state actors to have a voice, however small, in the decision-making processes of an international institution. The Panel is part of the broadening of the range of "actors" in international law and policy-making – a stage once restricted to national governments and the bureaucracies of international organizations.[15] One recent study characterizes this as part of the process of building "public space" where people, states and large institutions can better interact.[16]

As noted at the outset, the Panel opens a door for civil society to participate in ensuring compliance with international norms. As described in more detail below, it offers affected people a formal means to challenge whether an international institution (the World Bank) is complying with international norms (its operational policies and procedures). Because the Panel is required to publish all its reports and make relevant information publicly available, the Panel process contributes to the objective of enhancing transparency in the activities of international institutions.

In a sense, the Panel carries forward the mandates of the 1992 Rio Conference on Environment and Development and the 2002 Johannesburg World Summit on Sustainable Development. It has pioneered a new way to promote and support participation of civil society in development – especially participation of the poor and dispossessed, who otherwise lack the ability to have a voice in decisions that stand to affect them greatly.

The Inspection Panel is also an adaptation from another strand of international law: namely, the use of independent and impartial fact-finding bodies as a tool to understand and resolve problems. More than a century ago, the Hague Conventions of 1899 and 1907 established commissions of inquiry to investigate claims. The 1909 Boundary Waters case between Canada and the United States provided for a reference procedure to settle disputes, which is essentially a fact-finding procedure.[17] After 1919 many international agreements established permanent commissions of investigation, which could investigate and establish facts to aid the resolution of controversies.[18] More recently similar bodies have been used in a variety of international settings, which range from claims relating to human rights violations to disputes over transboundary watercourses.[19] The focus is on fact-finding. For fact-finding to be effective, the structure for implementing it must be independent and implementation must be impartial and objective. These characteristics are central to the work of the Inspection Panel.

As the *2006 Global Accountability Report* of the One World Trust makes clear,[20] there has been growing attention to the need for accountability in international institutions and to the effectiveness of instruments for ensuring this.[21] These trends and developments in "complaint and response mechanisms" may be characterized as an emerging part of what is referred to as "global administrative law", or the structural and normative framework which governs the operation of institutions at the international level.[22] Recently scholars have begun to expand the formerly rather narrow discussion of international administrative law to focus more broadly on "global administrative law". The latter reflects the growth of international institutions and the expanded roles that they serve.

Within this broader frame of reference of developments in international law and international institutions, the discussion below provides a more detailed review of the structure, mandate and activities of the World Bank Inspection Panel.

Structure of the Panel

Panel members

The Inspection Panel consists of three members of different nationalities from Bank member countries. The President, after consultation with the board of executive directors, nominates the members of the Panel to be appointed by the board.[23] The initial three Panel members were appointed on the basis of one for three years, one for four years and one for five years. Since that time, each vacancy is filled for a period of five years. No Panel member may serve for more than one term.

In terms of qualifications, a 1993 Panel resolution provides as follows:

> Members of the Panel shall be selected on the basis of their ability to deal thoroughly and fairly with the requests brought to them, their integrity and independence from the Bank's Management, and their exposure to developmental issues and to living conditions in developing countries. Knowledge and experience of the Bank's operations will also be desirable.[24]

This provision, among many others in the 1993 Panel resolution, highlights the basic foundations of independence, impartiality and integrity, and the fundamental importance of exposure to and understanding of issues of development and living conditions in developing countries.

The Panel resolution contains other provisions to support and ensure the independence of the Panel:

- executive directors, alternates, advisers and staff members of the World Bank Group may not serve on the Panel "until two years have elapsed since the end of their service in the Bank Group" (para. 4)
- Panel members are disqualified from participation in the hearing and investigation of any request related to a matter in which he/she has a personal interest or had significant involvement (para. 5)
- Panel members appoint their own chairperson for a period of one year, a practice which continues to the present day and is, again, an important feature in maintaining the independence of the Panel as an entity (para. 6)
- Panel members may be removed from office "only by decision of the Executive Directors, for cause" (para. 7).[25]

These provisions are critical to the effective functioning of the Panel. As described above, the Panel has a mandate to investigate the actions of Bank management in a particular project or programme. Depending on the facts, the Panel may issue a report finding that management has complied with applicable policies and procedures, or that it has failed to do so and this has contributed to, or may result in, significant harm to local communities and the environment. Or the Panel could find that the management has complied with some policies and procedures but not with others. The provisions in the resolution establishing the Panel reflect the premise that the Panel must remain free, structurally, from the possibility of interference or even retaliation by management (or others) in carrying out its responsibilities – whether through pressure on its budget, through pressure of removal, through an effort to intervene in the drafting of reports, or otherwise.

The Panel was also established at a high level within the Bank. It reports directly to the board of executive directors. The chair of the Inspection Panel has an appointment at the level of Vice-President of the World Bank.

Secretariat

A small secretariat of permanent staff supports and assists the Panel in carrying out its work and meeting its responsibilities.[26] The secretariat performs a broad range of tasks, and is headed by an executive secretary.[27] As provided in the 1993 panel resolution, the President makes the appointment after consultation with the board of executive directors.[28] If needed, one or more experts may be engaged to assist in a Panel investigation. These experts must be highly qualified and independent.

Relationship to board, management and staff

In line with its resolution, the Panel reports to the Bank's board of executive directors, and not to Bank management or any other entity. It is independent of Bank management and staff. This is important for several reasons. The reporting structure recognizes that the Panel serves the board. It provides the board with independent, carefully developed information regarding issues of Bank compliance with operational policies and procedures in the design, appraisal and implementation of Bank-funded projects. When local communities and civil society allege non-compliance and harm, the Panel serves as an independent body to which the board may turn in assessing and understanding the realities of the situation. The Panel's reports go directly to the board and are not submitted to management first. This achieves an essential premise of the Panel's work, which is to ensure that the Panel's independent findings are presented directly to the Bank's decision-making body for consideration and action.

Characteristics of the Panel

The Panel is an objective fact-finding body, independent from Bank management and staff. The principles of independence, impartiality and integrity are at the very heart of the Panel's mission and – indeed – effectiveness. The 1993 resolution creating the Panel begins with the words "There is established an *independent* Inspection Panel..." (emphasis added). The resolution contains many provisions designed to protect and reinforce the independence of the Panel, including the provisions for selection of Panel members and the executive secretary, described above. Another crucial element of the Panel's independence is the provision in the 1993 Panel resolution to secure its budget, which states that "The Panel shall be given such budgetary resources as shall be sufficient to carry out its activities."[29]

Impartiality and integrity are joined with independence for fact-finding to be effective. The qualifications for selection of Panel members noted previously include these characteristics. In carrying out its duties, the Panel often works with independent and highly regarded experts. All have to act objectively, so that the Panel can pursue the facts to wherever they may lead. This might mean, in some cases, that the claims of requesters are validated; in others, it might mean that they are not. The critical objective is to find the facts, put them in the light and bring them through the process to the top of the Bank for consideration and decision. The fact-finding process seeks input from a wide range of sources, and provides various opportunities for management to respond to claims presented in a request. In these ways, local community concerns may be heard, with fairness to all involved.

The Panel also is premised on the notion of transparency. Key documents relating to the processing of requests to the Panel are released to the public and posted on the Panel's website at various junctures throughout the process. The Panel's procedures, as well as some issues and concerns in this regard, are addressed below.

Panel process

Requests for inspection

The process by which the Panel may investigate Bank-funded projects is triggered by the submission of a request for inspection. In line with the Panel resolution, requests may be submitted by:

- a community of two or more affected people (in practice, even hundreds of affected people)
- a local organization or other duly appointed representative on behalf of the affected people
- a foreign organization, in exceptional circumstances, if no local representative is available
- an executive director of the World Bank.

All requests to date have been submitted through the first two means, except for an early request relating to a project in China. A request may be submitted in any language, and may be stated in very simple terms. No specific form is necessary – a letter will suffice. Requests must, however, be submitted in writing, dated and signed by the requesters, and contain name(s) and contact address.[30] The Panel has developed informal guidance, which includes information on eligibility criteria and a suggested format that may be followed to assist people and communities wishing to submit requests.[31]

Requesters to the Panel may ask that their names be kept confidential. This provision for confidentiality is no small matter. In some cases, requesters to the Panel have feared or faced retaliation for making their claims. This is of great concern in terms of the protection of individual human rights. It also raises a fundamental concern in the Panel process – that the possibility of retaliation would chill the making of requests and the assertion of rights by affected people. The Panel has placed the highest importance on respecting and protecting confidentiality when requested, and brings instances of potential or actual retaliation to the attention of responsible officials as a matter of the highest priority.

Once the Panel receives a request, it follows specified procedures to register the request and submit it to the board of executive directors. According to the Panel's operating procedures, a request will be registered for further process unless the chairperson determines that it is "without doubt manifestly outside the Panel's mandate".[32] The registration process was established by the Panel to facilitate the proper and effective processing of requests, and is used to notify the executive directors and President of the Bank of a request for inspection as required under the Panel resolution (para. 17). The Panel maintains a register of requests that it has registered for specific projects or programmes financed by the Bank. This register is publicly available on the Panel's website (www.inspectionpanel.org).

Once a request is registered, the Panel process may be divided into two phases: the eligibility phase and the investigation phase. These may be depicted as shown in table 13.1, and are described in more detail below.

Table 13.1 Eligibility and investigation

Eligibility – time bound	Investigation
• Request received • Management response to request (21 days) • Panel's eligibility report and recommendation on investigation (21 days) • Board decision (on non-objection basis)	• Upon board authorization, Panel conducts fact-finding investigation • Panel's investigation report • Management report and action plan in response to Panel's findings • Board meeting

Eligibility

Once the Panel registers a request and notifies the board and the President, Bank management has 21 working days to provide a written response to the claims in the request (the "initial Management Response"). Under the resolution and its 1999 clarifications, management will provide evidence that it has complied with the relevant Bank policies and procedures, or that there are serious failures attributable either to management, the borrower or other external factors, or some combination of these.[33] In practice, management submits detailed responses to the requests, which the Panel carefully reviews before determining whether the request is eligible for an inspection.

The Panel has 21 working days from the date of management's initial response to assess the eligibility of the request for inspection and recommend whether an investigation should be carried out. As part of this assessment, the Panel generally visits the location of the request to meet with the requesters and other relevant parties to determine whether the request meets specified criteria and, as a result, warrants a full investigation.

In this regard, the 1999 clarifications to the Panel resolution provide as follows:

> If the Panel so recommends, the Board will authorize an investigation without making a judgement on the merits of the claimants' request, and without discussion except with respect to the following technical eligibility criteria:
>
> a. The affected party consists of any two or more persons with common interests or concerns and who are in the borrower's territory (Resolution para. 12).
>
> b. The request does assert in substance that a serious violation by the Bank of its operational policies and procedures has or is likely to have a material adverse effect on the requester (Resolution paras. 12 and 14a).

c. The request does assert that its subject matter has been brought to Management's attention and that, in the requester's view, Management has failed to respond adequately demonstrating that it has followed or is taking steps to follow the Bank's polices and procedures (Resolution para. 13).
d. The matter is not related to procurement (Resolution para. 14b).
e. The related loan has not been closed or substantially disbursed (Resolution para. 14c).
f. The Panel has not previously made a recommendation on the subject matter or, if it has, that the request does assert that there is new evidence or circumstances not known at the time of the prior request (Resolution para. 14d).

These criteria reflect key operational features of the work of the Panel. The first two, for example, relate to requesters and the nature of the request. The third (subparagraph c) is based on the important notion that requesters should first bring their concerns to the attention of Bank management and staff before coming to the Panel, creating the opportunity to resolve problems before the mechanism of the Inspection Panel is applied to a particular situation. This creates an important incentive to respond to concerns that arise in connection with Bank-funded projects and improve the overall development process. The final three criteria (subparagraphs d, e and f) clarify situations that are not eligible for investigation. The Panel resolution of 1993 indicates that a loan is considered substantially disbursed (see subparagraph e) when at least 95 per cent of the loan proceeds have been disbursed.[34]

The specification of these criteria has been useful to the Panel process. In the early years of the Panel there were frequently difficult debates within the board of directors regarding whether a particular request for inspection should be considered eligible for full investigation, and on what basis to make this determination. In parallel, and following certain clarifications in 1996, there were circumstances where management produced early action plans or other steps prior to the Panel's recommendation on eligibility, which were viewed by some as a way to dissuade the board from accepting a Panel recommendation to carry out a full investigation.

With the 1999 clarifications, determinations regarding eligibility now benefit from criteria that are technical, transparent and clear. The clarifications further state that the Panel will determine the eligibility of a request for inspection "independently of any views that may be expressed by Management". These provisions reinforce the role of the Panel, in reporting to the board, as an independent entity that calls situations as it sees them in line with its mandate. Recommendations of the Panel regarding whether or not to carry out an investigation are considered by the board on a non-objection basis. Since the clarifications in 1999, the board has approved all the Panel's recommendations.

Investigation

Upon authorization by the board of directors, the Panel conducts an investigation into matters raised in a request. This investigation is not time-bound. Its length will depend on factors such as the complexity of issues, the types of information needed and logistical and practical issues (e.g. remoteness of places) relating to field investigations. In practice, investigations have ranged from a few months to 18 months. The length of time reflects not only the complexity of the request but the difficulty or ease of accessing the relevant areas in the country for the investigation.

The investigation involves a full-scale fact-finding process. For this purpose the Panel generally retains the services of one or more independent, highly qualified experts in fields relevant to the subject matter of the request, who are also familiar with the issues and conditions facing requesters and the communities they represent. For example, in claims involving forests and indigenous peoples who live in and depend on forests, the Panel has retained anthropologists, social forestry experts and environmental science and policy experts to assist in the investigation.

In its investigation, the Panel examines documents and other materials, including those relating to the project produced by the Bank and other sources – both at Bank headquarters and local Bank offices. The Panel carries out formal and informal interviews of Bank staff to learn more about the project, hear management and staff views, request additional information and, most importantly, try to establish the facts related to the claims. The Panel speaks with many different sources, including individual experts, staff of non-governmental organizations, local people and corporate personnel, as appropriate, to be sure that it receives all relevant information.

During its investigation, the Panel conducts on-site visits to areas allegedly affected by the project. It arranges and carries out a wide-ranging set of meetings, including with requesters and the people they represent, other members of local communities, national and local government officials, officials and representatives of the World Bank, interested members of civil society, including NGOs and private sector representatives as relevant, and representatives of other entities involved in or familiar with issues and conditions relevant to the request (e.g. other donors or intergovernmental organizations, universities and associations). The Panel examines conditions in the affected locations relevant to the type of project (e.g. hydropower, irrigation and drainage, transport, forestry, land use, etc.) and to the issues raised (e.g. harm to indigenous peoples, cultural property, forests and the environment). In all its work the Panel tries to avoid publicity, so that it can ascertain the facts objectively and its efforts do not become used for political purposes. The 1999 clarifications to the resolution establishing the Panel explicitly recognize "the need to conduct such work in an independent and low-profile manner" and provide that "the Panel – and Management – should decline media contacts while an investigation is pending or under way".[35]

On the basis of its investigation, the Panel develops a final investigation report. The report describes the Panel's findings in relation to the issues raised in the request, including its findings and conclusions on whether the Bank has complied with its operational policies and procedures, and whether any instances of non-compliance have led – or might lead – to harm to the requesters and those whom they represent. The Inspection Panel report includes a succinct executive summary, a detailed report and analysis, and one or more annexes. The full report varies in length; it is generally about 150–200 single-spaced pages in order to convey fully the findings, analysis and detailed documentation.

The Panel submits this report to the board of directors and the President of the Bank. Bank management then has six weeks to develop its response to the report and an action plan to deal with the Panel's findings. Management circulates its response and action plan to the board of directors and the Panel.

At this point, the board sets a date to consider the Panel's investigation report and management's response and action plan. At its meeting, the board may decide to accept the proposed management action plan or to require other (usually supplementary) actions to respond to the Panel's findings and the matters raised in the request. The ultimate decision on what action to take rests with the board of directors.

The thoroughness and specificity with which management's response and action plan address the Panel's findings are critical to the effectiveness of the Panel process. Sometimes the action plan may be quite general, in which case the board may ask for more specificity. In developing the action plan, management is instructed to "communicate to the Panel the nature and outcomes of the consultations with affected parties on the action plan".[36] Affected parties include those making the request. The Panel in turn "may submit to Executive Directors for their consideration a report in their view of the adequacy of consultations with affected parties in the preparation of the action plans". In practice, management has generally not consulted with the requesters in developing action plans and has not communicated to the Panel the nature and outcomes of consultations with affected parties. The Panel in turn has not provided the board with a report on this aspect. However, consultation with the affected parties is an important aspect of developing effective action plans, and this process deserves to be implemented.

Publication, transparency and accessibility

In accordance with its mandate and operating procedures, the Panel makes key documents relating to requests for inspection available to the public at various junctures of its review process. These documents are posted on the Panel website (www.inspectionpanel.org), and are also available upon request from the secretariat. For example:

- The notice of registration is made publicly available once submitted to the board and the President, and a "register" is established on the Inspection Panel website with information on key actions in processing the request.
- The request, the initial management response and the Panel eligibility report are made publicly available once the board determines whether or not to approve a Panel recommendation regarding eligibility for investigation.
- In cases involving an investigation, the Panel investigation report and the management response are made available once the board has met to review what actions are appropriate in response to the request, the Panel findings and management's response and proposed action plan.

Once the board of executive directors has taken its decision in relation to the Panel's findings and management's response and action plan, the Panel usually returns to the country to convey and discuss its findings with the requesters and with relevant authorities and interested parties.

The Panel's website contains a wide range of other information relating to requests. This includes a summary of the status of active requests and relevant press releases, usually prepared following the board decision on eligibility reports and final actions. The Panel's homepage and its annual reports provide additional information regarding its operations and procedures, its members and other matters relevant to its work.

Actions to promote awareness of the Inspection Panel among communities that might have an interest in seeking its help are of fundamental importance in ensuring that the Panel is able effectively to act as an accountability mechanism, and to provide a voice for people who might be affected by World Bank-financed projects. Building such awareness, however, is often no easy task. Such communities may live in remote areas and/or not have easy access to information about World Bank activities – let alone the Inspection Panel. Local communities also may speak languages not used by the World Bank in most of its project documents, or in meetings and consultations relating to those projects.

In its 1996 and 1999 reviews of the Panel, the board called on management to take actions to make the Panel better known in borrowing countries. For its part, the Panel has developed a range of informational materials, and has participated in events and meetings that promote information and awareness. The Panel has also translated a basic information brochure into 12 languages for dissemination. As noted, a request may be submitted in any language. But, to be sure, it continues to be a challenge to ensure that potentially affected people are aware of the Panel's existence.

The Panel wishes to ensure that the affected people who make a request are aware of its findings and management's response. The 1999 clarifications call upon management to provide specified documents from a Panel investigation to the claimants in their language, to the extent possible. The Panel now has the practice of providing a translation of the Panel's investigation report to the requesters in the country's local language.

Analysis of requests

Subject matter of requests

The Panel's mandate covers any project or programme financed at least in part by the International Bank for Reconstruction and Development (IBRD) or the International Development Association (IDA). This extends to projects under the Global Environment Facility which have the IBRD or IDA as the administrator, projects that may be jointly funded with the IFC or other sources, and guarantees issued by the IBRD or IDA. Since 1994, when it began its operations, the Panel has received 52 requests from 31 countries on a wide variety of projects, such as dams, municipal transport systems, waste disposal systems, forests, biodiversity, mining, pipelines and power-generating installations, and on structural adjustment and development policy loans. People from countries across the world, including Albania, Argentina, Bangladesh, Brazil, Cambodia, Chad, China, Colombia, Congo (DRC), Ecuador, Ghana, Honduras, India, Mexico, Nepal, Nigeria, Pakistan, Papua New Guinea, Paraguay, the Philippines, Romania and Uganda, have submitted requests to the Panel.

The Panel's annual reports contain updated information about requests received. For example, the annexes to the annual reports from 2003 to 2008 provide updated summary information on requests submitted to the Panel as of 30 June of the respective year. There are details on the date of each request, the type of project and the country involved, whether or not an investigation was recommended and carried out, and the policies and procedures raised by the request. The annual reports are available electronically at www.inspectionpanel.org and on request from the Inspection Panel secretariat.

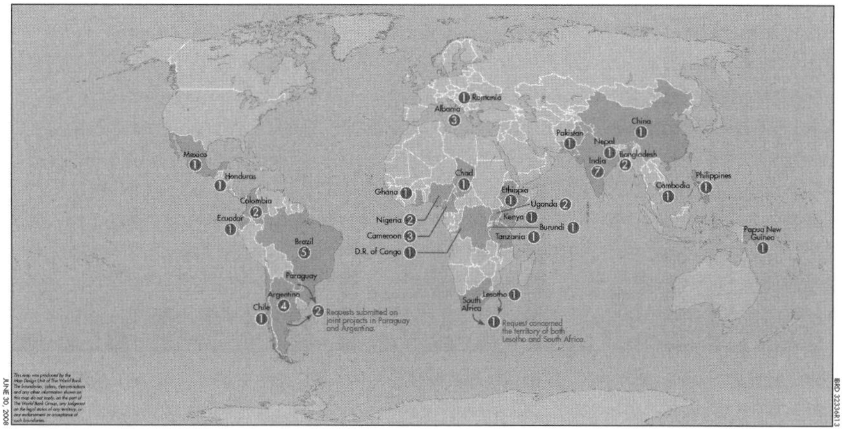

Figure 13.1 Geographical distribution of requests, as of 30 June 2008

Geographical distribution

Figure 13.1 illustrates the geographical distribution of requests submitted to the Panel since its creation in 1993, as of 30 June 2008.

Policies most often raised by requests

The current operational policies and procedures of the World Bank are on the World Bank website (www.worldbank.org), and the Panel's website provides a link to them. Bank policies may also be obtained from the Panel secretariat. The policies most often raised in requests for inspection, as of 30 June 2008, are indicated in figure 13.2.

The Panel's impact

The effects of the Inspection Panel may be considered along several different dimensions. These are discussed below.

Handling requests and outcomes for affected people

In considering the effects of the Inspection Panel over time, the first question involves what has happened to requests received. Several elements may be considered in this regard. Has the Panel been effective in processing and investigating the concerns raised by requesters, and presenting these to the Bank's board of executive directors for consideration and

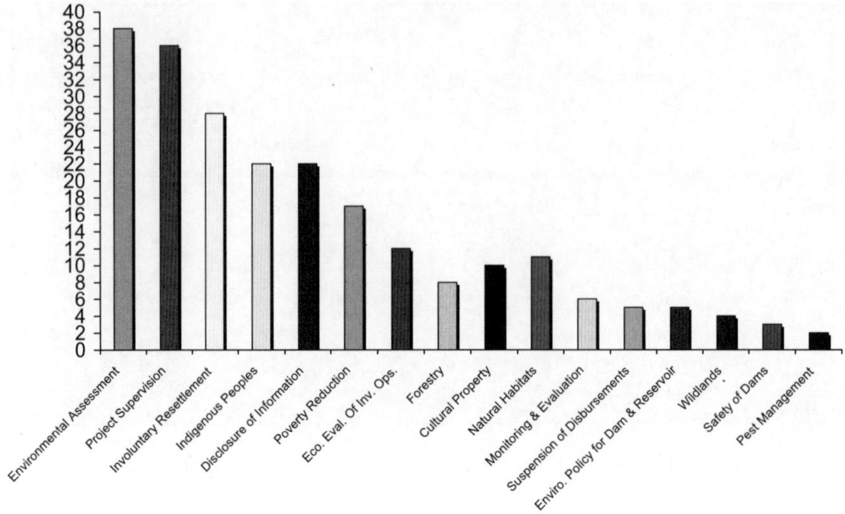

Figure 13.2 Policies most often raised in requests, as of 30 June 2008

action? What is the nature of the response by management to the findings of the Panel, including in particular any findings of non-compliance and harm? What has been the outcome on the ground for requesters as a result of the Panel's involvement?

As noted above, as of 30 June 2008 the Panel had received 52 requests since its establishment. It has conducted full investigations in response to slightly less than half of these requests. This is summarized on the Inspection Panel website and in the Panel's annual reports from 2003 to 2008. The website also contains the relevant final documents and related information on requests made to the Panel, including the requests, Panel eligibility and investigation reports, management responses and action plans, and press releases summarizing the discussions and decisions on each matter by the Bank's board of executive directors.

There is a growing literature on the Inspection Panel that reviews both the Panel and its case experience. The Panel's own publication, *Accountability at the World Bank: The Inspection Panel 10 Years On* (2003), provides a useful review of its achievements and difficulties in responding to specific requests at the time of its tenth anniversary. A number of recent books, articles and studies have also reviewed the Panel and its work as an instrument of accountability in response to requests from locally affected people and communities.[37]

This chapter includes a short case study of one recent request, involving a road transport project and major issues of displacement and resettlement in the city of Mumbai, India; prior to that, a few notes are given on two other recent cases – one in Cambodia, the other in Romania. The discussion does not intend to provide a framework for evaluating the effectiveness of the Panel process in meeting the needs of local communities, but rather some glimpses of the process and where it can lead.

The case in Cambodia involved a Bank-funded project relating to forest concession management and control. In that case, the NGO Forum on Cambodia and representatives of four villages in different parts of the country submitted a request complaining that the Bank, in its efforts to advise and support the Cambodian government in achieving improved management of forest concessions in the country, was instead serving to promote the interests of concession companies with a history of abusive and illegal logging. The request alleged non-compliance by the Bank with several of its policies, including environmental assessment, forests, indigenous peoples, cultural resources, natural habitat, disclosure of information and project supervision.

The request went through the eligibility phase of the process, and the Panel conducted a full investigation into the matters raised. In its final investigation report, the Panel noted the challenging context for work and decision-making in the forest sector in Cambodia and commended Bank management, in principle, for engaging in this work. The Panel found, however, that the Bank had failed to comply with a number of its policies, and that the "Projects' design created a structure likely to lead to inadequate levels of local involvement, community consultations and social and environmental assessments." The policy failures were of high significance in light of the reliance of local communities, including indigenous peoples, on the forests for their livelihoods and culture, and because of the world-class levels of natural habitat and biodiversity value of the forests. The Panel and its experts also found that the draft concession management plans prepared by concession companies with the guidance of technical materials developed or supported by the project were deficient in almost every respect, in terms of both process and content.[38]

The Panel report noted, at the same time, a number of actions by Bank management taken after the request was submitted, including a letter to the government of Cambodia in November 2005. This letter noted flaws in the draft concession proposals and recommended appropriate action, consistent with law, "to bring this unsatisfactory state of affairs to a quick conclusion".[39] The letter also referred to approaches other than concession-based logging for consideration, including community forestry initiatives. Management included many of these elements, and others, in the action plan and lessons-learned sections of its response to the Panel investigation, submitted to the board for its consideration. The board approved the proposed management action plan in June 2006, and asked management to report back on progress in its implementation. On 11 May 2007 management provided a progress report to the board.

This case highlights important aspects of the Panel process, and underscores the importance of the management response and action plan in presenting a way forward to address issues of harm and compliance identified by a Panel investigation. How this translates into effective action on the ground on behalf of the locally concerned and affected people, however, is still to be seen.

In other recent cases the Panel has faced a situation where – following the submission of a request – management initiated some significant actions to attempt to address and resolve concerns included in the request. For example, after the Panel received a request from Romania involving the impacts of a mine closure project on local communities, it found that the Bank initiated actions to address the issues. After the Panel's eligibility visit to the affected site and meeting with the requesters and others, it received a formal communication from the requesters indicating that the actions that had been initiated might resolve their concerns and requesting that the Panel allow a period of time (six months) before making a recommendation as to whether to carry out an investigation. In light of these circumstances, and the constructive nature of the actions being taken in response to the concerns of requesters, the Panel suggested to the board in its eligibility report that it refrain from issuing a recommendation at that time as to whether an investigation was warranted, and instead await further developments. As it turned out, further progress did occur and the requesters sent the Panel a "letter of contentment" regarding the response to their concerns.

Incentives for Bank compliance with policies and procedures in other projects and programmes

The Panel's impact is not confined to projects made subject to a request. Rather, it has a broader impact within the institution in promoting Bank management and staff compliance with Bank policies and procedures.

Experience has indicated that the simple existence of an independent panel, with the possibility of a request and board-approved investigation, reinforces incentives within management to be sure that policies and procedures are followed. This occurs at several levels: when affected people complain to the Bank about potential or actual harm, as is required before approaching the Inspection Panel; and secondly, and very importantly, when management and staff develop, appraise and supervise the implementation of Bank-financed projects. In some cases locally affected people have copied the Panel on correspondence to management, followed by important new actions.

This potential role of accountability mechanisms, such as the Inspection Panel, was recognized explicitly in the *2006 Global Accountability Report*.[40] The report states that mechanisms such as the Inspection Panel can, if rigorous, provide an incentive to ensure application of other types of accountability measures of international institutions (noted below).

The Panel is aware of many examples of this less tangible or measurable effect of the Panel in relation to the activities of the World Bank, and its role in promoting important actions to address social and environmental issues linked to Bank-funded projects.

To be sure, there are those who argue the Panel's existence promotes "Panel proofing" of projects, in that elements are not included simply because they might lead to complaints to the Panel, or works against taking risks in developing projects. However, these arguments often mask other reasons not to proceed in certain directions. The Panel has been very clear that risk-taking is integral to development, and that compliance with safeguard policies and procedures avoids harm to people and the environment and saves money in the long term.

Further development of Bank policies

The work of the Inspection Panel may also affect the further development of Bank policies. For example, the Panel's investigation report for the forestry project in Cambodia contributed to management's rethinking of its forest policy, both in Cambodia and in other countries with significant forest reserves.[41] A critical question, in this regard, is the extent to which these "lessons" or "new thinking" are actually applied in other settings.

Recognition for Panel achievements

The Panel, and similar mechanisms of accountability, can contribute to a higher degree of confidence in the work of an institution. The *2006 Global Accountability Report*, undertaken by One World Trust in London, studied 30 international institutions in terms of their accountability to people and societies affected by their actions.[42] The group included 10 international intergovernmental institutions, 10 transnational private sector companies and 10 international non-governmental organizations. The report identified four key dimensions of accountability: transparency, participation, evaluation, and complaint and response mechanisms. The report gave the World Bank, with its Inspection Panel, the highest rating (by far) among all the institutions along this fourth key dimension of accountability, and described the Panel as "good practice" or "best practice".

It is worth highlighting, in this regard, the tremendous contributions by civil society in the creation of the Panel and the ongoing fight for accountability. In addition, as described above, there remain significant challenges in making sure that people who come to the Panel get the kind of investigation *and* response they deserve. Nevertheless, as indicated by the *2006 Global Accountability Report*, the World Bank has kept its fundamental commitment over the years to having the Inspection Panel as an accountability mechanism to respond to complaints. This is no small achievement, and also makes an important contribution to the objectives of transparency and participation that are highlighted in the *2006 Global Accountability Report.*

Panel influence on accountability in other institutions

As noted above, the Inspection Panel has played a pioneering role in furthering development of accountability mechanisms in other international institutions and in several countries' national accountability instruments. Since the establishment of the Panel, other multilateral development banks have followed the lead of the World Bank and created their own accountability mechanisms, and in some cases subsequently revised them in light of the Panel's experience.[43] Canada, Japan and the United States have created national accountability mechanisms for their export or foreign investment institutions. The North American Agreement on Environmental Cooperation also provides for a procedure by which non-governmental entities and individuals can complain and trigger a fact-finding procedure.[44]

More broadly, the Inspection Panel offers a significant example of an internationally agreed mechanism to promote the involvement of civil society and local communities in the decision-making process of international law, cooperation and development. In this way it has made – and is still making – an important contribution in the continuing evolution towards greater rights of participation by non-state actors in the international law and policy-making process.[45]

The Mumbai Urban Transport Project (MUTP)

This chapter closes with a brief study of the recent Inspection Panel case involving a large-scale Bank-financed urban transport project in the city of Mumbai, India. The MUTP aims at the improvement and extension of rail and road infrastructure in the city by providing, *inter alia*, for the extension of two major east–west road links in Mumbai. It also has a resettlement component for persons affected by the project. It is the largest Bank-supported urban resettlement project ever undertaken outside

China. At project appraisal (2002), management estimated that at least 80,000 people would have to be resettled, and the number was revised upwards after project approval to some 120,000.[46]

Requests

The Panel received four successive requests for inspection related to the MUTP. The requests were submitted by a large number of affected people living in Mumbai, including families, other residents and shopkeepers with businesses of varying sizes facing resettlement.[47] All four requests pertained to the extension of two major roads under the MUTP and the resettlement of persons and shops affected by this. The requesters alleged that Bank operational policies and procedures were violated with respect to their resettlement and rehabilitation. As a result, the requesters claimed that they would suffer adverse effects. For reasons of economy and efficiency, the four requests were processed as one request, with the approval of the board for doing so.

The requesters complained that resettlement under the MUTP had not been planned appropriately, which in their view resulted in deficient baseline surveys of affected people and inadequate information and consultations. Moreover, the requesters claimed that the project failed to provide income restoration for displaced people, and would destroy their livelihoods. Particularly, the shopkeepers among the requesters feared that they would suffer irreparable damage to their well-established businesses and would lose their customer base at the resettlement sites. They expressed disagreement with the project resettlement and rehabilitation scheme that entitled them to an area of 225 square feet regardless of the actual area of their current premises affected by the project.

Under the project, most of the persons who presented the requests were to be moved to a resettlement site, which in their view offered unsuitable living and environmental conditions. The requesters complained that the site was not only too far away from their current location but also was located near the main municipal dump. They also claimed that the sites were lacking social services such as schools and medical facilities, and environmental services such as water supply. With regard to the new buildings, the requesters challenged the affordability of the maintenance charges. They also stated that they had no independent mechanism to revert to with their grievances.

Evolution of project

As noted, the MUTP today consists of both infrastructure and resettlement and rehabilitation components. The project's history holds the key to understanding many of the issues that the requesters raised and the project faced. Given the magnitude and complexity of displacement, the MUTP in 1995 was originally designed as two distinct full-scale "twin projects". One project was for transport infrastructure (MUTP) and one for resettlement, the Mumbai Urban Rehabilitation Project (MURP), with appropriate attention to the distinct design, content and institutional requirements of each.

However, after three years the Bank merged the two distinct projects into one. It reduced the complex resettlement and rehabilitation task from a full-scale project to a "subcomponent" within the MUTP infrastructure project. In this merger, the responsibility for implementing resettlement was shifted to the transportation authority, which did not have adequate capacity to deal with the resettlement of about 100,000 people. Under the MUTP, the resettlement component evolved into one focused primarily on restoration of housing, without explicit provisions for income restoration among the affected population. NGOs were contracted to implement the resettlement subcomponent of the project.

Key findings

On 21 December 2005 the Panel sent its investigation report[48] on the MUTP to the board. The report revealed several instances of non-compliance by the Bank, particularly with the policies on involuntary resettlement[49] and environmental assessment.[50]

The Panel investigation discovered that the shopkeepers' concerns had not been adequately addressed and that various issues of concern to them and their employees had been overlooked. Many of the shopkeepers, especially those with specific requirements, for example for their timber, textile and automotive enterprises, had valid and significant concerns which required full attention. Among other things, the Panel highlighted that the 225 square feet structures and the location of the resettlement sites – far away from the old customer base – would pose significant difficulties for many shopkeepers in restoring their businesses and maintaining incomes.

With regard to income restoration, the Panel noted that the Bank assumed that employment would not be problematic in Mumbai and thus did not anticipate major income losses. While many of the affected persons suffered from reduced income or job loss at the resettlement sites, they simultaneously faced very high costs at these sites, e.g. maintenance and transportation costs. In addition, the Panel identified serious issues relating to environmental and living conditions at the resettlement sites. Environmental and social services such as schools and medical facilities at the sites were inadequate when people were resettled, and many lacked sufficient access to water and sewerage. Housing societies had not been established in a timely fashion and funds for resettlement had not been transferred to the affected people. The Panel also identified flaws in the project's environmental assessment and found that the resettlement site that the requesters had to move to was close to the city's major waste dump. Moreover, the Panel noted the absence of an effective and independent grievance system that would enable project-affected persons to find recourse in the event of disagreements.

A major concern the Panel expressed was the Bank's failure to ensure that baseline surveys had been carried out adequately. In the view of the Panel, this failure resulted in, *inter alia*, highly conflicting demographic discrepancies in the estimates of affected people, including shopkeepers, as well as problems in assessing the costs and feasibility of resettlement and restoration of income. The Bank also overestimated the capacity of the implementing agency and the NGOs contracted to support project implementation.

The Panel linked many of the compliance issues raised by the requesters to the early decision to merge the initial two projects and make the resettlement action a subcomponent of the transport project. The Panel noted that the merger diverted attention away from the institutional capacity required to address resettlement issues effectively. Also, the estimate of the number of people to be resettled was reduced dramatically, as was the cost estimate for resettlement, before it was submitted to the board for approval, but then increased to about the original estimate some time following approval. Moreover, the reference to the problem of shopkeepers, initially identified in the separate resettlement project, seems to have been dropped from consideration after the merger.

Management response and actions

Bank management's report and recommendation in response to the Panel's findings acknowledged these findings in most instances.[51] Management recognized that it failed to identify the project's effects on middle-income shopkeepers. Among other issues, management agreed that special attention to the specific needs of the shopkeepers and their employees was necessary, and that it had to address their concerns regarding the suitable space allocation for shops of more than 225 square feet and their worries regarding the location of the new shops.

Management further agreed with the Panel's findings about the lack of institutional capacity of the implementing agency and the NGOs. It also acknowledged that consultations with affected people were limited and that the grievance mechanism needed serious improvement. Moreover, it acknowledged the Panel's finding that the surveys were inadequate and confirmed the conflicting estimates of affected people. Management confirmed significant delays in the establishing of functioning housing societies and in the transferring of funds aimed to assist the affected people to cope with resettlement. Moreover, management acknowledged the majority of the Panel's findings regarding the social and environmental conditions at the resettlement sites, such as the inadequate water supply and the absence of schools. However, management did not fully share the Panel's concerns about income restoration. Instead, it indicated that it had considered the issue of housing more important than the issue of employment.

Management agreed that a range of actions would be necessary to bring the project into compliance, and proposed an action plan consisting of several key actions to be undertaken by the implementing agency and management. Management proposed, *inter alia*, to expand the options of resettlement sites for the shopkeepers and to commence negotiations with the eligible shopkeepers. Moreover, the action plan provided for improvement in social and environmental services to the resettlement sites, e.g. through improving water supply and establishing housing cooperatives. Additionally, management included actions such as the establishment of a database and the improvement of the grievance redressal mechanism. Management also urged that MUTP's capacity for implementing resettlement be significantly strengthened.

Board decision and suspension of loan disbursement

On 1 March 2006, before the board met to deliberate on the investigation report and management's response, the Bank suspended disbursement on the road and resettlement components of the MUTP. The Bank asked the government of Maharashtra to complete a set of actions, consisting of 10 major action points, in a satisfactory manner before it would lift the suspension.

Soon thereafter, on 28 March 2006, the board of executive directors met to discuss the management report and recommendations and the Panel's investigation report. The board endorsed the action plan. It was agreed that management would submit a progress report to the board in no more than six months, and that the Panel would report on progress to the board.

On 29 June 2006 the Bank lifted the suspension of disbursement based on the conclusion that the state of Maharashtra had substantially met the conditions for lifting it.

Follow-up

In May 2006 the Panel visited Delhi and Mumbai and met with the requesters, government authorities and Bank staff to discuss and convey the findings of the investigation report. Management submitted its progress report to the board on 1 March 2007, after a significant delay, and the Panel reviewed the progress report in great detail for the board.[52] Both management's progress report and the Panel's review of management's progress report are available on the Panel's website.

Conclusion

The World Bank Inspection Panel has been in operation for more than a dozen years. During these years it has provided a forum for communities around the world to give voice to their concerns about the adverse social and environmental impacts of projects funded by the World Bank, to establish the facts in relation to those concerns and to report findings to the decision-making chamber of the Bank for consideration and action. The Panel has a well-developed body of procedures and practice on which to build for the future and assess the past.

The Panel's experience has considerable relevance for future efforts within the UN system to establish or strengthen institutions for ensuring accountability by management and staff. It suggests that it is important to establish such a body as structurally independent of management and staff, and to give it the attributes of a high-level body within the institution. To gain the trust of all parties, it is important that the reports be transparent, that the body communicates directly with those making the complaint and returns to convey the results of the investigations to them, and that panel members and staff are able at all times to operate impartially and objectively. It is also important that the body is able to have access to all relevant documents and be thorough in its work. Most importantly, it must have the trust of all concerned.

The Inspection Panel at the World Bank provides an entryway for people and civil society into the decision-making process of a major international institution. The people who have come to the Panel over the years have been poor, often living in remote locations and, without much ability to influence decisions and actions that affect them greatly – the kind of people that the World Bank expressly intends to help and to bring into the development process in a positive way. The Inspection Panel, as a means to promote participation and accountability, is intended to enhance the legitimacy of the World Bank as a development institution and to help ensure that development is effective and aids the poorest people of the world.

The key to this involves more than process; it needs to include outcomes. Where the World Bank has complied with its policies and procedures, this needs to be understood. Where things go awry – and they have – people will want to know and see what has been done, practically, to address their concerns. In the continuing fight for accountability, this issue merits careful and continuing attention. Good accountability helps ensure that development meets the needs of the poorest in the world.

Notes

1. The 1987 report of the World Commission on Environment and Development provides a landmark narrative on these issues, including connections between the dogged and fierce problem of poverty around the world and issues of social and environmental progress. See World Commission on Environment and Development (1987) *Report of the World Commission on Environment and Development: Our Common Future* ("Brundtland Report") UN Doc. A/42/427/Annex, Oxford: Oxford University Press.
2. The summit highlighted the need for positive integration of social, environmental and economic policies, and recognized that social equity and the fight against poverty were core to this effort. It also stressed financial support to developing countries and the active participation by civil society in the achievement of sustainable development. See principles 10, 20–22 of Rio Declaration on Environment and Development (1992) UN Doc. A/CONF. 151/5/ Rev. 1, 14 June, reprinted in *International Legal Materials* 31(4), pp. 876–880; Agenda 21 (adopted at Rio de Janeiro on 14 June 1992), UN Doc. A/CONF.151/26/Rev.1 (Vol. I), available at www.un.org/esa/sustdev/documents/agenda21/index.htm, ch. 33 (financial resources and mechanisms) and chs 23–32 (strengthening the role of major groups).
3. The International Bank for Reconstruction and Development (IBRD), commonly known as the World Bank, was established at Bretton Woods in 1944. Since then, the World Bank has evolved into a group of entities which include the IBRD, the International Finance Corporation (IFC, founded in 1956), the International Development Association (IDA, founded in 1960), the Multilateral Investment Guarantee Agency (MIGA, founded in 1988) and the Global Environment Facility (GEF, founded in 1990). The IBRD provides loans to support development-related projects and programmes in low- and middle-income countries. The IDA generally provides interest-free loans or grants to the poorest countries (through "credits"), on a highly concessional basis. The IDA is funded by contributions from richer member countries, and is periodically replenished. The IFC lends to the private sector.
4. The policies addressing social and environmental issues are sometimes referred to as "safeguard policies". They include those on involuntary resettlement, indigenous peoples, poverty reduction, cultural resources, environmental assessment, forests, natural habitat, pest management and safety of dams. Other important policies include those on project supervision, economic evaluation of investment opportunities and disclosure of information. The Bank's policies have evolved significantly over time.
5. See Clark, Dana L. (2003) "Understanding the World Bank Inspection Panel", in Dana L. Clark, Jonathan Fox and Kay Treakle, eds, *Demanding Accountability: Civil Society Claims and the World Bank Inspection Panel*, Lanham, MD: Rowman & Littlefield, pp. 1–24; Hunter, David and Lori Udall (1994) "The World Bank's New Inspection Panel: Will It Increase the Bank Accountability?", *Environment*, November, p. 1, also published as Center for International Environmental Law, Brief No. 1, April, available at www.ciel.org/Publications/issue1.html.
6. Clark, ibid., p. 3; Ramachandra, Komala (2006) "Sardar Sarovar: An Experience Retained?", *Harvard Human Rights Journal* 19, pp. 275–281. Many other projects were also highlighted as a source of concern, including dam projects in Thailand, Brazil and

the Argentine-Brazil border, forestry projects in Côte d'Ivoire and Gabon and a transmigration project in Indonesia. See Hunter and Udall, ibid.; Chatterjee, Pratap (1994) "Wapenhans Summary and Update", *Multinational Monitor*, October, available at www.globalpolicy.org/socecon/bwi-wto/critics/1994/9410wap.htm.

7. The Commission was headed by Bradford Morse, retired administrator of the UN Development Programme (UNDP), and Thomas Berger, former justice of the Supreme Court of British Columbia, Canada.
8. See Morse, Bradford and Thomas Berger (1995) "Findings and Recommendations of the Independent Review", in William F. Fisher, ed., *Toward Sustainable Development? Struggling Over India's Narmada River*, Armonk, NY: M. E. Sharpe, pp. 371–380; Clark, note 5 above, p. 5.
9. See IBRD Inspection Panel (2003) *Accountability at the World Bank: The Inspection Panel 10 Years On*, Washington, DC: International Bank for Reconstruction and Development, available at www.inspectionpanel.org, p. 8; Clark, note 5 above, p. 5; Chatterjee, note 6 above; IBRD Portfolio Management Task Force (1992) "Records of the Portfolio Management Task Force ('Wapenhans Report') and Follow-up", WB IBRD/IDA 03-07-02-01, July.
10. Hunter and Udall, note 5 above; Clark, note 5 above.
11. Clark, note 5 above, pp. 5–6.
12. IBRD International Development Association (1993) "The World Bank Inspection Panel", Res. No. IBRD 93-10, Res. No. IDA 93-6, 22 September ("1993 Panel resolution"). There have also been two "Clarifications of Certain Aspects of the Resolution", the first issued in 1996 and the second in 1999. See IBRD Inspection Panel (2006) "Final Panel Investigation Report Cambodia: Forest Concession Management and Control Pilot Project", available at www.inspectionpanel.org.
13. See 1993 Panel resolution, ibid.. See also IBRD Inspection Panel, note 9 above.
14. IBRD Inspection Panel (1994) "Panel Operating Procedures, August 19, 1994 (Purpose)", available at www.inspectionpanel.org. The Panel developed its own operating procedures early in its existence, which is consistent with its status as an independent entity.
15. See e.g. Sohn, Louis B. (1982) "The New International Law: Protection of the Rights of Individuals Rather than States", *American University Law Review* 32(1), pp. 1–64. See also Brown Weiss, Edith (1995) "New Directions in International Environmental Law: Address before the United Nations Congress on Public International Law", 15 March; Lallas, Peter L. (2001) "The Role of Process and Participation in the Development of Effective International Environmental Agreements: A Study of the Global Treaty on Persistent Organic Pollutants (POPs)", *UCLA Journal of Environmental Law and Policy* 19(1), pp. 83–152; Shelton, Dinah (2002) "Human Rights and the Environment: Jurisprudence of Human Rights Bodies", Background Paper No. 2, Joint UNEP-OHCHR Expert Seminar on Human Rights and the Environment, Geneva, 14–16 January, available at http://www2.ohchr.org/english/issues/environment/environ/bp2.htm.
16. See Boisson de Chazournes, Laurence (2005) "The World Bank Inspection Panel: About Public Participation and Dispute Settlement", in Tullio Treves, Marco Frigessi di Rattalma, Attila Tanzi, Alessandro Fodella, Cesare Pitea and Chiara Ragni, eds, *Civil Society, International Courts and Compliance Bodies*, The Hague: TMC Asser Press, pp. 187–203.
17. Washington Treaty Relating to the Boundary Waters and Questions Arising Along the Boundary Between the United States and Canada, 11 January 1909.
18. See e.g. Brown Weiss, Edith (1989) "New Directions for the Great Lakes Water Quality Agreement: A Commentary", *Chicago-Kent Law Review* 65(2), pp. 375–386, at pp. 380–384, regarding commissions of inquiry.

19. See e.g. UN Office of the UN High Commissioner for Human Rights (2007) "Strategic Management Plan 2006–2007", ATAR SA, Geneva: pp. 26–28 (supporting human rights thematic fact-finding procedures); UN Office of the UN High Commissioner for Human Rights (undated) "Complaints Procedures", available at www.unhcr.ch/html/men2/complain.htm; UN Convention on the Law of Non-Navigational Use of International Watercourses, 31 May 1997, UN Doc. A/RES/51/229, available at http://untreaty.un.org/ilc/texts/instruments/english/conventions18_3_1997.pdf, article 33.3 (providing for the submission of a dispute to impartial fact-finding under specified conditions).
20. See Blagescu, Monica and Robert Lloyd (2006) *2006 Global Accountability Report: Holding Power to Account*, London: One World Trust.
21. See Brown Weiss, Edith, Stephen McCaffrey, Daniel Magraw and A. Dan Tarlock (2006) *International Environmental Law and Policy*, 2nd edn, New York: Aspen Publishers, pp. 1024–1058.
22. See Kingsbury, Benedict, Nico Krisch and Richard Stewart (2005) "The Emergence of Global Administrative Law", *Law and Contemporary Problems* 68(3/4), pp. 15–62; Gunton, Dave, Mike Livermore and Antonios Tzanakopoulos (2005) "A Global Administrative Law Bibliography", *Law and Contemporary Problems* 68(3/4), pp. 357–378; Krisch, Nico and Benedict Kingsbury (2006) "Introduction: Global Governance and Global Administrative Law in the International Legal Order", *European Journal of International Law* 17(1), pp. 1–13.
23. IBRD 1993 Panel resolution, note 12 above, para. 2.
24. Ibid., para. 4.
25. Ibid., para. 7; see also para. 10 (containing further provisions relating to the status and remuneration of Panel members).
26. As of 1 December 2007 the secretariat had seven permanent staff, including professional and administrative.
27. The authors wish to express a special note of appreciation for the contributions of Eduardo Abbott, the first executive secretary of the Panel, who served the Panel continuously from his appointment on 4 April 1994 to his retirement on 31 December 2006.
28. See IBRD 1993 Panel resolution, note 12 above, para. 11. The decision is made by the President of the World Bank, in consultation with the board of executive directors – another element of the independence of the Panel from management and staff. In the recent process to select a new executive secretary, a representative of civil society, selected by civil society, participated.
29. Ibid., paras 1, 11.
30. See IBRD Inspection Panel, note 14 above, paras 6–15.
31. Annual report and website, available at www.inspectionpanel.org.
32. IBRD Inspection Panel, note 14 above, para. 22 (for example, the claim does not relate to a Bank project, or the project is already closed or the request is "manifestly frivolous").
33. See International Development Association (1999) "International Bank for Reconstruction and Development, Inspection Panel, Clarification of the Board's Second Review of the Inspection Panel", available at www.inspectionpanel.org, para. 3.
34. See IBRD 1993 Panel resolution, note 12 above, note 2.
35. Paragraph 12 provides that the profile of Panel activities, in-country during the course of an investigation, should be "kept as low as possible in keeping with its role as a fact-finding body on behalf of the Board... the Panel – and Management – should decline media contacts while an investigation is pending or underway". IBRD Inspection Panel, note 33 above, para. 12.
36. Ibid., para. 15.
37. IBRD Inspection Panel, note 9 above. See Bruch, Carl (2007) "Compliance", in *Compendium of Relevant Practices for Improved Decision-Making, Planning and Manage-*

ment of Dams and Their Alternatives, case study of Inspection Panel Request 2001 involving proposed Bujagali Dam in Uganda, Washington, DC: UN Environment Programme; Boisson de Chazournes, note 16 above; Orakhelashvili, Alexander (2005) "The World Bank Inspection Panel in Context: Institutional Aspects of the Accountability of International Organizations", *International Organizations Law Review* 2(1), pp. 57–102; Malone, Linda A. and Scott Pasternack (2004) *Defending the Environment: Civil Society Strategies to Enforce International Environmental Law*, Ardsley, NY: Transnational Publishers; Clark, Dana L., Jonathan Fox and Kay Treakle, eds (2003) *Demanding Accountability: Civil-Society Claims and the World Bank Inspection Panel*, Lanham, MD: Rowman & Littlefield Publishers; Hunter, David (2003) "Using the World Bank Inspection Panel to Defend the Interests of Project-Affected People", *Chicago Journal of International Law* 4(1), pp. 201–211; Freestone, David (2003) "The Environment and Social Safeguard Policies of the World Bank and the Evolving Role of the Inspection Panel", in Alexandre Kiss, Dinah Shelton and Kanami Ishibashi, eds, *Economic Globalization and Compliance with International Environmental Agreements*, The Hague and New York: Kluwer Law International, pp. 139–156; Clark, Dana L. (2002) "The World Bank and Human Rights: The Need for Greater Accountability", *Harvard Human Rights Journal* 15, pp. 205–226, especially the section on "The Inspection Panel: Recourse But Often No Redress"; Fox, Jonathan (2002) "The World Bank Inspection Panel and the Limits of Accountability", in Jonathan R. Pincus and Jeffrey A. Winters, eds, *Reinventing the World Bank*, Ithaca, NY, and London: Cornell University Press, pp. 131–163; Alfredsson, Gudmundur and Rolf Ring, eds (2001) *The Inspection Panel of the World Bank: A Different Complaints Procedure*, The Hague, London and Boston, MA: Martinus Nijhoff Publishers; Gowlland Gualtieri, Alix (2001) "The Environmental Accountability of the World Bank to Non-State Actors: Insights from the Inspection Panel", *British Yearbook of International Law* 72, pp. 213–253 (analysing experience to the year 2000).

38. See IBRD Inspection Panel, note 12 above.
39. Ibid. (noting and discussing management letter).
40. Blagescu and Lloyd, note 20 above.
41. The management response and action plan includes specific sections on "lessons learned" by the Bank to be applied not only in future work in Cambodia but also in forest-related work more generally. See IBRD Inspection Panel, note 12 above.
42. Blagescu and Lloyd, note 20 above.
43. Brown Weiss et al., note 21 above, ch. 19.
44. See North American Agreement on Environmental Cooperation: Between the Government of Canada, the Government of the United Mexican States and the Government of the United States of America (1993), available at www.worldtradelaw.net/nafta/naaec.pdf, articles 14 and 15. The nature and scope of this public submission process is described in more detail at www.cec.org and in Brown Weiss et al., note 21 above, ch. 18.
45. See Sohn, note 15 above; Brown Weiss, note 15 above; Lallas, note 15 above.
46. See IBRD Inspection Panel (2006) "Inspection Panel Investigation Report, India: Mumbai Urban Transport Project", 9 January, INSP/R2005-0005, available at www.inspectionpanel.org. The large change in figures reported was a significant issue addressed in the report.
47. The Panel received the first request on 28 April 2004 and the second request on 24 June 2004. On 29 November 2004 the third request was received and on 23 December 2004 the Panel received the fourth request for inspection.
48. IBRD Inspection Panel, note 46 above.
49. International Bank for Reconstruction and Development (1990) "Involuntary Resettlement", June, OD 4.30.

50. International Bank for Reconstruction and Development (1999) "Environmental Assessment", January, OP 4.01.
51. The term "management report" refers to the Bank management's report and recommendation in response to the Inspection Panel Investigation Report, 7 March 2006. See IBRD Inspection Panel, note 46 above.
52. The Panel submitted its report to the board on 11 May 2007, after revisiting the project site and meeting with affected people.

14

Improving accountability at the Asian Development Bank

Suresh Nanwani

Introduction

The inaugural workshop of the UNU Tokyo Symposium on Accountability, aimed to prepare concrete policy recommendations for the UN system organizations based on theoretical and empirical analyses, was timely. The practices of multilateral development banks (MDBs), including the Asian Development Bank (ADB), on the accountability of their operations to the public at large are relevant for consideration by the United Nations to enhance the accountability of UN system organizations to the global community. The focus of this chapter is on ADB measures to improve accountability.

This chapter outlines the key features of the concept of accountability; the role the ADB plays in addressing internal accountability issues through organizational, policy and other reforms and changes; and the ADB's provision of a window of access to address citizen complaints on ADB-assisted projects through its accountability mechanism policy. It also discusses emerging trends and challenges in MDBs and other development institutions to improve their citizen-complaint mechanisms to enhance the accountability of their operations and the participation of external stakeholders in their decision-making processes. The chapter concludes that there is progress in ADB efforts on improving accountability. The chapter reflects on the limitations of accountability mechanisms as internal governance tools, and highlights areas for improvement.

Envisioning reform: Enhancing UN accountability in the twenty-first century, Kuyama and Fowler (eds), United Nations University Press, 2009, ISBN 978-92-808-1170-4

Meanings of accountability

Although the term "accountability" for international organizations has been increasingly used in at least the past decade, it remains difficult to define and at best has many meanings. Professor Malcolm Shaw, co-rapporteur of the International Law Association London conference on the accountability of international organizations, stated that the term was "difficult to define".[1] Lewis Carroll's Humpty Dumpty in *Alice in Wonderland* would not have a problem with the term, as it would mean just what he chose it to mean – "neither more nor less". We all know that Alice questioned Humpty Dumpty on whether the word can mean different things.

Let me start with a dictionary definition. The *Oxford English Dictionary*'s definition of the term "accountable" is "(of a person, organization, or institution) required or expected to justify actions or decisions; responsible".[2] Merriam-Webster OnLine Dictionary defines the term "accountability" as "the quality or state of being accountable; especially: an obligation or willingness to accept responsibility or to account for one's actions".[3] In terms of forms of accountability in international organizations, the International Law Association has articulated four: legal, political, administrative and financial.[4] Ruth Grant and Robert Keohane take a different approach, defining seven mechanisms to hold international organizations accountable: supervisory, legal, market, peer, hierarchical, public reputational and fiscal.[5] The author's view of "accountability" of an international organization is the responsibility for action/inaction taken in terms of being answerable on why it was taken, the process by which it was carried out and the outcome. This institutional accountability, in turn, cascades down to teams and individuals in the organization.

Demands for accountability from multilateral development banks

Since the UN's establishment in 1945 there has been a proliferation of multilateral development banks promoting economic development. These include the World Bank, International Finance Corporation (IFC), Multilateral Investment Guarantee Agency (MIGA), Inter-American Development Bank (IDB), African Development Bank (AfDB), and Asian Development Bank (ADB) in the first 25 years, and the European Bank for Reconstruction and Development (EBRD) in 1991. These MDBs focus on lending to their members in both public and private sector operations to support economic growth or development in their borrowing member countries.

Over the past two decades various MDBs have adopted environmental and social policies such as those relating to involuntary resettlement, governance, anti-corruption, environment, indigenous peoples, public information disclosure and accountability mechanisms. The driving forces behind these policies are to improve institutional development effectiveness and enhance project quality; to have environmental and social safeguards to mitigate adverse project impacts; to emphasize the interests of affected communities through accessing information and through participation in project planning and implementation; to be abreast with various international agreements and developments, such as the Rio Declaration and Agenda 21 in 1992 and related conventions; and to address donor concerns through replenishment funds of the institutions and statements issued at meetings of the G-7 countries.[6] The demands for accountability are increasing, and as recently as September 2006 the Global Transparency Initiative launched its Transparency Charter for International Financial Institutions on the standards to which these institutions' disclosure information policies should conform.[7]

Strengthening accountability at the ADB

Concomitant with the adoption of these policies over this period and in response to criticisms of the organization's project management and operations performance, the ADB carried out organizational changes by establishing an Environment Division and a Social Dimensions Unit in 1987 and 1992, respectively, and merging them in 1995. In 1993 the ADB established the Task Force on Improving Project Quality to carry out an internal review of the Bank's portfolio of projects, including the work of the operations departments which are responsible for all aspects of the institution's lending operations at the country level. The report of this Task Force[8] addressed *internal accountability*,[9] and also noted "approval culture"[10] in the organization where excessive emphasis was placed on achieving annual levels of programmed lending; this can result in inadequate project design and insufficient consideration of beneficiary participation and local needs and demands. The Task Force also reiterated the theme of accountability for project quality: the ADB "cannot escape the need to restructure and reorient itself to strengthen the clarity of roles and *accountability* for quality at various levels in the organization"[11] (emphasis added).

The ADB's measures in improving accountability

Over the past decade the ADB has implemented various tools and measures to improve accountability, including the reorganization of the ADB in 2002; institutional changes and developments, such as the creation in 1999 of the Anticorruption Unit in the Office of the Auditor General (renamed the Integrity Division in 2005) and the enhancement of the Operations Evaluation Department (OED) in 2004; the adoption of a managing for development results (MfDR)[12] approach in 2003 to improve accountability through its emphasis on results in the institution and its country and project operations;[13] and formulation and revision of policies directly impacting on communities affected by ADB-assisted projects and the public at large (including the information and disclosure policies, which the public communications policy replaced,[14] and the inspection function policy, which the accountability mechanism policy replaced).[15]

The objective of the ADB reorganization in 2002[16] was to address its capacity to implement effectively its Long-Term Strategic Framework 2001–2015, which charts the ADB's agenda for these years. The reorganization noted the change of the ADB's role from its origins as a traditional project financier to that of a project financier and promoter of policy reforms in the 1980s and 1990s, and to a "full-fledged development institution"[17] in 2001. This reorganization also addressed the issue of responsibility on departments and positions in these departments which should be held accountable for results. It resulted in the creation of five regional departments to implement the ADB's strategic agenda for its developing member countries in the Asia-Pacific region and carry out its operational activities in each country. In 2004 an independent assessment panel consisting of three external experts carried out an evaluation of the effectiveness of the 2002 reorganization. The findings noted that while the creation of the regional departments in 2002 was a major step forward in terms of accountability for country operations, there was a need to clarify accountability for various products at different levels of staff, and a need to have greater empowerment of managers and staff to make decisions and be held accountable for results. This panel's findings were, in turn, used in the ADB's new human resources strategy in 2004, where managers and staff at senior levels are required to take on greater responsibilities and accountabilities in all aspects relating to staff management and "improving staff *accountability* at all levels of the organization"[18] (emphasis added). They were also used in April 2006 in realigning ADB regional departments, which are responsible for project administration and management of the portfolio of countries covered by the department.[19]

Enhancing the independence of the ADB Operations Evaluation Department

The OED evaluates ADB projects, programmes and technical assistance carried out by operations departments; the ongoing project portfolio; the broader thematic issues, policies and practices; the effectiveness of ADB operations at the country level; and the sector assistance programme. The OED is the first ADB department reporting to the board of directors, helping the ADB to "improve its development effectiveness and *accountability* to its stakeholders"[20] (emphasis added).

In 2004 the OED's independence and effectiveness was enhanced as an instrument of independent accountability. It now reports directly to the board of directors through the Development Effectiveness Committee (DEC), a board standing committee, instead of to the President. This change reflects the need to ensure four criteria are complied with by a number of official evaluation and audit organizations:[21] organizational independence, behavioural independence, protection from outside influence and avoidance of conflicts of interest.[22] As the board of directors is the policy-making organ of the ADB and is ultimately responsible for the development effectiveness of ADB operations, the OED reporting to the board through a board standing committee provides structural autonomy.

The board appoints, upon the joint recommendation of the DEC and the President, the Director-General heading the OED for an initial term of three years, which may be renewed for a maximum of two years. Upon completion of the term, the Director-General is ineligible for any other staff position in the ADB, including as a staff consultant. These provisions ensure independence to maintain the credibility of its evaluation and of the ADB as a whole.

From its initial establishment in 1978, when evaluation was geared towards specific ADB projects and programmes, the OED's role has increased in response to the need for increased accountability and results manifested in the growing focus and scope of evaluations. OED evaluation reports (except those on private sector operations which will be redacted if they contain confidential business information or other matters covered by the public communications policy), ADB management's[23] response, the OED's response to management, if any, and the DEC chair's summary are posted on the ADB website.[24]

With these improvements, objective evaluations are ensured and the lessons learned can be fed back by ADB management and staff into ADB operations. Also, external stakeholders have better access to information on the decision-making processes at the ADB – of management, the OED and the DEC – and can use the information to understand the institution and its activities better. For example, a non-governmental organization (NGO) has noted that "too many OED recommendations have not been acted upon by operations departments".[25] With the DEC's 2005 annual report, which recommended that "a system be established for monitoring the cumulative progress of actions on OED's recommendations",[26] the question of what prevented the ADB from establishing such a mechanism in the first place is now being asked.[27] The OED's annual evaluation review report of September 2006 also highlights governance and accountability issues such as "approval culture".[28] The need to address this matter, 14 years on from the 1992 Task Force report when it was first mentioned, is still relevant and challenging. A "reliable, tested system to measure ADB's contributions to achieving development results"[29] also needs to be developed. This report is also the "first attempt in ADB to examine ADB's staff accountability and project success".[30]

Increased transparency and availability of information through the public communications policy

In 2005 the ADB adopted its public communications policy,[31] which replaced its former information and disclosure policies. This policy aims to enhance stakeholders' trust in and ability to engage with the institution and to ensure that ADB operations have greater development impact. It promotes participatory development and a two-way flow of information between the ADB and its stakeholders, including affected people. This policy requires the ADB to make its documents publicly available, i.e. posted on the ADB website, "unless doing so will result in harm to ADB, its members, or another organization that entrusted ADB with the information".[32] A unique feature illustrative of this external accountability is that if a requester believes that the request for information has been unreasonably denied or the policy has been interpreted improperly, the person can submit a written request to an ADB committee – the Public Disclosure Advisory Committee (PDAC) – to address complaints regarding information disclosure denied by ADB departments. The PDAC consists of four ADB managers and senior staff; it will acknowledge receipt of the request within five working days, convene as soon as possible to consider the complaint, and give the requester its decision no later than 30 calendar days after receiving the request. Under this policy, the ADB will issue an annual report containing the results of its monitoring of the information activities, a summary of refusals to provide information to the public and any recommendations for changes to the policy. The first annual report was expected to be issued by December 2006. As of 5 October 2006 no complaints had been filed with the PDAC.

Addressing complaints on fraud and corruption

The ADB's anti-corruption policy[33] in 1999 opened up another window of access for anyone in the ADB or externally to submit to the ADB concerns about fraud or corruption in any ADB-financed activity, including

ADB staff involvement in such activity. Prior to this policy there were no publicized independent channels whereby incidents of fraud or corruption could be reported for investigation. One important objective of this policy is that ADB projects and staff adhere to the highest ethical standards. Any complaint can be brought to the attention of the ADB Integrity Division (called the Office of the Auditor General Integrity – OAGI), which is tasked by the Office of the Auditor General to handle and investigate all allegations of fraud or corruption among ADB-financed projects or ADB staff. If requested, the OAGI will protect the identity of the complainant and the information provided. The OAGI publishes annual reports on how it handles the allegations brought to its attention. The OAGI's 2005 annual report of January 2006[34] states that 199 complaints were received, and after screening on whether they relate to its mandate of ADB-financed activities or staff, it opened 102 investigations and closed 59 complaints after concluding that further investigation was not required.

This report also notes a total of 21 (including five involving ADB staff) fraud and corruption investigations in 1998 against 102 (including 15 involving ADB staff) such investigations in 2005, indicating the increase of complaints and investigations over the years, and provides summaries of OAGI investigative findings.[35] Measures include declaration of firms and individuals ineligible to participate in ADB-financed activity, suspension or cancellation of loans and sanctions on staff, from written censure to summary dismissal. There have been calls by some ADB member countries, NGOs and other stakeholders criticizing the ADB's policy not to disclose publicly the names of sanctioned individuals and entities. The Office of the Auditor General has considered and reassessed this matter, and concluded that the current policy of not publicizing the names of entities listed on the anti-corruption sanction list issued by the OAGI provides the best balance in addressing fraud and corruption related to ADB-financed activity, and allows the ADB to implement the anti-corruption policy in the best way.[36]

Handling complaints on procurement irregularities

Any person can refer a complaint concerning the recruitment and short-listing of consultants and the prequalification, bidding and bid evaluation process for procuring goods and works under an ADB-financed project to the ADB Central Operations Services Office (COSO).[37] COSO oversees ADB procurement and consulting services, and is responsible for reviewing ADB borrowers' procurement activities, selecting and engaging consultants required by the ADB and reviewing borrowers' selection and engagement of consultants under ADB loans. This office will consider the complaint and check that the actions are carried out in accordance with ADB policies, applicable guidelines[38] and the applicable loan agreements.

As there is currently no formal system for filing complaints, these have been filed in various ways, such as direct referrals to COSO by unsuccessful bidders, applicants or interested persons, or through members of the ADB board of directors who in turn bring them to COSO's attention. In one case where the ADB Compliance Review Panel was determining the eligibility of a request for compliance review, the Panel referred the matter to COSO as the requesters alleged procurement irregularities and violations of ADB procedures, and the subject matter did not fall within the Panel's remit under the accountability mechanism policy. COSO considered the matter and responded to the requesters, with a copy to the Panel.[39] Unlike the OAGI, which issues an annual report, COSO does not publish an annual report on complaints received and their disposal.

Obtaining civil society inputs in policy review and implementation

In the past decade the ADB has actively solicited specific civil society inputs from the outset to assist it to implement or review its policies as these impact on people. For instance, the ADB policy on gender and development (GAD)[40] provides for the establishment of the External Forum on Gender and Development (EFG) to promote and facilitate dialogue between the ADB and external groups on relevant issues. The EFG was established in 2001 and has been meeting annually since then as part of the ADB's initiative to promote and facilitate dialogue with this group on GAD issues. The Forum is a 10-member panel of experts on GAD and women's rights from different ADB member countries, and its members represent a variety of disciplines and perspectives.[41] This policy provides for a review of implementation experience after five years. The review commenced in 2004: its process involved consultations with governments and other stakeholders, including technical input by the EFG, resulting in the issue of the draft final report on the review of the GAD policy in June 2006 for public comment prior to finalization of the report.

Similarly, the ADB engaged a panel of external experts to review the implementation of its water policy in 2005. A panel of six members representing developing member country officials, civil society, bilateral donors and the private sector was appointed for a year to ensure broad stakeholder participation, transparent proceedings and reporting, and wide dissemination of results and recommendations. This panel had meetings, participated in in-country or regional consultations and contributed to the preparation of the final report for ADB management.

The panel's work was completed in May 2006 with the submission of a report containing its assessment of the implementation of the water policy. ADB management accepted the challenges given by the panel, and its Water Committee took into consideration the panel's suggestions for discussion with clients, partners and stakeholders in a consultation organized in 2006.

Providing information and communicating with stakeholders on the progress of the ADB reform agenda

The ADB's adoption of a reform agenda in 2004, whose foundation rests on MfDR, is an illustrative example which clearly spells out who has "*responsibility and ultimate accountability* for carrying out this reform agenda" (emphasis added) – ADB management under the overall guidance of the President. The reform agenda consists of 19 ADB-wide reform initiatives to deliver five outcomes related to internal changes and realignment.[42] The downward delegation of responsibility is also specified – that is, the "main responsibility for implementing a specific reform initiative and monitoring its progress lies with the focal department or office concerned". These two quoted provisions are highlighted in the annual progress report on the implementation of the reform agenda of March 2006.[43] The reform agenda also highlights the improvement of the human resources strategy, where a "new performance management system clearly defines staff responsibilities and accountabilities in an annual work plan agreed between staff and managers".[44] A dedicated ADB website on the reform agenda, containing information and progress reports, was launched in 2004 to facilitate communication with stakeholders.[45] Through the reform agenda, the ADB is actively pursuing automatic disclosure of information on its website for communication with its external stakeholders.

Demands for MDB accountability mechanisms to address citizen-based grievances

The examples above illustrate the changes in the ADB to be more inclusive of the needs of external stakeholders – project beneficiaries, pressure groups, affected communities and civil society at large – in its lending operations. This is still short of various calls and proposals, ranging from one extreme of cessation of lending activities (the role of the World Bank and regional development banks in lending operations should be significantly reduced and focused more on technical assistance, as recommended by the Meltzer Commission) to the other extreme of an organization engaged in "deliberative decision-making"[46] to democratize, pluralize and gain legitimacy. However, given the structure of MDBs and their weighted voting power according to the share subscription of their member states, the ground reality is that decision-making in most cases is led by their most powerful member states.[47] With the issuance of the Morse Commission Report (described below) and the Wapenhans Report,[48] there was a change in the global decision-making process at the World Bank, with pressure mounted by NGOs in proposals for an independent mechanism to allow adversely affected people to air their grievances on World Bank-assisted projects.[49]

The first MDB accountability mechanism and rippling effects on other MDBs

In 1991, for the first time in the operations of any MDB, the World Bank established a panel of outside experts (the Morse Commission) to review its Sardar Sarovar projects in India. The Commission was lauded for its well-documented investigation and clear analysis of the Sardar Sarovar projects, which involved construction of a large concrete dam and were expected to cause major environmental impacts and resettlement of about 70,000 people (this figure has at least trebled, according to a 2003 report by Environmental Defense, Friends of the Earth and International Rivers Network[50]). This Commission found that the "problems besetting the Sardar Sarovar Projects are more the rule than the exception to resettlement operations supported by the Bank in India".[51] The government of India as the borrower cancelled the remaining portion of the World Bank loan in 1993. The Sardar Sarovar projects continue to be a *cause célèbre* of World Bank responsibility for social hardship and economic and ecological damages resulting from its projects, due to its role in the crucial initial phases of the projects.[52] The Morse Commission turned out to be a catalyst in setting the tone and prototype for establishing the World Bank Inspection Panel in 1993 and other accountability mechanisms in other MDBs. The ripple effect of the global decision-making process in having the same major shareholders in each MDB also resulted in the creation of other MDB accountability mechanisms. The IDB had its independent investigation mechanism one year later in 1994, followed by the ADB's inspection function in 1995 (replaced by the ADB accountability mechanism in 2003) and the creation of the IFC/MIGA's Compliance/Advisor Ombudsman (CAO) in 1999, the EBRD's independent recourse mechanism in 2003 (operationalized in 2004) and the AfDB's independent review mechanism (established in 2004 and effective in early 2006).[53]

The ADB accountability mechanism: Review process leading to the new system

This chapter will not go into the working details, or the efficacy, of the new ADB accountability mechanism; the full impact of this mechanism – through views from various stakeholders, including the ADB, project affectees who have used the mechanism, potential claimants using the mechanism, NGOs which serve as watchdogs to check on how the ADB responds to institutional and staff accountability, and ADB member countries – can be known in several ways, including a review of the policy.[54] Rather, the focus is to highlight the process by which the new mechanism came into place as a result of extensive internal and external consultations, and to show the contributions made in providing a system that is more responsive to the needs of people affected by ADB-assisted projects than the former inspection function, which the new system replaced. The inspection function process and procedures were lengthy, confusing and complex for most stakeholders, both inside and outside the ADB. The first full inspection of the Samut Prakarn Wastewater Management Project in Thailand also raised concerns about independence, credibility, transparency and information dissemination, and effectiveness of the inspection function.[55] This upfronting of the inspection function review set the tone for a meaningful consultation process. The review process was both internal (involving the ADB board of directors, management and staff at headquarters and in country offices) and external (representatives from the governments in both donor and developing member countries (DMCs), civil society including NGOs, academe, project affectees under previous inspection requests, roster members under the previous inspection function and the private sector). The external participants numbered 300. The consultations were held in 10 venues, spread over ADB member countries for maximum coverage, over a four-month period in 2002. The process involved discussions on the first draft of the working paper, followed by a second draft which was used as a basis to prepare the final report. The first draft of the working paper was discussed in Tokyo, Frankfurt, Washington, DC, Ottawa, in Manila at a regional workshop for ADB DMCs and in Karachi at a special consultation workshop for NGOs and requesters involved in a project which went through the inspection process. The second draft was discussed in Phnom Penh, Kathmandu, Beijing and Sydney at subregional workshops for ADB DMCs for enhanced inputs. The consultations were carried out with the ADB's engagement of two civil society experts with experience on MDB accountability mechanisms.[56] E-mail comments were maintained during the process, with a dedicated e-mail address on the ADB website.

The ADB financed the cost of travel and accommodation for DMC participants – one government representative and one civil society representative from each country for the Manila workshop; and two government representatives and two civil society representatives from each country for the subregional workshops. The ADB translated documents in local languages (Urdu and Sinhalese),[57] hired translators and fielded facilitators at the workshops. The ADB also paid for selected project-affected people who went through the inspection process to attend the workshops. Overall the consultations were fruitful, though not every group got what it wanted. The transcripts, working papers produced and comments received during the review process are all documented on the ADB website,[58] with transparency as the foremost consideration. The inspection function review took about a year and a half from October 2001, when a steering committee supported by a working group were set up to carry out the review, to May 2003, when the board of directors approved the policy. The review process was long but the results gained were commendable. The most significant comment on the process can be summed up by a letter from 10 NGOs to the ADB President of 29 August 2002 saying that "while there are areas that can definitely be improved, this review process is perhaps the best that the Bank has ever conducted. We would like to encourage you to make this the minimum standard for future Bank consultations on policy development and reviews."[59] The ADB received accolades from several major advocacy groups for showing "strong leadership when it established the Accountability Mechanism and included elements – such as monitoring – that improved upon features of other International Financial Institutions' accountability panels".[60] The ADB used a similar consultation review process internally and externally in revising its information policy and disclosure policy into the public communications policy.[61] This review process took two years, from the establishment of the screening committee in May 2003 to board approval of the final policy paper in April 2005, and a lesson learned is that it does take time and resources to carry out a meaningful consultative process.

The ADB accountability mechanism and emerging trends and challenges in MDB accountability mechanisms

Six significant contributions from the inspection function review process were made the cornerstones of the accountability mechanism policy: a dual approach of a problem-solving/consultation phase followed by a compliance review/investigation phase; the policy was extended to cover private sector operations; the replacement of a roster of experts by a permanent three-member Compliance Review Panel to investigate requests;

the opportunity given to a requester filing a request for a compliance review to comment on the Compliance Review Panel's draft report before it is finalized by the Panel (in the inspection function and in other MDB accountability mechanisms, no such right to due process is given); the time for filing a claim extended from the so-called 95 per cent loan disbursement limit to the issuance of the project completion report (typically one to two years from physical completion of a project); and the introduction of a monitoring phase to review annually the outcomes of the problem-solving and compliance review phases after management or the board has made the decision. These contributions have also served as yardsticks for improvements to MDBs and bilaterals that wish to establish or review their accountability mechanisms.

The ADB accountability mechanism has two related but separate phases: problem-solving/consultation, followed by investigation/compliance review. The problem-solving/consultation approach is to find a solution using consensus-based methods, without attributing blame to any party (borrower, private project sponsor or claimant).[62] The investigation/compliance review phase investigates the compliance review request and determines fault – on the part of ADB management – if there is a violation of ADB operational policies and procedures, as well as making recommendations to the board of directors to ensure project compliance, for the board to decide on remedial actions.

The ADB accountability mechanism is the first MDB mechanism formulating and introducing this dual approach, where private individuals can file claims for problem-solving followed by requests for compliance review.[63] The IFC/MIGA's CAO has a triple function of compliance audit, advisory and ombudsman (problem-solving), and the compliance audit may be triggered by the CAO if compliance issues are raised or uncovered during the course of the ombudsman assessment of the complaint. This dual approach has been emulated with various shades and nuances by other MDB accountability mechanisms at the EBRD, AfDB and in the IDB's proposals to enhance its independent investigation mechanism.[64] The approach has also been taken on board by the accountability mechanism systems at other development institutions, including the Japan Bank for International Cooperation (JBIC) ("Procedures to Submit Objections concerning JBIC Guidelines for Confirmation of Environmental and Social Considerations"), Japan International Cooperation Agency (JICA) ("Modus Operandi of the Objection System regarding Compliance with JICA Guidelines for Environmental and Social Considerations") and Overseas Private Investment Corporation USA (accountability and advisory mechanism).

The accountability mechanism covers both private and public sector operations. Under the previous system, private sector operations were excluded. The compliance review phase of the ADB accountability mechanism is carried out by a permanent three-member panel instead of a roster of experts, as was the case in the previous system. This roster of experts did not work well; in its place, a permanent panel (each member serving a fixed term, appointed by and reporting to the board, independent from management and with an absolute employment bar with the organization after completion of the term) would be more knowledgeable about the institution and able to make the panel more accessible to potential requesters. In the ADB accountability mechanism, claimants are given a stronger voice than under the previous system. They are given due process, with the opportunity to have their views recorded during the investigation process and not be shut out of the equation and have a long wait in the tunnel before knowing the decision from the board of directors. They can file claims in any official or national language of ADB DMCs.

Confidentiality of the claimants' names is provided if requested. Also, the claimants' responses are posted on the Compliance Review Panel website as attachments to the Panel's final report, together with ADB management's response. This equality of treatment of both entities – ADB management and private individuals as requesters – means that both are treated on an equal footing in having the same opportunity and right to respond to the Panel's draft report.

The cut-off point for filing a claim under the new system has now been extended to issuance of the project completion report, which is typically one to two years after physical completion of the project. The World Bank and IDB accountability systems and the ADB's former inspection function did not allow claims to be filed for completed projects or for projects where at least 95 per cent of the loan financing was disbursed (the so-called 95 per cent disbursement limit of the World Bank Inspection Panel). The question of accountability is independent of the status of the project administration or the amount of the loan proceeds disbursed, and so the cut-off point is at best arbitrary and susceptible to manipulation. The replacement of the 95 per cent disbursement limit by the issuance of the project completion report reflects a willingness to be more accountable in terms of the duration of the project, and has been used by the accountability mechanism systems at the EBRD and AfDB. The JBIC does not use the issuance of a project completion report as a cut-off; its system allows claims to be filed up to completion of disbursement, and after this event if the request refers to non-compliance with the monitoring provisions of the JBIC's Guidelines for Confirmation of Environmental and Social Considerations during the period the JBIC was monitoring the project pursuant to these guidelines.

The new system introduced the need for monitoring outcomes, which was absent under the old system and in other MDB accountability systems at the World Bank and IDB. The need for monitoring is important, as this ensures that the outcomes and project improvements decided by the President or the board are indeed carried out. The monitoring of outcomes is used in the accountability mechanisms at the AfDB, EBRD and JBIC.

Under the ADB accountability mechanism, claims filed with the compliance review phase must first go through the consultation phase in view of the limited remedies under the compliance review, which may not necessarily resolve the claimant's immediate problems on the ground. The board of directors in approving the accountability mechanism policy also reserved a right for any board member in special cases to file a request for compliance review.

The experience of the ADB accountability mechanism is limited, given the few claims received since its operations started in December 2003. As of 5 October 2006 seven claims had been filed with the special project facilitator who handles the consultation phase of the mechanism: three have gone through the consultation process beyond the eligibility stage; three were held ineligible by the special project facilitator; and one is at the eligibility stage. To date only one complaint has gone through the full process of the consultation phase,[65] and one request has gone through the full process of the compliance review phase.[66]

The special project facilitator reports to the President, and is independent from ADB operations departments. The Panel is independent from ADB management and reports to the board on all matters, except for clearing its terms of reference on a compliance review and reviewing its draft monitoring reports, where it reports to a board standing committee – the Board Compliance Review Committee. Consistent with the transparency objective of the accountability mechanism policy, many reports – including the special project facilitator's eligibility report, final report and annual report, the Panel's eligibility report, draft report and final report in investigating claims, the Panel's monitoring report and the Panel's annual report – are posted on the website.[67]

The Compliance Review Panel found one request under the Melamchi Water Supply Project in Nepal ineligible, but it determined the request under the Southern Transport Development Project in Sri Lanka eligible. This project involved the construction of a 128 km highway linking Colombo to Matara, the district capital of the south of Sri Lanka. The Panel kept confidential the identities of 25 individual claimants, as the requesters, the Joint Organization of the Affected Communities on Colombo-Matara Highway, asked. The claims of the requesters stemmed from a change of highway trace for which required studies and consultations were not properly done, and adverse effects including loss of homes and livelihoods, damage to the environment and resettlement problems. The Panel investigated the request, holding hearings and discussions with various stakeholders, including the requesters and other project affectees, and provided its draft report to ADB management and the requesters for comments. The Panel took into account their responses in finalizing its report, which was provided to the board along with the responses attached to the Panel's final report. After the board made its decision on the Panel's findings and recommendations, the Panel informed the requesters of the outcome of the decision and its report, together with the responses of ADB management and the requesters, were all posted on the Panel website.

The Panel determined that the ADB violated seven operational policies and procedures from project processing to implementation of the Southern Transport Development Project: environmental considerations in Bank operations; gender and development in Bank operations; benefit monitoring and evaluation; formulation and implementation of loan covenants; incorporation of social dimensions in Bank operations; involuntary resettlement; and change in project scope or implementation arrangements. The Panel made 19 recommendations to ensure project compliance, which the board approved. These recommendations included compensating affected persons fully before they are moved; assisting in the income restoration programme and the establishment of household benchmarks in the resettlement implementation plan; ensuring full project information, especially essential elements in the resettlement implementation plan, is provided in an appropriate language to each affected household; and reviewing selected road projects to see to how changes of scope may make the application of environmental and resettlement policies difficult. The Panel is presently monitoring ADB management's work on the remedial actions. The monitoring is done at least annually, usually for a period of five years unless the board specifies a different timetable. The Panel's first annual monitoring report of August 2006 reported the progress made by ADB management in complying with the recommendations and the Panel's determination on the compliance status (complied with, not complied with or partially complied with). This report is also posted on the Panel website and was provided to the requesters.

Additionally, in 2004 the board tasked the Compliance Review Panel to monitor ADB management's implementation of the remedial actions in the board decision on the inspection request of the Chashma Right Bank Irrigation Project Stage III in Pakistan. This request was investigated under the previous inspection function. The Panel has been carrying out this monitoring mandate annually, and as frequently as needed.

The road ahead for accountability, including MDB accountability mechanisms

At the ADB progress has been made to enhance accountability, as indicated by the measures outlined above. Recent developments such as the enhancement of the OED's independence, reports and evaluations, and its monitoring of management's actions on OED recommendations will continue to be a challenge. The ongoing ADB reform agenda is a clear instance where responsibility and accountability issues are squarely looked at. There will be tensions – internal and external – on harmonization, use of country systems and other areas, but viewed from an accountability perspective, the need for transparency is paramount to ensure that decision-making processes involve the participation of external stakeholders. Citizen-based grievance mechanisms are a critical aspect of accountability. That the window of access has been opened to individuals by the creation of any MDB accountability mechanism is groundbreaking – for the first time, citizens are given a voice and an opportunity to participate in the decision-making processes of an international organization which consists of member states and to which individuals are not parties even though they are project beneficiaries. There is no perfect fit of the "best" MDB accountability mechanism in terms of being most responsive to citizens. Various mechanisms are in place today, and with the same set of donors in each MDB driving the agenda for enhanced accountability, it may be surprising that no attempt is made to harmonize the accountability systems and rationalize donor activities to make these systems as cost-effective as possible under the Paris Declaration on Aid Effectiveness of March 2005. However, with the proliferation of various MDB accountability mechanisms, forum shopping, frowned upon in some common law jurisdictions, appears to be open for potential requesters to use the systems they think can best address their claims. The principal officers of MDB accountability mechanisms and related development institutions, including the Japan Bank for International Cooperation and Overseas Private Investment Corporation USA, have been meeting annually since 2003. They discuss and share experiences under their mechanisms and exchange views on matters of common interest, including improving the implementation of their mechanisms.

There are, however, limitations on any MDB accountability mechanism. These mechanisms serve as internal governance tools, independent of local jurisdiction, from which the ADB and other MDBs are immune, to enhance development effectiveness and ensure project compliance. They are not adjudicative and do not provide judicial remedies such as damages or injunctions. The remit of the accountability mechanism is limited, in that the Panel's investigative work is confined to institutional accountability and not individuals and does not include staff sanction, which is within the purview of the President. Yet broader questions remain on institutional responsibility for harm and damages resulting from policy violation, and staff sanctions for those not complying with institutional policies and procedures. Civil society concerns have been expressed on whether staff responsible for planning and implementing problematic projects should be rewarded with promotions or be sanctioned, since the ADB, like any other MDB, is a public institution committed to "improving the welfare of the people in Asia and the Pacific", and must be accountable to these people and its "rhetoric must match its actions on the ground".[68]

The dictates of accountability of an international organization are that the accountability is a multifaceted phenomenon, with the grounded reality that "the ultimate decision to raise and effectively implement accountability will always remain a political one".[69] With this reality check, the door of access, once opened, cannot be closed; it can only be opened further with improvements and enhanced accountability of international organizations. The institution can incorporate and feed back the lessons learned under the accountability mechanism into the organization's development effectiveness, and take steps to promote accountability within the institution and among staff.

A spin-off from this momentum on calls for accountability in international organizations is that pressure is now on accountability from various other entities, including NGOs and financial institutions adopting the Equator Principles (EPFIs),[70] to be accountable for their operations to project beneficiaries. In the case of NGOs, Oxfam has set up a pilot complaint mechanism for beneficiaries at local levels, and there is a growing movement for development NGOs to set up complaint mechanisms for beneficiaries. Similarly, in the case of EPFIs applying the Equator Principles in addressing environmental and social issues in project financing operations of $10 million or more, there is growing pressure for them to be subject to an independent third-party appraisal for compliance in their conduct with local communities adversely affected by their projects.

Acknowledgements

This chapter is based on the paper presented by the author at the UNU Tokyo Symposium on Accountability held on 16–17 October 2006.

The author wishes to thank Mr Richard Bissell, Professor Leslie Moran, Dr Eisuke Suzuki, Ms Mishka Zaman and Mr Rolf Zelius for their comments in the preparation of this paper, as well as Ms Josefina C. Miranda and Ms Marie Antoinette Virtucio for their research assistance. The views expressed in the chapter are those of the author and do not necessarily reflect those of the Asian Development Bank or the Compliance Review Panel.

Notes

1. International Law Association (2000) "Report of the International Law Association Committee on Accountability of International Organizations", presented at International Law Association Sixty-ninth Conference, London, 25–29 July, p. 894.
2. Oxford University Press (1998) *New Oxford Dictionary of English*, New York: Oxford University Press, p. 12.
3. Merriam-Webster OnLine Dictionary, available at www.m-w.com/dictionary/accountability.
4. International Law Association (2004) "Final Report of the International Law Association Committee on Accountability of International Organizations", presented at International Law Association Seventy-first Conference, Berlin, 16–21 August, p. 168.
5. Grant, Ruth W. and Robert O. Keohane (2005) "Accountability and Abuses of Power in World Politics", *American Political Science Review* 99(1), pp. 29–43, available at http://journals.cambridge.org/production/action/cjoGetFulltext? fulltextid=290953.
6. See, for example, Group of Seven (2001) "Statement of G-7 Finance Ministers and Central Bank Governors at Palermo, Italy, 17 February 2001", available at www.g7.utoronto.ca/finance/fm20010217.htm. Paragraph 12 states, among other things, that MDBs should "further improve and strengthen accountability and transparency, including through the establishment or the reinforcement of central control mechanisms to ensure compliance with agreed policies and safeguards".
7. Global Transparency Initiative Project Secretariat (2006) "Transparency Charter for International Financial Institutions: Claiming the Right to Know", available at www.ifitransparency.org/doc/charter_en.pdf.
8. Asian Development Bank (1994) "Report of the Task Force on Improving Project Quality", available at www.adb.org/Documents/Policies/Project_Quality/project_quality.pdf.
9. Ibid., p. iii. The World Bank conducted a similar exercise through its Wapenhans Report: World Bank (1992) *Report of the World Bank's Portfolio Management Task Force. Effective Implementation: Key to Development Impact*, Washington, DC: World Bank. This also focused on internal accountability within the organization for portfolio results, such as ensuring that a country portfolio was made the unit of "managerial accountability" in composition, size and performance (p. v).
10. Asian Development Bank, note 8 above. The Wapenhans Report (ibid.) also noted the "approval culture" pervasive within the organization, and recommended improvement of quality of projects entering the portfolio through project analysis, appraisal methodology and contractual arrangements.
11. Asian Development Bank, note 8 above, para. 48.
12. MfDR is "a management approach to improve planning, monitoring, and evaluating operations in order to achieve and sustain intended development results". See Asian Development Bank (2006) "Managing for Development Results in ADB: Revised Action

Plan of August 2006", available at www.adb.org/Documents/Policies/Revised-Action-Plan/MfDR-Revised-Action-Plan.pdf, para. 2.

13. van Zant, Eric (2006) "Ensuring Accountability", *ADB Review* 38(2), p. 6, available at www.adb.org/Documents/Periodicals/ADB_Review/2006/vol38-2/vol38-2.pdf.
14. Asian Development Bank (2005) "The Public Communications Policy of the Asian Development Bank: Disclosure and Exchange of Information", available at www.adb.org/Documents/Policies/PCP/default.asp?p=disclose.
15. Asian Development Bank (2003) "Accountability Mechanism", available at www.adb.org/Accountability-Mechanism/default.asp.
16. Asian Development Bank (2001) "Reorganization of the Asian Development Bank", available at www.adb.org/Documents/Policies/Reorganization_ADB/reorganization_ADB.pdf.
17. Ibid., para. 9.
18. See van Zant, note 13 above, p. 10.
19. Asian Development Bank (2006) "Realignment of Regional Departments", available at www.adb. org/About/realignment-paper.pdf.
20. Leonard, R. Keith and Iris de Guzman (2006) "Impartial Observer", *ADB Review* 38(2), available at www.adb.org/Documents/Periodicals/ADB_Review/2006/vol38-2/vol38-2.pdf, p. 12.
21. These would include organizations such as the Canadian International Development Agency, the Organisation for Economic Co-operation and Development (OECD)/Development Assistance Committee and the US General Accounting Office.
22. Evaluation Cooperation Group (undated) "Template for Assessing the Independence of Evaluation Organizations", available at http://siteresources.worldbank.org/EXTGLOREGPARPRO/Resources/ECG_AssessingIndependence.pdf.
23. "ADB management" refers to the President and the four Vice-Presidents.
24. See the Operations Evaluation Department webpage, available at www.adb.org/OED/default.asp.
25. Zaman, Mishka (2006) "Rhetoric Must Match Action", *ADB Review* 38(2), p. 11, available at www.adb.org/Documents/Periodicals/ADB_Review/2006/vol38-2/vol38-2.pdf, p. 11.
26. Asian Development Bank (2005) "Annual Report of the Development Effectiveness Committee", available at www.adb.org/Documents/Board/Committee-Reports/2005/Dev-Effect/dec-ar05.pdf, p. 16.
27. Zaman, note 25 above, p. 11.
28. ADB Operations Evaluation Department (2006) "2006 Annual Evaluation Review", available at http://adb.org/Documents/Reports/ Evaluation/2006-AER.pdf.
29. Ibid., p. vii.
30. Ibid.
31. Asian Development Bank, note 14 above.
32. Malvicini, Cindy (2006) "Open and Accessible", *ADB Review* 38(2), p. 20, available at www.adb.org/Documents/Periodicals/ADB_Review/2006/vol38-2/vol38-2.pdf.
33. Asian Development Bank (1998) "Anticorruption", available at www.adb.org/Documents/Policies/Anticorruption/anticorruption.pdf.
34. ADB Office of the Auditor General (2006) "Integrity Division: 2005 Annual Report", available at www.adb.org/documents/reports/Anticorruption/OAGA-Annual-Report-2005.pdf.
35. These measures can be taken by ADB management on representatives of the borrower or a beneficiary of the loan engaged in corrupt or fraudulent practices, or by the ADB Integrity Oversight Committee on bidders, consultants, contractors, suppliers or other

parties to ADB-financed activity (other than ADB staff, as the budget, personnel and management systems department is responsible for staff disciplinary action).

36. The reasons for reaching this conclusion are provided in "Issues on Publicizing ADB's Anticorruption Sanctions List", available at www.adb.org/Integrity/issues.asp.
37. This information is available at www.adb.org/Business/Opportunities/default.asp.
38. There are two applicable guidelines, one for consulting services and one for procurement: Asian Development Bank (2006) "Guidelines on the Use of Consultants by Asian Development Bank and Its Borrowers", April, available at www.adb.org/Documents/Guidelines/Consulting/consultant-guidelines-April-2006.pdf; Asian Development Bank (2006) "Procurement Guidelines", April, available at www.adb.org/Documents/Guidelines/Procurement/guidelines-April-2006.pdf. These guidelines promote specific requirements, including enhancing transparency in the procurement and consultancy selection process.
39. ADB Compliance Review Panel (2004) "Report on Eligibility on the Request under the Southern Transport Development Project (Loan No. 1711-SRI[SF]) – CRP Request No. 2004/1", available at www.compliance.adb.org/dir0035p.nsf/attachments/STDP-EligibilityReport.pdf/$FILE/STDP-EligibilityReport.pdf.
40. Asian Development Bank (1998) "Gender and Development", available at www.adb.org/Documents/Policies/Gender/gender-policy.pdf.
41. The list of members of the External Forum on Gender and Development is available at www.adb.org/gender/forum/members.asp.
42. These outcomes are improving operational policies, strategies and approaches; mainstreaming MfDR; refining organizational process and structure; reinforcing knowledge management; and improving human resources management and staff incentives.
43. Asian Development Bank (2006) "Annual Progress Report on the Implementation of the Asian Development Bank's Reform Agenda", available at www.adb.org/Documents/Reports/Reform-Agenda/reform-agenda-mar2006.pdf, para. 4.
44. Ibid., para. 24.
45. Available at www.adb.org/ReformAgenda/default.asp.
46. Verweij, Marco and Timothy E. Josling (2003) "Special Issue: Deliberately Democratizing Multilateral Organization", *Governance: International Journal of Policy, Administration and Institutions* 16(1), pp. 1–21, at p. 10.
47. Suzuki, Eisuke and Suresh Nanwani (2005) "Responsibility of International Organizations: The Accountability Mechanisms of Multilateral Development Banks ", *Michigan Journal of International Law* 27(1), pp. 177–225, at p. 185.
48. World Bank, note 9 above.
49. Suzuki and Nanwani, note 47 above, p. 187.
50. Environmental Defense, Friends of the Earth and International Rivers Network (2003) "The World Bank and Large Dams: Failure to Learn from History in Gambling with People's Lives", available at www.environmentaldefense.org/documents/3006_GamblingWithPeoplesLives_0903.pdf, p. 32.
51. Morse, Bradford and Thomas Berger (1992) *Sardar Sarovar: Report of the Independent Review*, Ottawa: Resources Future International, pp. 53–54.
52. See Manibeli Declaration Calling for a Moratorium on World Bank Funding of Large Dams (1994) available at www.rivernet.org/manibeli.htm; letter to the World Bank President by 90 NGOs in 24 countries on the Sardar Sarovar Project, available at www.narmada.org/sardar-sarovar/wbletter.19991110.html; South Asia Citizens Wire, 5 May 2004, available at www.mail-archive.com/sacw@insaf.net/msg00115.html.
53. Outside MDBs, accountability mechanisms have also been set up. The Japan Bank for International Cooperation introduced its "Summary of Procedures to Submit

Objections Concerning JBIC Guidelines for Confirmation of Environmental and Social Considerations (Objection Procedures)" in 2003; the Japan International Cooperation Agency enacted its "Modus Operandi of the Objection System Regarding Compliance with JICA Guidelines for Environmental and Social Considerations" in 2004; and the Overseas Private Investment Corporation USA established its accountability and advisory mechanism in 2004.

54. The accountability mechanism policy provides that a review will be carried out three years from the effectiveness of the mechanism. The mechanism became effective in December 2003.
55. There have been many criticisms of the inspection process in the Samut Prakarn Wastewater Management Project. See, for example, the findings of Probe International of 30 July 2002, posted on the ADB website as part the review process in revising the accountability system, available at www.adb.org/inspection/comments_probe.pdf.
56. These were Ms Lori Udall and Mr David Hunter.
57. Translations were made in these languages to reach a wider civil society audience and get the views of requesters who filed inspection requests in Pakistan and Sri Lanka.
58. Available at www.adb.org/inspection/review.asp#Process.
59. Available at www.adb.org/inspection/comments_10ngos.pdf.
60. Letter from Oxfam Australia, NGO Forum on ADB and 11 other NGOs to the ADB President of 6 September 2006, available at www.forum-adb.org/PDF-Other/Joint20letter20to20ADB20President20on20SPF20060906.pdf.
61. The schedule of consultations and other activities is available at www.adb.org/Disclosure/public-communications.asp.
62. A claimant under the consultation or compliance review phase refers to two or more individuals or groups of individuals having common interests or concerns who claim to be adversely affected by the ADB-assisted project.
63. See also van Putten, Maartje (2006) "'Policing the World': Accountability Mechanisms for Multilateral Financial Institutions and Private Financial Institutions", unpublished PhD dissertation, Tilburg University, Netherlands/McGill University, Montreal, Canada, p. 129.
64. IDB (2005) "Proposal for Enhancements to the Independent Investigation Mechanism – Draft Consultation and Compliance Review Policy", 3 February, available at http://idbdocs.iadb.org/wsdocs/getdocument.aspx?docnum=474362.
65. Community Empowerment Rural Development Project in Indonesia (Loan Nos 1765(SF)/1766-INO); see steps taken and milestone events in the Special Project Facilitator Registry for this complaint, available at www.adb.org/SPF/cerp-complaint-registry.asp.
66. Southern Transport Development Project in Sri Lanka (Loan No. 1711-SRI(SF)); see steps taken and milestone events in the Compliance Review Panel Registry for this request, available at www.compliance.adb.org/dir0035p.nsf/alldocs/ELLN-6NH8JG?OpenDocument.
67. Available at www.adb.org/SPF/default.asp for the Special Project Facilitator and www.compliance.adb.org for the Compliance Review Panel.
68. Issues posed by Bank Information Center USA, an NGO, in Zaman, note 25 above, p. 11.
69. International Law Association (1998) "Report of the International Law Association Committee on Accountability of International Organizations", presented at International Law Association Sixty-eighth Conference, Taipei, 24–30 May, p. 603.
70. As of 5 October 2006 there were 44 EPFIs.

Part V

Conclusion

Conclusion

Michael Ross Fowler and Sumihiro Kuyama

Various of the contributors to this volume noted that, here at the beginning of a new millennium, people across the globe hope, and some expect, that the UN organizations can play a key role in helping international society to overcome or better manage the world's many difficulties. Reflective of that public sentiment, the Member States continue to assign the Organization an ever-longer list of tasks, some critically important, others less so, but all of them requiring energy and resources to undertake. And yet the longstanding questions that have continuously been raised about the efficiency and effectiveness with which the United Nations must function have by no means dissipated.

Within this context the term *accountability* has come to be employed much more frequently at the United Nations than in past eras. One finds increasing references to accountability in speeches and reports by the Secretary-General, in General Assembly debates and resolutions, and in analyses of the Organization by leading institutes[1] and academia. The concern that has concentrated much thinking at and about the United Nations in recent years is that neither governments nor their key domestic constituencies are likely to continue to support an organization that is unaccountable for its actions.

While all this is reasonably clear, one may wonder why exactly the subject of accountability in the UN system has suddenly captured the attention of so many. Part of the answer may be that scholars and policymakers have increasingly attended to the subject of *global governance* – that is, "the sum of the many ways individuals and institutions, public and

Envisioning reform: Enhancing UN accountability in the twenty-first century, Kuyama and Fowler (eds), United Nations University Press, 2009, ISBN 978-92-808-1170-4

private, manage their common affairs".[2] Anne-Marie Slaughter wrote, "As the bipolar state system of the Cold War disappeared and nonstate, substate, and supranational actors rode the tide of globalization, pundits and many scholars began heralding the era of complex, multilevel, global governance..."[3]

Actually, with the end of the Cold War a heightened attention to accountability has surfaced in many different contexts. At just the time that processes of globalization have come to pose new challenges for those attempting to address collectively problems that transcend state boundaries, people have come to analyse more rigorously modes of international problem-solving, enquiring as to how different interests might better be reconciled through structures and regimes, norms and laws. This has brought to the forefront of discussion issues of the accountability of key pieces of global governance. Besides UN organizations, the issue has arisen with respect to other international organizations, such as multilateral development banks, the Group of 8, government networks and prominent non-governmental organizations.[4] As Koji Fukuda wrote in this volume, "Accountability can be viewed as an important method of attaining good governance and ensuring governmental objectives are reached."

One might also note that various trends in the activities of the United Nations have themselves brought a spotlight of public scrutiny to accountability concerns. The introduction of far-ranging objectives, such as those found in the Millennium Development Goals, has both raised expectations and provided a yardstick by which to measure UN activities. In addition, the extraordinary expansion of peacekeeping operations, with military units at work in dangerous circumstances under various chains of command, has raised concerns about how they might be brought to account. Furthermore, as Edward Luck pointed out, "potential troop-contributing countries are asking pointed questions about who will be accountable for any lapses in oversight, communications, mission planning or adjustment to changing circumstances on the ground".

The Organization's involvement in extensive disaster management operations, detailed by Tadanori Inomata in chapter 6, and the development cooperation, humanitarian emergencies and peacebuilding field operations referenced by Kazuo Takahashi in chapter 11 have had the similar effect of bringing attention to accountability. As Takahashi pointed out, when, for example, Cambodia was flooded with 20,000 people associated with UN peacebuilding or when Bosnia and Herzegovina absorbed more than 40,000, the question of accountability must have been addressed with respect to these immense operations and the new and emerging structures that accompanied them. By the same token, as Inomata pointed out, the UN work in environmental matters is so multifaceted that fully 27 "mechanisms" have been created simply to coordinate all of the diverse organizations working in the multitude of existing programmes, frameworks and conventions. With so many at work on common problems and with administrators striving to overcome duplicated or overlapping responsibilities, issues of accountability can quickly become quite murky, leaving observers ill at ease.

In trying to determine why accountability has suddenly come to the forefront of concerns about the United Nations, one might also note that UN programmes are no longer being carried out solely by UN-associated employees or actors, but increasingly encompass independent actors of various sorts. This is seen as part of the trend towards, as Tatsuro Kunugi described, the "multi-stakeholder partnerships" in the public sphere of governance, and this has played an important part in the increased focus on accountability as well. Actually, various of the component parts of the United Nations, including the Office of the UN High Commissioner for Refugees (UNHCR), have partnered with numerous non-governmental organizations to provide a vast array of services, ranging from emergency relief to child and refugee protection.[5] As partnerships with other entities become more frequent, attention is drawn to these ever-more-complex arrangements and how the entities that the United Nations contracts or otherwise works with might be held accountable.

In the earlier decades of the Organization's operations, when the principle of article 2(7)[6] had rarely been questioned, when the ongoing Cold War frequently inhibited cooperation and when the United Nations was a smaller operation, with a more manageable roster of Member States and a far lesser set of ongoing activities, accountability garnered much less attention. Now, however, in an era marked by increasing interdependence and globalization, the typical view is that legal and moral constraints on intervention by international organizations in the affairs of sovereign states are coming to be rather outmoded, especially in light of the world's many pressing needs for peace, democracy and human rights.[7] Kunugi argued that in the post–Cold War era the concept of legitimacy has shifted away from traditional criteria, such as law, towards "the core characteristics of democratic governance, e.g. respect for human rights, popular participation, informed consent, transparency and accountability of the exercise of power". While the newly interventionist behaviour characteristic of the period in which we live has had certain positive motivations related to building, stabilizing and improving the functioning of states,[8] it has also raised concerns about the abusive exercise of powers. This, too, has put accountability on the political map as never before.

Finally, as a vital pre-condition to resolving or ameliorating the global problems and challenges of the twenty-first century, the many entities that find a place under the UN umbrella must themselves improve their efficiency and effectiveness. As the UN budget has soared ever higher,[9] as more resources have been engaged and more activities undertaken, as the world has come to be more interdependent and the business and authority of international organizations have seemingly increased, accountability issues have grown more and more important. Edward Luck noted, "At a point when the United Nations is coming to play an increasingly ubiquitous and even indispensable role in addressing critical public policy challenges, its persistent accountability deficits threaten to undermine the prospects for sustained and effective international cooperation when it is most needed [and] accountability – or more often the lack of it – has become a pervasive and central challenge to UN reformers." And yet there exists some mistrust between various Member States over the issue of accountability and, especially, the policy implications and consequences of the increasing focus on the term. This is exacerbated by "the apparent absence of a strong sense of political community at the global level", in the words of Jochen Prantl. In order to arrive at useful recommendations for reform, it is thus important to illuminate the contours of accountability as it relates to the United Nations, with a view to arriving at common ground, identifying cardinal issues for further analysis and formulating an initial set of proposals, if only tentative ones.

As mentioned in the introduction, this volume has emerged from the further reflections of the participants at the Tokyo Symposium on Accountability, hosted by the United Nations University (UNU) in the fall of 2006. In this conclusion we distil certain of the lessons suggested by this diverse group of scholars and practitioners in their reflections on UN accountability, highlighting some of the most salient points and key themes that emerged in the foregoing chapters.

The concept of accountability in the UN context

When a diverse group comes together to analyse a complex and understudied subject, particularly when the scholars hail from various different countries, speak several different first languages and are trained in different intellectual traditions, carefully defining terms takes on added importance. Since it is difficult to advance cogent reform proposals when core ideas are glossed over in ambiguous or over-broad language, the Tokyo participants took pains to explore whether a common approach to accountability, including its definition, is feasible in the UN context. In other words, in the light of divergent views and perspectives on an array of issues related to accountability, no a priori common approach was taken to the term's definition. Instead, the matter was left to each author to present on the basis of his or her own perspective, coloured, no doubt, by their different academic disciplines and experiences. Nevertheless, among the contributors a basic convergence did eventually emerge on matters related to the concept of accountability.

First, as Edward Luck noted, "Few concepts have been invoked with greater frequency or less precision around the United Nations in recent times than accountability." Despite repeated use of the term, accountability is a sufficiently elusive concept that views and opinions on it frequently diverge. The contributors to this volume generally agreed that, since UN accountability is a topic capable of a wide variety of interpretations – some narrowly focused, others more sweeping in scope – the community of international organization scholars and practitioners would benefit from forging an early consensus on what the phrase might best be taken to mean under the particular circumstances of the United Nations. A number of contributors further emphasized that how the term is defined bears directly on that cardinal question: who is accountable to whom, and for what?

Second, numerous contributions provided a wealth of evidence on how the subject of accountability is much more complicated in the UN context than is generally perceived. Not only is the UN system immense in its size and the scope of its activities, but it is both fragmented and very multidimensional in containing a number of distinct power centres, including the Member States or the legislative organs (particularly the Security Council and General Assembly), the Secretariat (including the Secretary-General atop the Secretariat) and the specialized agencies. Then, of fundamental importance for grasping properly the concept of accountability in the UN context, the framers of the Charter and the government representatives who adopted it acknowledged an authority of "the peoples of the United Nations". It is far from obvious how the different pieces of the UN system interact, and to whom and how accountability ought to flow under different circumstances.

Third, within the chapters of this volume elements of a common definition of accountability clearly emerge. For instance, many of the contributors focused on authorization: namely, when an individual, group or organization is entrusted with some financial, human or other resources, that individual, group or organization ought subsequently to give an account of the use (or non-use) of the resources. One important dimension of this is, as Koji Fukuda pointed out, that the definitions of accountability "all have the 'principal-agent relationship' in common". That is, the agent to whom the power is delegated has a responsibility to justify decisions and actions to the principal.

Furthermore, many of the contributors discussed the relationship between responsibility and accountability. Apart from what we have already noted in the introduction (see, for instance, the discussion by Kyoji Kawasaki), Michael Fowler stated, "At core, responsibility in public affairs involves the direct or indirect assignment and the consequent acceptance of particular tasks. Accountability focuses on the evaluation of those tasks: the manner in which they have been executed over a particular time period." Fowler concluded, "for an entity to be seen as properly accountable, duties must be defined, an adequate accounting to an appropriate body must occur, the results of the external evaluation must be communicated effectively to the entity being evaluated and the assessment must then be absorbed and, ideally, acted upon in some productive manner". However, the many contributors who referred to an accountability "gap" or "deficit" at the United Nations argued that, within this complex system, accountability "holdees" have often failed to assess carefully what has occurred. Perhaps even less frequently have they communicated a comprehensible critique to accountability "holders".[10]

A number of the contributors focus on problems of accountability at the United Nations through the lens of a developing problem in legitimacy: that is, as Jochen Prantl wrote, "the justification of legal and political authority exercised by an international institution through its procedures (or input) and output". Edith Brown Weiss, Peter Lallas and Anna Herken declared, "There is broad consensus that institutions need to be legitimate, both in the eyes of those who establish them and in the eyes of those whom they serve or affect. Legitimacy is essential if people are to accept the actions of institutions as valid and entitled to respect. For institutions to be legitimate, they need to be accountable, both for compliance with their policies and procedures and for the effectiveness of their operations." In this vein Tatsuo Sato (appendix I) likewise observed, "it seems quite natural that the more the decisions of international organizations have serious implications for private persons in national societies...the more they should be subject to the same standards of legitimacy required of national governments". Prantl wrote, "Legitimacy and accountability have become touchstones for the effective management of globalization and the regulation of conflicts arising out of the asymmetries of power and influence, and the global distribution of wealth and welfare. They help to establish a wider perception of justice and fairness in international society."

Prantl focused special attention on the "striking need to take better advantage of flexible mechanisms and multiple forms of legitimacy and accountability that we can see already in modern democracies". Since participation has become a key aspect of international legitimacy, Prantl contended that a "productive trade-off" needs to be found "between the competing demands of inclusiveness, efficiency, informality, transparency and accountability". In Prantl's formulation, "Legitimacy and accountability... constitute instrumental values that UN Member States need to trade off against competing demands, such as efficiency or informality. The balance between those demands is fluid and context-driven. It needs to be struck on a case-by-case basis." Most specifically, Prantl suggested that the legitimacy of Security Council decision-making might be improved, not merely through measures aimed at enhancing its efficiency and transparency, but via informal consultations and informal groupings of states.

The chapter authors were not in discord on the basic distinction between *managerial accountability* and *political accountability*, as laid out in the introduction and elaborated, in particular, by Edward Luck in his opening chapter.

Most fundamentally, enhancing *managerial accountability* at the United Nations would involve doing a better job of holding those with delegated authority accountable for the actions taken in accordance with their delineated responsibilities. Here the focus would be upon how competently and effectively programmes were managed. Given the existing mandates or policy directives, was the delegated authority properly executed or did problems emerge, for example, in the line-management structure? Were the expected actions duly carried out and expected results accomplished, or were they not satisfactory; and if not, why not? Managerial accountability would apply at all levels of the Organization, from the executive heads, such as the Secretary-General, down to lower-level managers and other staff members.

The various chapters then referenced examples of problematic managerial accountability from which lessons may be learned. Difficulties for proper managerial accountability are due partly to the fact that resolutions by the legislative organs are often stated in general and abstract terms, rather than specific and actionable ones. In this context, Edward Luck made pertinent remarks: "the intergovernmental bodies that produce the UN's core mandates thrive on creative ambiguity, even vagueness, in the pursuit of convergence and consensus among the Member States". A number of authors specifically mentioned the Oil-for-Food Programme scandal and the problems found in numerous peacekeeping operations, including those in Cambodia, Somalia, Rwanda and Bosnia. In such cases the intra-organizational coordination and responsibility to manage administrative matters properly were very much at issue. And, the contributors concluded, the processes of sound managerial accountability often left much to be desired.

Political accountability, by contrast, focuses upon an organization's need to account for its behaviour to the constituencies and stakeholders affected by its decisions, actions or inactions. Here the emphasis would be on assessing what the Organization chose to do, or opted not to do.

What mandates and policy directives were issued? What were their rationales? How did they relate to the basic purposes or mission objectives of the Organization in light both of the Charter and the norms derived from various endeavours, such as international conferences, that illuminate the principles found therein? Political accountability would involve exercises to scrutinize how UN decisions, and the actions or inactions that followed, affected individuals, communities and, ultimately, "the peoples of the United Nations".

Deficiencies in the political accountability of those in leadership positions, and especially the Security Council, absorbed the attention of various contributors. As referred to already, in his chapter Jochen Prantl focused especially on how working methods and procedures might best be adapted to the present era, with suggestions as to how to capitalize upon informal consultations and informal groupings of states. For his part, Edward Luck highlighted the issue of omissions to act as well as ambiguities in the developing doctrine of a "responsibility to protect". He observed: "What remains unclear . . . is who is responsible when the United Nations and the so-called international community fail collectively to uphold their side of the equation even in well-publicized situations of genocide, as in Darfur. The question of whether or how international leaders and national decision-makers should be held accountable for such failures of will has hardly entered the mainstream debate, much less produced any convergence of views."

Several of the authors suggested that political accountability might be enhanced if, to the extent possible, "relevant" stakeholders were much more involved, directly or indirectly, in UN decision-making. The guiding principle might be that those affected in major ways by a particular decision, programme or other UN action should be given some role in devising, or revising, the policies and mandates of the part of the United Nations involved. The fact that, to date, they are not usually involved in such a process at all points to a major shortcoming in the political accountability of the United Nations. One important aspect of accountability involves transparency, particularly for stakeholders, and here Kyoji Kawasaki pointed not only to access to information and a "participatory decision-making process", but to the international law principle of "stating the reasons for decisions or a particular course of action".

Mikoto Usui, in his commentary (see appendix I), pursued further the issue of the interrelationship between political and managerial accountability. Organizations, he pointed out, are necessarily "Janus-faced" in that they mix "politics" and "action programmes"; politics consists "primarily of talks and decisions that reflect the diverse demands and ideologies of its external stakeholders", whereas action programmes focus upon delivering promised products in as rational and efficient a manner as possible. It could be said that managerial and political accountability apply to different facets of the operations of the Organization, and speak to different challenges that the Organization faces. And yet both must be enhanced in a concerted manner if the United Nations is to function more efficiently and respond more effectively to the manifold challenges of the twenty-first century. As Luck argued, "The distinction between what is managerial and what is political is rarely clean cut. The United Nations needs to do far better at both. It cannot move with assurance down either path, moreover, without substantial progress on the other. This will require a degree of joint effort and mutual confidence between the Member States and the Secretariat."

As alluded to in the introduction, devising policy directives or mandates is, *de jure*, a basic function of the legislative organs. Since, however, it is often the practice that the Secretariat formulates policy options for consideration by the legislative organs, devising a mandate is, *de facto*, a joint endeavour. Furthermore, the legislative organs are expected to oversee the secretariats as they carry out their managerial responsibilities. Consequently, the legislative organs and the Secretariat have a shared obligation to strengthen the accountability of the UN Organization. This underscores the need to treat political and managerial accountability in a comprehensive manner in designing effective and comprehensive UN reforms. In any event, the question of how to ensure that political and managerial accountability act like the two halves of a pair of scissors, working usefully together, is one of the topics identified in appendix II as worthy of additional future study and considerations.

Routes towards enhanced accountability of the UN system

While the approaches of the various authors differed, depending among other factors on their particular specialities and fields of expertise, a number of themes emerged as to where and how accountability might be enhanced in the UN system. Many authors underscored both the challenge and the importance of better defining and articulating standards. Within the complex political landscape of the United Nations, the benchmarks to be used in bringing the distinct parts of the UN system to account have not been as well defined as might be hoped, particularly with respect to the more politicized dimensions of the Organization. Determining who is responsible when the United Nations acts, or fails to act, in response to situations of violence, humanitarian emergencies, human rights abuses and the like can be quite vexing. Circumstances on the ground can change rapidly, as when political opportunities emerge for fleeting periods and then vanish. The United Nations can be simply one of a significant number of actors, and complete resolution of the many problems laid before different parts of the Organization may well be exceedingly difficult to accomplish. In focusing especially on key development and security issues, Edward Luck noted "the UN's modest role as one of many actors in these fields, in which it often exercises relatively little control over events and developments".

To enhance political accountability under such difficult circumstances, Kyoji Kawasaki and Michael Fowler suggested that, in the first instance, one might look to the words of the UN Charter, and in effect subject the Organization to the Charter. However, both hastened to point out problems with this approach. Kawasaki noted, "if we look in detail into the Charter provisions, we will find that the rights and obligations enumerated there are directed to the Member States. In contrast, what the Charter endows to the organs of the United Nations are functions and powers." Fowler pointed out: "throughout the Organization's existence differing ideologies and national interests have regularly pulled the Member States towards pragmatic policies and away from the principled behaviour, the notions of how international politics ought to work, described in the Charter".

Similarly difficult problems afflict efforts to improve managerial accountability. One theme that runs through many of the contributions is that both results and performance need to be measured in a timely, defined and broadly accepted manner. Here the United Nations has made important first steps, but nonetheless has far to go. As part of what Hideaki Shiroyama characterized as "the backdrop of a worldwide wave of reform in management", in 1997 then Secretary-General Kofi Annan introduced a new set of management reforms. This was eventually highlighted by the 2001 effort to move to results-based budgeting (RBB), with an eye to better measurement of productivity and performance or results within the UN system. However, Luck noted that RBB has not provided an answer for problems of political accountability, has operated better in certain policy sectors than others and has been a less than wholly satisfactory answer "on core development issues and security issues of wide visibility and high public concern". Shiroyama further observed, "The determination of indicators is a difficult task even for a national administration, but becomes even more complicated in the case of an international organization, in which a variety of complex factors are involved. There is no simple solution, but if international organizations are to be managed as a system, then a concerted effort should be made to determine suitable evaluation indicators." And, Shiroyama continued, "indicators are frequently established hastily and without an essential understanding of the activities of the Organization, making evaluation ineffective". Certainly, there still remains considerable work to be done in this important area of managerial accountability.

In critically assessing managerial and political accountability at the United Nations, various contributors agreed that no one-size-fits-all strategy exists that would markedly enhance the accountability of all the UN organizations. For one, the targets at which different parts of the UN system aim can be quite different. Hence, as Edward Luck observed, "In an organization as intrinsically political as the United Nations, it makes little sense to employ standard management criteria for assessing whether it has succeeded in carrying out those mandates that are highly political or have a more aspirational or symbolic quality." Furthermore, the forms that the accountability of an international organization may take, counselled Kyoji Kawasaki, may be legal, political, administrative or financial. Tatsuo Sato added the thought that "Rules of accountability are not restricted to positive law, [but] ... include social customs, moral laws, institutional practices and political culture."

In trying to specify steps the United Nations might take to enhance the Organization's accountability to those whose projects it affects, Edith Brown Weiss, Peter Lallas and Anna Herken urged the United Nations to consider the advances made by the World Bank Inspection Panel. They suggested that the United Nations, too, should create a forum in which affected individuals and communities might voice their concerns over projects and be confident that findings would then be reported to decision-makers for consideration and action, whenever appropriate. Brown Weiss, Lallas and Herken concluded:

> it is important to establish such a body as structurally independent of management and staff, and to give it the attributes of a high-level body within the institution. To gain the trust of all parties, it is important that the reports be transparent, that the body communicates directly with those making the complaints and returns to convey the results of the investigations to them, and that panel members and staff are able at all times to operate impartially and objectively. It is also important that the body is able to have access to all relevant documents and be thorough in its work. Most importantly, it must have the trust of all concerned.

While accountability processes will have to be tailored to the wide variety of circumstances found within the different parts of the UN system, certain fundamental factors aimed at enhancing accountability may be drawn upon by multiple organizations. Drawing on the various contributions to this volume, we thus turn next to the presentation of a preliminary normative framework for strengthening UN accountability. We are presenting such a framework with full recognition, as referred to repeatedly in this volume, that no one-size-fits-all solution to enhance accountability will suit even part of the UN system, since different UN entities have distinctive functional, organizational, political, historical or other special considerations. In other words, we do not deny the principle that "legitimate difference... preserves diversity within a framework of a specified degree of convergence", as advocated by Anne-Marie Slaughter.[11] Nevertheless, we do hope that a normative framework, such as that presented below, could eventually serve as a common ground for enhancing accountability within, and of, the UN system.

A normative framework for strengthening UN accountability

In most cases, for any entity to be seen as properly accountable, a strategic plan and measurable goals and objectives must be defined. Necessary actions must be clearly identified, declaring who should carry out the action and how much resources should be devoted to the effort to achieve the goals. As Luck observed, "the mandate or policy task to be undertaken must be defined, articulated and communicated with sufficient clarity, precision and timeliness that all of the relevant players and stakeholders have a clear and common understanding of what is being undertaken".

Thereafter, progress should be monitored in relation to measurable factors. Attention must be paid to how measurement and evaluation ought to be conducted and then, in a timely and objective manner, critically assessed. And the results and performance must be communicated, in due course, to pertinent stakeholders. Here, of course, who constitutes a stakeholder may be an issue in dispute. While it may be suggested, most simply, that those affected by UN actions constitute stakeholders, agreement needs to be reached primarily on who are the relevant stakeholders. Depending on the activity at issue, those who wish to join the circle of participants acknowledged as relevant stakeholders and welcomed into discourse about an activity may encompass not simply certain individuals, local communities or special groups (such as religious groups), but any group or individuals, including civil society organizations, private sector entities (including multinational corporations) and numerous non-governmental organizations and advocacy groups of various sorts, who can affect or are affected by UN decisions and activities.[12] Here the United Nations might usefully tap into the experiences of the multilateral development banks. For instance, in his chapter on the Asian Development Bank Suresh Nanwani noted that external (relevant) stakeholders are now conceived as including "project beneficiaries, pressure groups, affected communities and civil society at large".

Within the Organization, critical evaluation needs to be conducted as well. The assessment of results ought to be used to provide feedback for the eventual improvement of future actions and performance. What makes this especially challenging is that those the United Nations is trying to help – including the poor, those in ill health, those displaced from their homes and those vulnerable to violence or natural disasters – are often precisely the stakeholders who are least able to communicate effectively about UN actions. Hence considerable work may have to be devoted to eliciting the collective viewpoints of affected constituencies.

Finally, something productive must happen at the end of the accountability process. Not just sanctions, but more importantly incentives must be incorporated in the accountability process, to work towards ensuring not only avoidance of replication of past errors but also better actions and performance in the future. But this is difficult at the international level, since the clear pathways by which people and institutions are brought to account domestically may be much more obscure in the international context. Edward Luck asked, "Are there rewards for good performance and punishment for bad? Are there increments along the way? Who determines these, and who is capable of carrying them out?... Neither punishment nor reward... comes easily or surely for the United Nations."

In sum, while by no means impossible to achieve, it will certainly be challenging to incorporate these reform elements into UN operations. It would thus be useful if broad agreement could be reached on central underlying ideas. For instance, one step forward would be explicit endorsement of the premise that if the failings of an organization – whether misconceived strategies or faulty programme implementation – are frankly confronted and rigorously scrutinized, with stakeholders informed and involved, then, in the long run, the entity will be stronger for it.

Based on these considerations, to facilitate the strengthening of UN accountability as a whole it would be useful to establish a normative general framework covering both managerial and political accountability. Such a framework could encompass elements such as the following.

1. Formulation (or reformulation), by each organization, of a strategic plan, which would include *inter alia* the following:

- articulation of quantitative and qualitative goals and objectives
- establishment of clear policy statements (tasks) or mandates on how these goals and objectives are to be achieved, with indication of necessary programmes
- anticipated accomplishments, including logical indicators that can be used to measure achievement

- identification of the key external factors that could affect achievement of the goals.

2. Implementation of the programme, which would include performance management and measurements based on a performance management system.
3. Timely communication or reporting, coupled with enhanced transparency, to the states and relevant non-state actors of the results, outcomes or performance, which should be based on a systematic evaluation of programme effectiveness in terms of achieving goals and objectives, as well as managerial efficiency concerning implementation of mandated programmes.
4. Feedback from the recipients, including relevant stakeholders, on the organization's reports and other communications in point 3 above, as inputs for point 5 below.
5. Development (decision-making) of new (or revised) policies or mandates, by fully taking into account evaluation findings and comments (critiques) received, as the basis for the next new cycle of activities.

If properly managed, such a framework could be a continuous process for improvement. In visual terms it could form a spiral, moving constantly upwards, helping to bring about more relevant policies and mandates and better programme performance. All this may lead, in turn, to greater effectiveness and efficiency of the UN organizations. However, in order to realize this, a number of preconditions should be met, including in particular a need to ensure that policies or mandates of the UN organizations reflect, in one way or another, diverse views and interests drawn from the international community as a whole. This is especially necessary at the stage of the policy development process as well as at the stage of feedback, through appropriate mechanisms to be established or strengthened, together with identification, in particular, of the relevant stakeholders in the respective fields or issues concerned.

Beyond this, since the legislative organs must be involved and must eventually give their blessing to the principles and guidelines embodied in such a framework and give the directives needed to operationalize it, some possible mistrust between Member States over the perception of accountability and ensuing policy implications and consequences must be overcome.

To conclude

More than six decades after the founding of the United Nations, observers continue to ask exactly how it is accountable for what it does. As Jochen Prantl noted, "Enhancing the legitimacy and accountability of the UN system has become a key concern in the discussion of how to adapt the world organization to the challenges of the twenty-first century. It is also part and parcel of a wider debate about the development of international norms and procedures for the good governance of globalization." Focusing on the problems of the United Nations in particular, former Secretary-General Kofi Annan noted, "A key ingredient of any successful organization is an ethical and accountable culture pervading its staff from top to bottom."[13] Opinion polls suggest that "we the peoples" often approve of multilateral action within the UN framework, as opposed to unilateral or allied or regional undertakings, but a significant number doubt that the Organization is sufficiently accountable, and hence they question the wisdom of devoting more of their resources to it.

Enhanced accountability thus amounts to a cardinal objective for the United Nations at the start of the twenty-first century. As Hirohide Takikawa emphasized, "accountability mechanisms may ensure that those exercising power comply with authorized rules, guarding against the abuse of power. The process of giving an account can check the activities and decisions of those in power. More importantly, merely anticipating giving an account can help prevent the abuse of power." The problem is not that the United Nations has been completely oblivious to the need for better accountability. Notable institutional developments have included the creation of the Ethics Office and strengthening oversight mechanisms. Procedural advances have encompassed enhanced oversight, whistleblower protection, financial disclosure measures and post-employment restrictions on UN officials. Nevertheless, the problem is broad in scope, and the measures taken to date have neither met the problem nor allayed public concerns in a sufficient manner.

Indeed, as UN undertakings have become ever more ambitious, have involved more and more actors and have aimed to play an ever more significant role in the lives that they affect, the lack of clear accountability for UN actions has become a source of grave concern. Perceptions of UN relevance, efficiency, effectiveness and credibility are closely related to accountability. The Organization is unlikely to receive the resources necessary to carry out its ambitious programmes and projects so long as its accountability is seen as deficient. Only when the accountability of UN organizations is enhanced can we become confident that their performance will not further deteriorate and that they will play an effective key role in global governance in the years ahead.

Notes

1. See, for instance, US Institute of Peace (2005) *American Interests and UN Reform: Report of the Task Force on the United Nations*, Washington, DC: US Institute of Peace, ch. 3.

2. Karns, Margaret P. and Karen Mingst (2004) *International Organizations: The Politics and Processes of Global Governance*, Boulder, CO and London: Lynne Rienner, p. 4. Anne-Marie Slaughter added the thought that global governance is a looser and less threatening conception of collective organization and regulation without coercion than would be world government. Slaughter, Anne-Marie (2004) *A New World Order*, Princeton, NJ: Princeton University Press, p. 9.
3. Slaughter, ibid., p. 42.
4. Ibid., p. 29.
5. Dickinson, Laura A. (2006) "Public Law Values in a Privatized World", *Yale Journal of International Law* 31(2), pp. 383–426, citing UN Office of the High Commissioner for Refugees (2004) "NGO Partnerships in Refugee Protection", available at www.unhcr.org/cgi-in/texis/vtx/partners/opendoc.pdf?tbl=PARTNERS&id=41c162d04.
6. This provision reads, in its pertinent part: "Nothing contained in the present Charter shall authorize the United Nations to intervene in matters which are essentially within the domestic jurisdiction of any state . . . " UN Charter, article 2(7). Note that in the appended commentaries Tatsuo Sato observed: "because international organizations are forced to adapt themselves to changing international society, their activities sometimes step out of the original agreement among Member States".
7. Inis Claude has termed this period the "new interventionism". Claude, Inis L. Jr (1995) "The United States and Changing Approaches to National Security and World Order", *Naval War College Review*, Summer, pp. 49–61, at p. 48. See also Claude, Inis L. Jr (1994) "Moral Dilemmas in International Relations", in K. W. Thompson, ed., *The Virginia Papers on the Presidency*, Vol. XXVIII, Miller Center Forums, 1988–1993, Lanham, MD: University Press of America.
8. See Watson, Adam (2007) *Hegemony and History*, London and New York: Routledge, p. 83, quoting Inis Claude: "most of our interventions have the ostensible purpose – if not always the actual result – of making the target state *more* capable and more effective (as well as more acceptable) in meeting the needs of its society".
9. Lynch, Colum (2008) "Expenses at U.N. Balloon 25 Percent", *Washington Post*, 21 March, p. A1.
10. See Behn, Robert D. (2001) *Rethinking Democratic Accountability*, Washington, DC: Brookings Institution, p. 64.
11. Slaughter, note 2 above, p. 249.
12. Freeman, R. Edward (1984) *Strategic Management: A Stakeholder Approach*, Boston, MA: Pitman.
13. Annan, Kofi (2006) "Investing in the United Nations: For a Stronger Organization Worldwide", UN Doc. A/60/692, 7 March, p. 13, box 1.

Appendix I

Commentaries made at the United Nations University Tokyo Symposium on Accountability

Tetsuo Sato, Mariko Shoji and Mikoto Usui

At the Tokyo Symposium on Accountability hosted by the United Nations University at UN House on 16–17 October 2006, several scholars were asked to comment on the papers that formed the original basis for the chapters in this volume. Accordingly, the commentaries made by these discussants are reproduced below as a part of the contributions to this volume. The discussants were asked to comment on particular groups of papers divided by the different parts of the book. The fourth discussant was Sumihiro Kuyama, whose observations have now been incorporated into the introduction and conclusion to this book.

Commentary: General analysis of accountability in the UN context

Tetsuo Sato

Let me briefly explain the general background of the phenomenon [of accountability], so that we can put the arguments by the authors in their proper perspective.

While the legitimacy of domestic government has been a central focus of political theory since the time of Hobbes and Locke, the legitimacy of international organizations has, until recently, received little attention. There are two reasons for this discrepancy. Firstly, until recently,

Envisioning reform: Enhancing UN accountability in the twenty-first century, Kuyama and Fowler (eds), United Nations University Press, 2009, ISBN 978-92-808-1170-4

international organizations have generally been so weak in terms of their powers and influence that the issue of their legitimacy has barely come up as a political problem. Secondly, to the extent that international organizations do influence the behavior of states, i.e. to the extent that we can speak of international governance, their powers have generally been self-imposed in the sense that they rest on the consent of the very states to which they apply. While theories of legitimacy focus on the problem of domination, the imposition of one will upon another, international organizations are usually established by multilateral treaties, agreements among Member States.

Logically speaking, the disappearance of these two reasons could be considered to have brought the issue of legitimacy to the forefront of international organization discourse. In addition, two new developments are worthy of note.

Firstly, international organizations have begun to play a larger role, particularly since the end of the Cold War, as is symbolized by the reinvigoration of the Security Council and the *de facto* compulsory jurisdiction of the WTO dispute settlement mechanism. Secondly, because international organizations are forced to adapt themselves to changing international society, their activities sometimes step out of the original agreement among Member States by having recourse to such concepts as the doctrine of implied powers or the teleological interpretation of their constituent instruments, as is evidenced by international legislation by the Security Council under Chapter VII of the UN Charter regarding the fight against international terrorism (Resolution 1373 (2001)) or the non-proliferation of weapons of mass destruction (Resolution 1540 (2004)).

I would like to add, however, a third point. The quality of the influence exerted by international organizations has changed in the sense that their decisions not only influence the behavior of States but also have serious implications for private persons, legal persons such as companies and corporations, and relevant industries in the domestic societies of the targeted states. As Professor Prantl expressed it, the intrusiveness of international norms, adopted at the global level, affect[s] domestic debates on how societies should organize themselves. Globalization and with it the intrusiveness of international norms and transnational laws and regulations have indeed started to concern and activate citizens. This is exemplified by the serious negative effect of economic sanctions imposed by the Security Council, and the large-scale negative effect of infrastructure projects financed by the World Bank.

Thus, it seems quite natural that the more the decisions of international organizations have serious implications for private persons in national societies, just as they do for national governments, the more they should be subject to the same standards of legitimacy required of national governments. Hence, the issue of legitimacy-deficit or democratic deficit has come to the forefront of international organizations. However, we have to distinguish between legitimacy-deficit and democratic deficit because it is not easy to bring democratic mechanisms into the framework of international organizations where the principle of sovereign equality usually prevails. Now let me move on to the chapters and point out several important problems clarified and analyzed by the contributors.

The first point is what is accountability? Here, Professor Takikawa made an excellent analysis of the structure of accountability and the process of responsibility. Frequently, the question of accountability is presented as who should be accountable to whom for what? But, as Professor Takikawa points out, accountable entities have an obligation to account because rules stipulate them to do so. Rules are the most fundamental component in the structure of accountability because rules stipulate all other components. I think it quite important to keep this premise explicit, as we tend to take it for granted and end up making our analysis confusing. Rules of accountability are not restricted to positive law, and include social customs, moral laws, institutional practices, and political culture. When it comes to positive law, however, it becomes a question of legal responsibility, as was treated by Professor Kawasaki. I would say, however, while legal responsibility is a powerful mechanism of accountability in general, it is relatively undeveloped in the case of international organizations. In fact, Professor Kawasaki makes the observation that at present, customary international law does not provide for sufficiently clear rules which would oblige international organizations to observe standards of due process *vis-à-vis* individuals

The second point is to keep in mind that the United Nations system is multi-dimensional. Professor Fowler is quite right in pointing out that the question of accountability must be analyzed according to each different aspect of the United Nations system such as the United Nations of the Secretariat, the United Nations of the Security Council, the plenary United Nations, and the United Nations system as a whole. Furthermore, although these different United Nations are not mutually exclusive bodies, they are often connected and intertwined in a complex manner. Therefore, I would like to emphasize that we must always pay enough attention to this entangled relationship among different United Nations whenever we analyze the propriety of the accountability mechanisms corresponding to each aspect of the United Nations.

In this connection, Professor Fowler might have caught the essence of the problem when he writes that: within this large and complex organization, composed of so many competing as well as cooperating units of different sizes and shapes, there are few clear hierarchies, [and] it is by no means always clear to whom accountability is owed, and that rather than a tidy, carefully planned, systematic approach, the push and pull of international politics has determined the extent to which particular parts of the UN were, or were not, brought to account.

The third and crucial point is the relationship among accountability, democracy and effectiveness. I have the impression that we are in consensus with regard to the preliminary point that there is no universally applicable accountability mechanism, or no one-size-fits-all strategy to make UN politics more legitimate and accountable, as was pointed out by both Professor Takikawa and Professor Fowler. As a starting point for discussing the relationship between accountability and democracy, I would like to cite a paragraph by Professor Takikawa. He says:

> accountability does not always go hand in hand with democracy. The relation between accountability and democracy is much more complicated than typically supposed. On the one hand, accountable governance does not necessarily presuppose democracy. Rather, accountability has been emphasized because of the so-called democratic deficit.
>
> On the other hand, accountability does rely on the idea of democracy. Democracy is a system in which political legitimacy flows from the people. Any public decisions must be ultimately justified to the people to acquire legitimacy. [A]ccountability may enhance the legitimacy of decisions. Democracy as the legitimacy principle requires accountability.
>
> In other words, we can say that democratic accountability is drawn from the principle of legitimacy.

Here one of the practical questions is how to coordinate frequently incompatible requirements of democratization, accountability and effectiveness. As was pointed out by Professor Fowler, however defined, democratization seems certain to imply the involvement of a greater number of voices. It is difficult to see how adding multitudes of more or less conflicting voices to those conceiving or implementing policies will improve the efficiency of the policy-making process or its final product. Thus, increased democratization or enhanced accountability could sometimes end up decreasing the effectiveness in achieving a certain purpose for which the Organization was established.

Professor Prantl also states that legitimacy and accountability should not be treated as absolute goods. They rather constitute instrumental values that UN Member States need to trade off against competing demands such as efficiency or informality. The balance between those demands is fluid and context-driven. It needs to be struck on a case-by-case basis. And he says, here is a strong case for softening overly rigid principles of international law in order to enhance the effectiveness of international organizations. Thus, Professor Prantl, applying his idea to the Security Council, concludes that the proliferation of informal groupings of states in the post–Cold War era, [such as] contact groups, core groups, groups of friends, can be explained as one important response to the tension resulting from those competing demands. However, I would like to draw your attention to the fact that Professor Prantl also admits that: these complementary functions of informal groups of states are, however, contingent upon whether informal groups of states operate within the objectives of the United Nations or whether they act on their own account. I would point out that, in other words, this mechanism primarily depends on the good faith of these States and to that extent [is] fragile if not unreliable.

Another relevant point is, as was pointed out by Professor Fowler, when a sizeable percentage of the Member States are not themselves democracies, how can we bring elements of democratization within the United Nations system? In other words, to whom is the United Nations accountable? While the preamble of the UN Charter seems to assume the existence of a global *demos*, that is the peoples, the United Nations essentially is a global institution composed of Member States. It might be wise if we follow the realistic advice of Professor Prantl as follows: any discussion of how to enhance legitimacy and accountability of the United Nations must take into account the limits of applying democratic standards and best practices in the absence of a strong sense of political community.

Another point is related to non-governmental organizations (NGOs). One might suggest that building stronger links between civil society and UN policy-making is of particular concern. Here, international institutions must provide opportunities for the expression of voice. It is true that NGOs might be used in some capacity to help to reflect the will of the people in non-democratic states. However, as Professor Fowler correctly points out, NGOs have their own problems of accountability

A final point concerns the role of national parliaments. It is well known (Professor Prantl) that foreign policy belongs to the most difficult areas where democratic control, and with it legitimacy and accountability, can be achieved at the national level. However, I also think and agree with Professor Prantl that accountability in fact starts at home by, for example, strengthening domestic procedures such as the enhanced involvement of national parliaments in foreign policy-making. As I pointed out at the beginning, the quality of the influence exerted by international organizations has changed in the sense that the decisions of international organizations now have serious implications for private persons. For private persons, national parliaments are the primary mechanism through which their interests are expected to be asserted and protected. These key questions must be carried over to Part III: Political Accountability.

Commentary: Political accountability (democratic accountability)

Mariko Shoji

In this short essay, I would like to focus upon the following three points: (1) the possession of democracy in the world; (2) democracy and the United Nations; and (3) questions for global democracy.

In the first place, I would like to make a short comment on the papers, which are excellent and gave me so much inspiration. Professor Kazuo Takahashi described how democracy is affected when an emphasis is put on governance. And he analyzed three major components of democracy, namely, participation, transparency and the rule of law. He mentioned the autocratic nature of UN operational activity. His is interesting analysis, and I was quite inspired. Tatsuro Kunugi suggested steps towards multi-stakeholder partnerships for enhancing legitimacy and accountability. He provides an ambitious idea, but a well-considered future vision.

The possession of democracy in the world

Both papers mentioned multiple actors in the world, such as nation states, international organizations, civil society organizations, transnational organizations and so on. Which, among all of these, has democratic accountability? For both papers, non-governmental organizations are a critical factor. Nevertheless, there is an important question as to whether NGOs are the real representatives of global civil society. I think there is a difference between the representatives of NGOs and the representatives of civil society in the sense of the world people.

Democracy and the UN

Three categories describe the relationship between the UN and democracy: (1) democracy in the UN as a deliberative body, (2) democracy of the UN as an operational body, and (3) democracy by the UN as an advisory body.

Democracy in the UN as a deliberative body

In the United Nations system, there are many kinds of deliberative bodies such as the United Nations General Assembly, the United Nations Security Council, the International Monetary Fund (IMF) Board of Governors, and the International Labour Conference of the International Labour Organization (ILO). Each deliberative organ has its specific decision-making system. The UN General Assembly has the "one state one vote" system. The UN Security Council has 15 Member States. Five permanent members have veto power, but the other 10 non-permanent Member States do not. The IMF Board of Governors has its weighted voting system. Each Member shall have 250 votes plus one additional vote for each part of its quota equivalent to 100,000 special drawing rights.[1] And, the International Labour Conference of the ILO has its three composition system. Each Member State is represented by a delegation consisting of two government delegates, an employer delegate, a worker delegate, and their respective advisers. Every delegate has the same rights, and all can express themselves freely and vote as they wish. So it happens that worker and employer delegates sometimes vote against their government's representatives or against each other.[2] Sovereign equality is not always an appropriate democratic procedure. In the international society, there is variety among Member States in terms of size, finance and population. We should seek the type of decision-making procedure that is most appropriate for global democracy.

Democracy of the UN as an operational body

Professor Takahashi examined this precise point. The UN dispatches many kinds of operational field activities, such as peacekeeping operations, humanitarian agencies and development cooperation. And, he analyzed rightly the three major components of democracy – participation, transparency and rule of law.

Of course, the United Nations has some kind of political authority in the world. But, that does not justify authoritarian intervention by the UN in its operations. The UN operational activities are not for the staff, but for the people the activities are designed to assist. The UN should not intervene too authoritatively in the matters in question.

Democracy by the UN as an advisory body

In many cases, people in a post-conflict society do not understand the concept of democracy. For peace-building activities, to teach people how to freely express their will and participate in democratic elections are very important things. There are great numbers of people who do not know the meaning of democracy. And, most of them cannot express their free will.

For democracy, it is most important to express the free will of the people not by forcible measures but by peaceful measures. At the post-conflict stage, many scholars believe in the theory of democratic peace. In the field of political science, after the Cold War, Michael Doyle[3] and Bruce Russett[4] have become leading democratic peace theorists. Russett explained "democratic peace" as follows: "The image of a world of peaceful relations among democracies represents an extension of democratic politics within states generally, and of immediate interpersonal relations."[5]

To attain a global democratic peace, however, there are some problems. A first problem is that democracy is not always a panacea for peace for a society in conflict. A second problem lies in imposing democracy. I would like to focus for a moment on democracy as a panacea for peace. Maybe the theory of democratic peace can apply to international conflicts. The number of conflicts will lessen if the political systems of aggressive states become democratic. But, after the Cold War, most conflicts are not inter-state wars but civil wars or other internal conflicts. In the field of domestic struggle, democracy cannot always be a panacea for peace. It is interesting to note that, after democratic elections, conflicts have broken out within many African countries.[6]

We should respect the will of people in post-conflict societies. But we should keep in mind that the people's free will, expressed through democracy, does not always bring peace. I would suggest that in this context democratic accountability by the UN means becoming an advisory body for the domestic democratization of states. And, it is most important for the UN to advise people to express their free will not by forcible measures but by peaceful measures.

Questions for global democracy

To realize global democracy, there are many obstacles and problems. Here, the following four problems should be examined: (1) democracy and tyranny of the majority, (2) "no representation without taxation", (3) people and democracy, and (4) inter-sovereign-state society.

Democracy and tyranny of the majority

When we think of democracy, how to prevent the tyranny of the majority is a very critical matter. This is a classic debate with respect to the decision-making process of the UN General Assembly with its "one state one vote" system. The number of founding Member States in 1945 was only 51 countries. In the 1960s many decolonized countries, newly independent from European powers, entered the United Nations. At the end of the 1960s, the number of Member States had risen from 51 to 126. Here is the contradiction of the UN General Assembly. Contrary to international power politics, in the General Assembly forum third world countries have a preponderance of numeric power. Developed countries complain about this tyranny of the majority by the third world. The majority does not always make collective judgements or choices. But normally, democratic procedure means the numeric majority has the power to make a decision. In the sense of a numerical majority, democratic accountability is achieved, but numbers do not necessarily signify responsibility.

No representation without taxation

In the decision-making process of the UN, people do not have any voting power, because they do not have to pay any tax directly to the UN. In the process of UN reform, so many times civil society and NGOs have offered to pay taxes directly to the UN. But the UN rejected these offers, because it is the privileged association of sovereign states. People and civil society do not have such a status. We know the slogan "no taxation without representation". In reverse, there is the phenomenon that no representation is offered without taxation for people and civil society.

Recently and in the future, an international tax will be realized globally. In the Outcome Document of the World Summit at the UN in September 2005, we can see an international tax. This is almost the first time that the UN takes up the subject of an international tax. In this Outcome Document, paragraph 23(d) mentioned the International Finance Facility.[7]

People and democracy

It is most important to consider how to teach the notion of democracy to the people in the domestic societies of states. We should not impose democracy on the people in a domestic society. Professor Fujiwara wrote *The Empire of Democracy*.[8] In this book, he mentioned the US government imposes democracy upon people who have different cultures. I think, in the case of the United States, democracy has two aspects: domestic and international. Domestically, President Bush was elected through democratic election. His appointment was the reflection of American citizens' will. On the other hand, internationally, his war against Iraq in 2003 was neither peaceful nor democratic. He enforced democracy upon Iraq.[9]

The role of the UN for democratization is not to enforce democracy but to assist elections technically. In the United Nations Secretariat, there is the electoral assistance unit in the Department of Political Affairs. The major tasks of this division are to conduct a realistic evaluation of varied elections and to assess the basic electoral needs of the country.[10] Beyond such matters, there are limits for the UN to take into account in the process of domestic democratization. The ultimate accountability for democratization is situated in the people and the government of the assisted state.

Inter-sovereign-state society

It would be ideal for us to realize the vision of Professor Kunugi. His work is praiseworthy because it is difficult to draw an ideal future world. But there is also the problem of how to realize the ideal vision of a multi-stakeholder system.

Sovereign states today do not easily hand over to other entities their privileged status to join the UN deliberative organs with voting rights. It is difficult for the non-state actors to join the UN deliberative organs with voting power. The world today is essentially an inter-sovereign-state society. But, gradually, international society transformed global society. Professor Held proposes "cosmopolitan democracy". He wrote, "In this world, there are many issues stretching beyond the borders of countries and challenging the relevance of those borders in key respects." And he continued, "The theory of cosmopolitan democracy suggests this is not only a real necessity but also a real possibility. I also believe that in the future there will be an urgent need to envisage a worldwide democratic system with multi-stakeholder partnerships. I think, to take accountability means to take power. If non-state actors take accountability in the world today, they will take power. So that, if non-state actors would like to dispatch representatives to the UN, they should take accountability. And if non-state actors take accountability, it means they will have power in the field of international politics."[11]

Commentary: Case studies of accountability

Mikoto Usui

Let me limit myself to two kinds of remarks. First, I venture to offer a perspective for analytically framing the intricate interrelationships between management accountability and political (or democratic) accountability. I am motivated to do so since most of the contributors seem to have avoided explicitly looking into the characteristics of the interrelationships between political and management accountability. Second, after that, I should like to point out the critical importance of the case-specific complaint-based system for the evolution of law and institutions, and provide one or two examples pertaining to certain specific segments of UN policy activities.

On the dual basis of organizational legitimacy: Politics and action

At the United Nations University seminar, with reference to J. D. Stewart's "Ladder of Accountability", Ms Hasuo concluded her presentation by pointing out that the UN or any of the UN organizations had not yet entered the final fifth stage of "Policy Accountability". She said so in her own analytical context of management accountability, perhaps having in mind the UN system's various operational action programs, hence leaving aside predominantly political programs such as the General Assembly, the Economic and Social Council (ECOSOC), the Commission for Sustainable Development (CSD), the UN Conference on Trade and Development (UNCTAD) and so on. It is not my task to comment on that interesting chapter of hers, but I wondered why she did not climb one more step beyond and over the Stewart Ladder so that she could have said something about how the UN proper, or the more predominantly political programs in the UN system, are preoccupied primarily with "talks and decisions" in a manner that is usually a few steps removed from the system functionalistic "action" programs.

Every organization, be it public or domestic, national or international, has a dual basis for legitimacy. It is necessarily "*Janus*-faced" in the sense that it consists in a subtle mixture of two programmatic ideal types: *politics* and *action*. The political program of a given organization consists primarily of talks and decisions that "reflect", as faithfully as possible, the diverse, even mutually inconsistent, demands and ideologies of its external stakeholders (who may not be limited to target beneficiaries of specific action projects). Here I recall the cynicism of Nils Brunsson, author of *The Organization of Hypocrisy*, in which he wrote that "hypocrisy" is a fundamental type of behavior in political rhetoric and decisions that are to "talk in a way that satisfies one demand, to decide in a way that satisfies another, and to supply products in a way that satisfies a third".[12] Here, "participatory" or "democratic" accountability matters, indeed, calling for sort of "political rationality" in reflecting and accommodating inconsistent norms.

On the other hand, the same organization ought to have an "action" program as well. Each action specializes in one type of action or product, addressing one market niche or one type of stakeholder group. Action is geared to delivering solutions rather than discussing problems, and involves a consistent organizational ideology needed to produce and deliver promised products. There, management accountability matters, but with a focus primarily on technical rationality and efficiency, even though some sort of complaint-based system would be required to keep a window open for a degree of participatory accountability for project-specific stakeholders.

Both politics and action are indispensable for organizational legitimacy, but both are easier to achieve if they are managed separately, since they require different organizational ideologies and managerial skills. Talks and decisions may be used to justify a new action proposal or defend the implementation of an agreed action, for instance, why it can only partially meet the bigger demands received and the broader organizational responsibilities allocated to respond to them in the earlier decisions. There usually remain significant gaps between talks and decisions, on the one hand, and actions, on the other. Brunsson called this an "organizational hypocrisy" – perhaps too cynical an expression to be decent, as that sort of hypocrisy can be considered a necessary evil for successful organizational survival and growth. (It is actually a characteristic of "permanently failing" but perhaps never-dying big organizations like the United Nations.) In any event, it should be borne in mind that public-sector organizations must be skilled at politics, as they exist because people count on them for grappling with market-unfriendly, nearly insoluble problems in society.

For that matter, Wikipedia (as of October this year) offers an interesting comment, saying that accountability only enables negative feedback *after* a decision or action (while "transparency" also enables negative feedback *before* or *during* the decision or action).[13] Thus, accountability as an ethical concept is associated with strategic uses of excuses, apologies, justifications, rationalizations and other forms of account-giving behavior. In fact, the discrepancy between politics and action gives rise to a demand for repentance and a promise of reform. So, Brunsson says, "Reforms give management a chance to fulfill their intention to generate (new) action."[14] Thus, almost all reforms may look better *ex ante* than *ex post*, but they can demonstrate top management's ability to stave off despair and inspire hope.

It is essential to manage politics and action in a mutually complementary but not mutually interfering way. A great deal of ingenuity is required to satisfy that requirement. Certainly, different organizations live with different ways of combining politics with action, and their leaders have to strike an appropriate balance between the two. So, sometimes, the Organization may look like a federation, family or network rather than a hierarchical structure.

In this conjunction, we should note that, even in a predominantly action-oriented organization (such as the World Bank and the Asian Development Bank [ADB] whose management accountability systems are discussed in this seminar as well), boards and councils that make formal decisions on policy matters and project priorities (by way of a political organization) may often have little influence over the control of their own decisions, because the decision basis is usually prepared by experts, administrators or special technical committees who first investigate and assess alternatives and possible consequences.

Dr Reiterer described how the European Union worked on the basis of technocratic policies being "worked out in endless meetings" and decisions "taken by no doubt worthy élites for the people". Nevertheless the European Commission (EC) has launched a Transparency Initiative that would reveal "who lobbies for whom or which policy, who gets what money and how it is spent". According to him, this transparency initiative will seek to strengthen ethical standards across European institutions. He noted that it had been difficult to reach agreed standards across the varying cultural norms even within Europe. But similar attempts would be far more difficult in a global public institution like the UN and even in its various specialized "executing agencies", which have to struggle with deep-rooted and multi-faceted issues of the North-South Divide.

We would all agree, however, with Dr Reiterer's concluding remark that "management reform is only the technical part of reform. There must emerge an improved shared vision on the goals and values of the institution." This would certainly apply to the UN reform as well.

Citizens' complaint-based systems for institutional evolution

Now, let me move on to the second part of my comments.

Today, the case studies on the World Bank and the ADB showed that their accountability mechanisms were to address only the specific complaints registered by the people affected by specific projects. It is interesting to note that the ADB adopts a dual approach consisting of a problem-solving/consultation phase (that involves a fairly broad variety of external stakeholders), followed by the investigation/compliance review by the ADB Management. Thus, citizens' grievance-based mechanisms constitute a critical facet of management accountability and concomitant organizational policy development. I wonder to what extent the problem-solving consultation phase is intended to contribute to the "program accountability" stage (if not so much "policy accountability" stage) in terms of Stewart's Ladder.

In this respect, let me highlight the fact that our revered institution, the United Nations High Commission for Refugees (UNHCR), is being criticized for a serious democratic deficit in regard to its policy accountability mechanisms. UNHCR conducts, single-handedly and in a top-down fashion, refugee status determination in as many as 80 countries, and has handled nearly 80,000 asylum applications so far. The process seems to offer minimal scope for refugee participation in status determination, so that the current UNHCR mechanisms do not render UNHCR accountable to refugees. Indeed, legally speaking, UNHCR is not mandated for implementation of the Human Rights Treaty, but civil society activists' voices are now getting ever louder, favoring a "*human rights*"-based approach to refugee protection: namely they demand that refugees be regarded as holders of rights for protection and development, rather than just as beneficiaries of humanitarian assistance.[15]

A vital step for thinking about accountability is to have some relevant "standards" against which those who exercise power should be held accountable. Such standards may not necessarily be legally binding, but can be a type of soft law for pragmatic purposes, provided that they are politically viable.

For that matter, the *evolutionary theory of institution* suggests that reasonably well-shared ethical norms and principles can gain effective regulatory power on the strength of complaint-based systems. Now a complaints-based "specific instances" approach is being effected by the *National Contact Points*, newly established under the 2000 revision of the Organisation for Economic Co-operation and Development (OECD) *Guidelines for Multinational Enterprises* (MNEs),[16] even though the *Guidelines* themselves are voluntary in nature. Civil society and trade union activists' *watch-dog* function, coupled with their strategy of "naming and shaming" and sometimes even litigating when prevailing norms are breached, are now allowed to exert influence to MNEs and their home country governments for improved performances for fulfillment of "corporate social responsibility".

A recent development with the UN Global Compact

As for corporate social responsibility and accountability, the post-Rio decade witnessed a high-paced proliferation of voluntary codes of international significance. A large number of private "multi-stakeholder codes" have been derived from direct engagement between major business corporations and public-interest non-governmental organizations. Although they seem to embrace basically comparable ethical norms, it would prove difficult to reconcile or standardize them, given their individual "voluntaristic" nature, and given the complexity of the procedural tasks of monitoring, reporting, audit and certification. Under the circumstances, "complaint-based mechanisms" have come to attract increasing attention, with a focus on how to address specific instances of corporate breach of revered codes and guidelines.

The *UN Global Compact*[17] (GC) was born originally without any intention to evolve into any regulatory code books. However, there has recently been a noteworthy development towards a civil-regulatory approach to corporate accountability. The case in point is the *Draft UN Norms on Responsibilities of Transnational Corporations* (TNCs)[18] in the matter of Human Rights (HR). The Draft Norms were adopted in principle by the Human Rights Commission in 2004. It was an outcome of several years of drafting and consultation by the UN Sub-Commission for the Protection and Promotion of Human Rights. The HR Commission is well known for its unique system of special procedures for independent experts to observe and analyze human rights compliance by "theme" and by "country", and also a close engagement with civil society organizations.

In parallel to the Draft Norms, Mary Robinson (former High Commissioner for HR) began to support the "Business Leaders Initiatives on HR" working out a "*Guide for Integrating HR into Business Management*". By December 2005, the draft *Guide* has acquired the status of "joint report" with the GC Office and Office of the High Commissioner for Human Rights (OHCHR). The HR Commission, in turn, authorized the UN Secretary-General to appoint his Special Representative on Business and HR (Professor John Ruggie, former Special Adviser to the SG on the *Global Compact*). Soon, the GC Office issued a proposal (as of August 2005) "The GC's Next Phase" for the Secretary-General's approval. The proposal retains the GC's voluntary and network-based character but contains a new element, called "Integrity Measures". It adopts a complaint-based system for protecting the GC logo from misuse. Now, against these backgrounds, the GC initiative has finally enjoyed broader formal political support, even from an increasing number of developing countries, by the time the 2005 World Summit was held. And the General Assembly unanimously adopted as of 15 December 2005, a Resolution called *Towards Global Partnerships*.[19] It will help provide stronger legitimacy to the GC and its future work, we hope.

Notes

1. See www.imf.org/external/pubs/ft/aa/aa12.htm.
2. See www.ilo.org/public/english/standards/relm/ilc/.
3. See, for instance, Doyle, Michael W. (1997) *Ways of War and Peace*. New York: W. W. Norton.
4. See, for instance, Russett, Bruce (1994) *Grasping the Democratic Peace*, Princeton, NJ: Princeton University Press.
5. Ibid., p. 129.

6. Shoji, Mariko (2005) "The Challenge for Democracy: A New Approach on Security Problems", *Daxiyangguo – Revista Portuguesa de Estudos Asiáticos*, Universidade Técnica de Lisboa, No. 8, available at www.macaulogia.blogspot.com/2006/06/daxiyang-guo-revista-portuguesa-de.html, p. 88.
7. United Nations (2005) "2005 World Summit Outcome: Programme Budget Implications of Draft Resolution", A/60/L.1, 15 September, para. 23(d).
8. See, for instance, Fujiwara, Kiichi (2002) *Democracy no Teikoku* (*Empire of Democracy*), Tokyo: Iwanami Shinsho.
9. Shoji, note 6 above, pp. 87–88.
10. Joyner, Christopher C. (1999) "The United Nations and Democracy", *Global Governance* 5(3), pp. 333–357, at pp. 342–352.
11. Held, David (1997) "Democracy and Globalization", *Global Governance* 3(3), pp. 251–267.
12. Brunsson, Nils (1989) *The Organization of Hypocrisy*, New York: John Wiley & Sons, p. 27.
13. *Accountability*, available at www.answers.com/topic/accountability.
14. Brunsson, note 11 above, p. 226.
15. This observation is based on Pallis, Mark (2005) "The Operation of UNHCR's Accountability Mechanisms", Institute for International Law and Justice Working Paper 2005/12, New York University School of Law.
16. Organisation for Economic Co-operation and Development (2000) "Guidelines for Multinational Enterprises", 27 June, available at www.oecd.org/document/28/0, 2340, en 2649 34889 2397532 1 1 1 1,00.html.
17. As Wikipedia noted, the Global Compact was "an initiative to encourage businesses worldwide to adopt sustainable and socially responsible policies and to report on them": UN Global Compact, available at www.wikipedia.org/wiki/UN_Global_Compact. It was first announced by UN Secretary-General Kofi Annan in an address to the World Economic Forum on 31 January 1999, and is available at www.unglobalcompact.org/.
18. UN Subcommission on the Promotion and Protection of Human Rights (2003) "Draft Norms on the Responsibilities of Transnational Corporations and Other Business Enterprises with Regard to Human Rights", UN Doc. E/CN.4/Sub. 2/2003/R/Rev. 2.
19. GA Res. 215, UN GAOR, A/RES/60/215, 15 December 2005.

Appendix II

Areas for further study

In the conclusion to this volume we highlighted a number of important points regarding the accountability of the United Nations in which the thinking of many of the authors converged. By the same token, however, it has also come to the surface that there are various issues on which scholars and practitioners, coming from divergent backgrounds and areas of expertise, differ in their thinking. And a number of them cited dimensions of UN accountability in which we might advance our understanding through more research, thinking and discourse. Thus, in view of the preliminary nature of the discussions at the UNU Tokyo Symposium on Accountability and the consequent limits to the scope of this volume, the following issues – some practical, others philosophical; some of immediate concern, others of future interest – have been identified, by way of illustration, as areas for further study.

- How to ensure enhancement of both political and managerial accountability in a concerted and comprehensive manner in order for the United Nations to respond to global challenges more effectively and efficiently.
- In this context, how could the normative framework for UN accountability be refined?
- What is the conceptual distinction, if any, between political accountability and democratic accountability?
- What exactly is the distinction between accountability and responsibility?

Envisioning reform: Enhancing UN accountability in the twenty-first century, Kuyama and Fowler (eds), United Nations University Press, 2009, ISBN 978-92-808-1170-4

- What can be said of the relationship among accountability, legitimacy and democracy?
- What mechanisms might facilitate direct or indirect participation of stakeholders in the UN policy development and feedback processes, and, in this context, how might relevant stakeholders be identified?
- How could the lessons-learned capacities and coherence be strengthened for enhancing accountability within the UN system?
- What specific reforms might enhance accountability with respect to UN peace operations?
- How could the Security Council be brought to account, and to whom ought it be accountable?
- How might non-governmental organizations be brought into the process of enhancing accountability, while themselves becoming more accountable?

Index

"f" refers to figures; "t" table; "n" notes.

ABM. *See* activity-based management [EU] (ABM)
ACABQ. *See* Advisory Committee on Administrative and Budgetary Questions [UN] (ACABQ)
ACC. *See* Administrative Committee on Coordination [UN] (ACC); Chief Executives Board for Coordination [UN] (CEB)
accountability
  accountable, who to hold, 83
  accountable for what, 5, 83
  action, 88
  concept of, 3–5, 73–76, 176–79
  deficit/gap, 5, 43
  definition, 75
  democracy and, 91, 215
  democratic, 215–24, 253–55
  distribution problems of, 91–92
  elusive idea, 74
  explaining and justifying, 85–86
  financial, 83–84
  foundation for, 3
  framework, 338–40
  global governance and, 1, 199–203
  holder and holdee, 5
  independence and, 90–91
  internal/external, 82–83
  justification and, 88
  legitimacy and, 13–14, 97–112, 209–11
  managerial and political, 5–8, 19–20, 22–24, 177–78, 232–33
  mechanisms, 90–93
  network of, 93
  obligation for, 87–88
  to people/we the peoples, 4, 19, 80–81
  performance, 84–85
  political and democratic, 8, 11, 24, 194–97, 256, 348–52
  process of, 86–90, 87f3.2
  regularity of, 84
  responsibility and, 75–76, 203–205
  rule, 77–78, 77f3.1
  sanctions, 87f3.2, 88–89, 89f3.3
  stakeholder/relevant stakeholder, 6, 78–82
  structure, 76–86, 77f3.1
  to superiors, 79–80
  transparency and, 92–93
  to whom?, 6, 78
  UN General Assembly (Member States) and, 1
  why?, 9, 73–74, 174–75

accountability and international law
  article 15: decisions, recommendations and authorizations, 128–29
  basic aspects of, 117t5.1
  conclusions, 129
  introduction, 116–18, 117t5.1
  from normative to operational, 122
  from obligation of solidarity to global legislator, 123–24
  from operational to normative, 122–23
  ultra vires acts and legal consequences, 120–22
  UN and international obligations, 124–26
  UN and international community, 118–24
  UN and international law, 124–29
  UN and breaches of obligations and legal consequences, 127–28
  UN Charter, exercise of powers, 118–20
accountability and legitimacy
  achieving, five hypotheses for, 103–4
  concept and context, 98–104
  foreign policy and democracy, 98–100
  institutional authority and its discontents, 111–12
  introduction, 97–98
  UN Security Council, informal consultation of, 105, 106f4.1, 107f4.2, 108
  UN Security Council, practice, 104–11
  UN Security Council and Article 24 crisis, 108–9, 109f4.3
  UN Security Council and informal groups of states, 109–11
  why?, 100–102
accountability of different United Nations
  accountability, lacking political tradition, 47–48
  conclusion, 59–63
  constitutional guidance, lack of, 43–46
  "democratization", shortcomings of further, 56–59
  hierarchies, lacking well-defined/effective, 49–56
  introduction, 37–38
  standards and objectives, 46–47
  UN, accountability gap at, 43–59
  UN, accountability within, 38–39
  UN, disaggregating pieces of the, 40–43
  UN reports, shortcomings of, 48–49
activity-based management [EU] (ABM), 235, 260
ADB. *See* Asian Development Bank (ADB)
Ad Hoc Committee of Experts to Examine the Finances of the UN and the Specialized Agencies, 182, 189n40
Administrative Committee on Coordination [UN] (ACC), 139–40, 160n7
Advisory Committee on Administrative and Budgetary Questions [UN] (ACABQ), 16n3
African Development Bank (AfDB), 304, 312, 315–17
An Agenda for Democratization (Boutros-Ghali), 197, 212n9
AIDCO. *See* EuropeAid Co-operation Office (AIDCO)
Annan, Secretary-General Kofi, 214n31, 249, 336, 341, 358n17
"Annual Review of Development Effectiveness" (World Bank), 169
Anti-Terrorism Special Measures Law [Japan], 233
Arendt, Hannah, 92, 96n65
Asian Development Bank (ADB)
  about, 303
  accountability, meanings of, 304
  accountability, strengthening, 305–11
  accountability demands from multilateral development banks, 304–5
  accountability mechanisms, effect on other MDBs, 312
  accountability mechanisms, review process, 313–14
  accountability mechanisms and citizen-based grievances, 311–19
  accountability mechanisms and emerging trends, 314–19
  accountability mechanisms and future accountability, 319–20
  Chashma Right Bank Irrigation Project [Pakistan], 318–19
  civil society inputs and policy review/implementation, 310–11
  Development Effectiveness Committee (DEC), 307
  fraud and corruption, addressing, 308–9
  Global Transparency Initiative, 305, 321n7
  Joint Organization of the Affected Communities on Colombo-Matara Highway, 317–18

Melamchi Water Supply Project [Nepal], 317
Morse Commission Report, 274, 321
Operations Evaluation Department, 306–8
organization, action-oriented, 354
Paris Declaration on Aid Effectiveness, 319
procurement irregularities, 309–10
public communications policy and transparency, 308
Public Disclosure Advisory Committee (PDAC), 308
reform agenda, progress of, 311
Sardar Sarovar projects, 274, 298, 312, 323n51–52
Southern Transport Development Project [Sri Lanka], 317–18
stakeholders of, 338–39

Ban Ki-moon, Secretary-General, 1, 4, 15, 19, 23, 26, 249
Barroso Commission [EU], 264
Basel Convention on the Control of Trans-boundary Movements of Hazardous Wastes and Their Disposal, 156t6.3
Behn, Robert D., 28, 34n31, 85
Bentham, Jeremy, 231–32
Bertrand, Maurice, 182, 189n43–44
Borins, Sandford, 234
Boutros-Ghali, Secretary-General Boutros, 169, 198
Bretton Woods institutions, 139
Brown Weiss, Edith, x, 13, 271–302, 299n15, 299n18, 300n21, 301n43–45, 332, 337

CAO. *See* Compliance/Advisor Ombudsman (CAO) [IFC/MIGA]
CAP. *See* Consolidated Appeals Process (CAP)
Cardoso Report, 206–9
Carroll, Lewis, 97, 112, 304
"Cartagena Package", 152, 161n26
CCA. *See* Common Country Assessment (CCA)
CCA/UNDAF. *See* UN Development Assistance Framework (CCA/UNDAF)
CEB. *See* Chief Executives Board for Coordination [UN] (CEB)
Central Emergency Response Fund (CERF), 145f6.1, 147
Centre for Disaster Prevention in Central America (CEPREDENAC), 145f6.1
CEPREDENAC. *See* Centre for Disaster Prevention in Central America (CEPREDENAC)
CERF. *See* Central Emergency Response Fund (CERF)
CHAP. *See* Common Humanitarian Action Plan (CHAP)
Chashma Right Bank Irrigation Project [Pakistan], 318–19
Chief Executives Board for Coordination [UN] (CEB), 139, 141, 153–54, 159n3, 159n6, 160n8, 161n29. *See also* Administrative Committee on Coordination [UN] (ACC)
CITES. *See* Convention on International Trade in Endangered Species of Wild Fauna and Flora (CITES),
citizens' complaint-based systems, 355–56
Citizens Network for Sustainable Development, 198
CMS. *See* Convention on Migratory Species (CMS)
Code of Conduct for the International Red Cross and NGOs in Disaster Relief, 202
Commission on Global Governance, 197–98, 212n10
Commission on Sustainable Development [UN] (CSD), 6, 17n16, 150, 153, 353
Committee of Independent Experts [EU], 236t11.1, 237t11.2, 239, 241, 243, 245t11.4, 251n39–40, 254
Committee on Accountability of International Organizations, 116, 130n2, 321n1, 321n4, 321n69
Common Country Assessment (CCA), 153–54, 158
Common Humanitarian Action Plan (CHAP), 145f6.1
Common Responsibility in the 1990s: The Stockholm Initiative on Global Security and Governance, 201, 213n13
Compliance/Advisor Ombudsman (CAO) [IFC/MIGA], 312, 315
Comprehensive Nuclear-Test-Ban Treaty Organization, 139

Conférence des Organs Spécialisés en Affaires Communautaires (COSAC), 236t11.1
Consolidated Appeals Process (CAP), 143t6.2
Convention on International Trade in Endangered Species of Wild Fauna and Flora (CITES), 156t6.3
Convention on Migratory Species (CMS), 156t6.3
Convention on Protection of World Cultural Heritage, 156t6.3
convention on the law of environmental treaties, 155
COSAC. *See* Conférence des Organs Spécialisés en Affaires Communautaires (COSAC)
Council of Ministers [EU], 236, 238–42, 258, 266
CSD. *See* Commission on Sustainable Development [UN] (CSD)

DAC. *See* OECD Development Assistance Committee (DAC)
Dahl, Robert, 99, 103, 113n7, 114n22
DEC. *See* Development Effectiveness Committee (DEC)
Declaration of Accountability for Global Governance, 197–200
DECODE. *See* Dessiner la Commission de Demain (DECODE)
"Delivering as One: Report of the Secretary-General's High-level Panel on UN System-wide Coherence in the Areas of Development, Humanitarian Assistance, and the Environment", 224, 224n9
De Mello, Sergio Vieira, 25
democracy deficits, 195
democratic accountability, *See* accountability
democratic accountability in UN field operations
  development cooperation principle, 219–20
  difficulties and contradictions, 215–17
  emerging principles, 219–23
  field operations, primacy of, 217–19
  humanitarian intervention, 221–22
  participation principle, 220–23
  PKO/interim administration operations, 222–23
  rule of law principle, 220–23
  transparency principle, 220–23
  UN reform exercise, 223–24
Department of Peacekeeping Operations [UN] (DPKO), 65n12, 114n30
Dessiner la Commission de Demain (DECODE), 235, 251n26
Development Effectiveness Committee (DEC), 307
DG. *See* directorate-general [EU] (DG); Director-General [UN] (DG)
directorate-general [EU] (DG), 237t11.2, 263
DPKO. *See* Department of Peacekeeping Operations [UN] (DPKO)
Dubnick, Melvyn, 81, 94n24

EAEC. *See* European Atomic Energy Community (EAEC)
Earth Charter, 202, 213n19
EBRD. *See* European Bank for Reconstruction and Development (EBRD)
EC. *See* European Commission (EC)
ECE. *See* Economic Commission for Europe (ECE)
ECHA. *See* Executive Committee on Humanitarian Affairs (ECHA)
ECJ. *See* European Court of Justice (ECJ)
Economic and Social Commission for Asia and the Pacific (ESCAP), 156
Economic and Social Commission for Western Asia (ESCWA), 156
Economic and Social Council [UN] (ECOSOC), 6, 17n16, 44, 55, 71n95, 150, 159, 159n6, 164, 353
Economic Commission for Europe (ECE), 156t6.3
ECOSOC. *See* Economic and Social Council [UN] (ECOSOC)
ECSC. *See* European Coal and Steel Community (ECSC)
EEC. *See* European Economic Community (EEC)
EFSA. *See* European Food Safety Authority (EFSA)
EMG. *See* Environmental Management Group (EMG)
environmental governance
  coordination mechanisms, 153–54

environmental agreements, 155–56, 156t6.3
environment-related initiatives, 150
expenditures on normative and operational environmental activities, 157t6.4
intergovernmental ownership in interagency coordination, 154
Kyoto and Montreal Protocol, control measures between, 152, 155–56, 156t6.3
multilateral environmental agreements (MEAs), 150, 155–56
Environmental Management Group (EMG), 153
EPFIs. *See* Equator Principles (EPFIs)
EPTA. *See* Expanded Programme of Technical Assistance (EPTA)
Equator Principles (EPFIs), 320
ESCAP. *See* Economic and Social Commission for Asia and the Pacific (ESCAP)
ESCWA. *See* Economic and Social Commission for Western Asia (ESCWA)
EU. *See* European Union (EU)
EUROJUST. *See* European Judicial Cooperation Office (EUROJUST)
EuropeAid Cooperation Office (AIDCO), 263
European Anti-Fraud Office (OLAF), 236t11.1, 237t11.2, 245t11.4, 253, 259
European Atomic Energy Community (EAEC), 236t11.1
European Bank for Reconstruction and Development (EBRD), 304, 312, 315–17
European Coal and Steel Community (ECSC), 236t11.1, 256
European Commission (EC)
accountability of, 238–40
accountability to European citizens, 242
Committee of Independent Experts, 236t11.1, 237t11.2, 239, 241, 243, 245t11.4, 251n39–40, 254
Council of Ministers, 236, 238–42, 258, 266
culture of communication with civil society, 265
democratic control, lacking, 254
directorates-general and accountability, 237t11.2, 245t11.4
European governance, white paper on, 254
European Parliament, 236, 236t11.1, 237t11.2, 238–40, 243, 245t11.4, 251n34, 251n38
evaluation system, new, 246
governance and NPM reform, 13, 233–36
hierarchical control *vs.* direct bonds, 238
internal organization of, 258
legal personality, 243
lobbies and transparency, 265
management "plus" reform, 263
Nice Treaty, 240–41
proposals, legislative and policy-defining, 264
responsibilities, collective, 236
Standard Eurobarometer, 21, 33n10
Transparency Initiative, 265, 355
European Court of Justice (ECJ), 237t11.2, 254–55
European Economic Community (EEC), 236, 236t11.1
European Food Safety Authority (EFSA), 243, 244t11.3
European Judicial Cooperation Office (EUROJUST), 236t11.1, 237t11.2, 244t11.3, 245t11.4
European Ombudsman, 237t11.2, 245t11.4, 248
European Parliament
European Commission (EC), 236, 236t11.1, 237t11.2, 238–40, 243, 245t11.4, 251n34, 251n38
European Union (EU), 253–54, 258, 260, 262, 264, 269n14
European Police Office (EUROPOL), 244t11.3
European Union (EU)
accountability, concepts and mechanisms, 231–38
accountability, democratic, 13, 253–55
accountability, evolution and types of, 231–32, 236–38, 236t11.1, 237t11.2
accountability, legal, 255–56
accountability, modern understanding, 237t11.2
accountability, political and managerial, 232–33, 256
accountability by new agencies and evaluation systems, 242–46, 244t11.3, 245t11.4

European Union (EU) (cont.)
accountability mechanisms, evolution of, 245t11.4
accountability reforms, chronological overview, 236t11.1
agencies, 244t11.3
Barroso Commission, 264
conclusion, 248–49, 266–68
Council of Ministers, accountability, 240–42
Directorate-General for External Relations (RELEX), 263
EU and UN, parallel developments, 256–58
EuropeAid Cooperation Office (AIDCO), 263
European Anti-Fraud Office (OLAF), 253, 259
European Commission, accountability of, 238–40
European Commission and Council of Ministers, 238–42
European Parliament, 253–54, 258, 260, 262, 264, 269n14
Internal Audit Service (IAS), 259
introduction, 229–31, 253
Laeken Declaration, 230, 249n3
management "plus" reform, 263–66
managing change, 261–63
NPM and European Commission, 13, 233–36
principle of subsidiarity, 60
reform, 258–61
sanctions, targeted, 126
Santer Commission, 234, 240, 253–54, 259
stakeholders, loss of confidence by key, 13, 33n10
Transparency Initiative, 265, 270n27, 355
EUROPOL. *See* European Police Office (EUROPOL)
Evans, Gareth, 208, 214n28, 214n36
Executive Committee on Humanitarian Affairs (ECHA), 145f6.1
Exit Strategy for Humanitarian Actors in Conflict Situations, 143t6.2
Exit Strategy for Humanitarian Actors in the Context of Complex Emergencies, 143t6.2
Exit Strategy from Relief to Development, 143t6.2
Expanded Programme of Technical Assistance (EPTA), 217

FAO. *See* Food and Agricultural Organization (FAO)
Fassbender, Bardo, 120, 126, 130n13
Field Guidelines for Assessing the Humanitarian Implications of Sanctions, 143t6.2
"Financing an Effective United Nations" (Volcker and Ogata), 169, 173n8
Finer, Herman, 82, 94–95n27
Food and Agricultural Organization (FAO), 154, 156, 160n14, 201
Fowler, Michael R., x, 3–17, 37–72, 67n44, 67n48, 69n76–77, 327–42, 345–47
Friedrich, Carl, 82, 94–95n27
Fukuda, Koji, xi, 12–13, 229–52, 249n5, 251n28–29, 251n31, 251n38, 328, 331

G-77. *See* Group of 77 (G-77)
GA. *See* General Assembly [UN] (GA)
Gallup survey, 20
GAO. *See* Government Accountability Office [US] (GAO)
GC. *See* Global Compact [UN] (GC)
GC/GMEF. *See* Governing Council/Global Ministerial Environment Forum (GC/GMEF) [UNEP]
GEF. *See* Global Environment Facility (GEF)
GEMS. *See* Global Environment Monitoring System (GEMS)
gender equality and empowerment of women, 168, 207
General Assembly [UN] (GA)
accountability, 1, 44
accountability and financial transparency, 149
article 7(1) of the Charter, 71n93
article 15 of the Charter, 67n51
article 17 of the Charter, 138
article 19 of the Charter, 69n78
article 41 of the Charter, 119
article 60 of the Charter, 67n50
article 98 of the Charter, 69n69
budgets of specialized agencies, administrative, 55
democracy, 23–24
democratic governance, 46, 57
Earth Summit, 17n16

Environmental Management Group (EMG), 153
Fifth Committee, 24, 26
as Governing Body of the Secretariat, 29
humanitarian assistance and, 141–42, 144
International Law Commission, 48–49
mechanisms for interagency coordination, 160n14
Preparatory Commission and, 29
reform, organizational, 58
resolution 53/35, 64n3; 60/260, 1; 61/245, 16n2
results-based budgeting and management, 140
results-based management (RBM), xvi, 10
Secretary-General and, 22, 31–32, 50–51
Security Council and, 4, 121–22
specialized intergovernmental support bodies (absence of), 148
state responsibilities and, 127
sustainable development governance, 150
Trusteeship Council and, 45
"Zionism as a form of racism," 71n91
Global Accountability Project, 27
Global Accountability Report (World Bank), 291–92
Global Accountability Report (One World Trust) (2006), 276, 291, 300n20
Global Alliance for Vaccines and Immunization, 211
Global Biodiversity Forum, 211
Global Compact [UN] (GC), 164, 203, 207, 213n24, 356–57, 358n17
Global Environment Facility (GEF), 150, 154, 156t6.3, 166, 211, 286, 298, 298n3
Global Environment Monitoring System (GEMS), 154
Global Platform for Disaster Risk Reduction, 147
Global Programme of Action for the Protection of the Marine Environment from Land-based Activities (GPA), 154
Global Transparency Initiative, 305, 321n7
Global Water Partnership, 211
Governing Council/Global Ministerial Environment Forum (GC/GMEF) [UNEP], 150–51, 153, 161n26
Government Accountability Office [US] (GAO), 16n5
GPA. *See* Global Programme of Action for the Protection of the Marine Environment from Land-based Activities (GPA)
Group of 77 (G-77), 24, 71n102
Growing the Sheltering Tree: Protecting Rights Through Humanitarian Action, 143t6.2
Guidelines for Field Staff Promoting Reintegration, 143t6.2
Guidelines for Flash Appeals, 143t6.2
Guidelines for HIV/AIDS Interventions in Emergency Settings, 143t6.2
Guidelines on the Use of Military and Civil Defence Assets in Disaster Relief, 143t6.2
Guidelines on the Use of Military and Civil Defence Assets to Support United Nations Humanitarian Activities in Complex Emergencies, 143t6.2
Guiding and Operating Principles for the Use of Military and Civil Defence Assets in Support of Humanitarian Operations, 143t6.2
Guiding Principles on Internal Displacement, 143t6.2

Hammarskjöld, Secretary-General Dag, 51, 53
Hart, H. L. A., 86–88, 95n44
Hasuo, Ikuyo, xi, 11, 17, 174–90, 353
Herken, Anna S., xi, 13, 271–302, 332, 337
High-level Panel on Threats, Challenges and Change, 204, 224
HIV/AIDS, 6, 143t6.2, 168, 211
Hohfeld, Wesley Newcomb, 45, 67n47
Hollingsworth, Kathryn, 81, 91, 94n19, 94n23, 177–79, 188n14
Hood, Christopher, 173, 234
Humanitarian Information Centres, 147
Humanitarian Supply Management System (SUMA), 145f6.1
Human Rights Council, 211
Humpty Dumpty, 97, 112, 304
Hurd, Ian, 111, 115n35
Hurrell, Andrew, 100–101, 113n12–13
Hyogo Framework for Action, 147

IACSD. *See* Inter-Agency Committee on Sustainable Development [UN] (IACSD)

IAS. *See* Internal Audit Service (IAS) [EU]
IASC. *See* Inter-Agency Standing Committee [UN] (IASC)
IATF. *See* Inter-Agency Task Force for Disaster Reduction [UN] (IATF)
IBRD. *See* International Bank for Reconstruction and Development (IBRD)
ICJ. *See* International Court of Justice (ICJ)
ICRC. *See* International Committee of the Red Cross (ICRC)
ICT. *See* international criminal tribunal (ICT)
ICTY. *See* International Criminal Tribunal for the Former Yugoslavia (ICTY)
ICVA. *See* International Council of Voluntary Agencies (ICVA)
IDA. *See* International Development Association (IDA)
IDB. *See* Inter-American Development Bank (IDB)
IDP. *See* internally displaced person (IDP)
IFC. *See* International Finance Corporation (IFC)
IFRC. *See* International Federation of Red Cross and Red Crescent Societies (IFRC)
IGO. *See* intergovernmental organization (IGO)
Ikenberry, G. John, 102, 113n18
ILA. *See* International Law Association (ILA)
ILC. *See* International Law Commission [UN] (ILC)
ILO. *See* International Labour Organization (ILO)
IMF. *See* International Monetary Fund (IMF)
IMO. *See* International Maritime Organization (IMO)
Independent Advisory Group on UN Finances, 169, 173n8
Independent Inquiry Committee into the UN Oil-for-Food Programme, 21, 33n11
Independent Panel on the Safety and Security of UN Personnel in Iraq, 4, 17n10, 34n21
Indian Ocean tsunami, 144, 146f6.2, 147–49, 149f6.3, 161n22
In Larger Freedom: Towards Development, Security, and Human Rights for All [UN], 93n1, 206–7, 214n31
Inomata, Tadanori, xi–xii, 10–11, 34n36, 48, 135–61, 159n2, 328
INSARAG. *See* International Search and Rescue Advisory Group (INSARAG)
Integrated Regional Information Networks [UN] (IRIN), 147
Inter-Agency Committee on Sustainable Development [UN] (IACSD), 153
Inter-Agency Contingency Planning Guidelines for Humanitarian Assistance, 143t6.2
Inter-Agency Standing Committee [UN] (IASC), 142, 143t6.2, 144, 147, 160n14, 160n17
Inter-Agency Task Force for Disaster Reduction [UN] (IATF), 144, 147
Inter-American Development Bank (IDB), 304, 312, 315–17, 324n64
intergovernmental organization (IGO)
  accountability, 52
  due process, standards of, 126
  evolutionary path, 209
  global governance, 201
  humanitarian agencies, code for operational, 213
  non-state actors and representatives, 210
  political reality and financial contribution, 59
  World Bank Panel and, 283
Internal Audit Service (IAS) [EU], 259
internally displaced person (IDP), 143t6.2
International Atomic Energy Agency, 155
International Bank for Reconstruction and Development (IBRD), 271, 286, 298n3, 299n9, 299n12, 299n14, 300n28, 300n32–300n33
International Commission on Intervention and State Sovereignty, 203–5, 214n26
International Committee of the Red Cross (ICRC), 160n14
International Council of Voluntary Agencies (ICVA), 160n14, 195, 212n2
International Court of Justice (ICJ), 44, 46, 71n93, 120–22, 124, 129n1, 130n4
International Criminal Court, 26, 139, 159n5, 205
international criminal tribunal (ICT)
  budget for, 140t6.1
  for Rwanda, 139

International Criminal Tribunal for the Former Yugoslavia (ICTY), 122, 131n24, 139
International Development Association (IDA), 274, 286, 298n3, 299n12
International Federation of Red Cross and Red Crescent Societies (IFRC), 160n14
International Finance Corporation (IFC), 154, 286, 298n3, 304, 312, 315
International Labour Organization (ILO), 6, 154, 197, 201, 349
International Law Association (ILA), 33n13, 116, 120, 130n2, 304, 321n1, 321n4, 324n69
International Law Commission [UN] (ILC), 10, 48–49, 118, 125, 127, 132n43, 132n46, 132n49
"Responsibility of International Organizations", 33n13, 118, 125, 127, 132n46, 132n49, 323n47
International Maritime Organization (IMO), 154
International Monetary Fund (IMF), 78, 187n4, 195, 198, 349
International Organization for Migration (IOM), 160n14
International Search and Rescue Advisory Group (INSARAG), 145f6.1
International Strategy for Disaster Reduction (ISDR), 145f6.1, 146–47, 153–54
International Telecommunication Union (ITU), 163–65
Inter-Parliamentary Union, 207, 214n34
inter-sovereign-state society, 352
IOM. *See* International Organization for Migration (IOM)
IRIN. *See* Integrated Regional Information Networks [UN] (IRIN)
ISDR. *See* International Strategy for Disaster Reduction (ISDR)
ITU. *See* International Telecommunication Union (ITU)

Jacques Santer Commission, 234
Japan Bank for International Cooperation (JBIC), 315–17, 319, 323n53, 324n53
Japanese Self-Defense Forces, 233
Japan International Cooperation Agency (JICA), 315, 324n53
Japan Social Development Fund (JSDF), 165
JBIC. *See* Japan Bank for International Cooperation (JBIC)
JICA. *See* Japan International Cooperation Agency (JICA)
JIU. *See* Joint Inspection Unit [UN] (JIU)
Joint Inspection Unit [UN] (JIU)
accountability, compliance and process, 181
accountability gap, UN, 43
money spent by UN system, 139
programme accountability, 183
report by, 17n9, 188n37, 189n52, 190n59, 190n66–67
source documents, 146n6.2, 149f6.3, 156t6.3, 159n1–2
Joint Organization of the Affected Communities on Colombo-Matara Highway, 317–18
Joint UN Programme on HIV/AIDS (UNAIDS), 6, 211
JPO. *See* Junior Professional Officer (JPO) Programme
JSDF. *See* Japan Social Development Fund (JSDF)
Junior Professional Officer (JPO) Programme, 169

Kawasaki, Kyoji, xii, 10, 34n22, 116–32, 131n33, 332, 334, 336–37, 345
Kelsen, Hans, 86–87, 95n39
Keohane, Robert O., 16n6, 66n31–33, 68n64, 70n90, 71n97, 78, 83, 92, 94n13, 94n22, 99, 101, 113n10, 113n14, 196, 212n7, 304, 321n5
Kunugi, Tatsuro, xii, 7, 12, 17n12, 18n21, 33n17, 193–214, 212n11, 213n14, 213n20, 213n22, 214n38–39, 225n11, 329, 348, 352
Kuyama, Sumihiro, xii, 1–16, 327–41
Kyoto Protocol, 152, 155

"ladder of accountability" (Stewart), 11, 176, 180, 180f8.3, 181, 184, 353, 355
Laeken Declaration [EU], 230, 249n3
Lallas, Peter L., xii–xiii, 13, 271–302, 299n15, 301n45, 332, 337
Lamy, Pascal, 196
League of Nations, 44, 49
Lie, Secretary-General Trygve, 51
Luck, Edward C., xiii, xvii, 3–4, 6, 8–9, 11, 17n19, 19–34, 33n18, 34n37, 65n15, 71n102, 114n23, 175, 204, 328, 330–31, 333–39

Luhmann, Niklas, 103, 114n20
Luntz Maslansky Strategic Research, 20

management accountability and its subconcepts
accountability, concept of, 176–79, 177f8.1
accountability, how to address, 175–76
accountability, ladder of, 174, 179–85
accountability, why?, 174–75
conclusion, 185–86, 186f8.4
introduction, 174–76
"A ladder of accountability" (Stewart), 11, 176, 180, 180f8.3, 181, 184, 353, 355
managerial accountability, concept of, 176–79
managerial accountability in government, 178, 178f8.2
managerial accountability in UN, 178f8.2, 179–85
management reform for enhancing accountability
about, 162–63
evaluation, over-emphasis on, 171
evaluation and revitalized assemblies, councils, board of directors, 171–72
evaluation by third party Member States, 172–73
evaluation indicators, development and application of, 170–71
financial systems reform of international organizations, 168–69
management and opaque financial systems, 165–67
Millennium Development Goals, 168
NPM and reform/evaluation of international organizations, 167–69
partnerships with private sector organizations, 164–65
performance indicators, lack of, 164
results-based budgeting, 167–68
transparency of funds and information, 170
managerial accountability and UN system
about, 135
accountability, management and financial, 148–49, 149f6.3
budget of UN system, total, 140t6.1
budget principle, zero-growth, 139
conclusions, 158–59
coordination mechanism, 153–54
disaster reduction and response, 145t6.1
environmental activities, multilateral resources for, 156t6.3
environmental governance, 150–58, 151f6.4, 152
environment-related initiatives, proliferation of, 150, 151f6.4
expenditures on normative and operational environmental activities, 157t6.4
expenditures on operational activities of UN by sector, 149f6.3
follow-up and implementation, lacking coherent, 138
governance and management framework for large-scale disasters, 147–48
governance framework and current management, 136–41
humanitarian assistance at disaster management stages, 146f6.2
humanitarian assistance system, 141–42, 143t6.2
humanitarian system, institutional deficiencies in, 144, 145f6.1, 146–47, 146f6.2
Indian Ocean tsunami disaster, 142
interagency coordination and intergovernmental ownership, 154–55
interagency coordination concept, 141
Inter-Agency Standing Committee, policies, principles and guidelines, 143t6.2
international humanitarian assistance, 142, 144
management and oversight lacunae, 137, 141–58
management framework and no single governance, 137
management of resources, 157–58, 157t6.4
multilateral environmental agreements and control measures, 155–56
normative activities and operational activities, 138–39
programming and budgeting, dichotomy between, 138
sustainable development governance, 150–52
system-wide coordination instrument, 154
system-wide management tools, lacking, 139–41, 140t6.1

managerial and political accountability, 5–8, 19–20, 22–24, 177–78, 232–33
Manin, Bernard, 90, 95n51, 95n53, 250n8–9, 250n11
MAP 2000. *See* "Modernization of Administration and Personnel Policy" (MAP 2000)
Marrakesh Process, 153
MDB. *See* multilateral development bank (MBD)
MDG. *See* Millennium Development Goal (MDG)
MEAs (multilateral environmental agreements), *See* environmental governance
meeting of interested parties (MIP), 166
member of the European Parliament (MEP), 245t11.4
Member States
 accountability, 1, 52
 accountability check by, 31
 General Assembly resolutions, 1
 participation by non-, 114n26
 Secretariat and, 32, 52–53, 335
 Security Council directives, 69n75
 Security Council resolutions, 52
 third party evaluation of, 172–73
MEP. *See* member of the European Parliament (MEP)
MIGA. *See* Multilateral Investment Guarantee Agency (MIGA)
Millennium Declaration [UN], 29, 168, 173n7, 203, 207, 213n25, 216
Millennium Development Goal (MDG), 10, 29, 154, 162, 167–68, 266, 328
Millennium Ecosystem Assessment, 154
"Millennium Report", 193
MIP. *See* meeting of interested parties (MIP)
"Modernization of Administration and Personnel Policy" (MAP 2000), 234, 250n22
Montreal Protocol, 150, 152, 155, 156t6.3
multilateral development bank (MDB), 6, 14, 272, 292, 303–5, 323n47, 328, 338
multilateral environmental agreements (MEAs), *See* environmental governance
Multilateral Fund for the Implementation of the Montreal Protocol, 150, 156t6.3
Multilateral Investment Guarantee Agency (MIGA), 298n3, 304, 312, 315
multi-stakeholder partnerships, 209–211

Nanwani, Suresh, xiii, 14, 303–24, 323n47, 323n49, 338
Nasser, President Gamel Abdel, 46–47
NATO. *See* North Atlantic Treaty Organization (NATO)
new public management (NPM)
 European Commission, 13, 233–36
 European Union, 229–31, 233–35, 246–49
 international organizations, 167–69, 173n1
 results-based budgeting (RBB), 162
 UN accountability, 174, 246–48
 UN management reform, 162, 174, 185–86, 187n4, 229
NGO. *See* non-governmental organization (NGO)
Nice Treaty [EU], 240–41
"no representation without taxation", 351
Nolan, Janne, 208, 214n37
non-governmental organization (NGO)
 Asian Development Bank and, 3
 democratic governance and, 80
 in non-democratic states, 58
 northern-based, 31
 partnership with, 164
 problems of accountability, 347
 public-interest, 356
 relationship contradictions, 216
 Save the Children, 38
 south-south, 31
 UN accountability and, 338
 UNHCR and, 329
 World Bank Panel, 283, 291
Normanton, E. L., 84, 91, 94n5, 95n32, 176, 188n15
North Atlantic Treaty Organization (NATO), 110, 232
NPM. *See* new public management (NPM)
Nye, Joseph, 94n22, 99, 101, 113n10, 113n14, 196, 212n7

OCHA. *See* Office for the Coordination of Humanitarian Affairs [UN] (OCHA)
ODA. *See* official development assistance (ODA)
OECD. *See* Organisation for Economic Co-operation and Development (OECD)

OECD Development Assistance Committee (DAC), 157, 219, 322n21
Office for the Coordination of Humanitarian Affairs [UN] (OCHA), 147–49, 160n14
Office of the High Commissioner for Human Rights [UN] (OHCHR), 160n14, 342n5, 357
Office of the UN High Commissioner for Refugees (UNHCR), 138, 163, 218, 329, 342
official development assistance (ODA), 157, 185
Ogata, Shijuro, 169, 173n8
OHCHR. *See* Office of the High Commissioner for Human Rights [UN] (OHCHR); UN High Commissioner for Human Rights (OHCHR)
Oil-for-Food Programme
  about, 23, 187n9
  aid programme, UN's largest, 229
  expenses of, 139, 140t6.1
  fraud, corruption and mismanagement of, 37–38
  oversight and accountability mechanisms, overtaxed UN's, 4–6
  Report of the Independent Inquiry Committee, 33n11
  reports on, 64n6
  responsibility of Secretariat and Security Council, 17n19, 23
  scandal, corruption, 6, 8, 20, 175, 333
  Volcker-led inquiry into, 26
OLAF. *See* European Anti-Fraud Office (OLAF)
Operational Guidelines of Human Rights in Natural Disasters, 143t6.2
Organisation for Economic Co-operation and Development (OECD), 11, 100, 174, 201, 219, 322n21, 356, 358n16
organizational legitimacy, dual basis of, 353–55
Osterwalder, Konrad, xvi–xvii
Outcome Document (2005), 25–26

Paris Declaration on Aid Effectiveness, 319
Parliamentary Oversight of the Security Sector – Principles, Mechanisms and Practices, 208, 214n34
Paul, Samuel, 183, 189n51
PDAC. *See* Public Disclosure Advisory Committee (PDAC)
Peacebuilding Commission, 211, 222
peacekeeping operations (PKOs)
  administrative functions, large-scale, 181
  autocratic nature, 216
  budget of, 140t6.1, 165
  in Congo, 182
  expansion of, 328
  field operations of the UN system, 216–19
  funds from wealthier states, 72n110
  General Assembly and, 122
  humanitarian law rules, international, 118
  interim administration operations, 222–23
  International Court of Justice, 122
  model status-forces agreement, 127
  as operational activities, 119
  programme scandal and problems, 38, 333
  reports, 65n11–12, 132n44, 159n4, 190n66
  results-based management, 186
  role of, 163
  rule of law, 223
  sexual abuses, 25, 38, 65n12, 217
  statistics on 2006, 114n30
  subcontractors/service provider for, 166
  in Sudan, 38
  UN Article 24, 108
  UN budget and, 184
  UN operational activities, 126
  zero-growth-budget principle and, 139
Peace Support Operations, Parliaments and Legislation, 208, 214n35
Pérez de Cuéllar, Secretary-General Javier, 66n22
Pew Research Center for the People and the Press, 33n9
Pew survey, 20
PHRDF. *See* Policy and Human Resources Development Fund (PHRDF)
PKOs. *See* peacekeeping operations (PKOs)
planning-programming-budgeting system [UN] (PPBS), 182–83, 189n42, 189n45
Plan of Action on Protection from Sexual Exploitation in Humanitarian Crises, 143t6.2
Platform for the Promotion of Early Warning (PPEW), 145f6.1
Policy and Human Resources Development Fund (PHRDF), 165
Policy Paper for Protection for IDPs, 143t6.2

Policy Statement for the Integration of a Gender Perspective in Humanitarian Assistance, 143t6.2
political accountability, *See* accountability
political accountability by multi-stakeholders
  accountability, political and democratic, 24, 194–97
  Cardoso Report, 206–9
  codes of conduct, 200–203
  conclusion, 211–12
  Declaration of Accountability for Global Governance, 197–200
  introduction, 193–94
  "Millennium Report" and, 193
  multi-stakeholder partnerships, 209–11
  responsibility and accountability for peace and security, 203–6
Power Without Accountability, 27, 34n29
PPBS. *See* planning-programming-budgeting system [UN] (PPBS)
PPEW. *See* Platform for the Promotion of Early Warning (PPEW)
Prantl, Jochen, xiii, 9–10, 16n7, 33n15, 97–115, 114n24, 114n28, 114n31, 330, 332–33, 340, 344, 346–47
Prezeworski, Adam, 90, 95n51, 95n53, 250n8–9, 250n11
Prodi Commission [EU], 234–35
Public Disclosure Advisory Committee (PDAC), 308

R2P. *See* responsibility to protect (R2P)
RBB. *See* results-based budgeting [UN] (RBB)
RBBM. *See* results-based budgeting and management [UN] (RBBM)
RBM. *See* results-based management [UN] (RBM)
Recommendations on UN/Non-UN Field Security Collaboration, 143t6.2
"Regulations Governing Programme Planning, the Programme Aspects of the Budget, the Monitoring of Implementation and the Methods of Evaluation", 183, 189n49
Reiterer, Michael, xiii–xiv, 8, 13, 253–70, 270n28, 355
RELEX. *See* Directorate-General for External Relations (RELEX)
ReliefWeb, 147
"Renewing the United Nations: A Programme for Reform", 167, 173n4, 175, 187n5
Report of the Independent Inquiry Committee: The Management of the United Nations Oil-for-Food Programme, 33n11
"Report of the Independent Inquiry into the Actions of the United Nations during the 1994 Genocide in Rwanda", 64n2
Report of the Panel of Eminent Persons on UN-Civil Society Relations (Cardoso Report), 206–9, 214n29
"Report on the Manipulation of the Oil-for-Food Programme", 64n6
Respect for Humanitarian Mandates in Conflict Situations (policy), 143t6.2
"Responsibility of International Organizations" [ILC], 33n13, 118, 125, 127, 132n46, 132n49, 323n47
responsibility to protect (R2P), 25, 204–6, 214n26, 214n28, 334
Result-Oriented Annual Report [UNDP] (ROAR), 169
results-based budgeting and management [UN] (RBBM), 10, 140, 167
results-based budgeting [UN] (RBB)
  about, 167–68
  accountability, management, 84, 167–68
  accountability, performance-based, 183–85
  NPM as, 162
  performance, 84
  report, 173n5, 187n6–7, 190n63, 190n66
  UN's adoption of, 175, 336
results-based management [UN] (RBM)
  about, 10–11
  benchmarking framework, 140–41
  management, overall, 186
  reports, 16n2, 160n9, 189n55
  traditional management *vs.*, 175
Rio Earth Summit, 150
ROAR. *See* Result-Oriented Annual Report [UNDP] (ROAR)
Romzek, Barbara, 81, 94n24
Rosenau, James, 195, 212n3
Rotterdam Convention on Prior Informed Consent Procedure for Certain Hazardous Chemicals and Pesticides in International Trade, 156t6.3

SAL. *See* structural adjustment lending (SAL)
Santer Commission [EU], 234, 240, 253–54, 259
Sardar Sarovar projects, 274, 298, 312, 323n51–52
Sato, Tetsuo, xiv, 332, 337, 342n6, 343–60
SC. *See* Security Council [UN] (SC)
Secretary-General of the EU Commission, 259, 261
"Secretary-General's Bulletin: Observance by United Nations Forces of International Humanitarian Law", 126, 132n41
Secretary-General [UN] (SG). *See also* Oil-for-Food Programme; UN Secretariat
accountability, 16n3, 40, 48, 51, 55
accountability, managerial and political, 22–23, 333
accountability, political/democratic, 272
accountability architecture, 16n2
accountability check by Member States, 31
accountability in speeches and reports, 327
accountability of actions, 5
accountability of member states, 52
administrative reforms, 185
An Agenda for Democratization, 197, 212n9
Annan, Kofi, 1, 10, 15, 19, 23–24, 26–27, 34n27, 73, 167, 172, 174–75, 185, 214n31, 249, 336, 341, 358n17
annual reports, 52
appointment of, 188n29
article 98 of the Charter, 69n69
article 100 of the Charter, 70n82
articles 10 and 11 of the Charter, 196
articles 98 and 99 of the Charter, 66n22
Ban Ki-moon, 1, 4, 15, 19, 23, 26, 249
Boutros-Ghali, Boutros, 169, 198
bulletin, 126
as chief administrative officer, 40, 50
control over UN organization, 52–53
corruption scandal, 229
"Delivering as One: Report of the Secretary-General's High-level Panel on UN System-wide Coherence in the Areas of Development, Humanitarian Assistance, and the Environment", 224, 224n9
democratization employed by, 71n98
ethical and accountable culture, 341
Global Compact, 358n17
Hammarskjöld, Dag, 51, 53
High-level Panel, 224
historical record, 34n26
HR Commission and, 357
human displacement principles, 160n13
humanitarian and humanitarian-related matters, 148
as international statesman, 50–51
In Larger Freedom: Towards Development, Security, and Human Rights for All, 93n1, 206–7, 214n31
leverage and control, reduced, 32
Libya and, 131n29
Lie, Trygve, 51
managerial accountability, 25, 179
to the Member States, 1
Member States and, 41
"Millennium Report", 193
new public management (NPM), 174, 247
peacekeeping operations and, 127
Pérez de Cuéllar, 66n22
plan to reform the bureaucracy, 50
power centres, 331
powers from Charter, 118–19
priorities, articulating, 63
privileges and immunities, 51, 63
programme accountability, 183
R2P, principle of, 204–5
removal from office, 51
"Renewing the United Nations: A Programme for Reform", 167, 173n4, 175, 187n5
reports, 64n3, 65n12, 93, 131n37, 131n41, 159n3, 161n28, 224n9
results-based budgeting (RBB), 167, 175, 336
role of, 50
UN independent inquiry, 50
U Thant, 47, 69n77
Security Council [UN] (SC). *See also* UN peacekeeping operations (PKOs)
accountability, 4, 53, 68n57, 331
accountability, political, 334
accountability, public, 45
accountability, transparency and enforceability, 196
accountability and collective legitimization, 61

accountability context, 197
activities, normative and operational, 122
activities not in conformity with the Charter, 121–22
Arria formula meetings, 203
article 24 crisis, 108–9, 109f4.3, 112
article 37, paragraph 2 of Chapter VI, 124
article 39 of Chapter VII, 124
article 41, 123, 130n5
articles 23, 27, 28 and 32, 119
articles 42, 123, 131n25
authorization "to speak and act in the name of the UN", 41
Chapter VII, 123, 204, 344
Charter's key tasks for, 44
China as permanent member, 24
Cold War, 217, 344
conflict in Namibia, El Salvador and Kosovo, 114n24
decision-making, legitimacy of, 333
decolonization and apartheid, 114n27
delisting request, 120
democracy, 56, 349
democracy deficits, 195
exceptional rules, 205
as "executive United Nations", 8
exercise of power, 17n12
expansion of, 24
General Assembly and, 51
genocide and mass atrocities, 204
genocide in Rwanda, 50, 64n2
humanitarian calamities in Rwanda, Srebrenica and Darfur, 28
informal consultation of, 105, 106f4.1, 107f4.2, 108
informal groups of states, 109–11
jurisdiction, limits of, 46
jus cogens rules of international law, 118, 124, 131n34
lapses, management and governance, 28
legitimacy and accountability, 9, 98, 104
Member States and, 52, 69n75
militaries of the permanent members, 41
non-Member States and, 114n26
Oil-for-Food Programme, 4–5, 17n19, 23, 26, 33n11, 37–38, 64n6, 139, 140t6.1, 175, 187n9, 229, 333
Parliamentary Oversight of the Security Sector – Principles, Mechanisms and Practices, 208, 214n34
partnerships, multi-stakeholder, 209
peacekeepers and malfeasance and nonfeasance charges, 53
peacekeeping mission mandates, 70n84
peace operations, high-risk, 25
peace operations in Rwanda, Srebrenica or Baghdad, 25
Peace Support Operations, Parliaments and Legislation, 208, 214n35
permanent members, 267, 349
power, discretion in exercising, 117
practice, 104–11
private sector and civil society, 208
Provisional Rules of Procedure, 105
reform, structural, 196
reform of, 24, 33n18
reports, annual and special, 67n51
resolution 276, 130n17
resolution 662, 129
resolution 678, 123
resolution 706, 175
resolution 731, 131n29
resolution 748, 123
resolution 1373, 124
resolution 1730, 120
Rwanda, responses to events in, 37
"safe area" of Srebrenica in Bosnia and Herzegovina, 37, 108
sanctions, economic, 119, 123, 344
sanctions lists, 120
sanctions regimes, 117, 126
Secretary-General and, 188n29
security, political perspective of, 171
sexual abuse of children by UN peacekeepers, 25, 38, 65n12, 217
special status within, 70n87
structure and procedures, 53–54, 349
symbolic power of, 115
transparency, 61
SEM 2000. *See* "Sound and Effective Management 2000" (SEM 2000)
SG. *See* Secretary-General [UN] (SG)
shared responsibility, 7
Shiroyama, Hideaki, xiv, 10–11, 162–73, 173n2–3, 173n9, 336
Shoji, Mariko, xiv, 343–60, 358n6, 358n9
SIDS. *See* Sustainable Development of Small Island Developing States (SIDS)
Slaughter, Anne-Marie, 18n25, 52, 69n79, 72n113, 72n117, 328, 338, 342n2

SMART. *See* specific, measurable, achievable, relevant and time-bound (objectives) [UN] (SMART)
"Sound and Effective Management 2000" (SEM 2000), 234, 250n21
Southern Transport Development Project [Sri Lanka], 317–18
specific, measurable, achievable, relevant and time-bound (objectives) [UN] (SMART), 140
Standard Eurobarometer, 20–21, 33n10
Stewart, J. D., 11, 176, 180–81, 180f8.3, 184, 188n13, 237, 251n30, 300n22, 353, 355
Stockholm Convention on Persistent Organic Pollutants, 156t6.3
Stokes, Susan, 90, 95n51, 95n53, 250n8–9, 250n11
structural adjustment lending (SAL), 195
Sustainable Development of Small Island Developing States (SIDS), 15
Sustainable Development Summit, 216

Takahashi, Kazuo, xiv–xv, 8, 12, 34n34, 215–25, 225n11, 328, 348–49
Takikawa, Hirohide, xv, 9, 33n14, 73–96, 341, 345–46
Tampere Convention on the Provision of Telecommunications Resources for Disaster Mitigation and Relief Operations, 144
TNC. *See* transnational corporation (TNC)
Tocqueville, Alexis de, 98–99, 113n5
transnational corporation (TNC), 83, 101, 198, 357, 358n18
Transparency Initiative [EU], 265, 270n27, 355

UK National Audit Office, 84
UNAIDS. *See* Joint UN Programme on HIV/AIDS (UNAIDS)
UNAMI. *See* UN Assistance Mission for Iraq (UNAMI)
UNAMIR. *See* UN Assistance Mission for Rwanda (UNAMIR)
UN Assistance Mission for Iraq (UNAMI), 25
UN Assistance Mission for Rwanda (UNAMIR), 50
UNCCD. *See* UN Convention to Combat Desertification (UNCCD)
UNCED. *See* UN Conference on Environment and Development (UNCED)
UN Children's Fund (UNICEF)
  activities, normative and operational, 138
  environment activities, 156t6.3, 157t6.4, 158
  funding, 72n110
  funds, extra-budgetary, 166
  goals of, 172
  humanitarian activities of, 163
  humanitarian interventions, 221
  IASC members, 160n14
  income, sources of, 164
  policy disputes, 171
UNCLOS. *See* UN Convention on the Law of the Sea (UNCLOS)
UN Conference on Environment and Development (UNCED), 17n16, 153, 276
UN Conference on Trade and Development (UNCTAD), 154, 353
UN Convention on the Law of Non-Navigational Use of International Watercourses, 300n19
UN Convention on the Law of the Sea (UNCLOS), 156t6.3
UN Convention to Combat Desertification (UNCCD), 154, 156t6.3
UNCTAD. *See* UN Conference on Trade and Development (UNCTAD)
UNDAF. *See* UN Development Assistance Framework (CCA/UNDAF)
UN Declaration on a Culture of Peace, 202, 210, 213n16
UN Development Assistance Framework (CCA/UNDAF), 153–54, 158–59
UN Development Programme (UNDP)
  about, 72n110, 187n1, 190n58, 190n61
  accountability, managerial, 179
  agency, implementing, 166
  aid organization, multilateral development, 185
  budget from voluntary contributions, 165
  core budget programme, 138
  creation of, 217
  developmental agency, 147, 154, 157t6.4, 158
  development goals, 172
  evaluation of, 171
  funds for technical assistance, 166

IASC, 160n14
programme evaluation, 185
"Result-Oriented Annual Report" (ROAR), 169
UN Educational, Scientific and Cultural Organization (UNESCO), 154, 156t6.3
UNEF. *See* UN Emergency Force (UNEF)
UN Emergency Force (UNEF), 46–47, 121
UN Environment Programme (UNEP), 150, 161n26, 166, 301n37
UNEP. *See* UN Environment Programme (UNEP)
UNESCO. *See* UN Educational, Scientific and Cultural Organization (UNESCO)
UNFCCC. *See* UN Framework Convention on Climate Change (UNFCCC)
UNFIP. *See* UN Fund for International Partnerships (UNFIP)
UNFPA. *See* UN Population Fund (UNFPA)
UN Framework Convention on Climate Change (UNFCCC), 154, 156t6.3, 157t6.4
UN Fund for International Partnerships (UNFIP), 211
UN-HABITAT. *See* UN Human Settlements Programme (UN-HABITAT)
UNHCR. *See* Office of the UN High Commissioner for Refugees (UNHCR)
UN High Commissioner for Human Rights (OHCHR), 120, 160n14, 300n19, 357
UN Human Settlements Programme (UN-HABITAT), 154
UNICEF. *See* UN Children's Fund (UNICEF)
UN Independent Inquiry Committee, 4, 17n11, 64n2, 64n6, 68n63
UN Institute for Training and Research (UNITAR), 154, 156t6.3
UNITAR. *See* UN Institute for Training and Research (UNITAR)
United Nations (UN)
accountability, 27–32, 38–39, 327–35
accountability, enhanced, 335–38
accountability, normative framework of, 338–40
accountability gap at, 43
Ad Hoc Committee of Experts to Examine the Finances of the UN and the Specialized Agencies, 182, 189n40
Administrative Committee on Coordination (ACC), 139–40, 160n7
Advisory Committee on Administrative and Budgetary Questions (ACABQ), 16n3
Assistant Secretaries-General, 179
bombing of UN headquarters [Baghdad], 25
breaches of obligations and legal consequences, 127–28
Charter, proper exercise of powers from, 118–20
Chief Executives Board for Coordination (CEB), 139, 141, 153–54, 159n3, 159n6, 160n8, 161n29
codes of conduct, 201–2, 210, 213n11, 213n14
Commission on Sustainable Development (CSD), 6, 17n16, 150, 153, 353
democracy, 348–50
Department of Peacekeeping Operations (DPKO), 65n12, 114n30
Deputy Secretaries-General, 179
Development Group, 172
Economic and Social Council (ECOSOC), 6, 17n16, 44, 55, 71n95, 150, 159, 159n6, 164, 353
Ethics Office, 26, 43, 341
Executive Committee on Economic and Social Affairs, 172
Executive Committee on Humanitarian Affairs, 172
Executive Committee on Peace and Security, 172
"Financing an Effective United Nations", 169, 173n8
Food and Agricultural Organization (FAO), 154, 156, 160n14, 201
Global Compact (GC), 164, 203, 207, 213n24, 356–57, 358n17
Guiding Principles on Internal Displacement, 142, 143t6.2, 160n13
Independent Advisory Group on UN Finances, 169, 173n8
Independent Steering Committee on the Comprehensive Review of Governance and Oversight, 27–28, 34n30

United Nations (UN) (cont.)
Integrated Regional Information Networks (IRIN), 147
Inter-Agency Committee on Sustainable Development (IACSD), 153
Inter-Agency Standing Committee (IASC), 142, 143t6.2, 144, 147, 160n14, 160n17
Inter-Agency Task Force for Disaster Reduction (IATF), 144, 147
international community, 118–24
international law, 124–29
International Law Commission (ILC), 10, 48–49, 118, 125, 127, 132n43, 132n46, 132n49
international obligations incumbent upon, 124–26
Junior Professional Officer (JPO) Programme, 169
Millennium Declaration, 29, 168, 173n7, 203, 207, 213n25, 216
NPM-guided reforms, 246–48
Office for the Coordination of Humanitarian Affairs (OCHA), 147–49, 160n14
Office of Internal Oversight Services, 43, 174
Office of Legal Affairs, 30n13, 125
Office of the High Commissioner for Human Rights (OHCHR), 160n14, 342n5, 357
Office of the UN High Commissioner for Refugees (UNHCR), 138, 163, 218, 329, 342
planning-programming-budgeting system (PPBS), 182–83, 189n42, 189n45
Preparatory Commission, 29, 34n33
"Regulations Governing Programme Planning, the Programme Aspects of the Budget, the Monitoring of Implementation and the Methods of Evaluation", 183, 189n49
reports, shortcomings of, 48–49
responsibility to protect (R2P), 25, 204–6, 214n26, 214n28, 334
results-based budgeting and management (RBBM), 10, 140, 167
specific, measurable, achievable, relevant and time-bound (objectives) (SMART), 140
Trusteeship Council, 44–45, 49, 67n49, 71n93
Under-Secretaries-General, 179
"United Nations Secretariat First Consolidated Report 2005", 130n11
Universal Declaration of Human Responsibilities, 202, 210, 213n18
whistleblower protection, 26, 43, 93, 259, 341
"United Nations Secretariat First Consolidated Report 2005", 130n11
United Nations University (UNU), 2, 22, 32, 63, 65n20, 155, 187, 330, 343, 353
Universal Declaration of Human Responsibilities, 202, 210, 213n18
UNMIBH. *See* UN Mission in Bosnia and Herzegovina (UNMIBH)
UN Millennium Summit, 168
UN Mission in Bosnia and Herzegovina (UNMIBH), 218
UNO. *See* UN Organization (UNO)
UN-Oceans, 153–54
UN Office for Project Services (UNOPS), 154
UN Organization (UNO), 187n1
UN Panel of Eminent Persons on United Nations-Civil Society, 214n29
UN peacekeeping operations (PKOs), *See* peacekeeping operations (PKOs)
UN Population Fund (UNFPA), 154, 160n14, 179, 185, 190n62, 218
UN Relief and Works Agency for Palestine Refugees in the Near East (UNRWA), 156t6.3
UNRWA. *See* UN Relief and Works Agency for Palestine Refugees in the Near East (UNRWA)
UN Secretariat. *See also* Secretary-General [UN] (SG)
about, 16n3, 17n19, 19, 34n26, 40–43, 48, 66n30, 67n40, 71n96, 173n3
accountability, financial/fiscal and managerial, 223–24
accountability, managerial, 179
accountability, perception of lack of, 28–29
accountability, performance-based, 183
accountability for UN administration and actions, 246
accountable to "we the peoples", 4, 23–24
administrative burden, increased, 182
administrative management and control, internal, 174

administrators, lower-level, 22
article 7(1) of the UN Charter, 71n93
assistance for elections, democracy and technical, 351
delegation of authority, 249
democratic accountability and, 23
disaster risk reduction and mitigation efforts, 147
Governing Body of the, 29
internal evaluation, 183
lapses, management and governance, 28
managers, disciplinary action towards, 31
material and human resources, 24
McCarthy-era and, 70n83
Member States and, 32, 52–53, 172, 335
mistrust with, 26
reforms, administrative, 185
responsibility for carrying out decisions of intergovernmental organs, 23
results-based budgeting (RBB), 167, 185
results-based management, 175
Secretary-General and, 52–53
Security Council and, 51, 107–8
transparency and accountability, 73
UN independent inquiry and, 50
"United Nations Secretariat First Consolidated Report 2005", 130n11
UNTAC. *See* UN Transitional Authority in Cambodia (UNTAC)
UN Transitional Authority in Cambodia (UNTAC), 218
UNU. *See* United Nations University (UNU)
UNU-IAS. *See* UNU Institute of Advanced Studies (UNU-IAS)
UNU Institute of Advanced Studies (UNU-IAS), 154
UN-Water, 153–54
UNWTO. *See* World Tourism Organization (UNWTO)
US Agency for International Development (US AID), 7, 17n20
US AID. *See* US Agency for International Development (US AID)
Usui, Mikoto, xv, 334, 343–60
U Thant, Secretary-General, 47, 69n77

value for money (VFM), 68n56, 84, 234, 250n20
VFM. *See* value for money (VFM)
Vienna Convention for the Protection of the Ozone Layer, 156t6.3
Vienna Convention on the Law of Treaties between States and International Organization or between International Organizations, 126, 131n40, 156t6.3
Volcker, Paul, 21, 26, 33n12, 169, 173n8

we the peoples, 4, 19
WFP. *See* World Food Programme (WFP)
White, Fidelma, 81, 91, 94n19, 94n23, 177–79, 188n14
WHO. *See* World Health Organization (WHO)
WIPO. *See* World Intellectual Property Organization (WIPO)
WMO. *See* World Meteorological Organization (WMO)
Wolfensohn, James, 169
World Bank Inspection Panel
about, 271–73
affected people, handling requests and outcomes for, 287–90
"Annual Review of Development Effectiveness", 169
Bank policies, further development of, 291
complaint-based systems, citizens', 355
conclusion, 297–98
decision-making process, global, 312
developmental cooperation, 219
eligibility, 281–82
evaluation, 171–72
IDB accountability systems, 316–17
incentives for Bank compliance with policies and procedures, 290–91
Independent Evaluation Group, 68n55
infrastructure projects, 344
Inspection Panel, 68n55, 312, 337
inspection requests, 279–80, 281t13.1
International Council of Voluntary Agencies (ICVA), 160n14, 195, 212n2
investigation, 283–84
lending operations, 311
Manibeli Declaration and, 323n52
Morse Commission, 312
Mumbai Urban Transport Project (MUTP), 292–97
NGO dialogue with, 212n2
NGO Working Groups, 194–95
Panel, characteristics of, 279

World Bank Inspection Panel (cont.)
Panel, establishing, 273–75
Panel, history of, 273–77
Panel, impact of, 287–92
Panel, purpose of, 275
Panel achievements, 291–92
Panel influence on accountability in other institutions, 292
Panel and international legal system, 275–77
Panel members, 277–78
Panel process, 279–86
Panel's relationships to board, management and staff, 278–79
Panel structure, 277–79
programmes, critical evaluation of, 47, 68n56
publications, transparency of, 285–86
requests, analysis of, 286–87
requests, geographical distribution, 287, 287f13.1
requests, subject matter of, 286
requests and policies, 287, 288f13.2
Sardar Sarovar Projects, 312
Secretariat, 278
stakeholders, non-state, 6
structural adjustment lending (SAL), 195
transparency, 78
World Conference on Disaster Reduction, 147
World Food Programme (WFP)
General Assembly resolution 46/182, 160n14
humanitarian disasters, large-scale, 218
World Health Organization (WHO), 160n14, 163, 201, 218
World Intellectual Property Organization (WIPO), 185, 190n60
World Meteorological Organization (WMO), 154
World Summit on Sustainable Development (WSSD), 150, 152, 276
World Summit Outcome Document, 20, 205, 207, 212n6
World Tourism Organization (UNWTO), 256
World Trade Organization (WTO), 78, 195–98, 344
WSSD. *See* World Summit on Sustainable Development (WSSD)
WTO. *See* World Trade Organization (WTO)